Ultimate Recipes

Chinese

Ultimate Recipes

Chinese

p

Notes

Use all metric or all imperial quantities, as the two are not interchangeable.
Cup measurements in this book are for American cups. Tablespoons are assumed to be 15 ml.
Unless otherwise stated, milk is assumed to be full fat, eggs are medium and pepper is freshly
ground black pepper.

The nutritional information provided for each recipe is per serving or per portion.
Optional ingredients, variations or serving suggestions have not been included in the
calculations. The times given for each recipe are an approximate guide only as the
preparation times may differ as a result of the type of oven used.

Contents

Introduction   10

Soups

Appetizers

Appetizers (continued)

Salads & Pickles

Poultry

Meat

Fish & Seafood

Vegetables

Tofu

Rice

Rice
(continued)

Noodles

Desserts

Introduction

The abundance of Chinese restaurants testify to the fact that Chinese cuisine is hugely popular in the West. This book will show you how to recreate authentic Chinese dishes in your own home. Along with the more famous Cantonese and Szechuan specialities, there are also less familiar but equally delicious recipes from other regions for you to try.

There can be few places in the world nowadays that are unfamiliar with Chinese cuisine. It first became known in the West with the arrival of Chinese workers in the United States during the Gold rush years and today there are Chinese restaurants from San Francisco to Helsinki and from Sydney to Edinburgh. Home-cooked Chinese food is a more recent phenomenon – at least, in the Western kitchen – but, once the ingredients and the wok became easily available and people realized how quick and easy it is to prepare, it soon became popular.

Besides being quite delicious, which is undoubtedly its most attractive characteristic, Chinese food is both healthy and economic. Carbohydrates, such as rice, which release energy slowly and are recommended by nutritionists as an important part of a healthy diet, are served at every meal. Vegetables, too, play a starring role and they are cooked in ways, such as stir-frying and steaming, which preserve most

Introduction

of their vitamins and minerals. With a few exceptions, high-cholesterol, high-fat ingredients, such as dairy products and red meat, are either absent altogether or are served sparingly.

To a considerable extent, the distinctive flavours of Chinese food resulted from the need to be economical. Bulky but bland foods, such as noodles, were served in relatively large amounts to satisfy the appetite. Expensive ingredients, such as meat and fish, could be used in only small quantities, so they had to

be prepared in ways that made the most of them – combined with herbs, spices and other flavourings. As a result, Chinese cuisine probably has the largest repertoire of any in the world. Fuel was scarce, so 'fast food' was a necessity, resulting in the art of stir-frying in which ingredients are tossed in a round-based, cast iron wok over a high heat to cook in a short time. This preserves their flavour, colour, texture and nutrients. Steaming, also a favourite Chinese cooking technique, similarly results in flavoursome, attractive and nutritious dishes. Bamboo baskets are stacked one above another over a single heat source, thus saving fuel.

A desire for balance and harmony has permeated all aspects of Chinese life since the days of Confucius and this applies to food as well as everything else. Spicy dishes are complemented by sweet-and-sour ones, dry-cooked dishes are balanced with those bathed in sauce, meat is matched with seafood. Dishes are chosen to complement each other in texture, flavour and colour and it is not considered correct to serve more than one dish with the same main ingredient or to cook them using the same technique. Consciously or unconsciously, Chinese cooks, from the housewife to the professional chef, all work to this ancient Taoist principle of Yin and Yang in which balance and contrast are the key. Mealtimes, too, are a time of harmony, when the family – often three generations – gather and share a selection of different dishes, as well as their daily news.

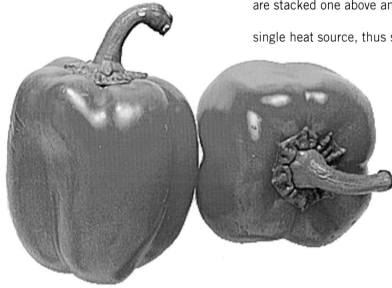

Regional Cooking

China is a huge country and the terrain and climate vary dramatically from one region to another. The crops grown and the livestock raised are equally diverse, giving rise to distinctive regional culinary traditions.

The North

Beijing has been the capital of China for about 1,000 years and, as befits such an important city, its culinary tradition is venerable. The Emperor's chief chef was a highly respected figure whose responsibilities included maintaining the health of the Imperial family through a careful balance of herbs, spices and other ingredients, not simply creating appetizing dishes. Each newly appointed chef considered it a matter of honour to outdo his predecessors and there was also much rivalry with visiting chefs who accompanied dignitaries from other provinces when they came to Beijing. As a result, Beijing cuisine, which still tends to be called Peking in culinary circles, is varied and elegant. It has also been influenced by the Moslem culinary traditions of Central Asia through a number of Tartar invasions. Sesame seeds and the oil and paste made from them, which now feature in the cooking of all regions of China, were originally introduced by the Tartars. The popularity of lamb, rather than pork, unique to the Northern provinces, is probably also a result of Moslem influences. Outside the city, the cooking is simpler and lacks the light-handed touch that is characteristic of Beijing. Sauces and dips tend to be strongly flavoured and leeks, onions and garlic are popular vegetables. Mongolian or chrysanthemum fire pot dishes – a kind of stock-based fondue – are a speciality.

Wheat, rather than rice, is the staple ingredient in Northern Chinese cuisine and it is used to make noodles, dumplings, pancakes and steamed buns. The climate can be quite harsh, but produce in this region includes pak choi, onions, grapes and peaches. Freshwater fish, especially carp, are popular in the area around the Huang Ho River and prawns (shrimp) and other seafood are abundant in the coastal regions. Drying, smoking and pickling are typical preserving techniques.

The South

The first Chinese emigrants came from Kwangtung in the nineteenth century, so this is probably the best-known style of Chinese cuisine in the West. The capital of the province, Canton, was the first major trading port in the country and so was open to many foreign influences. However,

Regional Cooking

probably the most important influence, from the culinary point of view, was internal. In 1644 the Ming dynasty was overthrown and the Imperial Household, together with its retinue of chefs, fled to Canton from Beijing. This has resulted in a style of cooking that is renowned for its variety, sophistication and excellence.

Steaming is a characteristic technique in Southern China and small fish, little parcels of meat or patties and, above all, dumplings are often cooked this way. Dim sum, which literally means 'to please the heart' are a Cantonese speciality. These small, steamed, filled dumplings are as popular in the West as they are in China, but there, they are never served as an appetizer. Rather, they are eaten as snacks at teahouses in the morning or afternoon. In fact, an alternative way of saying going to a dim sum restaurant is going out for morning tea.

Char siu roasting is another Cantonese technique. No kind of roasting is common in Chinese homes, which often do not have ovens, but this method is popular in restaurants. Meat is seasoned and marinated well and then roasted at a very high temperature for a short time. This results in the marinade becoming encrusted on the meat in a crisp outer layer, while the inside remains succulent and juicy. Only very tender cuts of meat, particularly pork, can be prepared in this way.

Agricultural produce in this semi-tropical region is abundant and varied. Vegetables are often simply stir-fried and served plain or just with oyster sauce. They may also be combined with meat or fish. Spinach, pak choi and dried mushrooms feature widely. Fresh fruit, frequently served on its own as a dessert, may also be combined with meat or fish in sweet-and-sour dishes. Fish and seafood, particularly abalone, crab, lobster, prawns (shrimp) and scallops, are plentiful. They are usually stir-fried or steamed, often flavoured with ginger, and cooking meat with fish is typically Cantonese. Generally, food is not highly spiced, as the Cantonese prefer to enjoy the natural flavours of the ingredients. Light soy sauce is a popular flavouring and other typical sauces include hoisin, oyster, black bean and plum.

The East

The delta of the Yangtse River makes this one of the most fertile regions in China. The abundant produce includes broccoli, spring onions (scallions), sweet potatoes, pak choi, soya beans, tea, wheat, rice, maize and nuts and the region is well known for its superb vegetarian

Regional Cooking

dishes, noodles and dumplings. Freshwater fish are found in the many streams and lakes, especially in Kiangsu, which also has a long tradition of deep-sea fishing.

The provinces that comprise this region each have a particular style of cooking, but all are characterized by their richness. The vast cosmopolitan city of Shanghai has assimilated many influences from both other parts of China and abroad. Its cuisine is unusual in that it features dairy products and uses lavish quantities of lard. Shanghai dishes are typically rich, sweet and beautifully presented. The school of cooking in the surrounding area is known as Kiangche, the name being an amalgamation of the two provinces of Kiangsu and Chekiang. Duck, ham

and fish dishes are specialities, often prepared with piquant spices. This region produces the best rice wine in the country. It is one of the most prosperous parts of China and has a long gourmet tradition. In Fukien to the South, the cuisine is less sophisticated, relying mainly on fish and a wealth of fresh produce. It is strongly influenced by neighbouring Kwangtung.

The West

Surrounded by mountains, Szechuan has a mild, humid climate and rich fertile soil. Its cuisine is most noted for its robust, richly coloured dishes flavoured with hot spices, such as chillies and Szechuan peppercorns. Strongly flavoured ingredients, such as garlic, ginger, onions, leeks and sesame seed paste

are typical and hot pickles are a speciality. Food preservation techniques, for which Western China is famous, include smoking, drying, salting and pickling. Yunnan, to the South of Szechuan, produces superb cured, smoked raw ham.

Szechuan cooking is traditionally described as having seven kinds of flavours - sweet, salty, sour, bitter, fragrant, sesame and hot - based respectively on honey or sugar, soy sauce, vinegar, onions or leeks, garlic or ginger, sesame seeds and, finally, chillies. Methods of cooking are varied, ranging from dry-frying with very little oil and no additional liquid to cooking in a clear, well-flavoured broth, which is then reduced to make a thick rich sauce. Deep-fried, paper-wrapped parcels of marinated meat or fish are a Szechuan speciality.

Equipment

It is not essential to buy a vast array of special equipment for Chinese cooking, but some items, especially a good-quality wok, are easier to use than their Western equivalents and will result in more authentic-tasting dishes. Most utensils are inexpensive and easily available from Chinese supermarkets and good kitchenware shops.

Wok

This bowl-shaped 'frying pan' with sloping sides is designed to ensure that heat spreads quickly and evenly over the surface so that food can be cooked rapidly, which is crucial for stir-frying. Once the ingredients have been added to the wok, they are tossed and stirred constantly for a short time over a very high heat. It is possible to stir-fry in a Western-style frying pan (skillet), but it is more difficult and the texture of the dish is likely to be less crisp. Woks can also be used for a variety of other cooking techniques, including braising, deep-frying and steaming.

Traditionally made from cast iron, they are now available in a variety of metals and in a wide range of prices. Carbon steel is a good choice, but stainless steel tends to scorch. Non-stick woks are also manufactured, but the lining cannot really withstand the high temperature required for stir-frying. Handles may be single or double, semi-circular or long, or a combination of the two. Wooden handles are safer than metal ones. It is important that a wok is large enough for the ingredients to be stirred and tossed all the time they are cooking and a range of sizes is available. One with a diameter of about 35 cm/14 inches is adequate for most Western families without being so heavy, whatever it is made of, that it is an effort to use. Flat-based woks are now manufactured for use on electric hobs.

New woks, apart from those with a non-stick lining, must be seasoned before they are used. First wash well with hot water and cream cleanser to remove the protective coating of oil. Rinse and dry the wok and then place it over a low heat and add about 2 tablespoons of vegetable oil. Rub the oil all over the inner surface of the wok with a thick pad of kitchen paper, taking care not to burn your fingers. Heat the oil for about 10 minutes, then wipe it off with a fresh pad of kitchen paper, which will become black. Repeat this heating and wiping process until the kitchen paper remains clean; it will take quite a long time.

Once the wok has been seasoned, it should not be washed with cream cleanser or detergent. Simply wipe it out with kitchen paper, wash in hot water and dry thoroughly. If the wok is used only occasionally, it may become rusty. In this case, scour the rust off and season again.

Wok Accessories

Some woks are supplied with lids, but if not, these can be bought separately. They are dome-shaped, usually made of aluminium and are tight-fitting. A lid is necessary when the wok is used for steaming, but a dome-shaped saucepan lid will work as satisfactorily.

A metal stand is an essential safety feature when the wok is used for steaming, braising or deep-frying. It may be an open-sided frame or a perforated metal ring.

A wok scoop is a bowl-shaped spatula with a long handle. Some resemble a perforated spoon and others are made from reinforced wire mesh. The handle may be wood or metal. The scoop makes it easier to toss the ingredients during stir-frying, but a long-handled spoon is an adequate substitute. Chinese cooks also use the scoop for adding ingredients to the wok.

A trivet is used for steaming. It is placed in the base of the wok and supports the dish or plate containing the food above the water level. It may be made of wood or metal. A wok brush of split bamboo is used for cleaning the wok.

Bamboo Steamer

Bamboo baskets with lids are available in a range of sizes and can be stacked one on top of another. They are designed to rest on the sloping sides of the wok above the water level.

Cleaver

This finely balanced tool is seen in every Chinese kitchen and is used for virtually all cutting tasks, from chopping spare ribs and halving duck to slashing fish and deveining prawns. Cleavers are available in a variety of weights and sizes and although they look unwieldy, they are precision instruments. The blade should be kept razor sharp.

Chopsticks

Long wooden chopsticks may be used for adding ingredients to the wok, fluffing rice, separating noodles and general stirring. They are not essential, but are useful and add a feeling of authenticity. Because they have a lighter touch than a spoon or fork, they are less likely to break up or squash delicate ingredients. Chopsticks are easy to handle once you have acquired the knack. Place one chopstick in the angle between your thumb and index finger, with the lower part resting on your middle finger. Hold the other chopstick between the thumb and index finger as you would hold a pencil; this is the one you manipulate.

Ingredients

Many ingredients used in Chinese cooking are also typically found in the Western kitchen – eggs, meat, poultry, fish, (bell) peppers, spring onions, carrots cucumbers and so on. Some, such as bean sprouts and soy sauce, have become familiar. A few, such as wonton wrappers and chilli sauce, may not be so well known. A comprehensive range of specialist ingredients can be obtained from Chinese foodstores and many can be purchased from good supermarkets.

Bamboo Shoots

Used for their texture rather than their flavour, which is very bland, bamboo shoots are readily available in cans. Fresh young bamboo shoots can sometimes be obtained. To prepare them, remove the tough outer skin and boil them in water for 40–50 minutes. Adding two red (bell) peppers to the water helps to remove the bitter taste.

Bean sauce

Also known as bean paste, this savoury purée may be black or yellow. It is made from crushed, salted soya beans, flour and spices and is often used instead of soy sauce when a thicker consistency is required. It is available in cans and jars. Sweet bean sauce is red and is used as a basis for sweet sauces and as an accompaniment to char siu dishes.

Bean Sprouts

This term usually refers to the shoots of the mung bean, although the shoots of many other pulses and grains can also be eaten. They are widely available, fresh and in cans from supermarkets. It is easy to sprout beans at home to provide a fresh supply when needed. They are used to give texture to dishes and can be stored in the refrigerator for two or three days.

Black Beans

Salted fermented soy beans are available in cans and packets. They should be soaked in cold water for 5–10 minutes before use to remove some of their saltiness. They have a distinctive flavour and are always combined with other ingredients, such as meat or fish.

Cellophane Noodles

Also known as transparent noodles or bean threads, these opaque white noodles are sold in bundles that resemble candy floss in appearance. They should be soaked in hot water for 5 minutes before using, when they will become translucent. They

Ingredients

are never eaten on their own and are good combined with soups and soupy dishes because they absorb a lot of liquid, making them very tasty.

Chilli Bean Sauce

This fermented soya bean sauce flavoured with chillies and other spices is available in cans and jars. Some varieties are fiery hot, so use with caution.

Chilli Oil

This is a very hot, red-coloured oil used for flavouring spicy dishes. It should always be used with caution. Some varieties contain chilli flakes. You can make your own by adding a few dried chillies to a small bottle of bland vegetable oil.

Chillies

Many varieties of both red and green fresh chillies are widely available and they range from relatively mild to scorchingly hot. It is often not possible to tell which variety you are buying and some look very similar to each other, but taste quite different. As a general rule, large, round chillies are usually milder than small, pointed ones. The seeds are the hottest part, so if you prefer a milder flavour, remove and discard them before use. Take care when handling chillies, as the juice can burn. Wear protective gloves if you have sensitive skin and avoid touching your face, especially the eyes. Always wash you hands thoroughly afterwards. Dried red chillies are also used in Chinese cooking. They are often hotter than fresh chillies and can also burn.

Chinese Five-spice Powder

This flavouring contains star anise, fennel seeds, cinnamon, cloves and Szechuan pepper. It has a distinctive taste and a pungent aroma, so it should be used sparingly. It is a popular flavouring for soy-braised dishes and roast meat. It will keep more or less indefinitely in an airtight container. When buying, make sure you look for Chinese five-spice powder because the Indian flavouring is a different mixture.

Chinese Leaves

Also known as Chinese cabbage, the commonest variety of this leafy vegetable resembles a tightly packed, pale green Cos lettuce. Another variety is rounder with curly yellow

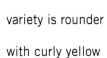

leaves. A large proportion of the vegetable consists of the crunchy stems, which add texture to stir-fries and other dishes.

Chinese Pancakes

These are made from flour and water and are available fresh and frozen. Frozen pancakes should be thawed before steaming.

Chinese Pickles

A variety of pickles is available from Chinese foodstores in jars and cans. They include salted cabbage, salted mustard greens, Szechuan hot pickle, made from kohlrabi, and Szechuan preserved vegetable, made from the root of mustard greens. They should be rinsed well before using.

Chinese Rice Vinegar

White rice vinegar, which is distilled from Chinese rice wine, has a stronger flavour than the red variety, which is made from fermented rice. Cider vinegar or white wine vinegar may used as a substitute.

Chinese Rice Wine

Made from glutinous rice, this has a rich, sherry-like flavour and is golden in colour. In fact, its alternative name is yellow wine. The best type, called Shaoxing, comes from Chekiang in Western China and is made from glutinous rice, millet, ordinary rice and mineral water. Another famous wine, Chen Gang, comes from nearby Fukien. These are both well-matured and quite expensive. Ordinary quality rice wine, made from glutinous rice alone, is adequate for cooking and dry or medium sherry may be used as a substitute. Be careful not to buy Mao Tai, which is also sometimes marketed as a 'wine', as it is a spirit distilled from sorghum and is even stronger than pure vodka.

Coriander (Cilantro)

Also known as Chinese parsley, the fresh leaves are widely used in Chinese cooking. Tearing the leaves, rather than chopping them, produces a more subtle flavour. Although it resembles flat leaf parsley in appearance, coriander (cilantro) tastes quite different.

Dried Mushrooms

Dried Chinese or shiitake mushrooms are used many dishes. They are expensive, but as their flavour is very strong, only a few are required. Soak them in hot water for 20–30 minutes before using. The soaking water can be used as stock. Dried mushrooms keep more or less indefinitely in a cool, dry place.

Ingredients

Egg Noodles

These yellow noodles range in size and shape from long, narrow strands, like spaghetti, to broad, flat ribbons, like tagliatelle. They are available both fresh and dried.

Ginger

The fresh root is an essential ingredient in many Chinese dishes. Ground ginger is no substitute, as it will burn during stir-frying and does not impart the same delicate flavour to other dishes. Choose plump sections of root with shiny, unblemished skins. To use, peel with a swivel vegetable peeler or a small sharp knife and thinly slice, finely chop or grate, according to the recipe. Fresh root ginger will keep for several weeks in a cool, dry place.

Hoisin Sauce

Sweet and spicy, this dark brownish red sauce is made from soya beans, sugar, flour, vinegar, garlic, chillies, sesame oil and salt. It is often combined with soy sauce for flavouring stir-fried dishes and may also be used on its own when cooking seafood, spare ribs and duck. It is sometimes provided in a small bowl at the table as a dipping sauce.

Lemon Grass

This aromatic herb has a mild citrus flavour. It is available fresh, in jars or powdered. Use only the lower part of the stem, which should either be removed from the dish before serving or very finely chopped, as it is quite woody.

Lily Buds

Tiger lily buds, also called golden needles, are dried flower buds with a rather musty flavour that is something of an acquired taste. They should be soaked in water for 20 minutes before use.

Lotus Leaves

The leaves of the lotus plant are very large and are used to enclose food to be steamed and although they are not eaten, they impart a subtle flavour to the contents of the parcels. They are sold dried and should be soaked in warm water for 20 minutes before use.

Lotus Root

Available dried or canned, lotus root is cooked as part of a mixed vegetable dish. Soak the dried root in cold water overnight before use. Fresh lotus root is not usually available in the West.

Ingredients

Lotus Seeds

These oval seeds, about 1 cm/^{1}/$_2$ inch long, are available dried or canned. They are used in vegetable dishes and soups.

Oyster Sauce

Made from boiled oysters and soy sauce, this salty, brown sauce should be used moderately. It is widely used in Cantonese cooking. Vegetarians can use soy sauce as a substitute. Oyster sauce will keep in the refrigerator for several months.

Pak Choi

Also known as bok choy, this is an attractive vegetable with white stems and dark green leaves.

Plum Sauce

Especially popular in Cantonese cooking, this thick, rich, spicy fruit sauce is available in jars and cans.

Rice Stick Noodles

About 25 cm/10 inches long, these white thread noodles are more popular in Southern than Northern cuisine and go well with fish. They do not require soaking before cooking.

Sesame Oil

Made from toasted sesame seeds, this oil is strongly flavoured and aromatic. It is rarely used for frying, but a little is often added to a dish at the end of the cooking time for extra flavour. Be sure to buy a Chinese variety, as Middle Eastern sesame oil is less aromatic and flavoursome.

Sesame Seeds

Widely used in all Chinese cooking, sesame seeds add a nutty flavour, pleasant aroma and crunchy texture to many dishes.

Soy Sauce

This is the sauce most widely used in Chinese cooking and is made from fermented soy beans, salt, yeast and sugar. Light soy sauce has a stronger flavour than dark and is mainly used in cooking. Dark soy sauce is sweeter and richer and is frequently used as a condiment. When used in cooking, it imparts a rich colour to the food and is integral to the technique known as red-cooking. Japanese soy sauce has a much lighter flavour and is not an adequate substitute.

Spring Roll Wrappers

These are made from wheat flour or rice flour and water and are wafer thin. They are available in a variety of sizes. Wheat-flour wrappers are sold frozen and should be thoroughly thawed before separating and using them. Rice-flour wrappers must be soaked before use.

Straw Mushrooms

Named because they grow on beds of rice straw, these mushrooms are used for their unusual slippery texture rather than their flavour, which is quite bland. They are widely available in cans, but fresh straw mushrooms cannot be obtained in the West.

Szechuan Peppercorns

These reddish brown or pink peppercorns, also known as farchiew, grow wild in Western China. They are very aromatic, but not so hot as either black or white peppercorns. They are often roasted and ground before use.

Tofu

Also known as bean curd, this soya bean product is used extensively in Chinese cooking. It has a fairly bland flavour, but readily absorbs the flavours of other ingredients. Firm tofu, ideal for stir-frying, is usually sold in cakes. It should be handled carefully, as it breaks up fairly easily. It can be sliced, diced or shredded. Silken tofu has a more jelly-like consistency. Tofu is high in protein, making it a very popular vegetarian food. It can be stored, submerged in water and covered, in the refrigerator for several days. Dried tofu is sold in cakes and can be cut into strips or slices before being cooked with other ingredients. Smoked and marinated tofu is also available, but these are less suitable for Chinese cooking.

Water Chestnuts

These roots of an aquatic plant resemble chestnuts in appearance only and peeling them reveals crisp, white, sweet-tasting flesh. They are available fresh and in cans, but the latter have less flavour and texture. Store fresh water chestnuts, submerged in water and covered, in the refrigerator for up to a month, changing the water every two or three days.

Wonton Wrappers

These are made from flour, egg and water. You can make your own or buy them ready-made.

Wood Ears

Dried fungi that grow on trees, wood ears and the similar cloud ears are like mushrooms. They are used more for their texture than flavour and provide contrasting colour in some dishes. They are available dried and should be soaked in hot water for 20-30 minutes and thoroughly rinsed before use. Discard the soaking water.

Basic Recipes

Chinese Stock

This basic stock is used in Chinese cooking not only as the basis for soup-making, but also whenever liquid is required instead of plain water.

MAKES 2.5L/4½ PINTS/10 CUPS

750 g/1 lb 10 oz chicken pieces

750 g/1 lb 10 oz pork spare ribs

3.75 litres/6½ pints/15 cups cold water

3-4 pieces ginger root, crushed

3-4 spring onions (scallions), each tied into a knot

3-4 tbsp Chinese rice wine or dry sherry

1 Trim off any excess fat from the chicken and spare ribs; chop them into large pieces.

2 Place the chicken and pork in a large pan with the water; add the ginger and spring onion (scallion) knots.

3 Bring to the boil, and skim off the scum. Reduce the heat and simmer uncovered for at least 2-3 hours.

4 Strain the stock, discarding the chicken, pork, ginger and spring onions (scallions); add the wine and return to the boil, simmer for 2-3 minutes.

5 Refrigerate the stock when cool; it will keep for up to 4-5 days. Alternatively, it can be frozen in small containers and be defrosted as required.

Fresh Chicken Stock

MAKES 1.75 LITRES/3 PINTS/7½ CUPS

1 kg/2 lb 4 oz chicken, skinned

2 celery sticks

1 onion

2 carrots

1 garlic clove

few sprigs of fresh parsley

2 litres/3½ pints/9 cups water

salt and pepper

1 Put all the ingredients into a large saucepan.

2 Bring to the boil. Skim away surface scum using a large flat spoon. Reduce the heat to a gentle simmer, partially cover, and cook for 2 hours. Allow to cool.

3 Line a sieve (strainer) with clean muslin (cheesecloth) and place over a large jug or bowl. Pour the stock through the sieve (strainer). The cooked chicken can be used in another recipe. Discard the other solids. Cover the stock and chill.

4 Skim away any fat that forms before using. Store in the refrigerator for 3-4 days, until required, or freeze in small batches.

Fresh Vegetable Stock

This can be kept chilled for up to three days or frozen for up to three months. Salt is not added when cooking the stock: it is better to season it according to the dish in which it its to be used.

MAKES 1.5 LITRES/2¾ PINTS/6¼ CUPS

250 g/9 oz shallots

1 large carrot, diced

1 celery stalk, chopped

½ fennel bulb

1 garlic clove

1 bay leaf

a few fresh parsley and tarragon sprigs

2 litres/ 3½ pints/8¾ cups water

pepper

1 Put all the ingredients in a large saucepan and bring to the boil.

2 Skim off the surface scum with a flat spoon and reduce to a gentle simmer. Partially cover and cook for 45 minutes. Leave to cool.

3 Line a sieve (strainer) with clean muslin (cheesecloth) and put over a large jug or bowl. Pour the stock through the sieve (strainer). Discard the herbs and vegetables.

4 Cover and store in small quantities in the refrigerator for up to three days.

Fresh Lamb Stock

MAKES 1.75 LITRES/3 PINTS/7½ CUPS

about 1 kg/2 lb 4 oz bones from a cooked joint or raw chopped lamb bones

2 onions, studded with 6 cloves, or sliced or chopped coarsely

2 carrots, sliced

1 leek, sliced

1-2 celery sticks, sliced

1 Bouquet Garni

about 2.25 litres/4 pints/2 quarts water

1 Chop or break up the bones and place in a large saucepan with the other ingredients.

2 Bring to the boil and remove any scum from the surface with a perforated spoon. Cover and simmer gently for 3-4 hours. Strain the stock and leave to cool.

3 Remove any fat from the surface and chill. If stored for more than 24 hours the stock must be boiled every day, cooled quickly and chilled again. The stock may be frozen for up to 2 months; place in a large plastic bag and seal, leaving at least 2.5 cm/1 inch of headspace to allow for expansion.

Fresh Fish Stock

MAKES 1.75 LITRES/3 PINTS/7½ CUPS

1 head of a cod or salmon, etc, plus the trimmings, skin and bones or just the trimmings, skin and bones

1-2 onions, sliced

1 carrot, sliced

1-2 celery sticks, sliced

good squeeze of lemon juice

1 Bouquet Garni or 2 fresh or dried bay leaves

1 Wash the fish head and trimmings and place in a saucepan. Cover with water and bring to the boil.

2 Remove any scum with a perforated spoon, then add the remaining ingredients. Cover and simmer for about 30 minutes.

3 Strain and cool. Store in the refrigerator and use within 2 days.

Cornflour (Cornstarch) Paste

Cornflour (cornstarch) paste is made by mixing 1 part cornflour (cornstarch) with about 1½ parts of cold water. Stir until smooth. The paste is used to thicken sauces.

Plain Rice

Use long-grain rice or patna rice, or better still, try fragrant Thai rice.

SERVES 4

250 g/9 oz long-grain rice

about 250 ml/9 fl oz/1 cup cold water

pinch of salt

½ tsp oil (optional)

1 Wash and rinse the rice just once. Place the rice in a saucepan and add enough water so that there is no more than 2 cm/¾ inch of water above the surface of the rice.

2 Bring to the boil, add salt and oil (if using), and stir to prevent the rice sticking to the bottom of the pan.

3 Reduce the heat to very, very low, cover and cook for 15-20 minutes.

4 Remove from the heat and let stand, covered, for 10 minutes or so. Fluff up the rice with a fork or spoon before serving.

Fresh Coconut Milk

To make it from fresh grated coconut, place about 250 g/9 oz grated coconut in a bowl, pour over about 600 ml/1 pint of boiling water to just cover and leave to stand for 1 hour. Strain through muslin, squeezing hard to extract as much 'thick' milk as possible. If you require coconut cream, leave to stand then skim the 'cream' from the surface for use. Unsweetened desiccated coconut can also be used in the same quantities.

How to Use This Book

Each recipe contains a wealth of useful information, including a breakdown of nutritional quantities, preparation and cooking times, and level of difficulty. All of this information is explained in detail below.

The nutritional information provided for each recipe is per serving or per portion. Optional ingredients, variations or serving suggestions have not been included in the calculations.

The number of chef's hats represents the difficulty of each recipe, ranging from easy (1 chef's hat) to difficult (5 chef's hats).

This amount of time represents the preparation of ingredients, including cooling, chilling and soaking times.

This represents the cooking time.

The ingredients for each recipe are listed in the order that they are used.

The method is clearly explained with step-by-step instructions that are easy to follow.

A full-colour photograph of the finished dish.

The method is illustrated with step-by-step photographs, making the recipe easy to follow.

Cook's tips and variations provide useful information regarding ingredients or cooking techniques.

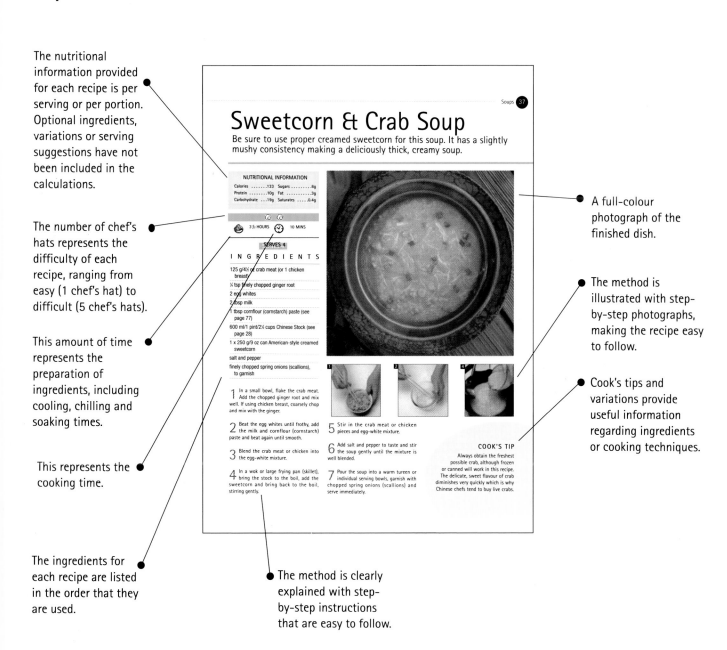

Soups 37

Sweetcorn & Crab Soup

Be sure to use proper creamed sweetcorn for this soup. It has a slightly mushy consistency making a deliciously thick, creamy soup.

NUTRITIONAL INFORMATION

Calories . . . . .133 Sugars 6g
Protein . . . . .10g Fat 3g
Carbohydrate . . .19g Saturates 0.4g

3½ HOURS   10 MINS

SERVES 4

INGREDIENTS

125 g/4½ oz crab meat (or 1 chicken breast)

¼ tsp finely chopped ginger root

2 egg whites

2 tbsp milk

1 tbsp cornflour (cornstarch) paste (see page 77)

600 ml/1 pint/2½ cups Chinese Stock (see page 28)

1 x 250 g/9 oz can American-style creamed sweetcorn

salt and pepper

finely chopped spring onions (scallions), to garnish

1 In a small bowl, flake the crab meat. Add the chopped ginger root and mix well. If using chicken breast, coarsely chop and mix with the ginger.

2 Beat the egg whites until frothy, add the milk and cornflour (cornstarch) paste and beat again until smooth.

3 Blend the crab meat or chicken into the egg-white mixture.

4 In a wok or large frying pan (skillet), bring the stock to the boil, add the sweetcorn and bring back to the boil, stirring gently.

5 Stir in the crab meat or chicken pieces and egg-white mixture.

6 Add salt and pepper to taste and stir the soup gently until the mixture is well blended.

7 Pour the soup into a warm tureen or individual serving bowls, garnish with chopped spring onions (scallions) and serve immediately.

COOK'S TIP

Always obtain the freshest possible crab, although frozen or canned will work in this recipe. The delicate, sweet flavour of crab diminishes very quickly which is why Chinese chefs tend to buy live crabs.

Soups

Soup is an integral part of the Chinese meal but is rarely served as a starter as it is in the Western world. Instead, soup is usually served between courses to clear the palate and act as a beverage throughout the meal. The soup is usually presented in a large tureen in the centre of the table for people to help themselves as the meal progresses.

The soups in this chapter combine a range of flavours and textures. There are thicker soups, thin clear consommés, and those which are served with wontons, dumplings, noodles or even rice in them. Ideally the soup should be made with fresh stock, but if this is unavailable, use a stock cube and reduce the amount of seasonings otherwise the soup will be too salty. It is always worth making your own Chinese Stock (see page 28) if you have time.

Chicken & Sweetcorn Soup

A hint of chilli and sherry flavour this soup while red (bell) pepper and tomato add colour.

NUTRITIONAL INFORMATION

Calories 199	Sugars 8g
Protein 12g	Fat 8g
Carbohydrate . . .19g	Saturates 1g

 5 MINS   20 MINS

SERVES 4

I N G R E D I E N T S

1 skinless, boneless chicken breast,
   about 175 g/6 oz

2 tbsp sunflower oil

2–3 spring onions (scallions),
   thinly sliced diagonally

1 small or ½ large red
   (bell) pepper, thinly sliced

1 garlic clove, crushed

125 g/4½ oz baby sweetcorn (corn-on-the-
   cob), thinly sliced

1 litre/1¾ pints/4 cups chicken stock

200 g/7 oz can of sweetcorn
   niblets, well drained

2 tbsp sherry

2–3 tsp bottled sweet chilli sauce

2–3 tsp cornflour (cornstarch)

2 tomatoes, quartered
   and deseeded, then sliced

salt and pepper

chopped fresh coriander (cilantro)
   or parsley, to garnish

1 Cut the chicken breast into 4 strips lengthways, then cut each strip into narrow slices across the grain.

2 Heat the oil in a wok or frying pan (skillet), swirling it around until it is really hot.

3 Add the chicken and stir-fry for 3–4 minutes, moving it around the wok until it is well sealed all over and almost cooked through.

4 Add the spring onions (scallions), (bell) pepper and garlic, and stir-fry for 2–3 minutes. Add the sweetcorn and stock and bring to the boil.

5 Add the sweetcorn niblets, sherry, sweet chilli sauce and salt to taste, and simmer for 5 minutes, stirring from time to time.

6 Blend the cornflour (cornstarch) with a little cold water. Add to the soup and bring to the boil, stirring until the sauce is thickened. Add the tomato slices, season to taste and simmer for 1–2 minutes.

7 Serve the chicken and sweetcorn soup hot, sprinkled with chopped coriander (cilantro) or parsley.

Sweetcorn & Crab Soup

Be sure to use proper creamed sweetcorn for this soup. It has a slightly mushy consistency making a deliciously thick, creamy soup.

NUTRITIONAL INFORMATION

Calories 133	Sugars 6g	
Protein 10g	Fat 3g	
Carbohydrate ...19g	Saturates 0.4g	

3¹/₂ HOURS   10 MINS

SERVES 4

INGREDIENTS

125 g/4½ oz crab meat (or 1 chicken breast)

¼ tsp finely chopped ginger root

2 egg whites

2 tbsp milk

1 tbsp cornflour (cornstarch) paste (see page 31)

600 ml/1 pint/2½ cups Chinese Stock (see page 30)

1 x 250 g/9 oz can American-style creamed sweetcorn

salt and pepper

finely chopped spring onions (scallions), to garnish

1 In a small bowl, flake the crab meat. Add the chopped ginger root and mix well. If using chicken breast, coarsely chop and mix with the ginger.

2 Beat the egg whites until frothy, add the milk and cornflour (cornstarch) paste and beat again until smooth.

3 Blend the crab meat or chicken into the egg-white mixture.

4 In a wok or large frying pan (skillet), bring the stock to the boil, add the sweetcorn and bring back to the boil, stirring gently.

5 Stir in the crab meat or chicken pieces and egg-white mixture.

6 Add salt and pepper to taste and stir the soup gently until the mixture is well blended.

7 Pour the soup into a warm tureen or individual serving bowls, garnish with chopped spring onions (scallions) and serve immediately.

COOK'S TIP

Always obtain the freshest possible crab, although frozen or canned will work in this recipe. The delicate, sweet flavour of crab diminishes very quickly which is why Chinese chefs tend to buy live crabs.

Seafood & Tofu Soup

Use prawn (shrimp), squid or scallops, or a combination of all three in this healthy soup.

NUTRITIONAL INFORMATION

Calories	97	Sugars 0g
Protein	........17g	Fat 2g
Carbohydrate	....3g	Saturates 0.4g

3½ HOURS   10 MINS

SERVES 4

INGREDIENTS

250 g/9 oz seafood: peeled prawns (shrimp), squid, scallops, etc., defrosted if frozen

½ egg white, lightly beaten

1 tbsp cornflour (cornstarch) paste (see page 31)

1 cake tofu (bean curd)

700 ml/1¼ pints/3 cups Chinese Stock (see page 30)

1 tbsp light soy sauce

salt and pepper

fresh coriander (cilantro) leaves, to garnish (optional)

1 Small prawns (shrimp) can be left whole; larger ones should be cut into smaller pieces; cut the squid and scallops into small pieces.

2 If raw, mix the prawns (shrimp) and scallops with the egg white and cornflour (cornstarch) paste to prevent them from becoming tough when they are cooked. Cut the cake of tofu into about 24 small cubes.

3 Bring the stock to a rolling boil. Add the tofu and soy sauce, bring back to the boil and simmer for 1 minute.

4 Stir in the seafood, raw pieces first, pre-cooked ones last. Bring back to the boil and simmer for just 1 minute.

5 Adjust the seasoning to taste and serve, garnished with coriander (cilantro) leaves, if liked.

COOK'S TIP

Tofu, also known as bean curd, is made from puréed yellow soya beans, which are very high in protein. Although almost tasteless, tofu absorbs the flavours of other ingredients. It is widely available in supermarkets, and Oriental and health-food stores.

Hot & Sour Soup

This well-known soup from Peking is unusual in that it is thickened. The 'hot' flavour is achieved by the addition of plenty of black pepper.

NUTRITIONAL INFORMATION

Calories ....124 Sugars 1g
Protein ....5g Fat 8g
Carbohydrate ....8g Saturates 1g

3½ HOURS 25 MINS

SERVES 4

INGREDIENTS

2 tbsp cornflour (cornstarch)

4 tbsp water

2 tbsp light soy sauce

3 tbsp rice wine vinegar

½ tsp ground black pepper

1 small fresh red chilli, finely chopped

1 egg

2 tbsp vegetable oil

1 onion, chopped

850 ml/1½ pints/3¾ cups chicken or beef consommé

1 open-cap mushroom, sliced

50 g/1¾ oz skinless chicken breast, cut into very thin strips

1 tsp sesame oil

1 In a mixing bowl, blend the cornflour (cornstarch) with the water to form a smooth paste.

2 Add the soy sauce, rice wine vinegar and black pepper.

3 Finely chop the red chilli and add to the ingredients in the bowl. Mix well.

4 Break the egg into a separate bowl and beat well. Set aside while you cook the other ingredients.

5 Heat the oil in a preheated wok and fry the onion for 1–2 minutes until softened.

6 Stir in the consommé, mushroom and chicken and bring to the boil. Cook for about 15 minutes or until the chicken is tender.

7 Gradually pour the cornflour (cornstarch) mixture into the soup and cook, stirring constantly, until it thickens.

8 As you are stirring, gradually drizzle the egg into the soup, to create threads of egg.

9 Pour the hot and sour soup into a warm tureen or individual serving bowls, sprinkle with the sesame oil and serve immediately.

Lamb & Rice Soup

This is a very filling soup, as it contains rice and tender pieces of lamb. Serve before a light main course.

NUTRITIONAL INFORMATION

Calories 116	Sugars 0.2g
Protein 9g	Fat 4g
Carbohydrate . . .12g	Saturates 2g

5 MINS   35 MINS

SERVES 4

INGREDIENTS

150 g/5½ oz lean lamb

50 g/1¾ oz/¼ cup rice

850 ml/1½ pints/3¾ cups
   lamb stock

1 leek, sliced

1 garlic clove, thinly sliced

2 tsp light soy sauce

1 tsp rice wine vinegar

1 medium open-cap mushroom,
   thinly sliced

salt

1 Using a sharp knife, trim any fat from the lamb and cut the meat into thin strips. Set aside until required.

2 Bring a large pan of lightly salted water to the boil and add the rice. Bring back to the boil, stir once, reduce the heat and cook for 10–15 minutes, until tender.

3 Drain the rice, rinse under cold running water, drain again and set aside until required.

4 Meanwhile, put the lamb stock in a large saucepan and bring to the boil.

5 Add the lamb strips, leek, garlic, soy sauce and rice wine vinegar to the stock in the pan. Reduce the heat, cover and leave to simmer for 10 minutes, or until the lamb is tender and cooked through.

6 Add the mushroom slices and the rice to the pan and cook for a further 2–3 minutes, or until the mushroom is completely cooked through.

7 Ladle the soup into 4 individual warmed soup bowls and serve immediately.

VARIATION

Use a few dried Chinese mushrooms, rehydrated according to the packet instructions and chopped, as an alternative to the open-cap mushroom. Add the Chinese mushrooms with the lamb in step 4.

Noodle & Mushroom Soup

This soup is very quickly and easily put together, and is cooked so that each ingredient can still be tasted in the finished dish.

NUTRITIONAL INFORMATION

Calories 74	Sugars 1g
Protein 13g	Fat 3g
Carbohydrate 9g	Saturates 0.4g

 4 HOURS   10 MINS

SERVES 4

INGREDIENTS

15 g/½ oz/¼ cup dried Chinese mushrooms or 125 g/4½ oz/1⅓ cups field or chestnut (crimini) mushrooms

1 litre/1¾ pints/4 cups hot Fresh Vegetable Stock (page 30)

125 g/4½ oz thread egg noodles

2 tsp sunflower oil

3 garlic cloves, crushed

2.5 cm/1 inch piece ginger, shredded finely

½ tsp mushroom ketchup

1 tsp light soy sauce

125 g/4½ oz/2 cups bean sprouts

coriander (cilantro) leaves, to garnish

1 Soak the dried Chinese mushrooms, if using, for at least 30 minutes in 300 ml/½ pint/1¼ cups of the hot vegetable stock. Remove the stalks and discard, then slice the mushrooms. Reserve the stock.

2 Cook the noodles for 2–3 minutes in boiling water. Drain, rinse and set aside until required.

3 Heat the oil over a high heat in a wok or large, heavy frying pan (skillet). Add the garlic and ginger, stir and add the mushrooms. Stir over a high heat for 2 minutes.

4 Add the remaining vegetable stock with the reserved stock and bring to the boil. Add the mushroom ketchup and soy sauce and mix well.

5 Stir in the bean sprouts and cook until tender. Serve over the noodles, garnished with coriander (cilantro) leaves.

COOK'S TIP

Dried mushrooms are highly fragrant and add a special flavour to Chinese dishes. There are many different varieties but Shiitake are the best. Although not cheap, a small amount will go a long way and they will keep indefinitely in an airtight jar.

Wonton Soup

The recipe for the wonton skins makes 24 but the soup requires only half this quantity. The other half can be frozen ready for another time.

NUTRITIONAL INFORMATION

Calories ....278 Sugars 2g
Protein ....10g Fat 5g
Carbohydrate ...50g Saturates 1g

45 MINS   5 MINS

SERVES 4

INGREDIENTS

WONTON SKINS

1 egg

6 tbsp water

250 g/9 oz/2 cups plain (all-purpose) flour, plus extra for dusting

FILLING

125 g/4½ oz/½ cup frozen chopped spinach, defrosted

15 g/½ oz/1 tbsp pine kernels (nuts), toasted and chopped

25 g/1 oz/¼ cup minced quorn (TVP)

salt

SOUP

600 ml/1 pint/2½ cups vegetable stock

1 tbsp dry sherry

1 tbsp light soy sauce

2 spring onions (scallions), chopped

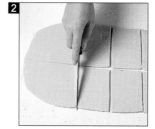

1 To make the wonton skins, beat the egg lightly in a bowl and mix with the water. Stir in the flour to form a stiff dough. Knead lightly, then cover with a damp cloth and leave to rest for 30 minutes.

2 Roll the dough out into a large sheet about 1.5 mm/¼ inch thick. Cut out 24 x 7 cm/3 inch squares. Dust each one lightly with flour. Only 12 squares are required for the soup so freeze the remainder to use on another occasion.

3 To make the filling, squeeze out the excess water from the spinach. Mix the spinach with the pine kernels (nuts) and quorn (TVP) until thoroughly combined. Season with salt.

4 Divide the mixture into 12 equal portions. Using a teaspoon, place one portion in the centre of each square. Seal the wontons by bringing the opposite corners of each square together and squeezing well.

5 To make the soup, bring the vegetable stock, sherry and soy sauce to the boil, add the wontons and boil rapidly for 2–3 minutes. Add the spring onions (scallions) and serve in warmed bowls immediately.

Spicy Chicken Noodle Soup

This filling soup is filled with spicy flavours and bright colours for a really attractive and hearty dish.

NUTRITIONAL INFORMATION

Calories 286   Sugars 21g
Protein ....22g   Fat 6g
Carbohydrate ...37g   Saturates 1g

15 MINS   20 MINS

SERVES 4

INGREDIENTS

2 tbsp tamarind paste

4 red chillies, finely chopped

2 cloves garlic, crushed

2.5 cm/1-inch piece Thai ginger, peeled and very finely chopped

4 tbsp fish sauce

2 tbsp palm sugar or caster (superfine) sugar

8 lime leaves, roughly torn

1.2 litres/2 pints/5 cups chicken stock

350 g/12 oz boneless chicken breast

100 g/3½ oz carrots, very thinly sliced

350 g/12 oz sweet potato, diced

100 g/3½ oz baby corn cobs, halved

3 tbsp fresh coriander (cilantro), roughly chopped

100 g/3½ oz cherry tomatoes, halved

150 g/5½ oz flat rice noodles

fresh coriander (cilantro), chopped, to garnish

1 Preheat a large wok or frying pan (skillet). Place the tamarind paste, chillies, garlic, ginger, fish sauce, sugar, lime leaves and chicken stock in the wok and bring to the boil, stirring constantly. Reduce the heat and cook for about 5 minutes.

2 Using a sharp knife, thinly slice the chicken. Add the chicken to the wok and cook for a further 5 minutes, stirring the mixture well.

3 Reduce the heat and add the carrots, sweet potato and baby corn cobs to the wok. Leave to simmer, uncovered, for 5 minutes, or until the vegetables are just tender and the chicken is completely cooked through.

4 Stir in the chopped fresh coriander (cilantro), cherry tomatoes and flat rice noodles.

5 Leave the soup to simmer for about 5 minutes, or until the noodles are tender.

6 Garnish the spicy chicken noodle soup with chopped fresh coriander (cilantro) and serve hot.

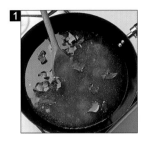

Spicy Prawn (Shrimp) Soup

Lime leaves are used as a flavouring in this soup to add tartness.

NUTRITIONAL INFORMATION

Calories 217	Sugars 16g
Protein 16g	Fat 4g
Carbohydrate . . .31g	Saturates 1g

 10 MINS   20 MINS

SERVES 4

INGREDIENTS

2 tbsp tamarind paste

4 red chilies, very finely chopped

2 cloves garlic, crushed

2.5 cm/1 inch piece Thai ginger, peeled and very finely chopped

4 tbsp fish sauce

2 tbsp palm sugar or caster (superfine) sugar

1.2 litres/2 pints/5 cups fish stock

8 lime leaves

100 g/3½ oz carrots, very thinly sliced

350 g/12 oz sweet potato, diced

100 g/3½ oz/1 cup baby corn cobs, halved

3 tbsp fresh coriander (cilantro), roughly chopped

100g/3½ oz cherry tomatoes, halved

225 g/8 oz fan-tail prawns (shrimp)

1 Place the tamarind paste, red chillies, garlic, ginger, fish sauce, sugar and fish stock in a preheated wok or large, heavy frying pan (skillet). Roughly tear the lime leaves and add to the wok. Bring to the boil, stirring constantly to blend the flavours.

2 Reduce the heat and add the carrot, sweet potato and baby corn cobs to the mixture in the wok.

3 Leave the soup to simmer, uncovered, for about 10 minutes, or until the vegetables are just tender.

4 Stir the coriander (cilantro), cherry tomatoes and prawns (shrimp) into the soup and heat through for 5 minutes.

5 Transfer the soup to a warm soup tureen or individual serving bowls and serve hot.

COOK'S TIP

Thai ginger or galangal is a member of the ginger family, but it is yellow in colour with pink sprouts. The flavour is aromatic and less pungent than ginger.

Chicken Wonton Soup

This Chinese-style soup is delicious as a starter to an oriental meal or as a light meal.

NUTRITIONAL INFORMATION

Calories . . . . .101 Sugars 0.3g
Protein . . . . .14g Fat 4g
Carbohydrate . . . .3g Saturates 1g

15 MINS   10 MINS

SERVES 4-6

INGREDIENTS

FILLING

350 g/12 oz minced (ground) chicken

1 tbsp soy sauce

1 tsp grated, fresh ginger root

1 garlic clove, crushed

2 tsp sherry

2 spring onions (scallions), chopped

1 tsp sesame oil

1 egg white

½ tsp cornflour (cornstarch)

½ tsp sugar

about 35 wonton wrappers

SOUP

1.5 litres/2¾ pints/6 cups chicken stock

1 tbsp light soy sauce

1 spring onion (scallion), shredded

1 small carrot, cut into very thin slices

1 Place all the ingredients for the filling in a large bowl and mix until thoroughly combined.

2 Place a small spoonful of the filling in the centre of each wonton wrapper.

3 Dampen the edges and gather up the wonton wrapper to form a small pouch enclosing the filling.

4 Cook the filled wontons in boiling water for 1 minute or until they float to the top. Remove with a slotted spoon and set aside.

5 Bring the chicken stock to the boil. Add the soy sauce, spring onion (scallion) and carrot.

6 Add the wontons to the soup and simmer gently for 2 minutes. Serve.

COOK'S TIP

Make double quantities of wonton skins and freeze the remainder. Place small squares of baking parchment in between each skin, then place in a freezer bag and freeze. Defrost thoroughly before using.

Vegetarian Hot & Sour Soup

This popular soup is easy to make and very filling. It can be eaten as a meal on its own or served as an appetizer before a light menu.

NUTRITIONAL INFORMATION

Calories 61	Sugars 1g	
Protein 5g	Fat 2g	
Carbohydrate 8g	Saturates 0.2g	

  30 MINS   10 MINS

SERVES 4

INGREDIENTS

4 Chinese dried mushrooms
(if unavailable, use open-cup
mushrooms)

125 g/4½ oz firm tofu (bean curd)

60 g/2 oz/1 cup canned bamboo
shoots

600 ml/1 pint/2½ cups vegetable stock
or water

60 g/2 oz/⅓ cup peas

1 tbsp dark soy sauce

2 tbsp white wine vinegar

2 tbsp cornflour (cornstarch)

salt and pepper

sesame oil, to serve

1 Place the Chinese dried mushrooms in a small bowl and cover with warm water. Leave to soak for about 20–25 minutes.

2 Drain the mushrooms and squeeze out the excess water, reserving this. Remove the tough centres and cut the mushrooms into thin shreds. Shred the tofu (bean curd) and bamboo shoots.

3 Bring the stock or water to the boil in a large saucepan. Add the mushrooms, tofu (bean curd), bamboo shoots and peas. Simmer for 2 minutes.

4 Mix together the soy sauce, vinegar and cornflour (cornstarch) with 2 tablespoons of the reserved mushroom liquid.

5 Stir the soy sauce and cornflour (cornstarch) mixture into the soup with the remaining mushroom liquid. Bring to the boil and season with salt and plenty of pepper. Simmer for 2 minutes.

6 Serve in warmed bowls with a few drops of sesame oil sprinkled over the top of each.

COOK'S TIP

If you use open-cup mushrooms instead of dried mushrooms, add an extra 150 ml/ ¼ pint/⅔ cup vegetable stock or water to the soup, as these mushrooms do not need soaking.

Sweetcorn & Lentil Soup

This pale-coloured soup is made with sweetcorn and green lentils, and is similar in style to the traditional crab and sweetcorn soup.

NUTRITIONAL INFORMATION

Calories 171	Sugars 9g
Protein 5g	Fat 2g
Carbohydrate . . .30g	Saturates 0.3g

 5 MINS   30 MINS

SERVES 4

INGREDIENTS

25 g/1 oz/2 tbsp green lentils

1 litre/1¾ pints/4 cups vegetable stock

1cm/½ inch piece ginger root, chopped finely

2 tsp soy sauce

1 tsp sugar

1 tbsp cornflour (cornstarch)

3 tbsp dry sherry

325 g/11½ oz can sweetcorn

1 egg white

1 tsp sesame oil

salt and pepper

TO GARNISH

spring onion (scallion), cut into strips

red chilli, cut into strips

1 Wash the lentils in a sieve (strainer). Place in a saucepan with the stock, ginger root, soy sauce and sugar. Bring to the boil and boil rapidly, uncovered, for 10 minutes. Skim off any froth on the surface. Reduce the heat, cover and simmer for 15 minutes.

2 Mix the cornflour (cornstarch) with the sherry in a small bowl. Add the sweetcorn with the liquid from the can and cornflour (cornstarch) mixture to the saucepan. Simmer for 2 minutes.

3 Whisk the egg white lightly with the sesame oil. Pour the egg mixture into the soup in a thin stream, remove from the heat and stir. The egg white will form white strands. Season with salt and pepper to taste.

4 Pour into 4 warmed soup bowls and garnish with strips of spring onion (scallion) and red chilli. Serve the soup immediately.

COOK'S TIP

To save time use a 425 g/15 oz can of green lentils instead of dried ones. Place the lentils and sweetcorn in a large saucepan with the stock and flavourings, bring to the boil and simmer for 2 minutes, then continue the recipe from step 2 as above.

Chinese Potato & Pork Broth

In this recipe the pork is seasoned with traditional Chinese flavourings – soy sauce, rice wine vinegar and a dash of sesame oil.

NUTRITIONAL INFORMATION

Calories	166	Sugars	.........2g
Protein	........10g	Fat	...........5g
Carbohydrate	...26g	Saturates	.......1g

 5 MINS 20 MINS

SERVES 4

I N G R E D I E N T S

1 litre/1¾ pints/4½ cups chicken stock

2 large potatoes, diced

2 tbsp rice wine vinegar

2 tbsp cornflour (cornstarch)

4 tbsp water

125 g/4½ oz pork fillet, sliced

1 tbsp light soy sauce

1 tsp sesame oil

1 carrot, cut into very thin strips

1 tsp ginger root, chopped

3 spring onions (scallions), sliced thinly

1 red (bell) pepper, sliced

225 g/8 oz can bamboo shoots, drained

1 Add the chicken stock, diced potatoes and 1 tbsp of the rice wine vinegar to a saucepan and bring to the boil. Reduce the heat until the stock is just simmering.

2 Mix the cornflour (cornstarch) with the water then stir into the hot stock.

3 Bring the stock back to the boil, stirring until thickened, then reduce the heat until it is just simmering again.

4 Place the pork slices in a dish and season with the remaining rice wine vinegar, the soy sauce and sesame oil.

5 Add the pork slices, carrot strips and ginger to the stock and cook for 10 minutes. Stir in the spring onions (scallions), red (bell) pepper and bamboo shoots. Cook for a further 5 minutes. Pour the soup into warmed bowls and serve immediately.

VARIATION

For extra heat, add 1 chopped red chilli or 1 tsp of chilli powder to the soup in step 5.

Lettuce & Tofu Soup

This is a delicate, clear soup of shredded lettuce and small chunks of tofu (bean curd) with sliced carrot and spring onion (scallion).

NUTRITIONAL INFORMATION

Calories 113
Sugars 2g
Protein 5g
Fat 8g
Carbohydrate 3g
Saturates 1g

 5 MINS   15 MINS

SERVES 4

INGREDIENTS

200 g/7 oz tofu (bean curd)

2 tbsp vegetable oil

1 carrot, sliced thinly

1 cm/½ inch piece ginger root,
    cut into thin shreds

3 spring onions (scallions), sliced
    diagonally

1.2 litres/2 pints/5 cups vegetable stock

2 tbsp soy sauce

2 tbsp dry sherry

1 tsp sugar

125 g/4½ oz/1½ cups cos (romaine) lettuce,
    shredded

salt and pepper

1 Using a sharp knife, cut the tofu (bean curd) into small cubes.

2 Heat the vegetable oil in a preheated wok or large saucepan, add the tofu (bean curd) and stir-fry until browned. Remove with a perforated spoon and drain on kitchen paper (paper towels).

3 Add the carrot, ginger root and spring onions (scallions) to the wok or saucepan and stir-fry for 2 minutes.

4 Add the vegetable stock, soy sauce, sherry and sugar. Stir well to mix all the ingredients. Bring to the boil and simmer for 1 minute.

5 Add the cos (romaine) lettuce to the wok or saucepan and stir until it has just wilted.

6 Return the tofu (bean curd) to the pan to reheat. Season with salt and pepper to taste and serve the soup immediately in warmed bowls.

COOK'S TIP

For a prettier effect, score grooves along the length of the carrot with a sharp knife before slicing. This will create a flower effect as the carrot is cut into rounds. You could also try slicing the carrot on the diagonal to make longer slices.

Chilli Fish Soup

Chinese mushrooms add an intense flavour to this soup which is unique. If they are unavailable, use open-cap mushrooms, sliced.

NUTRITIONAL INFORMATION

Calories 166	Sugars 1g	
Protein 23g	Fat 7g	
Carbohydrate 4g	Saturates 1g	

 15 MINS   15 MINS

SERVES 4

INGREDIENTS

15 g/½ oz Chinese dried mushrooms

2 tbsp sunflower oil

1 onion, sliced

100 g/3½ oz/1½ cups mangetout (snow peas)

100 g/3½ oz/1½ cups bamboo shoots

3 tbsp sweet chilli sauce

1.2 litres/2 pints/5 cups fish or vegetable stock

3 tbsp light soy sauce

2 tbsp fresh coriander (cilantro), plus extra to garnish

450 g/1 lb cod fillet, skinned and cubed

COOK'S TIP

Cod is used in this recipe as it is a meaty white fish. For real luxury, use monkfish tail instead.

There are many different varieties of dried mushrooms, but shiitake are best. They are not cheap, but a small amount will go a long way.

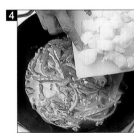

1 Place the mushrooms in a large bowl. Pour over enough boiling water to cover and leave to stand for 5 minutes. Drain the mushrooms thoroughly in a colander. Using a sharp knife, roughly chop the mushrooms.

2 Heat the sunflower oil in a preheated wok or large frying pan (skillet). Add the sliced onion to the wok and stir-fry for 5 minutes, or until softened.

3 Add the mangetout (snow peas), bamboo shoots, chilli sauce, stock and soy sauce to the wok and bring to the boil.

4 Add the coriander (cilantro) and cod and leave to simmer for 5 minutes or until the fish is cooked through.

5 Transfer the soup to warm bowls, garnish with extra coriander (cilantro), if wished, and serve hot.

Shrimp Dumpling Soup

These small dumplings filled with shrimp and pork may be made slightly larger and served as dim sum on their own, if you prefer.

NUTRITIONAL INFORMATION

Calories 311	Sugars 2g
Protein 18g	Fat 8g
Carbohydrate . . .41g	Saturates 2g

  20 MINS   10 MINS

SERVES 4

I N G R E D I E N T S

DUMPLINGS

150 g/5½ oz/1⅛ cups plain (all-purpose) flour

50 ml/2 fl oz/¼ cup boiling water

30 ml/1 fl oz/⅛ cup cold water

1½ tsp vegetable oil

FILLING

125 g/4½ oz minced (ground) pork

125 g/4½ oz cooked peeled shrimp, chopped

50 g/1¾ oz canned water chestnuts, drained, rinsed and chopped

1 celery stick, chopped

1 tsp cornflour (cornstarch)

1 tbsp sesame oil

1 tbsp light soy sauce

SOUP

850 ml/1½ pints/3¾ cups fish stock

50 g/1¾ oz cellophane noodles

1 tbsp dry sherry

chopped chives, to garnish

1 To make the dumplings, mix together the flour, boiling water, cold water and oil in a bowl until a pliable dough is formed.

2 Knead the dough on a lightly floured surface for 5 minutes. Cut the dough into 16 equal sized pieces.

3 Roll the dough pieces into rounds about 7.5 cm/ 3 inches in diameter.

4 Mix the filling ingredients together in a large bowl.

5 Spoon a little of the filling mixture into the centre of each round. Bring the edges of the dough together, scrunching them up to form a 'moneybag' shape. Twist the gathered edges to seal.

6 Pour the fish stock into a large saucepan and bring to the boil.

7 Add the cellophane noodles, dumplings and dry sherry to the pan and cook for 4–5 minutes, until the noodles and dumplings are tender. Garnish with chopped chives and serve immediately.

Chicken Noodle Soup

Quick to make, this hot and spicy soup is hearty and warming. If you like your food really fiery, add a chopped dried or fresh chilli with its seeds.

NUTRITIONAL INFORMATION

Calories 196	Sugars 4g	
Protein 16g	Fat 11g	
Carbohydrate 8g	Saturates 2g	

🍲 10 MINS 🕐 25 MINS

SERVES 4-6

INGREDIENTS

1 sheet of dried egg noodles
   from a 250 g/9 oz pack

1 tbsp oil

4 skinless, boneless
   chicken thighs, diced

1 bunch spring onions (scallions), sliced

2 garlic cloves, chopped

2 cm/¾ inch piece fresh
   ginger root, finely chopped

850 ml/1½ pints/3¾ cups chicken stock

200 ml/7 fl oz/scant 1 cup coconut milk

3 tsp red curry paste

3 tbsp peanut butter

2 tbsp light soy sauce

1 small red (bell) pepper, chopped

60 g/2 oz/½ cup frozen peas

salt and pepper

1 Put the noodles in a shallow dish and soak in boiling water as the pack directs.

2 Heat the oil in a large preheated saucepan or wok.

3 Add the diced chicken to the pan or wok and fry for 5 minutes, stirring until lightly browned.

4 Add the white part of the spring onions (scallions), the garlic and ginger and fry for 2 minutes, stirring.

5 Stir in the chicken stock, coconut milk, red curry paste, peanut butter and soy sauce.

6 Season with salt and pepper to taste. Bring to the boil, stirring, then simmer for 8 minutes, stirring occasionally.

7 Add the red (bell) pepper, peas and green spring onion tops and cook for 2 minutes.

8 Add the drained noodles and heat through. Spoon the chicken noodle soup into warmed bowls and serve with a spoon and fork.

VARIATION

Green curry paste can be used instead of red curry paste for a less fiery flavour.

Spinach & Tofu Soup

This is a very colourful and delicious soup. If spinach is not in season, watercress or lettuce can be used instead.

NUTRITIONAL INFORMATION

Calories 33	Sugar 1g	
Protein 4g	Fat 2g	
Carbohydrate 1g	Saturates 0.2g	

   3¹/₂ HOURS   10 MINS

SERVES 4

I N G R E D I E N T S

1 cake tofu (bean curd)

125 g/4½ oz spinach leaves without stems

700 ml/1¼ pints/3 cups Chinese Stock (see page 30) or water

1 tbsp light soy sauce

salt and pepper

1 Using a sharp knife, cut the tofu into small pieces about 5 mm (¼ inch) thick.

2 Wash the spinach leaves thoroughly under cold, running water and drain thoroughly.

3 Cut the spinach leaves into small pieces or shreds, discarding any discoloured leaves and tough stalks. (If possible, use fresh young spinach leaves, which have not yet developed tough ribs. Otherwise, it is important to cut out all the ribs and stems for this soup.) Set the spinach aside until required.

4 In a preheated wok or large frying pan (skillet), bring the Chinese stock or water to a rolling boil.

5 Add the tofu (bean curd) cubes and light soy sauce, bring back to the boil and simmer for about 2 minutes over a medium heat.

6 Add the shredded spinach leaves and simmer for 1 more minute, stirring gently. Skim the surface of the soup to make it clear, adjust the seasoning to taste.

7 Transfer the spinach and tofu (bean curd) soup to a warm soup tureen or individual serving bowls and serve with chopsticks, to pick up the pieces of food and a broad, shallow spoon for drinking the soup.

COOK'S TIP

Soup is an integral part of a Chinese meal; it is usually presented in a large bowl placed in the centre of the table, and consumed as the meal progresses. It serves as a refresher between different dishes and as a beverage throughout the meal.

Peking Duck Soup

This is a hearty and robustly flavoured soup, containing pieces of duck and vegetables cooked in a rich stock.

NUTRITIONAL INFORMATION

Calories	.92	Sugars	.3g
Protein	.8g	Fat	.5g
Carbohydrate	.3g	Saturates	.1g

 5 MINS   35 MINS

SERVES 4

INGREDIENTS

125 g/4½ oz lean duck breast meat

225 g/8 oz Chinese leaves (cabbage)

850 ml/1½ pints/3¾ cups chicken or duck stock

1 tbsp dry sherry or rice wine

1 tbsp light soy sauce

2 garlic cloves, crushed

pinch of ground star anise

1 tbsp sesame seeds

1 tsp sesame oil

1 tbsp chopped fresh parsley

1 Remove the skin from the duck breast and finely dice the flesh.

2 Using a sharp knife, shred the Chinese leaves (cabbage).

3 Put the stock in a large saucepan and bring to the boil. Add the sherry or rice wine, soy sauce, diced duck meat and shredded Chinese leaves and stir to mix thoroughly. Reduce the heat and leave to simmer gently for 15 minutes.

4 Stir in the garlic and star anise and cook over a low heat for a further 10–15 minutes, or until the duck is tender.

5 Meanwhile, dry-fry the sesame seeds in a preheated, heavy-based frying pan (skillet) or wok, stirring constantly.

6 Remove the sesame seeds from the pan and stir them into the soup, together with the sesame oil and chopped fresh parsley.

7 Spoon the soup into warm bowls and serve immediately.

VARIATION

If Chinese leaves (cabbage) are unavailable, use leafy green cabbage instead. You may wish to adjust the quantity to taste, as Western cabbage has a stronger flavour and odour than Chinese leaves (cabbage).

Prawn (Shrimp) Soup

This soup is an interesting mix of colours and textures. The egg may be made into a flat omelette and added as thin strips if preferred.

NUTRITIONAL INFORMATION

Calories ....123 Sugars 0.2g
Protein ....13g Fat 8g
Carbohydrate ....1g Saturates 1g

5 MINS   20 MINS

SERVES 4

INGREDIENTS

2 tbsp sunflower oil

2 spring onions (scallions), thinly sliced diagonally

1 carrot, coarsely grated

125 g/4½ oz large closed cup mushrooms, thinly sliced

1 litre/1¾ pints/4 cups fish or vegetable stock

½ tsp Chinese five-spice powder

1 tbsp light soy sauce

125 g/4½ oz large peeled prawns (shrimp) or peeled tiger prawns (shrimp), defrosted if frozen

½ bunch watercress, trimmed and roughly chopped

1 egg, well beaten

salt and pepper

4 large prawns (shrimp) in shells, to garnish (optional)

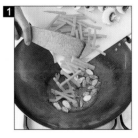
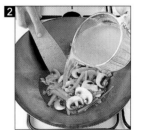

1 Heat the oil in a wok, swirling it around until really hot. Add the spring onions (scallions) and stir-fry for a minute then add the carrots and mushrooms and continue to cook for about 2 minutes.

2 Add the stock and bring to the boil then season to taste with salt and pepper, five-spice powder and soy sauce and simmer for 5 minutes.

3 If the prawns (shrimp) are really large, cut them in half before adding to the wok and simmer for 3-4 minutes.

4 Add the watercress to the wok and mix well, then slowly pour in the beaten egg in a circular movement so that it cooks in threads in the soup. Adjust the seasoning and serve each portion topped with a whole prawn (shrimp).

COOK'S TIP

The large open mushrooms with black gills give the best flavour but they tend to spoil the colour of the soup, making it very dark. Oyster mushrooms can also be used.

Clear Chicken & Egg Soup

This tasty chicken soup has the addition of poached eggs, making it both delicious and filling. Use fresh, home-made stock for a better flavour.

NUTRITIONAL INFORMATION

Calories 138   Sugars 1g
Protein ....16g   Fat 7g
Carbohydrate ....1g   Saturates 2g

5 MINS   35 MINS

SERVES 4

INGREDIENTS

1 tsp salt

1 tbsp rice wine vinegar

4 eggs

850 ml/1½ pints/3¾ cups
   chicken stock

1 leek, sliced

125 g/4½ oz broccoli florets

125 g/4½ oz/1 cup shredded
   cooked chicken

2 open-cap mushrooms, sliced

1 tbsp dry sherry

dash of chilli sauce

chilli powder, to garnish

VARIATION

You could use 4 dried Chinese mushrooms, rehydrated according to the packet instructions, instead of the open-cap mushrooms, if you prefer.

1 Bring a large saucepan of water to the boil and add the salt and rice wine vinegar.

2 Reduce the heat so that it is just simmering and carefully break the eggs into the water, one at a time. Poach the eggs for 1 minute.

3 Remove the poached eggs with a slotted spoon and set aside.

4 Bring the chicken stock to the boil in a separate pan and add the leek, broccoli, chicken, mushrooms and sherry and season with chilli sauce to taste. Cook for 10–15 minutes.

5 Add the poached eggs to the soup and cook for a further 2 minutes. Carefully transfer the soup and poached eggs to 4 soup bowls. Dust with a little chilli powder and serve immediately.

Curried Chicken & Corn Soup

Tender cooked chicken strips and baby corn cobs are the main flavours in this delicious clear soup, with just a hint of ginger.

NUTRITIONAL INFORMATION

Calories 206   Sugars 5g
Protein . . . . .29g   Fat 5g
Carbohydrate . . .13g   Saturates 1g

 5 MINS   30 MINS

SERVES 4

INGREDIENTS

175 g/6 oz can sweetcorn
(corn), drained

850 ml/1½ pints/3¾ cups
chicken stock

350 g/12 oz cooked, lean chicken,
cut into strips

16 baby corn cobs

1 tsp Chinese curry powder

1-cm/½-inch piece fresh root ginger
(ginger root), grated

3 tbsp light soy sauce

2 tbsp chopped chives

1 Place the canned sweetcorn (corn) in a food processor, together with 150 ml/¼ pint/⅔ cup of the chicken stock and process until the mixture forms a smooth purée.

2 Pass the sweetcorn purée through a fine sieve (strainer), pressing with the back of a spoon to remove any husks.

3 Pour the remaining chicken stock into a large saucepan and add the strips of cooked chicken. Stir in the sweetcorn (corn) purée.

4 Add the baby corn cobs and bring the soup to the boil. Boil the soup for 10 minutes.

5 Add the Chinese curry powder, grated fresh root ginger and light soy sauce and stir well to combine. Cook for a further 10–15 minutes.

6 Stir the chopped chives into the soup.

7 Transfer the curried chicken and corn soup to warm soup bowls and serve immediately.

COOK'S TIP

Prepare the soup up to 24 hours in advance without adding the chicken, cool, cover and store in the refrigerator. Add the chicken and heat the soup through thoroughly before serving.

Fish & Vegetable Soup

A chunky fish soup with strips of vegetables, all flavoured with ginger and lemon, makes a meal in itself.

NUTRITIONAL INFORMATION

Calories 88	Sugars 1g
Protein 12g	Fat 3g
Carbohydrate 3g	Saturates 0.5g

  40 MINS   20 MINS

SERVES 4

INGREDIENTS

250 g/9 oz white fish fillets (cod, halibut, haddock, sole etc)

½ tsp ground ginger

½ tsp salt

1 small leek, trimmed

2-4 crab sticks, defrosted if frozen (optional)

1 tbsp sunflower oil

1 large carrot, cut into julienne strips

8 canned water chestnuts, thinly sliced

1.2 litres/2 pints/5 cups fish or vegetable stock

1 tbsp lemon juice

1 tbsp light soy sauce

1 large courgette (zucchini), cut into julienne strips

black pepper

COOK'S TIP

To skin fish, place the fillet skin-side down and insert a sharp, flexible knife at one end between the flesh and the skin. Hold the skin tightly at the end and push the knife along, keeping the blade flat against the skin.

1 Remove any skin from the fish and cut into cubes, about 2.5 cm/1 inch. Combine the ground ginger and salt and use to rub into the pieces of fish. Leave to marinate for at least 30 minutes.

2 Meanwhile, divide the green and white parts of the leek. Cut each part into 2.5 cm/1 inch lengths and then into julienne strips down the length of each piece, keeping the two parts separate. Slice the crab sticks into 1 cm/ ½ inch pieces.

3 Heat the oil in the wok, swirling it around so it is really hot. Add the white part of the leek and stir-fry for a couple of minutes, then add the carrots and water chestnuts and continue to cook for 1-2 minutes, stirring thoroughly.

4 Add the stock and bring to the boil, then add the lemon juice and soy sauce and simmer for 2 minutes.

5 Add the fish and continue to cook for about 5 minutes until the fish begins to break up a little, then add the green part of the leek and the courgettes (zucchini) and simmer for about 1 minute. Add the sliced crab sticks, if using, and season to taste with black pepper. Simmer for a further minute or so and serve piping hot.

Three-Flavour Soup

Ideally, use raw prawns (shrimp) in this soup. If that is not possible, add ready-cooked ones at the very last stage.

NUTRITIONAL INFORMATION

Calories 117   Sugars 0g
Protein . . . . .20g   Fat 3g
Carbohydrate . . . .2g   Saturates 1g

3½ HOURS   10 MINS

SERVES 4

INGREDIENTS

125 g/4½ oz skinned, boned chicken breast

125 g/4½ oz raw peeled prawns (shrimp)

salt

½ egg white, lightly beaten

2 tsp cornflour (cornstarch) paste
   (see page 31)

125 g/4½ oz honey-roast ham

700 ml/1¼ pints/3 cups Chinese Stock
   (see page 30) or water

finely chopped spring onions (scallions), to
   garnish

1 Using a sharp knife or meat cleaver, thinly slice the chicken into small shreds. If the prawns (shrimp) are large, cut each in half lengthways, otherwise leave them whole.

2 Place the chicken and prawns (shrimps) in a bowl and mix with a pinch of salt, the egg white and cornflour (cornstarch) paste until well coated. Set aside until required.

3 Cut the honey-roast ham into small thin slices roughly the same size as the chicken pieces.

4 In a preheated wok or large, heavy frying pan (skillet), bring the Chinese stock or water to a rolling boil and add

the chicken, the raw prawns (shrimp) and the ham.

5 Bring the soup back to the boil, and simmer for 1 minute.

6 Adjust the seasoning to taste, then pour the soup into four warmed individual serving bowls, garnish with the spring onions (scallions) and serve immediately.

COOK'S TIP

Soups such as this are improved enormously in flavour if you use a well-flavoured stock. Either use a stock cube, or find time to make Chinese Stock – see the recipe on page 28. Better still, make double quantities and freeze some for future use.

Beef & Vegetable Noodle Soup

Thin strips of beef are marinated in soy sauce and garlic to form the basis of this delicious soup. Served with noodles, it is both filling and delicious.

NUTRITIONAL INFORMATION

Calories 186	Sugars 1g
Protein 17g	Fat 5g
Carbohydrate ...20g	Saturates 1g

 35 MINS   20 MINS

SERVES 4

INGREDIENTS

225 g/8 oz lean beef

1 garlic clove, crushed

2 spring onions (scallions), chopped

3 tbsp soy sauce

1 tsp sesame oil

225 g/8 oz egg noodles

850 ml/1½ pints/3¾ cups
beef stock

3 baby corn cobs, sliced

½ leek, shredded

125 g/4½ oz broccoli, cut into florets
(flowerets)

pinch of chilli powder

1 Using a sharp knife, cut the beef into thin strips and place in a bowl with the garlic, spring onions (scallions), soy sauce and sesame oil.

2 Mix together the ingredients in the bowl, turning the beef to coat. Cover and leave to marinate in the refrigerator for 30 minutes.

3 Cook the noodles in a saucepan of boiling water for 3–4 minutes. Drain the noodles thoroughly and set aside.

4 Put the beef stock in a large saucepan and bring to the boil. Add the beef, together with the marinade, the baby corn, leek and broccoli. Cover and leave to simmer over a low heat for 7–10 minutes, or until the beef and vegetables are tender and cooked through.

5 Stir in the noodles and chilli powder and cook for a further 2–3 minutes.

6 Transfer the soup to bowls and serve immediately.

VARIATION

Vary the vegetables used, or use those to hand.

If preferred, use a few drops of chilli sauce instead of chilli powder, but remember it is very hot!

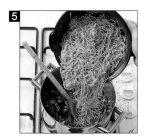

Chicken Soup with Almonds

This soup can also be made using pheasant breasts. For a really gamy flavour, make game stock from the carcass and use in the soup.

NUTRITIONAL INFORMATION

Calories 219   Sugars 2g
Protein . . . . .18g   Fat 15g
Carbohydrate . . . .2g   Saturates 2g

 10 MINS   20 MINS

SERVES 4

I N G R E D I E N T S

1 large or 2 small boneless skinned
  chicken breasts

1 tbsp sunflower oil

4 spring onions (scallions), thinly sliced
  diagonally

1 carrot, cut into julienne strips

700 ml/1¼ pints/3 cups chicken stock

finely grated rind of ½ lemon

40 g/1½ oz/⅓ cup ground almonds

1 tbsp light soy sauce

1 tbsp lemon juice

25 g/1 oz/¼ cup flaked almonds, toasted

salt and pepper

1 Cut each breast into 4 strips length-ways, then slice very thinly across the grain to give shreds of chicken.

2 Heat the oil in a wok, swirling it around until really hot.

3 Add the spring onions (scallions) and cook for 2 minutes, then add the chicken and toss it for 3-4 minutes until sealed and almost cooked through, stirring all the time. Add the carrot strips and stir.

4 Add the stock to the wok and bring to the boil. Add the lemon rind, ground almonds, soy sauce, lemon juice and plenty of seasoning. Bring back to the boil and simmer, uncovered, for 5 minutes, stirring from time to time.

5 Adjust the seasoning, add most of the toasted flaked almonds and continue to cook for a further 1-2 minutes.

6 Serve the soup very hot, in individual bowls, sprinkled with the remaining flaked almonds.

COOK'S TIP

To make game stock, break up a pheasant carcass and place in a pan with 2 litres/3½ pints/8 cups water. Bring to the boil slowly, skimming off any scum. Add 1 bouquet garni, 1 peeled onion and seasoning. Cover and simmer gently for 1½ hours. Strain, and skim any surface fat.

Oriental Fish Soup

This is a deliciously different fish soup which can be made quickly and easily in a microwave.

NUTRITIONAL INFORMATION

Calories 105	Sugars 1g	
Protein 13g	Fat 5g	
Carbohydrate 1g	Saturates 1g	

 20 MINS 🕐 10 MINS

SERVES 4

INGREDIENTS

1 egg

1 tsp sesame seeds, toasted

1 celery stick, chopped

1 carrot, cut into julienne strips

4 spring onions (scallions), sliced on the diagonal

1 tbsp oil

60 g/2 oz/1½ cups fresh spinach

850 ml/1½ pints/3½ cups hot vegetable stock

4 tsp light soy sauce

250 g/9 oz haddock, skinned and cut into small chunks

salt and pepper

VARIATION

Instead of topping the soup with omelette shreds, you could pour the beaten egg, without the sesame seeds, into the hot stock at the end of the cooking time. The egg will set in pretty strands to give a flowery look.

1 Beat the egg with the sesame seeds and seasoning. Lightly oil a plate and pour on the egg mixture. Cook on HIGH power for 1½ minutes until just setting in the centre. Leave to stand for a few minutes then remove from the plate. Roll up the egg and shred thinly.

2 Mix together the celery, carrot, spring onions (scallions) and oil. Cover and cook on HIGH power for 3 minutes.

3 Wash the spinach thoroughly under cold, running water. Cut off and discard any long stalks and drain well. Shred the spinach finely.

4 Add the hot stock, soy sauce, haddock and spinach to the vegetable mixture. Cover and cook on HIGH power for 5 minutes. Stir the soup and season to taste. Serve in warmed bowls with the shredded egg scattered over.

Mushroom Noodle Soup

A light, refreshing clear soup of mushrooms, cucumber and small pieces of rice noodles, flavoured with soy sauce and a touch of garlic.

NUTRITIONAL INFORMATION

Calories ....84 Sugars 1g
Protein ....1g   Fat 8g
Carbohydrate ....3g   Saturates 1g

 5 MINS   10 MINS

SERVES 4

INGREDIENTS

125 g/4½ oz flat or open-cup
   mushrooms

½ cucumber

2 spring onions (scallions)

1 garlic clove

2 tbsp vegetable oil

25 g/1 oz/¼ cup Chinese rice
   noodles

¾ tsp salt

1 tbsp soy sauce

1 Wash the mushrooms and pat dry on kitchen paper (paper towels). Slice thinly. Do not remove the peel as this adds more flavour.

2 Halve the cucumber lengthways. Scoop out the seeds, using a teaspoon, and slice the cucumber thinly.

3 Chop the spring onions (scallions) finely and cut the garlic clove into thin strips.

4 Heat the vegetable oil in a large saucepan or wok.

5 Add the spring onions (scallions) and garlic to the pan or wok and stir-fry for 30 seconds. Add the mushrooms and stir-fry for 2–3 minutes.

6 Stir in 600 ml/1 pint/2½ cups water. Break the noodles into short lengths and add to the soup. Bring to the boil, stirring occasionally.

7 Add the cucumber slices, salt and soy sauce, and simmer for 2–3 minutes.

8 Serve the mushroom noodle soup in warmed bowls, distributing the noodles and vegetables evenly.

COOK'S TIP

Scooping the seeds out from the cucumber gives it a prettier effect when sliced, and also helps to reduce any bitterness, but if you prefer, you can leave them in.

Fish Soup with Wontons

This soup is topped with small wontons filled with prawns (shrimp), making it both very tasty and satisfying.

NUTRITIONAL INFORMATION

Calories . . . . .115 Sugars 0g
Protein . . . . .16g Fat 5g
Carbohydrate . . . .1g Saturates 1g

🍲 10 MINS   🕐 15 MINS

SERVES 4

I N G R E D I E N T S

125 g/4½ oz large, cooked, peeled
  prawns (shrimp)

1 tsp chopped chives

1 small garlic clove, finely chopped

1 tbsp vegetable oil

12 wonton wrappers

1 small egg, beaten

850 ml/1½ pints/3¾ cups fish stock

175 g/6 oz white fish fillet, diced

dash of chilli sauce

sliced fresh red chilli and chives,
  to garnish

1 Roughly chop a quarter of the prawns (shrimp) and mix together with the chopped chives and garlic.

2 Heat the oil in a preheated wok or large frying pan (skillet) until it is really hot.

3 Stir-fry the prawn (shrimp) mixture for 1–2 minutes. Remove from the heat and set aside to cool completely.

4 Spread out the wonton wrappers on a work surface (counter). Spoon a little of the prawn (shrimp) filling into the centre of each wrapper. Brush the edges of the wrappers with beaten egg and press the edges together, scrunching them to form a 'moneybag' shape. Set aside while you are preparing the soup.

5 Pour the fish stock into a large saucepan and bring to the boil. Add the diced white fish and the remaining prawns (shrimp) and cook for 5 minutes.

6 Season to taste with the chilli sauce. Add the wontons and cook for a further 5 minutes.

7 Spoon into warmed serving bowls, garnish with sliced red chilli and chives and serve immediately.

VARIATION

Replace the prawns (shrimp) with cooked crabmeat for an alternative flavour.

Chicken, Noodle & Corn Soup

The vermicelli gives this Chinese-style soup an Italian twist, but you can use egg noodles if you prefer.

NUTRITIONAL INFORMATION

Calories 401   Sugars 6g
Protein . . . . .31g   Fat 24g
Carbohydrate . . .17g   Saturates 13g

 5 MINS   25 MINS

SERVES 4

INGREDIENTS

450 g/1 lb boned chicken breasts,
   cut into strips

1.2 litres/2 pints/5 cups chicken stock

150 ml/¼ pint/⅝ cup double (heavy)
   cream

100 g/3½ oz/¾ cup dried vermicelli

1 tbsp cornflour (cornstarch)

3 tbsp milk

175 g/6 oz sweetcorn (corn-on-the-cob)
   kernels

salt and pepper

finely chopped spring onion (scallions),
   to garnish (optional)

1 Put the chicken strips, chicken stock and double (heavy) cream into a large saucepan and bring to the boil over a low heat.

2 Reduce the heat slightly and simmer for about 20 minutes. Season the soup with salt and black pepper to taste.

3 Meanwhile, cook the vermicelli in lightly salted boiling water for 10-12 minutes, until just tender. Drain the pasta and keep warm.

4 In a small bowl, mix together the cornflour (cornstarch) and milk to make a smooth paste. Stir the cornflour

(cornstarch) paste into the soup until thickened.

5 Add the sweetcorn (corn-on-the-cob) and vermicelli to the pan and heat through.

6 Transfer the soup to a warm tureen or individual soup bowls, garnish with spring onions (scallions), if desired, and serve immediately.

VARIATION

For crab and sweetcorn soup, substitute 450 g/1 lb cooked crabmeat for the chicken breasts. Flake the crabmeat well before adding it to the saucepan and reduce the cooking time by 10 minutes.

Chicken & Coconut Soup

This fragrant soup combines citrus flavours with coconut and a hint of piquancy from chillies.

2¼ HOURS   15 MINS

SERVES 4

INGREDIENTS

350 g/12 oz/1¾ cups cooked, skinned chicken breast

125 g/4½ oz/1⅓ cups unsweetened desiccated coconut

500 ml/16 fl oz/2 cups boiling water

500 ml/18 fl oz/2 cups Fresh Chicken Stock (see page 30)

4 spring onions (scallions), white and green parts, sliced thinly

2 stalks lemon grass

1 lime

1 tsp grated ginger root

1 tbsp light soy sauce

2 tsp ground coriander

2 large fresh red chillies

1 tbsp chopped fresh coriander (cilantro)

1 tbsp cornflour (cornstarch), mixed with 2 tbsp cold water

salt and white pepper

chopped red chilli, to garnish

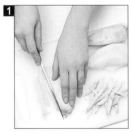

1 Using a sharp knife, slice the chicken into thin strips.

2 Place the coconut in a heatproof bowl and pour over the boiling water. Work the coconut mixture through a sieve (strainer). Pour the coconut water into a large saucepan and add the stock.

3 Add the spring onions (scallions) to the saucepan. Slice the base of each lemon grass and discard damaged leaves. Bruise the stalks and add to the saucepan.

4 Peel the rind from the lime in large strips. Extract the juice and add to the pan with the lime strips, ginger, soy sauce and coriander. Bruise the chillies with a fork then add to the pan. Heat the pan to just below boiling point.

5 Add the chicken and fresh coriander (cilantro) to the saucepan, bring to the boil, then simmer for 10 minutes.

6 Discard the lemon grass, lime rind and red chillies. Pour the blended cornflour (cornstarch) mixture into the saucepan and stir until slightly thickened. Season with salt and white pepper to taste and serve immediately, garnished with chopped red chilli.

Pork & Szechuan Vegetable

Sold in cans, Szechuan preserved vegetable is pickled mustard root which is quite hot and salty, so rinse in water before use.

NUTRITIONAL INFORMATION

Calories	135	Sugars	.........1g
Protein	........14g	Fat	...........7g
Carbohydrate	....3g	Saturates	.......2g

 5 MINS 5 MINS

SERVES 4

INGREDIENTS

250 g/9 oz pork fillet

2 tsp cornflour (cornstarch) paste (see page 31)

125 g/4½ oz Szechuan preserved vegetable

700 ml/1¼ pints/3 cups Chinese stock (see page 30) or water

salt and pepper

a few drops sesame oil (optional)

2-3 spring onions (scallions), sliced, to garnish

1 Preheat a wok or large, heavy-based frying pan (skillet).

2 Using a sharp knife, cut the pork across the grain into thin shreds.

3 Mix the pork with the cornflour (cornstarch) paste until the pork is completely coated in the mixture.

4 Thoroughly wash and rinse the Szechuan preserved vegetable, then pat dry on absorbent kitchen paper (paper towels). Cut the Szechuan preserved vegetable into thin shreds the same size as the pork.

5 Pour the Chinese stock or water into the wok or frying pan (skillet) and bring to a rolling boil. Add the pork to the wok and stir to separate the shreds. Return to the boil.

6 Add the shredded Szechuan preserved vegetable and bring back to the boil once more.

7 Adjust the seasoning to taste and sprinkle with sesame oil. Serve hot, garnished with spring onions (scallions).

COOK'S TIP

Szechuan preserved vegetable is actually mustard green root, pickled in salt and chillies. Available in cans from specialist Chinese supermarkets, it gives a crunchy, spicy taste to dishes. Rinse in cold water before use and store in the refrigerator.

Crab & Ginger Soup

Two classic ingredients in Chinese cooking are blended together in this recipe for a special soup.

NUTRITIONAL INFORMATION

Calories 32   Sugars 1g
Protein ....6g   Fat 0.4g
Carbohydrate ....1g   Saturates 0g

10 MINS   25 MINS

SERVES 4

INGREDIENTS

1 carrot

1 leek

1 bay leaf

850 ml/1½ pints/3¾ cups fish stock

2 medium-sized cooked crabs

2.5-cm/1-inch piece fresh root ginger (ginger root), grated

1 tsp light soy sauce

½ tsp ground star anise

salt and pepper

1 Using a sharp knife, chop the carrot and leek into small pieces and place in a large saucepan with the bay leaf and fish stock.

2 Bring the mixture in the saucepan to the boil.

3 Reduce the heat, cover and leave to simmer for about 10 minutes, or until the vegetables are nearly tender.

4 Remove all of the meat from the cooked crabs. Break off and reserve the claws, break the joints and remove the meat, using a fork or skewer.

5 Add the crabmeat to the pan of fish stock, together with the ginger, soy sauce and star anise and bring to the boil. Leave to simmer for about 10 minutes, or until the vegetables are tender and the crab is heated through.

6 Season the soup then ladle into a warmed soup tureen or individual serving bowls and garnish with crab claws. Serve immediately.

VARIATION

If fresh crabmeat is unavailable, use drained canned crabmeat or thawed frozen crabmeat instead.

Crab & Sweetcorn Soup

Crab and sweetcorn are classic ingredients in Chinese cookery. Here egg noodles are added for a filling dish.

NUTRITIONAL INFORMATION

Calories	324	Sugars	.........6g
Protein	........27g	Fat	..........8g
Carbohydrate	...39g	Saturates	.......2g

 5 MINS   20 MINS

SERVES 4

INGREDIENTS

1 tbsp sunflower oil

1 tsp Chinese five-spice powder

225 g/8 oz carrots, cut into sticks

150 g/5½ oz/½ cup canned or frozen sweetcorn

75 g/2¾ oz/¼ cup peas

6 spring onions (scallions), trimmed and sliced

1 red chilli, deseeded and very thinly sliced

2 x 200 g/7 oz can white crab meat

175 g/6 oz egg noodles

1.7 litres/3 pints/7½ cups fish stock

3 tbsp soy sauce

1 Heat the sunflower oil in a large preheated wok or heavy-based frying pan (skillet).

2 Add the Chinese five-spice powder, carrots, sweetcorn, peas, spring onions (scallions) and red chilli to the wok and cook for about 5 minutes, stirring constantly.

3 Add the crab meat to the wok and stir-fry the mixture for 1 minute, distributing the crab meat evenly.

4 Roughly break up the egg noodles and add to the wok.

5 Pour the fish stock and soy sauce into the mixture in the wok and bring to the boil.

6 Cover the wok or frying pan (skillet) and leave the soup to simmer for 5 minutes.

7 Stir once more, then transfer the soup to a warm soup tureen or individual serving bowls and serve at once.

COOK'S TIP

Chinese five-spice powder is a mixture of star anise, fennel, cloves, cinnamon and Szechuan pepper. It has an unmistakeable flavour. Use it sparingly, as it is very pungent.

Hot & Sour Mushroom Soup

Hot and sour soups are found across South East Asia in different forms. Reduce the number of chillies added if you prefer a milder dish.

NUTRITIONAL INFORMATION

Calories	.87	Sugars	.7g
Protein	.4g	Fat	.5g
Carbohydrate	.8g	Saturates	.1g

 10 MINS 20 MINS

SERVES 4

INGREDIENTS

2 tbsp tamarind paste

4 red chilies, very finely chopped

2 cloves garlic, crushed

2.5 cm/1 inch piece of Thai ginger, peeled and very finely chopped

4 tbsp fish sauce

2 tbsp palm sugar or caster (superfine) sugar

8 lime leaves, roughly torn

1.2 litres/2 pints/5 cups vegetable stock

100 g/3½ oz carrots, very thinly sliced

225 g/8 oz button mushrooms, halved

350 g/12 oz shredded white cabbage

100 g/3½ oz fine green beans, halved

3 tbsp fresh coriander (cilantro), roughly chopped

100 g/3½ oz cherry tomatoes, halved

COOK'S TIP

Tamarind is the dried fruit of the tamarind tree. Sold as a pulp or paste, it is used to give a special sweet and sour flavour to Oriental dishes.

1 Place the tamarind paste, red chillies, garlic, Thai ginger, fish sauce, palm or caster (superfine) sugar, lime leaves and vegetable stock in a large preheated wok or heavy-based frying pan (skillet). Bring the mixture to the boil, stirring occasionally.

2 Reduce the heat and add the carrots, mushrooms, white cabbage and green beans. Leave the soup to simmer, uncovered, for about 10 minutes, or until the vegetables are just tender.

3 Stir the fresh coriander (cilantro) and cherry tomatoes into the mixture in the wok and heat through for another 5 minutes.

4 Transfer the soup to a warm tureen or individual serving bowls and serve immediately.

Chinese Cabbage Soup

This is a piquant soup, which is slightly sweet-and-sour in flavour. It can be served as a hearty meal or appetizer.

NUTRITIONAL INFORMATION

Calories	.65	Sugars	.7g
Protein	.3g	Fat	.0.5g
Carbohydrate	.11g	Saturates	.0.1g

 5 MINS   30 MINS

SERVES 4

INGREDIENTS

450 g/1 lb pak choi

600 ml/1 pint/2½ cups vegetable stock

1 tbsp rice wine vinegar

1 tbsp light soy sauce

1 tbsp caster (superfine) sugar

1 tbsp dry sherry

1 fresh red chilli, thinly sliced

1 tbsp cornflour (cornstarch)

2 tbsp water

1 Wash the pak choi thoroughly under cold running water, rinse and drain. Pat dry on kitchen paper (paper towels) .

2 Trim the stems of the pak choi and shred the leaves.

3 Heat the vegetable stock in a large saucepan. Add the pak choi and cook for 10–15 minutes.

4 Mix together the rice wine vinegar, soy sauce, caster (superfine) sugar and sherry in a small bowl. Add this mixture to the stock, together with the sliced chilli.

5 Bring to the boil, lower the heat and cook for 2–3 minutes.

6 Blend the cornflour (cornstarch) with the water to form a smooth paste.

7 Gradually stir the cornflour (cornstarch) mixture into the soup. Cook, stirring constantly, until it thickens. Cook for a further 4–5 minutes.

8 Ladle the Chinese cabbage soup into individual warm serving bowls and serve immediately.

COOKS TIP

Pak choi, also known as bok choi or spoon cabbage, has long, white leaf stalks and fleshy, spoon-shaped, shiny green leaves. There are a number of varieties available, which differ mainly in size rather than flavour.

Mixed Vegetable Soup

Select 3 or 4 vegetables for this soup: the Chinese like to blend different colours, flavours and textures to create harmony as well as contrast.

NUTRITIONAL INFORMATION

Calories 38	Sugars 3g	
Protein 3g	Fat 2g	
Carbohydrate 4g	Saturates 0.2g	

  3¹/₂ HOURS   5 MINS

SERVES 4

INGREDIENTS

about 30-60 g/1-2 oz each of
  mushrooms, carrots, asparagus,
  mangetout (snow peas), bamboo
  shoots, baby sweetcorn, cucumber,
  tomatoes, spinach, lettuce,
  Chinese leaves (cabbage),
  tofu (bean curd) etc.

600 ml/1 pint/2 ½ cups Chinese Stock
  (see page 30)

1 tbsp light soy sauce

a few drops sesame oil (optional)

salt and pepper

finely chopped spring onions (scallions),
  to garnish

1 Preheat a wok or large heavy-based frying pan (skillet).

2 Using a sharp knife or cleaver, cut your selection of vegetables into roughly uniform shapes and sizes (slices, shreds or cubes).

3 Pour the Chinese stock into the wok or frying pan (skillet) and bring to a rolling boil.

4 Add the vegetables, bearing in mind that some require a longer cooking time than others: add carrots and baby sweetcorn first, cook for 2 minutes, then add asparagus, mushrooms, Chinese leaves (cabbage), tofu (bean curd), and cook for another minute.

5 Spinach, lettuce, watercress, cucumber and tomato are added last. Stir, and bring the soup back to the boil.

6 Add the soy sauce and the sesame oil, if wished, and adjust the seasoning to taste.

7 Transfer the mixed vegetable soup to warm serving bowls and serve hot, garnished with spring onions (scallions).

COOK'S TIP

Sesame oil is a low-saturate oil widely used for its nutty, aromatic flavour. Made from toasted sesame seeds it is used as a seasoning, not as a cooking oil. Thick and dark, it burns easily, so it should be added at the last moment.

Chilli & Watercress Soup

This delicious soup is a wonderful blend of colours and flavours. It is very hot, so if you prefer a milder taste, omit the seeds from the chillies.

NUTRITIONAL INFORMATION

Calories 90	Sugars 1g
Protein 7g	Fat 6g
Carbohydrate 2g	Saturates 1g

 10 MINS   15 MINS

SERVES 4

INGREDIENTS

1 tbsp sunflower oil

250 g/9 oz smoked tofu
(bean curd), sliced

90 g/3 oz/1 cup shiitake
mushrooms, sliced

2 tbsp chopped fresh coriander (cilantro)

125 g/4½ oz/2 cups watercress

1 red chilli, sliced finely, to garnish

STOCK

1 tbsp tamarind pulp

2 dried red chillies, chopped

2 kaffir lime leaves, torn in half

2.5 cm/1 inch piece ginger, chopped

5 cm/2 inch piece galangal, chopped

1 stalk lemon grass, chopped

1 onion, quartered

1 litre/1¾ pints/4 cups cold water

1 Put all the ingredients for the stock into a saucepan and bring to the boil.

2 Simmer the stock for 5 minutes. Remove from the heat and strain, reserving the stock.

3 Heat the sunflower oil in a wok or large, heavy frying pan (skillet) and cook the tofu (bean curd) over a high heat for about 2 minutes, stirring constantly so that the tofu (bean curd) cooks evenly on both sides. Add the strained stock.

4 Add the mushrooms and coriander (cilantro), and boil for 3 minutes.

5 Add the watercress and boil for 1 minute.

6 Serve immediately, garnished with red chilli slices.

VARIATION

You might like to try a mixture of different types of mushroom. Oyster, button and straw mushrooms are all suitable.

Appetizers

Appetizers are often served as starters in a Chinese meal. This chapter contains a range of old favourites and traditional Chinese dishes, and there is sure to be something to suit every occasion. One of the advantages of these dishes is that they can be prepared well in advance. The Chinese usually serve a selection of

appetizers together as an assorted hors d'oeuvres. Remember not to have more than one type of the same food. The ingredients should be chosen for their harmony and balance in colour, aroma, texture and flavour. A suitable selection might contain Crispy Seaweed, Sesame Prawn Toasts, Spare Ribs and Spring Rolls. Many of these dishes would also make an attractive addition to a buffet for example Filled Cucumber Cups and Aubergine (Eggplant) Dipping Platter.

Spicy Salt & Pepper Prawns

For best results, use raw tiger prawns (shrimp) in their shells. They are 7-10 cm/3-4 inches long, and you should get 18-20 per 500 g/1 lb 2 oz.

NUTRITIONAL INFORMATION

Calories	160	Sugars	.......0.2g
Protein	........17g	Fat	..........10g
Carbohydrate	...0.5g	Saturates	.......1g

 35 MINS   20 MINS

SERVES 4

I N G R E D I E N T S

250-300 g/9-10½ oz raw prawns (shrimp) in their shells, defrosted if frozen

1 tbsp light soy sauce

1 tsp Chinese rice wine or dry sherry

2 tsp cornflour (cornstarch)

vegetable oil, for deep-frying

2-3 spring onions (scallions), to garnish

S P I C Y   S A L T   A N D   P E P P E R

1 tbsp salt

1 tsp ground Szechuan peppercorns

1 tsp five-spice powder

1 Pull the soft legs off the prawns (shrimp), but keep the body shell on. Dry well on absorbent kitchen paper (paper towels).

2 Place the prawns (shrimp) in a bowl with the soy sauce, rice wine or sherry and cornflour (cornstarch). Turn the prawns (shrimp) to coat thoroughly in the mixture and leave to marinate for about 25-30 minutes.

3 To make the Spicy Salt and Pepper, mix the salt, ground Szechuan peppercorns and five-spice powder together. Place in a dry frying pan (skillet) and stir-fry for about 3-4 minutes over a low heat, stirring constantly to prevent the spices burning on the bottom of the pan. Remove from the heat and allow to cool.

4 Heat the vegetable oil in a preheated wok or large frying pan (skillet) until smoking, then deep-fry the prawns (shrimp) in batches until golden brown. Remove the prawns (shrimp) from the wok with a slotted spoon and drain on kitchen paper (paper towels).

5 Place the spring onions (scallions) in a bowl, pour on 1 tablespoon of the hot oil and leave for 30 seconds. Serve the prawns (shrimp) garnished with the spring onions (scallions), and with the Spicy Salt and Pepper as a dip.

COOK'S TIP

The roasted spice mixture made with Szechuan peppercorns is used throughout China as a dip for deep-fried food. The peppercorns are sometimes roasted first and then ground. Dry-frying is a way of releasing the flavours of the spices.

Pork with Chilli & Garlic

Any leftovers from this dish can be used for a number of other dishes, for example Twice-cooked Pork (page 225).

(page 225)

NUTRITIONAL INFORMATION

Calories	137	Sugars	0.1g
Protein	16g	Fat	8g
Carbohydrate	1g	Saturates	2g

5 HOURS   35 MINS

SERVES 4

INGREDIENTS

500 g/1 lb 2 oz leg of pork, boned but not skinned

SAUCE

1 tsp finely chopped garlic

1 tsp finely chopped spring onions (scallions)

2 tbsp light soy sauce

1 tsp red chilli oil

½ tsp sesame oil

sprig of fresh coriander (cilantro), to garnish (optional)

1 Place the pork, tied together in one piece, in a large saucepan, add enough cold water to cover, and bring to a rolling boil over a medium heat.

2 Using a slotted spoon, skim off the scum that rises to the surface, cover the pan with a lid and simmer gently for 25-30 minutes.

3 Leave the meat in the liquid to cool, under cover, for at least 1-2 hours.

4 Lift out the meat with 2 slotted spoons and leave to cool completely, skin-side up, for 2-3 hours.

5 To serve, cut off the skin, leaving a very thin layer of fat on top like a

ham joint. Cut the meat in small thin slices across the grain, and arrange on a plate in an overlapping pattern.

6 In a small bowl, mix together the sauce ingredients, and pour the sauce evenly over the pork.

7 Garnish the pork with a sprig of fresh coriander (cilantro), if wished, and serve at once.

COOK'S TIP

This is a very simple dish, but beautifully presented. Make sure you slice the meat as thinly and evenly as possible to make an elegantly arranged dish.

Butterfly Prawns (Shrimp)

Use unpeeled, raw king or tiger prawns (jumbo shrimp) which are about 7-10cm (3-4 inches) long.

NUTRITIONAL INFORMATION

Calories	157	Sugars	.......0.3g
Protein	.........8g	Fat	...........9g
Carbohydrate	....11g	Saturates	.......2g

25 MINS   10 MINS

SERVES 4

I N G R E D I E N T S

12 raw tiger prawns (jumbo shrimp) in their shells

2 tbsp light soy sauce

1 tbsp Chinese rice wine or dry sherry

1 tbsp cornflour (cornstarch)

vegetable oil, for deep-frying

2 eggs, lightly beaten

8-10 tbsp breadcrumbs

salt and pepper

shredded lettuce leaves, to serve

chopped spring onions (scallions), either raw or soaked for about 30 seconds in hot oil, to garnish

1 Shell and devein the prawns (shrimp) leaving the tails on. Split them in half from the underbelly about halfway along, leaving the tails still firmly attached. Mix together the salt, pepper, soy sauce, wine and cornflour (cornstarch), add the prawns (shrimp) and turn to coat. Leave to marinate for 10-15 minutes.

2 Heat the oil in a preheated wok. Pick up each prawn (shrimp) by the tail, dip it in the beaten egg then roll it in the breadcrumbs to coat well.

3 Deep-fry the prawns (shrimp) in batches until golden brown. Remove them with a slotted spoon and drain on paper towels.

4 To serve, arrange the prawns (shrimp) neatly on a bed of lettuce leaves and garnish with spring onions (scallions).

COOK'S TIP

To devein prawns (shrimp), first remove the shell. Make a shallow cut about three-quarters of the way along the back of each prawn (shrimp), then pull out and discard the black intestinal vein.

Barbecue Spare Ribs

This is a simplified version of the half saddle of pork ribs seen hanging in the windows of Cantonese restaurants.

NUTRITIONAL INFORMATION

Calories 271   Sugars 4g
Protein . . . . .13g   Fat 22g
Carbohydrate . . . .5g   Saturates 8g

6¹/₂ HOURS   50 MINS

SERVES 4

INGREDIENTS

500 g/1 lb 2 oz pork finger spare ribs

1 tbsp sugar

1 tbsp light soy sauce

1 tbsp dark soy sauce

3 tbsp hoi-sin sauce

1 tbsp rice wine or dry sherry

4-5 tbsp water or Chinese Stock
(see page 30)

mild chilli sauce, to dip

coriander (cilantro) leaves, to garnish

1 Using a sharp knife, trim off any excess fat from the spare ribs and cut into pieces. Place the ribs in a baking dish.

2 Mix together the sugar, light and dark soy sauce, hoi-sin sauce and wine. Pour over the ribs in the baking dish. Turn to coat the ribs thoroughly in the mixture and leave to marinate for about 2-3 hours.

3 Add the water or Chinese stock to the ribs and spread them out in the dish. Roast in a preheated hot oven for 15 minutes.

4 Turn the ribs over, lower the oven temperature and cook for 30-35 minutes longer.

5 To serve, chop each rib into 3-4 small, bite-sized pieces with a large knife or Chinese cleaver and arrange neatly on a serving dish.

6 Pour the sauce from the baking dish over the spare ribs and garnish with a few coriander (cilantro) leaves. Place some mild chilli sauce into a small dish and serve with the ribs as a dip. Serve immediately.

COOK'S TIP

Finger ribs are specially small, thin ribs. Ask your local butcher to cut some if you can't find the right size in the supermarket. Don't throw away any trimmings from the ribs – they can be used for soup or stock.

Spring Rolls

This classic Chinese dish is very popular in the West. Serve hot or chilled with a soy sauce or hoisin dip.

NUTRITIONAL INFORMATION

Calories 442   Sugars 4g
Protein . . . . .23g   Fat 21g
Carbohydrate . . .42g   Saturates 3g

🥟 🥟 🥟 🥟

🍲 45 MINS   🕒 45 MINS

SERVES 4

INGREDIENTS

175 g/6 oz cooked pork, chopped

75 g/2¾ oz cooked chicken, chopped

1 tsp light soy sauce

1 tsp light brown sugar

1 tsp sesame oil

1 tsp vegetable oil

225 g/8 oz bean sprouts

25 g/1 oz canned bamboo shoots, drained, rinsed and chopped

1 green (bell) pepper, seeded and chopped

2 spring onions (scallions), sliced

1 tsp cornflour (cornstarch)

2 tsp water

vegetable oil, for deep-frying

SKINS

125 g/4½ oz/1⅛ cups plain (all-purpose) flour

5 tbsp cornflour (cornstarch)

450 ml/16 fl oz/2 cups water

3 tbsp vegetable oil

1 Mix the pork, chicken, soy sauce, sugar and sesame oil. Cover and marinate for 30 minutes.

2 Heat the vegetable oil in a preheated wok. Add the bean sprouts, bamboo shoots, (bell) pepper and spring onions (scallions) to the wok and stir-fry for 2–3 minutes. Add the meat and the marinade to the wok and stir-fry for 2–3 minutes.

3 Blend the cornflour (cornstarch) with the water and stir the mixture into the wok. Set aside to cool completely.

4 To make the skins, mix the flour and cornflour (cornstarch) and gradually stir in the water, to make a smooth batter.

5 Heat a small, oiled frying pan (skillet). Swirl one-eighth of the batter over the base and cook for 2–3 minutes. Repeat with the remaining batter. Cover the skins with a damp tea towel (dish cloth) while frying the remaining skins.

6 Spread out the skins and spoon one-eighth of the filling along the centre of each. Brush the edges with water and fold in the sides, then roll up.

7 Heat the oil for deep-frying in a wok to 180°C/350°F. Cook the spring rolls, in batches, for 2–3 minutes, or until golden and crisp. Remove from the oil with a slotted spoon, drain and serve immediately.

Pot Sticker Dumplings

These dumplings obtain their name from the fact that they would stick to the pot when steamed if they were not fried crisply enough initially.

NUTRITIONAL INFORMATION

Calories 345	Sugar 3g	
Protein 13g	Fat 17g	
Carbohydrate ...36g	Saturates 2g	

50 MINS   25 MINS

SERVES 4

INGREDIENTS

DUMPLINGS

175 g/6 oz/1½ cups plain (all-purpose) flour

pinch of salt

3 tbsp vegetable oil

6–8 tbsp boiling water

oil, for deep-frying

125 ml/4 fl oz/½ cup water, for steaming

sliced spring onions (scallions) and chives, to garnish

soy sauce or hoisin sauce, to serve

FILLING

150 g/5½ oz lean chicken, very finely chopped

25 g/1 oz canned bamboo shoots, drained and chopped

2 spring onions (scallions), finely chopped

½ small red (bell) pepper, seeded and finely chopped

½ tsp Chinese curry powder

1 tbsp light soy sauce

1 tsp caster (superfine) sugar

1 tsp sesame oil

1 To make the dumplings, mix together the flour and salt in a bowl. Make a well in the centre, add the oil and water and mix well to form a soft dough. Knead the dough on a lightly floured surface, wrap in cling film (plastic wrap) and let stand for 30 minutes. Meanwhile, mix all of the filling ingredients together in a large bowl.

2 Divide the dough into 12 equal-sized pieces and roll each piece into a 12.5-cm/5-inch round. Spoon a portion of the filling on to one half of each round. Fold the dough over the filling to form a 'pasty', pressing the edges together to seal.

3 Pour a little oil into a frying pan (skillet) and cook the dumplings, in batches, until browned and slightly crisp.

4 Return all of the dumplings to the pan and add about 125 ml/4 fl oz/½ cup water. Cover and steam for 5 minutes, or until the dumplings are cooked through. Remove with a slotted spoon and garnish with spring onions (scallions) and chives. Serve with soy sauce or hoisin sauce.

Pancake Rolls

This classic *dim sum* dish is adaptable to almost any filling of your choice. Here the traditional mixture of pork and pak choi is used.

NUTRITIONAL INFORMATION

Calories 488   Sugars 19g
Protein . . . . .16g   Fat 24g
Carbohydrate . . .55g   Saturates 4g

 20 MINS   20 MINS

SERVES 4

I N G R E D I E N T S

4 tsp vegetable oil

1-2 garlic cloves, crushed

225 g/8 oz minced (ground) pork

225/8 oz pak choi, shredded

4½ tsp light soy sauce

½ tsp sesame oil

8 spring roll skins, 25 cm/10 inches square,
 thawed if frozen

oil, for deep-frying

C H I L L I   S A U C E

60 g/2 oz/¼ cup caster (superfine) sugar

50 ml/2 fl oz/¼ cup rice vinegar

2 tbsp water

2 red chillies, finely chopped

1 Heat the oil in a preheated wok. Add the garlic and stir-fry for 30 seconds. Add the pork and stir-fry for 2–3 minutes, until lightly coloured.

2 Add the pak choi, soy sauce and sesame oil to the wok and stir-fry for 2–3 minutes. Remove from the heat and set aside to cool.

3 Spread out the spring roll skins on a work surface (counter) and spoon 2 tablespoons of the pork mixture along one edge of each. Roll the skin over once and

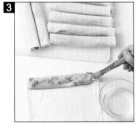

fold in the sides. Roll up completely to make a sausage shape, brushing the edges with a little water to seal. Set the pancake rolls aside for 10 minutes to seal firmly.

4 To make the chilli sauce, heat the sugar, vinegar and water in a small saucepan, stirring until the sugar dissolves. Bring the mixture to the boil and boil rapidly until a light syrup forms. Remove from the heat and stir in the

chopped red chillies. Leave the sauce to cool before serving.

5 Heat the oil for deep-frying in a wok until almost smoking. Reduce the heat slightly and fry the pancake rolls, in batches if necessary, for 3–4 minutes, until golden brown. Remove from the oil with a slotted spoon and drain on absorbent kitchen paper (paper towels). Serve with the chilli sauce.

Filled Cucumber Cups

These attractive little cups would make an impressive appetizer at a dinner party.

NUTRITIONAL INFORMATION

Calories 256   Sugars 7g
Protein ....10g   Fat 21g
Carbohydrate ....8g   Saturates 4g

10 MINS   0 MINS

SERVES 4

I N G R E D I E N T S

1 cucumber

4 spring onions (scallions),
  chopped finely

4 tbsp lime juice

2 small red chillies, deseeded and
  chopped finely

3 tsp sugar

150 g/5½ oz/1¼ cups ground roasted
  peanuts

¼ tsp salt

3 shallots, sliced finely and deep-fried,
  to garnish

1 Wash the cucumber thoroughly and pat dry with absorbent kitchen paper (paper towels).

2 To make the cucumber cups, cut the ends off the cucumber, and divide it into 3 equal lengths. Mark a line around the centre of each one as a guide.

3 Make a zigzag cut all the way around the centre of each section, always pointing the knife towards the centre of the cucumber.

4 Pull apart the two halves. Scoop out the centre of each cup with a melon baller or teaspoon, leaving a base on the bottom of each cup.

5 Put the spring onions (scallions), lime juice, red chillies, sugar, ground roasted peanuts and salt in a bowl and mix well to combine.

6 Divide the filling evenly between the 6 cucumber cups and arrange on a serving plate.

7 Garnish the cucumber cups with the deep-fried shallots and serve.

COOK'S TIP

Cherry tomatoes can also be hollowed out very simply with a melon baller and filled with this mixture. The two look very pretty arranged together on a serving dish.

Little Golden Parcels

These little parcels will draw admiring gasps from your guests, but they are fairly simple to prepare.

NUTRITIONAL INFORMATION

Calories 320   Sugars 1g
Protein . . . . .6g   Fat 21g
Carbohydrate . . .28g   Saturates 5g

35 MINS   35 MINS

SERVES 4

INGREDIENTS

1 garlic clove, crushed

1 tsp chopped coriander (cilantro) root

1 tsp pepper

250 g/9 oz/1 cup boiled mashed potato

175 g/6 oz/1 cup water chestnuts, chopped finely

1 tsp grated ginger root

2 tbsp ground roasted peanuts

2 tsp light soy sauce

½ tsp salt

½ tsp sugar

30 wonton sheets, defrosted

1 tsp cornflour (cornstarch), made into a paste with a little water

vegetable oil for deep-frying

fresh chives to garnish

sweet chilli sauce, to serve

VARIATION

If wonton sheets are not available, use spring roll sheets or filo pastry, and cut the large squares down to about 10 cm/ 4 inches square.

1 Mix together all the ingredients except the wonton sheets, cornflour (cornstarch) and oil.

2 Keeping the remainder of the wonton sheets covered with a damp cloth, lay 4 sheets out on a work surface (counter). Put a teaspoonful of the mixture on each. Make a line of the cornflour (cornstarch) paste around each sheet, about 1 cm/ ½ inch from the edge.

3 Bring all four corners to the centre and press together to form little bags. Repeat with all the wonton sheets.

4 Heat 5 cm/2 inches of the oil in a pan until a light haze appears on top and fry the parcels, in batches of 3, until golden brown. Remove and drain on paper towels. Tie a chive around the neck of each bag to garnish, and serve with a sweet chilli sauce for dipping.

Stuffed Courgettes (Zucchini)

Hollow out some courgettes (zucchini), fill them with a spicy beef mixture and bake them in the oven for a delicious side dish.

NUTRITIONAL INFORMATION

Calories 208	Sugars 3g
Protein 12g	Fat 9g
Carbohydrate . . .20g	Saturates 4g

45 MINS   35 MINS

SERVES 4

I N G R E D I E N T S

8 medium courgettes (zucchini)

1 tbsp sesame or vegetable oil

1 garlic clove, crushed

2 shallots, chopped finely

1 small red chilli, deseeded and chopped finely

250 g/9 oz/1 cup lean minced (ground) beef

1 tbsp fish sauce or mushroom ketchup

1 tbsp chopped fresh coriander (cilantro) or basil

2 tsp cornflour (cornstarch), blended with a little cold water

90 g/3 oz/½ cup cooked long-grain rice

salt and pepper

TO GARNISH

sprigs of fresh coriander (cilantro) or basil

carrot slices

1 Slice the courgettes (zucchini) in half horizontally and scoop out a channel down the middle, discarding all the seeds. Sprinkle with salt and set aside for 15 minutes.

2 Heat the oil in a wok or frying pan (skillet) and add the garlic, shallots and chilli. Stir-fry for 2 minutes, until golden. Add the minced (ground) beef and stir-fry briskly for about 5 minutes. Stir in the fish sauce or mushroom ketchup, the chopped coriander (cilantro) or basil and the blended cornflour (cornstarch), and cook for 2 minutes, stirring until thickened. Season with salt and pepper, then remove from the heat.

3 Rinse the courgettes (zucchini) in cold water and arrange them in a greased shallow ovenproof dish, cut side uppermost. Mix the cooked rice into the minced (ground) beef, then use this mixture to stuff the courgettes (zucchini).

4 Cover with foil and bake in a preheated oven at 190°C/375°F/ Gas Mark 5 for 20–25 minutes, removing the foil for the last 5 minutes of cooking time.

5 Serve at once, garnished with sprigs of fresh coriander (cilantro) or basil, and carrot slices.

Spare Ribs

Another classic favourite in Chinese restaurants, these sticky ribs are best eaten with your fingers.

NUTRITIONAL INFORMATION

Calories	436	Sugars	........3g
Protein	........21g	Fat	..........37g
Carbohydrate	....3g	Saturates	......14g

  1¼ HOURS 1 HOUR

SERVES 4

I N G R E D I E N T S

900 g/2 lb pork spare ribs

2 tbsp dark soy sauce

3 tbsp hoisin sauce

1 tbsp Chinese rice wine or dry sherry

pinch of Chinese five-spice powder

2 tsp dark brown sugar

¼ tsp chilli sauce

2 garlic cloves, crushed

coriander (cilantro) sprigs, to garnish
  (optional)

1 Cut the spare ribs into separate pieces if they are joined together. If desired, you can chop them into 5 cm/2-inch lengths, using a cleaver.

2 Mix together the soy sauce, hoisin sauce, Chinese rice wine or sherry, Chinese five-spice powder, dark brown sugar, chilli sauce and garlic in a large mixing bowl.

3 Place the ribs in a shallow dish and pour the mixture over them, turning to coat the ribs thoroughly. Cover with cling film (plastic wrap) and leave to marinate in the refrigerator, turning the ribs from time to time, for at least 1 hour.

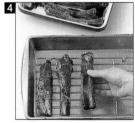

4 Remove the ribs from the marinade and arrange them in a single layer on a wire rack placed over a roasting tin (pan) half filled with warm water. Using a pastry brush, coat the ribs evenly with the marinade, reserving the remaining marinade.

5 Cook the ribs in a preheated oven, at 180°C/350°F/Gas Mark 4, for 30 minutes. Remove the roasting tin (pan) from the oven and turn the ribs over. Brush with the remaining marinade and return to the oven for a further 30 minutes, or until cooked through. Add more hot water to the roasting tin (pan) during cooking, if required. Do not allow it to dry out as the water steams the ribs and aids in their cooking.

6 Transfer the ribs to a warmed serving dish, garnish with the coriander (cilantro) sprigs (if using) and serve immediately.

Chinese Omelette

This is a fairly filling omelette, as it contains chicken and prawns (shrimp). It is cooked as a whole omelette and then sliced for serving.

NUTRITIONAL INFORMATION

Calories 309   Sugars 0g
Protein ....34g   Fat 19g
Carbohydrate ...0.2g   Saturates 5g

5 MINS   5 MINS

SERVES 4

I N G R E D I E N T S

8 eggs

225 g/8 oz/2 cups cooked chicken, shredded

12 tiger prawns (jumbo shrimp), peeled and deveined

2 tbsp chopped chives

2 tsp light soy sauce

dash of chilli sauce

2 tbsp vegetable oil

1 Lightly beat the eggs in a large mixing bowl.

2 Add the shredded chicken and tiger prawns (jumbo shrimp) to the eggs, mixing well.

3 Stir in the chopped chives, light soy sauce and chilli sauce, mixing well to combine all the ingredients.

4 Heat the vegetable oil in a large preheated frying pan (skillet) over a medium heat.

5 Add the egg mixture to the frying pan (skillet), tilting the pan to coat the base completely.

6 Cook over a medium heat, gently stirring the omelette with a fork, until the surface is just set and the underside is a golden brown colour.

7 When the omelette is set, slide it out of the pan, with the aid of a palette knife (spatula).

8 Cut the Chinese omelette into squares or slices and serve immediately. Alternatively, serve the omelette as a main course for two people.

VARIATION

You could add extra flavour to the omelette by stirring in 3 tablespoons of finely chopped fresh coriander (cilantro) or 1 teaspoon sesame seeds with the chives in step 3.

Prawn (Shrimp) Parcels

These small prawn (shrimp) bites are packed with the flavour of lime and coriander (cilantro) for a quick and tasty starter.

NUTRITIONAL INFORMATION

Calories 305   Sugars 2g
Protein ....15g   Fat 21g
Carbohydrate ...14g   Saturates 8g

15 MINS   20 MINS

SERVES 4

I N G R E D I E N T S

1 tbsp sunflower oil

1 red (bell) pepper, deseeded and very thinly sliced

75 g/2¾ oz/¾ cup beansprouts

finely grated zest and juice of 1 lime

1 red chili, deseeded and very finely chopped

1 cm/½ inch piece of root ginger, peeled and grated

225 g/8 oz peeled prawns (shrimp)

1 tbsp fish sauce

½ tsp arrowroot

2 tbsp chopped fresh coriander (cilantro)

8 sheets filo pastry

25 g/1 oz/2 tbsp butter

2 tsp sesame oil

oil, for frying

spring onion (scallion) tassels, to garnish

chilli sauce, to serve

COOK'S TIP

If using cooked prawns (shrimp), cook for 1 minute only otherwise the prawns (shrimp) will toughen.

1 Heat the sunflower oil in a large preheated wok. Add the red (bell) pepper and beansprouts and stir-fry for 2 minutes, or until the vegetables have softened.

2 Remove the wok from the heat and toss in the lime zest and juice, red chilli, ginger and prawns (shrimp), stirring well.

3 Mix the fish sauce with the arrowroot and stir the mixture into the wok juices. Return the wok to the heat and cook, stirring, for 2 minutes, or until the juices thicken. Toss in the coriander (cilantro) and mix well.

4 Lay the sheets of filo pastry out on a board. Melt the butter and sesame oil and brush each pastry sheet with the mixture.

5 Spoon a little of the prawn (shrimp) filling on to the top of each sheet, fold over each end, and roll up to enclose the filling.

6 Heat the oil in a large wok. Cook the parcels, in batches, for 2–3 minutes, or until crisp and golden. Garnish with spring onion (scallion) tassels and serve hot with a chilli dipping sauce.

Aubergine Dipping Platter

Dipping platters are a very sociable dish, bringing together all the diners at the table.

NUTRITIONAL INFORMATION

Calories 81	Sugars 4g
Protein 4g	Fat 5g
Carbohydrate 5g	Saturates 1g

🥘 15 MINS   🕐 10 MINS

SERVES 4

I N G R E D I E N T S

1 aubergine (eggplant), peeled and cut into 2.5 cm/1 inch cubes

3 tbsp sesame seeds, roasted in a dry pan over a low heat

1 tsp sesame oil

grated rind and juice of ½ lime

1 small shallot, diced

1 tsp sugar

1 red chilli, deseeded and sliced

125 g/4½ oz/1¼ cups broccoli florets

2 carrots, cut into matchsticks

125 g/4½ oz/8 baby corn, cut in half lengthways

2 celery stalks, cut into matchsticks

1 baby red cabbage, cut into 8 wedges, the leaves of each wedge held together by the core

salt and pepper

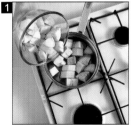 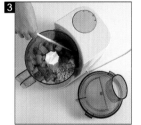 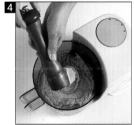

1 Cook the diced aubergine (eggplant) in a saucepan of boiling water for 7–8 minutes.

2 Meanwhile, grind the sesame seeds with the oil in a food processor or pestle and mortar.

3 Add the aubergine (eggplant), lime rind and juice, shallot, ½ tsp salt, pepper, sugar and chilli in that order to the sesame seeds. Process, or chop and mash by hand, until smooth.

4 Adjust the seasoning to taste then spoon the dip into a bowl.

5 Serve the aubergine (eggplant) dipping platter surrounded by the broccoli, carrots, baby corn, celery and red cabbage.

VARIATION

You can vary the selection of vegetables depending on your preference or whatever you have at hand. Other vegetables you could use are cauliflower florets and cucumber sticks.

Chilli Fish Cakes

These small fish cakes are quick to make and are delicious served with a chilli dip.

NUTRITIONAL INFORMATION

Calories . . . . . . .164 Sugars 1g
Protein . . . . .23g Fat 6g
Carbohydrate . . . .6g Saturates 1g

   5 MINS   40 MINS

SERVES 4

I N G R E D I E N T S

450 g/1 lb cod fillets, skinned

2 tbsp fish sauce

2 red chilies, deseeded and very finely chopped

2 cloves garlic, crushed

10 lime leaves, very finely chopped

2 tbsp fresh coriander (cilantro), chopped

1 large egg

25 g/1 oz/¼ cup plain (all-purpose) flour

100 g/3½ oz fine green beans, very finely sliced

groundnut oil, for frying

chilli dip, to serve

1 Using a sharp knife, roughly cut the cod fillets into bite-sized pieces.

2 Place the cod in a food processor together with the fish sauce, chillies, garlic, lime leaves, coriander (cilantro), egg and flour. Process until finely chopped and turn out into a large mixing bowl.

3 Add the green beans to the cod mixture and combine.

4 Divide the mixture into small balls. Flatten the balls between the palms of your hands to form rounds.

5 Heat a little oil in a preheated wok or large frying pan (skillet). Fry the fish cakes on both sides until brown and crispy on the outside.

6 Transfer the fish cakes to serving plates and serve hot with a chilli dip.

VARIATION

Almost any kind of fish fillets and seafood can used in this recipe, try haddock, crab meat or lobster.

Honeyed Chicken Wings

Chicken wings are ideal for a starter as they are small and perfect for eating with the fingers.

NUTRITIONAL INFORMATION

Calories 131   Sugars 4g
Protein . . . . .10g   Fat 8g
Carbohydrate . . . .4g   Saturates 2g

 5 MINS   40 MINS

SERVES 4

I N G R E D I E N T S

450 g/1 lb chicken wings

2 tbsp peanut oil

2 tbsp light soy sauce

2 tbsp hoisin sauce

2 tbsp clear honey

2 garlic cloves, crushed

1 tsp sesame seeds

M A R I N A D E

1 dried red chilli

½–1 tsp chilli powder

½–1 tsp ground ginger

finely grated rind of 1 lime

1 To make the marinade, crush the dried chilli in a pestle and mortar. Mix together the crushed dried chilli, chilli powder, ground ginger and lime rind in a small mixing bowl.

2 Thoroughly rub the spice mixture into the chicken wings with your fingertips. Set aside for at least 2 hours to allow the flavours to penetrate the chicken wings.

3 Heat the peanut oil in a large wok or frying pan (skillet).

4 Add the chicken wings and fry, turning frequently, for about 10–12 minutes, until golden and crisp. Drain off any excess oil.

5 Add the soy sauce, hoisin sauce, honey, garlic and sesame seeds to the wok, turning the chicken wings to coat.

6 Reduce the heat and cook for 20–25 minutes, turning the chicken wings frequently, until completely cooked through. Serve hot.

COOK'S TIP

Make the dish in advance and freeze the chicken wings. Defrost thoroughly, cover with foil and heat right through in a moderate oven.

Lettuce-Wrapped Meat

Serve the minced meat and lettuce leaves on separate dishes: each guest then wraps his or her own parcel.

NUTRITIONAL INFORMATION

Calories	159	Sugars	.......0.2g
Protein	........14g	Fat	..........10g
Carbohydrates	....1g	Saturates	.......2g

 5 MINS 5 MINS

SERVES 4

INGREDIENTS

250 g/9 oz minced (ground) pork or chicken

1 tbsp finely chopped Chinese mushrooms

1 tbsp finely chopped water chestnuts

pinch of sugar

1 tsp light soy sauce

1 tsp Chinese rice wine or dry sherry

1 tsp cornflour (cornstarch)

2-3 tbsp vegetable oil

½ tsp finely chopped ginger root

1 tsp finely chopped spring onions (scallions)

1 tbsp finely chopped Szechuan preserved vegetables (optional)

1 tbsp oyster sauce

a few drops of sesame oil

salt and pepper

8 crisp lettuce leaves, to serve

COOK'S TIP

Szechuan preserved vegetables are pickled mustard roots. Hot and salty with a peppery flavour, they are often used to intensify the spiciness of a dish. Once opened, store in the refrigerator in a tightly sealed jar.

1 Mix the minced (ground) pork or chicken with the Chinese mushrooms, water chestnuts, salt, pepper, sugar, soy sauce, rice wine or sherry and cornflour (cornstarch). Blend well until all the ingredients are thoroughly combined.

2 Heat the vegetable oil in a preheated wok or large frying pan (skillet).

3 Add the ginger and spring onions (scallions) to the wok or frying pan (skillet), followed by the minced (ground) meat. Stir-fry for 1 minute.

4 Add the Szechuan preserved vegetables (if using) and continue stirring for 1 more minute.

5 Add the oyster sauce and sesame oil, blend well and cook for 1 more minute. Remove the mixture in the wok to a warmed serving dish.

6 To serve: place about 2-3 tablespoons of the mixture on a lettuce leaf and roll it up tightly to form a small parcel. Eat with your fingers.

Bang-Bang Chicken

The cooked chicken meat is tenderized by being beaten with a rolling pin, hence the name for this very popular Szechuan dish.

NUTRITIONAL INFORMATION

Calories 82	Sugars 1g	
Protein 13g	Fat 3g	
Carbohydrate 2g	Saturates 1g	

1¼ HOURS   40 MINS

SERVES 4

I N G R E D I E N T S

1 litre/1¾ pints/4 cups water

2 chicken quarters (breast half and leg)

1 cucumber, cut into matchstick shreds

S A U C E

2 tbsp light soy sauce

1 tsp sugar

1 tbsp finely chopped spring onions
(scallions), plus extra to garnish

1 tsp red chilli oil

¼ tsp pepper

1 tsp white sesame seeds

2 tbsp peanut butter, creamed with a little
sesame oil, plus extra to garnish

1 Bring the water to a rolling boil in a wok or a large saucepan. Add the chicken pieces, reduce the heat, cover and cook for 30–35 minutes.

2 Remove the chicken from the wok or pan and immerse in a bowl of cold water for at least 1 hour to cool it, ready for shredding.

3 Remove the chicken pieces, drain and dry on absorbent kitchen paper (paper towels). Take the meat off the bone.

4 On a flat surface, pound the chicken with a rolling pin, then tear the meat

into shreds with 2 forks. Mix the chicken with the shredded cucumber and arrange in a serving dish.

5 To serve, mix together all the sauce ingredients until thoroughly combined and pour over the chicken and cucumber in the serving dish. Sprinkle some sesame seeds and chopped spring onions (scallions) over the sauce and serve.

COOK'S TIP

Take the time to tear the chicken meat into similar-sized shreds, to make an elegant-looking dish. You can do this quite efficiently with 2 forks, although Chinese cooks would do it with their fingers.

(Small) Shrimp Rolls

This variation of a spring roll is made with shrimps, stir-fried with shallots, carrot, cucumber, bamboo shoots and rice.

NUTRITIONAL INFORMATION

Calories	388	Sugars	........2g
Protein	.........9g	Fat	.........25g
Carbohydrate	...33g	Saturates	.......6g

10 MINS   15 MINS

SERVES 4

I N G R E D I E N T S

2 tbsp vegetable oil

3 shallots, chopped very finely

1 carrot, cut into matchstick pieces

7 cm/3 inch piece of cucumber, cut into matchstick pieces

60 g/2 oz/½ cup bamboo shoots, shredded finely

125 g/4½ oz/½ cup peeled (small) shrimps

90 g/3 oz/½ cup cooked long-grain rice

1 tbsp fish sauce or light soy sauce

1 tsp sugar

2 tsp cornflour (cornstarch), blended in 2 tbsp cold water

8 × 25 cm/10 inch spring roll wrappers

oil for deep-frying

salt and pepper

plum sauce, to serve

TO GARNISH

spring onion (scallion) brushes (see page 305)

sprigs of fresh coriander (cilantro)

1 Heat the oil in a wok and add the shallots, carrot, cucumber and bamboo shoots. Stir-fry briskly for 2–3 minutes. Add the shrimps and cooked rice, and cook for a further 2 minutes. Season.

2 Mix together the fish sauce or soy sauce, sugar and blended cornflour (cornstarch). Add to the stir-fry and cook, stirring constantly, for about 1 minute, until thickened. Leave to cool slightly.

3 Place spoonfuls of the shrimp and vegetable mixture on the spring roll wrappers. Dampen the edges and roll them up to enclose the filling completely.

4 Heat the oil for deep-frying and fry the spring rolls until crisp and golden brown. Drain on paper towels. Serve the rolls garnished with spring onion (scallion) brushes and fresh coriander (cilantro) and accompanied by the plum sauce.

Spinach Meatballs

Balls of pork mixture are coated in spinach and steamed before being served with a sesame and soy sauce dip.

NUTRITIONAL INFORMATION

Calories 137   Sugars 2g
Protein . . . . .13g   Fat 7g
Carbohydrate . . . .6g   Saturates 2g

20 MINS   25 MINS

SERVES 4

INGREDIENTS

125 g/4½ oz pork

1 small egg

1-cm/½-inch piece fresh root ginger (ginger root), chopped

1 small onion, finely chopped

1 tbsp boiling water

25 g/1 oz canned bamboo shoots, drained, rinsed and chopped

2 slices smoked ham, chopped

2 tsp cornflour (cornstarch)

450 g/1 lb fresh spinach

2 tsp sesame seeds

SAUCE

150 ml/¼ pint/⅔ cup vegetable stock

½ tsp cornflour (cornstarch)

1 tsp cold water

1 tsp light soy sauce

½ tsp sesame oil

1 tbsp chopped chives

1 Mince (grind) the pork very finely in a food processor. Lightly beat the egg in a bowl and stir into the pork.

2 Put the ginger and onion in a separate bowl, add the boiling water and let stand for 5 minutes. Drain and add to the pork mixture with the bamboo shoots, ham and cornflour (cornstarch). Mix thoroughly and roll into 12 balls.

3 Wash the spinach and remove the stalks. Blanch in boiling water for 10 seconds, drain well then slice into very thin strips and mix with the sesame seeds. Roll the meatballs in the mixture to coat.

4 Place the meatballs on a heatproof plate in the base of a steamer. Cover and steam for 8–10 minutes, until cooked through and tender.

5 Meanwhile, make the sauce. Put the stock in a saucepan and bring to the boil. Mix together the cornflour (cornstarch) and water to a smooth paste and stir it into the stock. Stir in the soy sauce, sesame oil and chives. Transfer the cooked meatballs to a warm plate and serve with the sauce.

Rice Paper Parcels

These special rice paper wrappers are available in Chinese supermarkets and health shops. Do not use the rice paper sold for making cakes.

NUTRITIONAL INFORMATION

Calories	133	Sugars	.........2g
Protein	........10g	Fat	...........8g
Carbohydrate	....5g	Saturates	.......1g

 5 MINS   15 MINS

SERVES 4

I N G R E D I E N T S

1 egg white

2 tsp cornflour (cornstarch)

2 tsp dry sherry

1 tsp caster (superfine) sugar

2 tsp hoisin sauce

225 g/8 oz peeled, cooked prawns (shrimp)

4 spring onions (scallions), sliced

25 g/1 oz canned water chestnuts, drained, rinsed and chopped

8 Chinese rice paper wrappers

vegetable oil, for deep-frying

hoisin sauce or plum sauce, to serve

1 Lightly beat the egg white in a bowl. Mix in the cornflour (cornstarch), dry sherry, sugar and hoisin sauce. Add the prawns (shrimp), spring onions (scallions) and water chestnuts, mixing thoroughly.

COOK'S TIP

Use this filling inside wonton skins (see page 42) if the rice paper wrappers are unavailable.

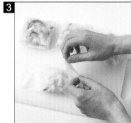

2 Soften the rice papers first by dipping them in a bowl of water one at a time. Spread them out on a clean work surface (counter).

3 Using a dessert spoon, place a little of the prawn (shrimp) mixture into the centre of each rice paper. Carefully wrap the rice paper around the filling to make a secure parcel. Repeat to make 8 parcels.

4 Heat the oil in a wok until it is almost smoking. Reduce the heat slightly, add the parcels, in batches if necessary, and deep-fry for 4–5 minutes, until crisp. Remove from the oil with a slotted spoon and drain on absorbent kitchen paper (paper towels).

5 Transfer the parcels to a warmed serving dish and serve immediately with a little hoisin or plum sauce.

Crispy Wontons

Mushroom-filled crispy wontons are served on skewers with a dipping sauce flavoured with chillies.

NUTRITIONAL INFORMATION

Calories ....302 Sugars 1g
Protein ....3g Fat 25
Carbohydrate ...15g Saturates 6g

45 MINS   20 MINS

SERVES 4

I N G R E D I E N T S

8 wooden skewers, soaked in cold water
   for 30 minutes

1 tbsp vegetable oil

1 tbsp chopped onion

1 small garlic clove, chopped

½ tsp chopped ginger root

60 g/2 oz/½ cup flat mushrooms,
   chopped

16 wonton skins (see page 42)

vegetable oil, for deep-frying

salt

S A U C E

2 tbsp vegetable oil

2 spring onions (scallions),
   shredded thinly

1 red and 1 green chilli, deseeded and
   shredded thinly

3 tbsp light soy sauce

1 tbsp vinegar

1 tbsp dry sherry

pinch of sugar

1 Heat the vegetable oil in a preheated
wok or frying pan (skillet).

2 Add the onion, garlic and ginger root
to the wok or pan and stir-fry for 2
minutes. Stir in the mushrooms and fry for

a further 2 minutes. Season well with salt and leave
to cool.

3 Place 1 teaspoon of the cooled mushroom filling in the
centre of each wonton skin.

4 Bring two opposite corners of each wonton skin
together to cover the mixture and pinch together to
seal. Repeat with the remaining corners.

5 Thread 2 wontons on to each skewer. Heat enough oil
in a large saucepan to deep-fry the wontons in batches
until golden and crisp. Do not overheat the oil or the
wontons will brown on the outside before they are
properly cooked inside. Remove the wontons with a
perforated spoon and drain on absorbent kitchen paper
(paper towels).

6 To make the sauce, heat the vegetable oil in a small
saucepan until quite hot or until a small cube of bread
dropped in the oil browns in a few seconds. Put the spring
onions (scallions) and chillies in a bowl and pour the hot oil
slowly on top. Mix in the remaining ingredients.

7 Transfer the crispy wontons to a serving dish and serve
with the dipping sauce.

Salt & Pepper Prawns

Szechuan peppercorns are very hot, adding heat and a red colour to the prawns (shrimp). They are effectively offset by the sugar in this recipe.

NUTRITIONAL INFORMATION

Calories 174   Sugars 1g
Protein . . . . .25g   Fat 8g
Carbohydrate . . . .1g   Saturates 1g

 5 MINS   10 MINS

SERVES 4

INGREDIENTS

2 tsp salt

1 tsp black pepper

2 tsp Szechuan peppercorns

1 tsp sugar

450 g/1 lb peeled raw tiger prawns (jumbo shrimp)

2 tbsp groundnut oil

1 red chilli, deseeded and finely chopped

1 tsp freshly grated ginger

3 cloves garlic, crushed

spring onions (scallions), sliced, to garnish

prawn (shrimp) crackers, to serve

1 Grind the salt, black pepper and Szechuan peppercorns in a pestle and mortar.

2 Mix the salt and pepper mixture with the sugar and set aside until required.

3 Rinse the tiger prawns (jumbo shrimp) under cold running water and pat dry with absorbent kitchen paper (paper towels).

4 Heat the oil in a preheated wok or large frying pan (skillet).

5 Add the prawns (shrimp), chopped red chilli, ginger and garlic to the wok or frying pan (skillet) and stir-fry for 4–5 minutes, or until the prawns (shrimp) are cooked through.

6 Add the salt and pepper mixture to the wok and stir-fry for 1 minute, stirring constantly so it does not burn on the base of the wok.

7 Transfer the prawns (shrimp) to warm serving bowls and garnish with spring onions (scallions). Serve hot with prawn (shrimp) crackers.

COOK'S TIP

Tiger prawns (jumbo shrimp) are widely available and have a lovely meaty texture. If using cooked tiger prawns (shrimp), add them with the salt and pepper mixture in step 5 – if the cooked prawns (shrimp) are added any earlier they will toughen up and be inedible.

Tofu (Bean Curd) Tempura

Crispy coated vegetables and tofu (bean curd) accompanied by a sweet, spicy dip give a real taste of the Orient in this Japanese-style dish.

NUTRITIONAL INFORMATION

Calories 582   Sugars 10g
Protein . . . . .16g   Fat 27g
Carbohydrate . . .65g   Saturates 4g

 15 MINS   20 MINS

SERVES 4

I N G R E D I E N T S

125 g/4½ oz baby courgettes (zucchini)

125 g/4½ oz baby carrots

125 g/4½ oz baby corn cobs

125 g/4½ oz baby leeks

2 baby aubergines (eggplants)

225 g/8 oz tofu (bean curd)

vegetable oil, for deep-frying

julienne strips of carrot, root ginger and
baby leek to garnish

noodles, to serve

B A T T E R

2 egg yolks

300 ml/½ pint/1¼ cups water

225 g/8 oz/2 cups plain (all-purpose) flour

D I P P I N G   S A U C E

5 tbsp mirin or dry sherry

5 tbsp Japanese soy sauce

2 tsp clear honey

1 garlic clove, crushed

1 tsp grated root ginger

1 Slice the courgettes (zucchini) and carrots in half lengthways. Trim the corn. Trim the leeks at both ends. Quarter the aubergines (eggplants). Cut the tofu (bean curd) into 2.5 cm/1 inch cubes.

2 To make the batter, mix the egg yolks with the water. Sift in 175 g/6 oz/1½ cups of the flour and beat with a balloon whisk to form a thick batter. Don't worry if there are any lumps. Heat the oil for deep-frying to 180°C/350°F or until a cube of bread browns in 30 seconds.

3 Place the remaining flour on a large plate and toss the vegetables and tofu (bean curd) until lightly coated.

4 Dip the tofu (bean curd) in the batter and deep-fry for 2–3 minutes, until lightly golden. Drain on kitchen paper (paper towels) and keep warm.

5 Dip the vegetables in the batter and deep-fry, a few at a time, for 3–4 minutes, until golden. Drain and place on a warmed serving plate.

6 To make the dipping sauce, mix all the ingredients together. Serve with the vegetables and tofu (bean curd), accompanied with noodles and garnished with julienne strips of vegetables.

Steamed Cabbage Rolls

These small cabbage parcels are quick and easy to prepare and cook. They are ideal for a speedy starter.

NUTRITIONAL INFORMATION

Calories	162	Sugars	.......0.3g
Protein	........24g	Fat	...........7g
Carbohydrates	....2g	Saturates	.......1g

 5 MINS 20 MINS

SERVES 4

I N G R E D I E N T S

8 cabbage leaves, trimmed

225 g/8 oz skinless, boneless chicken

175 g/6 oz peeled raw or cooked prawns (shrimp)

1 tsp cornflour (cornstarch)

½ tsp chilli powder

1 egg, lightly beaten

1 tbsp vegetable oil

1 leek, sliced

1 garlic clove, thinly sliced

sliced fresh red chilli, to garnish

1 Blanch the cabbage for 2 minutes. Drain and pat dry with absorbent kitchen paper (paper towels).

2 Mince (grind) the chicken and prawns (shrimp) in a food processor. Place in a bowl with the cornflour (cornstarch), chilli powder and egg. Mix well to combine all the ingredients.

3 Place 2 tablespoons of the chicken and prawn (shrimp) mixture towards one end of each cabbage leaf. Fold the sides of the cabbage leaf around the filling and roll up.

4 Arrange the parcels, seam-side down, in a single layer on a heatproof plate and cook in a steamer for 10 minutes.

5 Meanwhile, sauté the leek and garlic in the oil for 1–2 minutes.

6 Transfer the cabbage parcels to warmed individual serving plates and garnish with red chilli slices. Serve with the leek and garlic sauté.

COOK'S TIP

Use Chinese leaves (cabbage) or Savoy cabbage for this recipe, choosing leaves of a similar size for the parcels.

Chicken Spring Rolls

A cucumber dipping sauce tastes perfect with these delicious spring rolls, filled with chicken and fresh, crunchy vegetables.

NUTRITIONAL INFORMATION

Calories	367	Sugars	........18g
Protein	........13g	Fat	..........21g
Carbohydrate	...32g	Saturates	.......3g

 10 MINS   25 MINS

SERVES 4

I N G R E D I E N T S

2 tbsp vegetable oil

4 spring onions (scallions), trimmed and sliced very finely

1 carrot, cut into matchstick pieces

1 small green or red (bell) pepper, cored, deseeded and sliced finely

60 g/2 oz/⅔ cup button mushrooms, sliced

60 g/2 oz/1 cup bean-sprouts

175 g/6 oz/1 cup cooked chicken, shredded

1 tbsp light soy sauce

1 tsp sugar

2 tsp cornflour (cornstarch), blended in 2 tbsp cold water

12 × 20 cm/8 inch spring roll wrappers

oil for deep-frying

salt and pepper

spring onion (scallion) brushes to garnish

S A U C E

50 ml/2 fl oz/¼ cup light malt vinegar

60 g/2 oz/¼ cup light muscovado sugar

½ tsp salt

5 cm/2 inch piece of cucumber, peeled and chopped finely

4 spring onions (scallions), trimmed and sliced finely

1 small red or green chilli, deseeded and chopped very finely

1 Stir-fry the spring onions (scallions), carrot and (bell) pepper for 2–3 minutes. Add the mushrooms, bean-sprouts and chicken and cook for 2 minutes. Season. Mix the soy sauce, sugar and blended cornflour (cornstarch). Add to the wok and stir-fry for 1 minute. Leave to cool slightly. Spoon the chicken and vegetable mixture on to the spring roll wrappers. Dampen the edges and roll them up to enclose the filling completely.

2 To make the sauce, heat the vinegar, water, sugar and salt in a pan. Boil for 1 minute. Combine the cucumber, spring onions (scallions) and chilli and pour over the vinegar mixture. Leave to cool.

3 Heat the oil and fry the rolls until crisp and golden brown. Drain on paper towels, garnish with spring onion (scallion) brushes and serve with the cucumber dipping sauce.

Sesame Prawn Toasts

These are one of the most recognised and popular starters in Chinese restaurants in the Western world. They are also quick and easy to make.

NUTRITIONAL INFORMATION

Calories 237   Sugars 1g
Protein . . . . .18g   Fat 12g
Carbohydrate . . .15g   Saturates 2g

 5 MINS   🕐 10 MINS

SERVES 4

I N G R E D I E N T S

4 slices medium, thick-sliced white bread

225 g/8 oz cooked peeled prawns (shrimp)

1 tbsp soy sauce

2 cloves garlic, crushed

1 tbsp sesame oil

1 egg

25 g/1 oz/2 tbsp sesame seeds

oil, for deep-frying

sweet chilli sauce, to serve

1 Remove the crusts from the bread, if desired, then set aside until required.

2 Place the peeled prawns (shrimp), soy sauce, crushed garlic, sesame oil and egg into a food processor and blend until a smooth paste has formed.

VARIATION

Add 2 chopped spring onions (scallions) to the mixture in step 2 for added flavour and crunch.

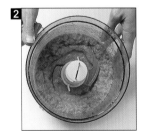 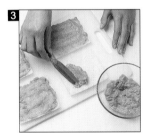 

3 Spread the prawn (shrimp) paste evenly over the 4 slices of bread. Sprinkle the sesame seeds over the top of the prawn (shrimp) mixture and press the seeds down with your hands so that they stick to the mixture. Cut each slice in half and in half again to form 4 triangles.

4 Heat the oil in a large wok or frying pan (skillet) and deep-fry the toasts,

sesame seed-side up, for 4-5 minutes, or until golden and crispy.

5 Remove the toasts with a slotted spoon and transfer to absorbent kitchen paper (paper towels) and leave to drain thoroughly.

6 Serve the sesame prawn (shrimp) toasts warm with sweet chilli sauce for dipping.

Pork Dim Sum

These small steamed parcels are traditionally served as an appetizer and are very adaptable to your favourite fillings.

NUTRITIONAL INFORMATION

Calories	478	Sugars	.........3g
Protein	........33g	Fat	..........29g
Carbohydrate	...21g	Saturates	.......9g

10 MINS   15 MINS

SERVES 4

INGREDIENTS

400 g/14 oz minced (ground) pork

2 spring onions (scallions), chopped

50 g/1¾ oz canned bamboo shoots, drained, rinsed and chopped

1 tbsp light soy sauce

1 tbsp dry sherry

2 tsp sesame oil

2 tsp caster (superfine) sugar

1 egg white, lightly beaten

4½ tsp cornflour (cornstarch)

24 wonton wrappers

1 Place the minced (ground) pork, spring onions (scallions), bamboo shoots, soy sauce, dry sherry, sesame oil, caster (superfine) sugar and beaten egg white in a large mixing bowl and mix until all the ingredients are thoroughly combined.

2 Stir in the cornflour (cornstarch), mixing until thoroughly incorporated with the other ingredients.

3 Spread out the wonton wrappers on a work surface (counter). Place a spoonful of the pork and vegetable mixture in the centre of each wonton wrapper and lightly brush the edges of the wrappers with water.

4 Bring the sides of the wrappers together in the centre of the filling, pinching firmly together.

5 Line a steamer with a clean, damp tea towel (dish cloth) and arrange the wontons inside.

6 Cover and steam for 5–7 minutes, until the dim sum are cooked through. Serve immediately.

COOK'S TIP

Bamboo steamers are designed to rest on the sloping sides of a wok above the water. They are available in a range of sizes.

Son-in-Law Eggs

This recipe is supposedly so called because it is an easy dish for a son-in-law to cook to impress his new mother-in-law!

NUTRITIONAL INFORMATION

Calories . . . . . . .229 Sugars 8g
Protein . . . . .9g Fat 18g
Carbohydrate . . . .8g Saturates 3g

15 MINS   15 MINS

SERVES 4

INGREDIENTS

6 eggs, hard-boiled (hard-cooked)
  and shelled

4 tbsp sunflower oil

1 onion, sliced thinly

2 fresh red chillies, sliced

2 tbsp sugar

1 tbsp water

2 tsp tamarind pulp

1 tbsp liquid seasoning, such
  as Maggi

rice, to serve

1 Prick the hard-boiled (hard-cooked) eggs 2 or 3 times with a cocktail stick (toothpick).

2 Heat the sunflower oil in a wok and fry the eggs until crispy and golden. Drain on absorbent kitchen paper (paper towels).

3 Halve the eggs lengthways and put on a serving dish.

4 Reserve one tablespoon of the oil, pour off the rest, then heat the tablespoonful in the wok. Cook the onion and chillies over a high heat until golden and slightly crisp. Drain on kitchen paper (paper towels).

5 Heat the sugar, water, tamarind pulp and liquid seasoning in the wok and simmer for 5 minutes until thickened.

6 Pour the sauce over the eggs and spoon over the onion and chillies. Serve immediately with rice.

COOK'S TIP

Tamarind pulp is sold in oriental stores, and is quite sour. If it is not available, use twice the amount of lemon juice in its place.

Chilli & Peanut Prawns

Peanut flavours are widely used in Far East and South East Asian cooking and complement many ingredients.

NUTRITIONAL INFORMATION

Calories ....478 Sugars 2g
Protein ....32g Fat 30g
Carbohydrate ...19g Saturates 11g

 15 MINS   10 MINS

SERVES 4

INGREDIENTS

450 g/1 lb king prawns (peeled apart from tail end)

3 tbsp crunchy peanut butter

1 tbsp chilli sauce

10 sheets filo pastry

25 g/1 oz butter, melted

50 g/1¾ oz fine egg noodles

oil, for frying

1 Using a sharp knife, make a small horizontal slit across the back of each prawn (shrimp). Press down on the prawns (shrimps) so that they lie flat.

2 Mix together the peanut butter and chilli sauce in a small bowl until well blended. Using a pastry brush, spread a little of the sauce on to each prawn (shrimp) so they are evenly coated.

3 Cut each pastry sheet in half and brush with melted butter.

4 Wrap each prawn (shrimp) in a piece of pastry, tucking the edges under to fully enclose the prawn (shrimp).

5 Place the fine egg noodles in a bowl, pour over enough boiling water to cover and leave to stand for 5 minutes. Drain the noodles thoroughly. Use 2–3

cooked noodles to tie around each prawn (shrimp) parcel.

6 Heat the oil in a preheated wok. Cook the prawns (shrimp) for 3–4 minutes, or until golden and crispy.

7 Remove the prawns (shrimp) with a slotted spoon, transfer to absorbent kitchen paper and leave to drain. Transfer to serving plates and serve warm.

COOK'S TIP

When using filo pastry, keep any unused pastry covered to prevent it drying out and becoming brittle.

Red Curry Fishcakes

You can use almost any kind of fish fillets or seafood for these delicious fishcakes which can be eaten as an appetizer or a light meal.

NUTRITIONAL INFORMATION

Calories 203   Sugars 1g
Protein ....32g   Fat 8g
Carbohydrate ....1g   Saturates 1g

15 MINS   15 MINS

SERVES 6

INGREDIENTS

1 kg/2 lb 4 oz fish fillets or prepared seafood, such as cod, haddock, prawns (shrimp), crab meat or lobster

1 egg, beaten

2 tbsp chopped fresh coriander (cilantro)

Red Curry Paste (see page 184)

1 bunch spring onions (scallions), finely chopped

vegetable oil, for deep-frying

chilli flowers, to garnish

CUCUMBER SALAD

1 large cucumber, peeled and grated

2 shallots, peeled and grated

2 red chillies, seeded and very finely chopped

2 tbsp fish sauce

2 tbsp dried powdered shrimps

1½-2 tbsp lime juice

COOK'S TIP

To save time, Red Curry Paste can be bought ready-made in jars from Chinese grocery stores or large supermarkets.

1 Place the fish in a blender or food processor with the egg, coriander (cilantro) and curry paste and purée until smooth and well blended.

2 Turn the mixture into a bowl, add the spring onions (scallions) and mix well to combine.

3 Taking 2 tablespoons of the fish mixture at a time, shape into balls, then flatten them slightly with your fingers to make fishcakes.

4 Heat the vegetable oil in a preheated wok or frying pan (skillet) until hot.

5 Add a few of the fishcakes to the wok or pan and deep-fry for a few minutes until brown and cooked through. Remove with a slotted spoon and drain on absorbent kitchen paper (paper towels). Keep warm while cooking the remaining fishcakes.

6 Meanwhile, to make the cucumber salad, mix the cucumber with the shallots, chillies, fish sauce, dried shrimps and lime juice.

7 Serve the cucumber salad immediately, with the warm fishcakes.

Vegetable Spring Rolls

There are many different versions of spring rolls throughout the Far East, a vegetable filling being the classic.

NUTRITIONAL INFORMATION

Calories	189	Sugars	........4g
Protein	.........2g	Fat	..........16g
Carbohydrate	....11g	Saturates	.......5g

 10 MINS   15 MINS

SERVES 4

INGREDIENTS

225 g/8 oz carrots

1 red (bell) pepper

1 tbsp sunflower oil, plus extra for frying

75 g/2¾ oz/¾ cup bean sprouts

finely grated zest and juice of 1 lime

1 red chilli, deseeded and very finely chopped

1 tbsp soy sauce

½ tsp arrowroot

2 tbsp chopped fresh coriander (cilantro)

8 sheets filo pastry

25 g/1 oz butter

2 tsp sesame oil

TO SERVE

chilli sauce

spring onion (scallion) tassels

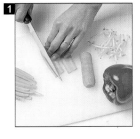  

1 Using a sharp knife, cut the carrots into thin sticks. Deseed the (bell) pepper and cut into thin slices.

2 Heat the sunflower oil in a large preheated wok.

3 Add the carrot, red (bell) pepper and bean sprouts and cook, stirring, for 2 minutes, or until softened. Remove the wok from the heat and toss in the lime zest and juice, and the red chilli.

4 Mix the soy sauce with the arrowroot. Stir the mixture into the wok, return to the heat and cook for 2 minutes or until the juices thicken.

5 Add the chopped fresh coriander (cilantro) to the wok and mix well.

6 Lay the sheets of filo pastry out on a board. Melt the butter and sesame oil and brush each sheet with the mixture.

7 Spoon a little of the vegetable filling at the top of each sheet, fold over each long side, and roll up.

8 Add a little oil to the wok and cook the spring rolls in batches, for 2–3 minutes, or until crisp and golden.

9 Transfer the spring rolls to a serving dish, garnish and serve hot with chilli dipping sauce.

Crispy Seaweed

This tasty Chinese starter is not all that it seems – the 'seaweed' is in fact pak choi which is then fried, salted and tossed with pine kernels.

NUTRITIONAL INFORMATION

Calories 214	Sugars 14g	
Protein 6g	Fat 15g	
Carbohydrate . . .15g	Saturates 2g	

 10 MINS 5 MINS

SERVES 4

INGREDIENTS

1 kg/2 lb 4 oz pak choi

groundnut oil, for deep-frying (about 850 ml/1½ pints/3¾ cups)

1 tsp salt

1 tbsp caster (superfine) sugar

50 g/1¾ oz/2½ tbsp toasted pine kernels (nuts)

1 Rinse the pak choi leaves under cold running water and then pat dry thoroughly with absorbent kitchen paper (paper towels).

2 Discarding any tough outer leaves, roll each pak choi leaf up, then slice

through thinly so that the leaves are finely shredded. Alternatively, use a food processor to shred the pak choi.

3 Heat the groundnut oil in a large wok or heavy-based frying pan (skillet).

4 Carefully add the shredded pak choi leaves to the wok or frying pan (skillet) and fry for about 30 seconds or until they shrivel up and become crispy

(you will probably need to do this in several batches, depending on the size of the wok).

5 Remove the crispy seaweed from the wok with a slotted spoon and drain on absorbent kitchen paper (paper towels).

6 Transfer the crispy seaweed to a large bowl and toss with the salt, sugar and pine kernels (nuts). Serve immediately.

COOK'S TIP

The tough, outer leaves of pak choi are discarded as these will spoil the overall taste and texture of the dish.

Use savoy cabbage instead of the pak choi if it is unavailable, drying the leaves thoroughly before frying.

Money Bags

These traditional steamed dumplings can be eaten on their own or dipped in a mixture of soy sauce, sherry and slivers of ginger root.

NUTRITIONAL INFORMATION

Calories	315	Sugars	. . . . .3g
Protein	. . . . .8g	Fat	. . . . .8g
Carbohydrate	. . .56g	Saturates	. . . . . . .1g

45 MINS 20 MINS

SERVES 4

INGREDIENTS

3 Chinese dried mushrooms
(if unavailable, use thinly sliced
open-cup mushrooms)

250 g/9 oz/2 cups plain (all-purpose) flour

1 egg, beaten

75 ml/3 fl oz/⅓ cup water

1 tsp baking powder

¾ tsp salt

2 tbsp vegetable oil

2 spring onions (scallions), chopped

90 g/3 oz/½ cup sweetcorn kernels

½ red chilli, deseeded and chopped

1 tbsp brown bean sauce

1 Place the dried mushrooms in a small bowl, cover with warm water and leave to soak for 20–25 minutes.

2 To make the wrappers, sift the plain (all-purpose) flour into a bowl. Add the beaten egg and mix in lightly. Stir in the water, baking powder and salt. Mix to make a soft dough.

3 Knead the dough lightly on a floured board. Cover with a damp tea towel (dish cloth) and set aside for 5–6 minutes. This allows the baking powder time to activate, so that the dumplings swell when steaming.

4 Drain the mushrooms, squeezing them dry. Remove the tough centres and chop the mushrooms.

5 Heat the vegetable oil in a wok or large frying pan (skillet) and stir-fry the mushrooms, spring onions (scallions), sweetcorn and chilli for 2 minutes.

6 Stir in the brown bean sauce and remove from the heat.

7 Roll the dough into a large sausage and cut into 24 even-sized pieces. Roll each piece out into a thin round and place a teaspoonful of the filling in the centre. Gather up the edges to a point, pinch together and twist to seal.

8 Stand the dumplings in an oiled steaming basket. Place over a saucepan of simmering water, cover and steam for 12–14 minutes before serving.

Vegetable Dim Sum

Dim sum are small Chinese parcels which may be filled with any variety of fillings, steamed or fried and served with a dipping sauce.

NUTRITIONAL INFORMATION

Calories 295	Sugars 1g
Protein 5g	Fat 22g
Carbohydrate . . .20g	Saturates 6g

15 MINS   15 MINS

SERVES 4

I N G R E D I E N T S

2 spring onions (scallions), chopped

25 g/1 oz green beans, chopped

½ small carrot, finely chopped

1 red chilli, chopped

25 g/1 oz/⅓ cup bean sprouts, chopped

25 g/1 oz/⅓ cup button mushrooms, chopped

25 g/1 oz/¼ cup unsalted cashew nuts, chopped

1 small egg, beaten

2 tbsp cornflour (cornstarch)

1 tsp light soy sauce

1 tsp hoisin sauce

1 tsp sesame oil

32 wonton wrappers

oil, for deep-frying

1 tbsp sesame seeds

1 Mix all of the vegetables together in a bowl. Add the nuts, egg, cornflour (cornstarch), soy sauce, hoi-sin sauce and sesame oil to the bowl. Mix well.

2 Lay the wonton wrappers out on a chopping board and spoon small quantities of the mixture into the centre of each. Gather the wrapper around the filling at the top, to make little parcels, leaving the top open.

3 Heat the oil for deep-frying in a wok to 180°C/350°F or until a cube of bread browns in 30 seconds. Fry the wontons, in batches, for 1–2 minutes or until golden brown. Drain on kitchen paper (paper towels) and keep warm whilst frying the remaining wontons.

4 Sprinkle the sesame seeds over the wontons. Serve the vegetable dim sum with a soy or plum dipping sauce.

COOK'S TIP

If preferred, arrange the wontons on a heatproof plate and then steam in a steamer for 5-7 minutes for a healthier cooking method.

Crispy Crab Wontons

These delicious wontons are a superb appetizer. Deep-fried until crisp and golden, they are delicious with a chilli dipping sauce.

NUTRITIONAL INFORMATION

Calories	266	Sugars	.......0.4g
Protein	........10g	Fat	..........17g
Carbohydrate	...18g	Saturates	.......5g

10 MINS   15 MINS

SERVES 4

INGREDIENTS

175 g/6 oz white crabmeat, flaked

50 g/1¾ oz canned water chestnuts, drained, rinsed and chopped

1 small fresh red chilli, chopped

1 spring onion (scallion), chopped

1 tbsp cornflour (cornstarch)

1 tsp dry sherry

1 tsp light soy sauce

½ tsp lime juice

24 wonton wrappers

vegetable oil, for deep-frying

sliced lime, to garnish

1 To make the filling, mix together the crabmeat, water chestnuts, chilli, spring onion (scallion), cornflour (cornstarch), sherry, soy sauce and lime juice.

2 Spread out the wonton wrappers on a work surface (counter) and spoon one portion of the filling into the centre of each wonton wrapper.

3 Dampen the edges of the wonton wrappers with a little water and fold them in half to form triangles. Fold the two pointed ends in towards the centre, moisten with a little water to secure and then pinch together to seal.

4 Heat the oil for deep-frying in a wok or deep-fryer to 180°C–190°C/350°F–375°F, or until a cube of bread browns in 30 seconds. Fry the wontons, in batches, for 2–3 minutes, until golden brown and crisp. Remove the wontons from the oil and leave to drain on kitchen paper (paper towels).

5 Serve the wontons hot, garnished with slices of lime.

COOK'S TIP

Handle wonton wrappers carefully as they can be easily damaged. Make sure that the wontons are sealed well and secured before deep-frying to prevent the filling coming out and the wontons unwrapping.

Aubergine (Eggplant) Satay

Aubergines (eggplants) and mushrooms are grilled on skewers and served with a satay sauce.

NUTRITIONAL INFORMATION

Calories . . . . . . .155 Sugars 2g
Protein . . . . .4g Fat 14g
Carbohydrate . . . .3g Saturates 3g

   2¼ HOURS   25 MINS

SERVES 4

I N G R E D I E N T S

2 aubergines (eggplants), cut into 2.5 cm/
  1 inch pieces

175 g/6 oz small chestnut mushrooms

M A R I N A D E

1 tsp cumin seeds

1 tsp coriander seeds

2.5 cm/1 inch piece ginger root, grated

2 garlic cloves, crushed lightly

½ stalk lemon grass, chopped roughly

4 tbsp light soy sauce

8 tbsp sunflower oil

2 tbsp lemon juice

P E A N U T   S A U C E

½ tsp cumin seeds

½ tsp coriander seeds

3 garlic cloves

1 small onion, puréed in a food processor or
  chopped very finely by hand

1 tbsp lemon juice

1 tsp salt

½ red chilli, deseeded and sliced

125 ml/4 fl oz/½ cup coconut milk

250 g/9 oz/1 cup crunchy peanut butter

250 ml/8 fl oz/1 cup water

1 Thread the vegetables on to eight metal or pre-soaked wooden skewers.

2 For the marinade, grind the cumin and coriander seeds, ginger, garlic and lemon grass. Stir-fry over a high heat until fragrant. Remove from the heat and add the remaining marinade ingredients. Place the skewers in a dish and spoon the marinade over. Leave to marinate for at least 2 hours and up to 8 hours.

3 To make the sauce, grind the cumin and coriander seeds with the garlic. Add all the ingredients except the water. Transfer to a pan and stir in the water. Bring to the boil and cook until thick.

4 Cook the skewers under a preheated very hot grill (broiler) for 15–20 minutes. Brush with the marinade frequently and turn once. Serve with the peanut sauce.

Spicy Sweetcorn Fritters

Cornmeal can be found in most supermarkets or health food shops.
Yellow in colour, it acts as a binding agent in this recipe.

NUTRITIONAL INFORMATION

Calories 213	Sugars 6g
Protein 5g	Fat 8g
Carbohydrate . . .30g	Saturates 1g

5 MINS   15 MINS

SERVES 4

I N G R E D I E N T S

225 g/8 oz/¾ cup canned or frozen
  sweetcorn

2 red chillies, deseeded and very finely
  chopped

2 cloves garlic, crushed

10 lime leaves, very finely chopped

2 tbsp fresh coriander (cilantro),
  chopped

1 large egg

75 g/2¾ oz/½ cup cornmeal

100 g/3½ oz fine green beans, very finely
  sliced

groundnut oil, for frying

1 Place the sweetcorn, chillies, garlic, lime leaves, coriander (cilantro), egg and cornmeal in a large mixing bowl, and stir to combine.

2 Add the green beans to the ingredients in the bowl and mix well, using a wooden spoon.

3 Divide the mixture into small, evenly sized balls. Flatten the balls of mixture between the palms of your hands to form rounds.

4 Heat a little groundnut oil in a preheated wok or large frying pan

(skillet) until really hot. Cook the fritters, in batches, until brown and crispy on the outside, turning occasionally.

5 Leave the fritters to drain on absorbent kitchen paper (paper towels) while frying the remaining fritters.

6 Transfer the fritters to warm serving plates and serve immediately.

COOK'S TIP

Kaffir lime leaves are dark green, glossy leaves that have a lemony-lime flavour. They can be bought from specialist Asian stores either fresh or dried. Fresh leaves impart the most delicious flavour.

Steamed Duck Buns

The dough used in this recipe may also be wrapped around chicken, pork or prawns (shrimp), or sweet fillings as an alternative.

NUTRITIONAL INFORMATION

Calories 307	Sugars 11g
Protein 17g	Fat 6g
Carbohydrate . . .50g	Saturates 1g

1½ HOURS   1 HOUR

SERVES 4

I N G R E D I E N T S

D U M P L I N G   D O U G H

300 g/10½ oz/2⅔ cups plain (all-purpose) flour

15 g/½ oz dried yeast

1 tsp caster (superfine) sugar

2 tbsp warm water

175 ml/6 fl oz/¾ cup warm milk

F I L L I N G

300 g/10½ oz duck breast

1 tbsp light brown sugar

1 tbsp light soy sauce

2 tbsp clear honey

1 tbsp hoisin sauce

1 tbsp vegetable oil

1 leek, finely chopped

1 garlic clove, crushed

1-cm/½-inch piece fresh root ginger (ginger root), grated

1 Place the duck breast in a large bowl. Mix together the light brown sugar, soy sauce, honey and hoisin sauce. Pour the mixture over the duck and marinate for 20 minutes.

2 Remove the duck from the marinade and cook on a rack set over a roasting tin (pan) in a preheated oven, at 200°C/400°F/Gas Mark 6, for 35–40 minutes, or until cooked through. Leave to cool, remove the meat from the bones and cut into small cubes.

3 Heat the vegetable oil in a preheated wok or frying pan (skillet) until really hot.

4 Add the leek, garlic and ginger to the wok and fry for 3 minutes. Mix with the duck meat.

5 Sift the plain (all-purpose) flour into a large bowl. Mix the yeast, caster (superfine) sugar and warm water in a separate bowl and leave in a warm place for 15 minutes.

6 Pour the yeast mixture into the flour, together with the warm milk, mixing to form a firm dough. Knead the dough on a floured surface for 5 minutes. Roll into a sausage shape, 2.5 cm/1 inch in diameter. Cut into 16 pieces, cover and let stand for 20–25 minutes.

7 Flatten the dough pieces into 10-cm/4-inch rounds. Place a spoonful of filling in the centre of each, draw up the sides to form a 'moneybag' shape and twist to seal.

8 Place the dumplings on a clean, damp tea towel (dish cloth) in the base of a steamer, cover and steam for 20 minutes. Serve immediately.

Barbecue Pork (Char Siu)

Also called honey-roasted pork, these are the strips of reddish meat sometimes seen hanging in the windows of Cantonese restaurants.

NUTRITIONAL INFORMATION

Calories	250	Sugar	.........8g
Protein	........27g	Fat	..........10g
Carbohydrate	....9g	Saturates	.......3g

4¼ HOURS   30 MINS

SERVES 4

INGREDIENTS

500 g/1 lb 2 oz pork fillet

150 ml/¼ pint/⅔ cup boiling water

1 tbsp honey, dissolved with a little hot water

MARINADE

1 tbsp sugar

1 tbsp crushed yellow bean sauce

1 tbsp light soy sauce

1 tbsp hoisin sauce

1 tbsp oyster sauce

½ tsp chilli sauce

1 tbsp brandy or rum

1 tsp sesame oil

shredded lettuce, to serve

1 Using a sharp knife or meat cleaver, cut the pork into strips about 2.5 cm/1 inch thick and 18-20 cm/7-8 inches long and place in a large shallow dish. Mix the marinade ingredients together and pour over the pork, turning until well coated. Cover, and leave to marinate for at least 3-4 hours, turning occasionally.

2 Remove the pork strips from the dish with a slotted spoon, reserving the marinade. Arrange the pork strips on a rack over a baking tin (pan). Place the tin (pan) in a preheated oven and pour in the boiling water. Roast the pork for about 10-15 minutes.

3 Lower the oven temperature. Baste the pork strips with the reserved marinade and turn over using metal tongs. Roast for a further 10 minutes.

4 Remove the pork from the oven, brush with the honey syrup, and lightly brown under a medium hot grill (broiler) for about 3-4 minutes, turning once or twice.

5 To serve, allow the pork to cool slightly before cutting it. Cut across the grain into thin slices and arrange neatly on a bed of shredded lettuce. Make a sauce by boiling the marinade and the drippings in the baking tin (pan) for a few minutes, strain and pour over the pork.

Fat Horses

A mixture of meats is flavoured with coconut milk, fish sauce and coriander (cilantro) in this curious sounding dish.

NUTRITIONAL INFORMATION

Calories	195	Sugars	.........1g
Protein	........23g	Fat	...........11g
Carbohydrate	....1g	Saturates	.......6g

🍲 10 MINS   ⏱ 30 MINS

SERVES 4

INGREDIENTS

25 g/1 oz/2 tbsp creamed coconut

125 g/4½ oz lean pork

125 g/4½ oz chicken breast, skin removed

125 g/4½ oz/½ cup canned crab meat, drained

2 eggs

2 garlic cloves, crushed

4 spring onions (scallions), trimmed and chopped

1 tbsp fish sauce

1 tbsp chopped fresh coriander (cilantro) leaves and stems

1 tbsp dark muscovado sugar

salt and pepper

TO GARNISH

finely sliced white radish (mooli) or turnip

chives

red chilli

sprigs of fresh coriander (cilantro)

1 Mix the coconut with 3 tbsp of hot water. Stir to dissolve the coconut.

2 Put the pork, chicken and crab meat into a food processor or blender and process for 10–15 seconds until minced (ground), or chop them finely by hand and put in a mixing bowl.

3 Add the coconut mixture to the food processor or blender with the eggs, garlic, spring onions (scallions), fish sauce, coriander (cilantro) and sugar. Season to taste and process for a few more seconds. Alternatively, mix these ingredients into the chopped pork, chicken and crab meat.

4 Grease 6 ramekin dishes with a little butter. Spoon in the minced (ground) mixture, levelling the surface. Place them in a steamer, then set the steamer over a pan of gently boiling water. Cook until set – about 30 minutes.

5 Lift out the dishes and leave to cool for a few minutes. Run a knife around the edge of each dish, then invert on to warmed plates. Serve garnished with finely sliced white radish (mooli) or turnip, chives, red chilli and sprigs of fresh coriander (cilantro).

Crispy-Fried Vegetables

A hot and sweet dipping sauce makes the perfect accompaniment to fresh vegetables coated in a light batter and deep-fried.

NUTRITIONAL INFORMATION

Calories	258	Sugars	........11g
Protein	.........6g	Fat	...........9g
Carbohydrate	...39g	Saturates	......11g

 40 MINS   10 MINS

SERVES 4

INGREDIENTS

vegetable oil for deep-frying

500 g/1 lb 2 oz selection of vegetables, such as cauliflower, broccoli, mushrooms, courgettes (zucchini), (bell) peppers and baby sweetcorn, cut into even-sized pieces

BATTER

125 g/4½ oz/1 cup plain (all-purpose) flour

½ tsp salt

1 tsp caster (superfine) sugar

1 tsp baking powder

3 tbsp vegetable oil

200 ml/7 fl oz/scant 1 cup warm water

SAUCE

6 tbsp light malt vinegar

2 tbsp fish sauce or light soy sauce

2 tbsp water

1 tbsp soft brown sugar

pinch of salt

2 garlic cloves, crushed

2 tsp grated ginger root

2 red chillies, deseeded and chopped finely

2 tbsp chopped fresh coriander (cilantro)

1 To make the batter, sift the flour, salt, sugar and baking powder into a bowl. Add the oil and most of the water. Whisk together to make a smooth batter, adding extra water to give it the consistency of single cream. Chill for 20–30 minutes.

2 Meanwhile, make the sauce. Heat the vinegar, fish sauce or soy sauce, water, sugar and salt until boiling. Remove from the heat and leave to cool.

3 Mix together the garlic, ginger, chillies and coriander (cilantro). Add the cooled vinegar mixture and stir well to combine.

4 Heat the oil for deep-frying in a wok. Dip the vegetables in the batter and fry, in batches, until crisp and golden – about 2 minutes. Drain on kitchen paper (paper towels). Serve the vegetables accompanied by the dipping sauce.

Pork Satay

Small pieces of tender pork are skewered on bamboo satay sticks, grilled (broiled) or barbecued, then served with a delicious peanut sauce.

NUTRITIONAL INFORMATION

Calories 397	Sugars 8g	
Protein 35g	Fat 24g	
Carbohydrate 11g	Saturates 6g	

 10 MINS   15 MINS

SERVES 4

INGREDIENTS

8 bamboo satay sticks, soaked in warm water

500 g/1 lb 2 oz pork fillet (tenderloin)

SAUCE

125 g/4½ oz/1 cup unsalted peanuts

2 tsp hot chilli sauce

175 ml/6 fl oz/¾ cup coconut milk

2 tbsp soy sauce

1 tbsp ground coriander

pinch of ground turmeric

1 tbsp dark muscovado sugar

salt

TO GARNISH

fresh flat leaf (Italian) parsley or coriander (cilantro)

cucumber leaves

red chillies

COOK'S TIP

To make cucumber leaves, slice a thick chunk from the side of a cucumber, and cut to shape. Cut grooves in the cucumber flesh in the shape of leaf veins.

1 To make the sauce, scatter the peanuts on a baking tray (cookie sheet) and toast under a preheated grill (broiler) until golden brown, turning them once or twice. Leave to cool, then grind them in a food processor, blender or food mill. Alternatively, chop the peanuts very finely.

2 Put the ground peanuts into a small saucepan with the hot chilli sauce, coconut milk, soy sauce, coriander, turmeric, sugar and salt. Heat gently, stirring constantly and taking care not to burn the sauce on the bottom of the pan. Reduce the heat to very low and cook gently for 5 minutes.

3 Meanwhile, trim any fat from the pork. Cut the pork into small cubes and thread it on to the bamboo satay sticks. Place the kebabs on a rack covered with foil in a grill (broiler) pan.

4 Put half the peanut sauce into a small serving bowl. Brush the skewered pork with the remaining satay sauce and place under a preheated grill (broiler) for about 10 minutes, turning and basting frequently, until cooked.

5 Serve the pork with the reserved peanut sauce and garnish with flat leaf (Italian) parsley or coriander (cilantro) leaves, cucumber leaves and red chillies.

Sweet & Sour Pork Ribs

Here I have used the spare rib, the traditional Chinese-style rib. Baby back ribs and loin ribs are also suitable in this recipe.

NUTRITIONAL INFORMATION

Calories 565	Sugars 29g
Protein 24g	Fat 37g
Carbohydrate . . .32g	Saturates 14g

2¼ HOURS   50 MINS

SERVES 4

INGREDIENTS

2 garlic cloves, crushed

5 cm/2 inch piece ginger, grated

150 ml/¼ pint/⅔ cup soy sauce

2 tbsp sugar

4 tbsp sweet sherry

4 tbsp tomato purée (paste)

300 g/10½ oz/2 cups pineapple, cubed

2 kg/4 lb 8 oz pork spare ribs

3 tbsp clear honey

300 g/10½ oz/5 pineapple rings, fresh or canned, to serve

1 Mix together the garlic, ginger, soy sauce, sugar, sherry, tomato purée (paste) and cubed pineapple in a non-porous dish.

2 Put the spare ribs into the dish and make sure that they are coated completely with the marinade.

3 Cover the dish with cling film (plastic wrap).

4 Leave the ribs to marinate at room temperature for 2 hours only.

5 Cook the ribs over a medium barbecue (grill) for 30–40 minutes, brushing with the honey after 20–30 minutes.

6 Baste the spare ribs with the reserved marinade frequently until cooked.

7 Cook the pineapple rings over the barbecue (grill) for about 10 minutes, turning once.

8 Transfer the sweet & sour ribs to a serving dish and serve with the barbecued (grilled) pineapple rings on the side.

COOK'S TIP

If a marinade contains soy sauce, the marinating time should be limited, usually to 2 hours. If allowed to marinate for too long, the meat will dry out and become tough.

Lentil Balls with Sauce

Crisp golden lentil balls are served in a sweet and sour sauce with (bell) peppers and pineapple chunks.

NUTRITIONAL INFORMATION

Calories 384   Sugars 15g
Protein ....17g   Fat 14g
Carbohydrate ...49g   Saturates 2g

 15 MINS   35 MINS

SERVES 4

INGREDIENTS

250 g/9 oz/1 cup red lentils

425 ml/¾ pint/scant 2 cups water

½ green chilli, deseeded and chopped

4 spring onions (scallions), chopped finely

1 garlic clove, crushed

1 tsp salt

4 tbsp pineapple juice from can

1 egg, beaten

vegetable oil for deep-frying

rice or noodles, to serve

SAUCE

3 tbsp white wine vinegar

2 tbsp sugar

2 tbsp tomato purée (paste)

1 tsp sesame oil

1 tsp cornflour (cornstarch)

½ tsp salt

6 tbsp water

2 tbsp vegetable oil

½ red (bell) pepper, cut into chunks

½ green (bell) pepper, cut into chunks

2 canned pineapple rings, cut into chunks

1 Wash the lentils, then place in a saucepan with the water and bring to the boil. Skim and boil rapidly for 10 minutes, uncovered. Reduce the heat and simmer for 5 minutes until you have a fairly dry mixture, stirring occasionally.

2 Remove from the heat and stir in the chilli, spring onions (scallions), garlic, salt and pineapple juice. Leave to cool for 10 minutes.

3 To make the sauce, mix together the vinegar, sugar, tomato purée (paste) sesame oil, cornflour (cornstarch), salt and water, and set aside.

4 Add the beaten egg to the lentil mixture. Heat the oil in a large pan or wok and deep-fry tablespoonfuls of the mixture in batches until crisp and golden. Remove with a perforated spoon and drain on paper towels.

5 Heat the 2 tablespoons oil in a wok or frying pan (skillet). Stir-fry the (bell) peppers for 2 minutes. Add the sauce mixture with the pineapple chunks. Bring to the boil, then reduce the heat and simmer for 1 minute, stirring constantly, until the sauce has thickened. Add the lentil balls and heat thoroughly, taking care not to break them up. Serve with rice or noodles.

Prawn (Shrimp) Omelette

This is called *Foo Yung* in China and is a classic dish which may be flavoured with any ingredients you have to hand.

NUTRITIONAL INFORMATION

Calories 320   Sugars 1g
Protein . . . . .31g   Fat 18g
Carbohydrate . . . .8g   Saturates 4g

5 MINS   10 MINS

SERVES 4

INGREDIENTS

3 tbsp sunflower oil

2 leeks, trimmed and sliced

350 g/12 oz raw tiger prawns (jumbo shrimp)

25 g/1 oz/4 tbsp cornflour (cornstarch)

1 tsp salt

175 g/6 oz mushrooms, sliced

175 g/6 oz/1½ cups bean sprouts

6 eggs

deep-fried leeks, to garnish (optional)

1 Heat the sunflower oil in a preheated wok or large frying pan (skillet). Add the sliced leeks and stir-fry for 3 minutes.

2 Rinse the prawns (shrimp) under cold running water and then pat dry with absorbent kitchen paper (paper towels).

3 Mix together the cornflour (cornstarch) and salt in a large bowl.

4 Add the prawns (shrimp) to the cornflour (cornstarch) and salt mixture and toss to coat all over.

5 Add the prawns (shrimp) to the wok or frying pan (skillet) and stir-fry for 2 minutes, or until the prawns (shrimp) are almost cooked through.

6 Add the mushrooms and bean sprouts to the wok and stir-fry for a further 2 minutes.

7 Beat the eggs with 3 tablespoons of cold water. Pour the egg mixture into the wok and cook until the egg sets, carefully turning over once. Turn the omelette out on to a clean board, divide into 4 and serve hot, garnished with deep-fried leeks (if using).

VARIATION

If liked, divide the mixture into 4 once the initial cooking has taken place in step 6 and cook 4 individual omelettes.

Chicken or Beef Satay

In this dish, strips of chicken or beef are threaded on to skewers, grilled (broiled) and served with a spicy peanut sauce.

NUTRITIONAL INFORMATION

Calories 314	Sugars 8g
Protein 32g	Fat 16g
Carbohydrate . . .10g	Saturates 4g

  🐔 🐔 🐔

2¼ HOURS   15 MINS

SERVES 6

INGREDIENTS

4 boneless, skinned chicken breasts or
  750 g/1 lb 10 oz rump steak, trimmed

MARINADE

1 small onion, finely chopped

1 garlic clove, crushed

2.5 cm/1 inch piece ginger root, peeled
  and grated

2 tbsp dark soy sauce

2 tsp chilli powder

1 tsp ground coriander

2 tsp dark brown sugar

1 tbsp lemon or lime juice

1 tbsp vegetable oil

SAUCE

300 ml/½ pint/1¼ cups coconut milk

4 tbsp/⅓ cup crunchy peanut butter

1 tbsp fish sauce

1 tsp lemon or lime juice

salt and pepper

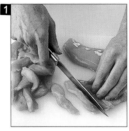  

1 Using a sharp knife, trim any fat from the chicken or beef then cut into thin strips, about 7 cm/3 inches long.

2 To make the marinade, place all the ingredients in a shallow dish and mix well. Add the chicken or beef strips and turn in the marinade until well coated.

Cover with cling film (plastic wrap) and leave to marinate for 2 hours or stand overnight in the refrigerator.

3 Remove the meat from the marinade and thread the pieces, concertina style, on pre-soaked bamboo or thin wooden skewers.

4 Grill (broil) the chicken and beef satays for 8-10 minutes, turning and

brushing occasionally with the marinade, until cooked through.

5 Meanwhile, to make the sauce, mix the coconut milk with the peanut butter, fish sauce and lemon or lime juice in a saucepan. Bring to the boil and cook for 3 minutes. Season to taste.

6 Transfer the sauce to a serving bowl and serve with the cooked satays.

Vegetable Rolls

In this recipe a mixed vegetable stuffing is wrapped in Chinese leaves (cabbage) and steamed until tender.

NUTRITIONAL INFORMATION

Calories 69	Sugars 1g
Protein 2g	Fat 5g
Carbohydrate 3g	Saturates 1g

🍲 10 MINS   🕐 20 MINS

SERVES 4

I N G R E D I E N T S

8 large Chinese leaves (cabbage)

FILLING

2 baby corn cobs, sliced

1 carrot, finely chopped

1 celery stick, chopped

4 spring onions (scallions), chopped

4 water chestnuts, chopped

2 tbsp unsalted cashews, chopped

1 garlic clove, chopped

1 tsp grated fresh root ginger

25 g/1 oz canned bamboo shoots, drained, rinsed and chopped

1 tsp sesame oil

2 tsp soy sauce

1 Place the Chinese leaves (cabbage) in a large bowl and pour over boiling water to soften them. Leave to stand for 1 minute and drain thoroughly.

2 Mix together the baby corn cobs, chopped carrot, celery, spring onions (scallions), water chestnuts, cashews, garlic, ginger and bamboo shoots in a large bowl.

3 In a separate bowl, mix together the sesame oil and soy sauce. Add this mixture to the vegetables, mixing well until the vegetables are thoroughly coated in the mixture.

4 Spread out the Chinese leaves (cabbage) on a chopping board and spoon an equal quantity of the filling mixture on to each leaf.

5 Roll the Chinese leaves (cabbage) up, folding in the sides, to make neat parcels. Secure the parcels with cocktail sticks (toothpicks).

6 Place the filled rolls in a small heatproof dish in a steamer, cover and cook for 15–20 minutes, until the parcels are cooked.

7 Transfer the vegetable rolls to a warm serving dish and serve with a soy or chilli sauce.

Crudites with Shrimp Sauce

In this recipe, fruit and vegetable crudités are served with a spicy, garlicky shrimp sauce.

NUTRITIONAL INFORMATION

Calories ....85 Sugars 11g
Protein ....7g Fat 1g
Carbohydrate ...12g Saturates 0.2g

12¼ HOURS   0 MINS

SERVES 4

I N G R E D I E N T S

about 750 g/1 lb10 oz prepared
   raw fruit and vegetables, such
   as broccoli, cauliflower, apple,
   pineapple, cucumber, celery, (bell)
   peppers and mushrooms

S A U C E

60 g/2 oz dried shrimps

1 cm/½ inch cube shrimp paste

3 garlic cloves, crushed

4 red chillies, seeded and chopped

6 stems fresh coriander (cilantro),
   coarsely chopped

juice of 2 limes

fish sauce, to taste

brown sugar, to taste

1 Soak the dried shrimps in warm water for 10 minutes.

2 To make the sauce, place the shrimp paste, drained shrimps, garlic, chillies and coriander (cilantro) in a food processor or blender and process until well chopped but not smooth.

3 Turn the sauce mixture into a bowl and add the lime juice, mixing well.

4 Add fish sauce and brown sugar to taste to the sauce. Mix well.

5 Cover the bowl tightly and chill the sauce in the refrigerator for at least 12 hours, or overnight.

6 To serve, arrange the fruit and vegetables attractively on a large serving plate. Place the prepared sauce in the centre for dipping.

COOK'S TIP

Hard-boiled quail's eggs are often added to this traditional fruit and vegetable platter and certainly would be offered on a special occasion.

Aspagarus Parcels

These small parcels are ideal as part of a main meal and irresistible as a quick snack with extra plum sauce for dipping.

NUTRITIONAL INFORMATION

Calories ....194 Sugars 2g
Protein ....3g Fat 16g
Carbohydrate ....11g Saturates 4g

 5 MINS ⏱ 25 MINS

SERVES 4

I N G R E D I E N T S

100 g/3½ oz fine tip asparagus

1 red (bell) pepper, deseeded and thinly sliced

50 g/1¾ oz/½ cup bean sprouts

2 tbsp plum sauce

1 egg yolk

8 sheets filo pastry

oil, for deep-frying

1 Place the asparagus, (bell) pepper and beansprouts in a large mixing bowl.

2 Add the plum sauce to the vegetables and mix until well-combined.

3 Beat the egg yolk and set aside until required.

4 Lay the sheets of filo pastry out on to a clean work surface (counter).

5 Place a little of the asparagus and red (bell) pepper filling at the top end of each filo pastry sheet. Brush the edges of the filo pastry with a little of the beaten egg yolk.

6 Roll up the filo pastry, tucking in the ends and enclosing the filling like a spring roll. Repeat with the remaining filo sheets.

7 Heat the oil for deep-frying in a large preheated wok. Carefully cook the parcels, 2 at a time, in the hot oil for 4–5 minutes or until crispy.

8 Remove the parcels with a slotted spoon and leave to drain on absorbent kitchen paper (paper towels).

9 Transfer the parcels to warm serving plates and serve immediately.

COOK'S TIP

Be sure to use fine-tipped asparagus as it is more tender than the larger stems.

Chicken Wontons

These deliciously crispy nibbles make an ideal introduction to a Chinese meal. Here they are filled with a chicken and mushroom mixture.

NUTRITIONAL INFORMATION

Calories 285	Sugars 1g
Protein 16g	Fat 19g
Carbohydrate ...14g	Saturates 5g

 20 MINS   35 MINS

SERVES 4

INGREDIENTS

250 g/9 oz boneless chicken breast, skinned

60 g/2 oz/⅔ cup mushrooms

1 garlic clove

2 shallots

1 tbsp fish sauce or mushroom ketchup

1 tbsp chopped fresh coriander (cilantro)

2 tbsp vegetable oil

about 50 wonton wrappers

oil, for deep-frying

salt and pepper

sliced spring onion (scallion), to garnish

sweet chilli sauce, to serve

1 Put the chicken, mushrooms, garlic, shallots, fish sauce or mushroom ketchup and coriander (cilantro) into a blender or food processor. Blend for 10–15 seconds. Alternatively, chop all the ingredients finely and mix together well.

2 Heat the vegetable oil in a wok or frying pan (skillet) and add the chicken mixture. Stir-fry for about 8 minutes, breaking up the mixture as it cooks, until it browns. Transfer to a bowl and leave to cool for 10–15 minutes.

3 Place the wonton wrappers on a clean, damp tea towel (dish cloth).

Layering 2 wrappers together at a time, place teaspoonfuls of the chicken mixture into the middle. Dampen the edges with water, then make small pouches, pressing the edges together to seal. Repeat with the remaining wrappers until all the mixture is used.

4 Heat the oil for deep-frying in a wok or deep fat fryer. Fry the wontons, a few at a time, for about 2–3 minutes until golden brown. Remove the won tons

from the oil with a perforated spoon and drain on kitchen paper (paper towels). Keep warm while frying the remaining wontons.

5 Transfer the wontons to a warmed serving platter and garnish with the sliced spring onion (scallion). Serve at once, accompanied by some sweet chilli sauce.

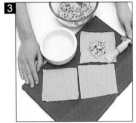

Deep-fried Chilli Corn Balls

These small corn balls have a wonderful hot and sweet flavour, offset by the pungent coriander (cilantro).

NUTRITIONAL INFORMATION

Calories	248	Sugars	.........6g
Protein	.........6g	Fat	12
Carbohydrate	...30g	Saturates	.......5g

15 MINS   30 MINS

SERVES 4

I N G R E D I E N T S

6 spring onions (scallions), sliced

3 tbsp fresh coriander (cilantro), chopped

225 g/8 oz canned sweetcorn

1 tsp mild chilli powder

1 tbsp sweet chilli sauce

25 g/1 oz/¼ cup desiccated (shredded) coconut

1 egg

75 g/2¾ oz/⅓ cup polenta (cornmeal)

oil, for deep-frying

extra sweet chilli sauce, to serve

1 In a large bowl, mix together the spring onions (scallions), coriander (cilantro), sweetcorn, chilli powder, chilli sauce, coconut, egg and polenta (cornmeal) until well blended.

2 Cover the bowl with cling film (plastic wrap) and leave to stand for about 10 minutes.

3 Heat the oil for deep-frying in a large preheated wok or frying pan (skillet) to 180°C/350°F or until a cube of bread browns in 30 seconds.

4 Carefully drop spoonfuls of the chilli and polenta (cornmeal) mixture into the hot oil. Deep-fry the chilli corn balls, in batches, for 4–5 minutes or until crispy and a deep golden brown colour.

5 Remove the chilli corn balls with a slotted spoon, transfer to absorbent kitchen paper (paper towels) and leave to drain thoroughly.

6 Transfer the chilli corn balls to serving plates and serve with an extra sweet chilli sauce for dipping.

COOK'S TIP

For safe deep-frying in a round-bottomed wok, place it on a wok rack so that it rests securely. Only half-fill the wok with oil. Never leave the wok unattended over a high heat.

Sesame Ginger Chicken

Chunks of chicken breast are marinated in a mixture of lime juice, garlic, sesame oil and fresh ginger to give them a great flavour.

NUTRITIONAL INFORMATION

Calories 204   Sugars 0g
Protein ....28g   Fat 10g
Carbohydrate ....1g   Saturates 2g

2¼ HOURS   10 MINS

SERVES 4

INGREDIENTS

4 wooden satay sticks, soaked in warm water

500 g/1 lb 2 oz boneless chicken breasts

sprigs of fresh mint, to garnish

MARINADE

1 garlic clove, crushed

1 shallot, chopped very finely

2 tbsp sesame oil

1 tbsp fish sauce or light soy sauce

finely grated rind of 1 lime or ½ lemon

2 tbsp lime juice or lemon juice

1 tsp sesame seeds

2 tsp finely grated fresh ginger root

2 tsp chopped fresh mint

salt and pepper

COOK'S TIP

The kebabs taste delicious if dipped into an accompanying bowl of hot chilli sauce.

1 To make the marinade, put the crushed garlic, chopped shallot, sesame oil, fish sauce or soy sauce, lime or lemon rind and juice, sesame seeds, grated ginger root and chopped mint into a large non-metallic bowl. Season with a little salt and pepper and mix together until all the ingredients are thoroughly combined.

2 Remove the skin from the chicken breasts and cut the flesh into chunks.

3 Add the chicken to the marinade, stirring to coat the chicken completely in the mixture. Cover with cling film (plastic wrap) and chill in the refrigerator for at least 2 hours so that the flavours are absorbed.

4 Thread the chicken on to wooden satay sticks. Place them on the rack of a grill (broiler) pan and baste with the marinade.

5 Place the kebabs under a preheated grill (broiler) for about 8–10 minutes. Turn them frequently, basting them with the remaining marinade.

6 Serve the chicken skewers at once, garnished with sprigs of fresh mint.

Deep-Fried Spare Ribs

The spare ribs should be chopped into small bite-sized pieces before or after cooking.

NUTRITIONAL INFORMATION

Calories	177	Sugars	........0.2g
Protein	.........6g	Fat	..........14g
Carbohydrate	....6g	Saturates	.......4g

5 MINS   2¼ HOURS

SERVES 4

I N G R E D I E N T S

8-10 finger spare ribs

1 tsp five-spice powder or 1 tbsp mild curry powder

1 tbsp rice wine or dry sherry

1 egg

2 tbsp flour

vegetable oil, for deep-frying

1 tsp finely shredded spring onions (scallions)

1 tsp finely shredded fresh green or red hot chillies, seeded

salt and pepper

Spicy Salt and Pepper (see page 76), to serve

1 Chop the ribs into 3-4 small pieces. Place the ribs in a bowl with salt, pepper, five-spice or curry powder and the wine. Turn to coat the ribs in the spices and leave to marinate for 1-2 hours.

2 Mix the egg and flour together to make a batter. Dip the ribs in the batter one by one to coat well.

3 Heat the oil in a preheated wok until smoking. Deep-fry the ribs for 4-5 minutes, then remove with chopsticks or a slotted spoon and drain on kitchen paper (paper towels).

4 Reheat the oil over a high heat and deep-fry the ribs once more for another minute. Remove and drain again on kitchen paper (paper towels).

5 Pour 1 tablespoon of the hot oil over the spring onions (scallions) and chillies and leave for 30-40 seconds. Serve the ribs with Spicy Salt and Pepper, garnished with the shredded spring onions (scallions) and chillies.

COOK'S TIP

To make finger ribs, cut the sheet of spare ribs into individual ribs down each side of the bones. These ribs are then chopped into bite-sized pieces for deep-frying.

Crab Ravioli

These small parcels are made from won ton wrappers, filled with mixed vegetables and crabmeat for a melt-in-the-mouth starter.

NUTRITIONAL INFORMATION

Calories 292   Sugars 1g
Protein . . . . .25g   Fat 17g
Carbohydrate . . . .11g   Saturates 5g

 20 MINS   25 MINS

SERVES 4

INGREDIENTS

450 g/1 lb crabmeat (fresh or canned and drained)

½ red (bell) pepper, seeded and finely diced

125 g/4½ oz Chinese leaves (cabbage), shredded

25 g/1 oz bean sprouts, roughly chopped

1 tbsp light soy sauce

1 tsp lime juice

16 wonton wrappers

1 small egg, beaten

2 tbsp peanut oil

1 tsp sesame oil

salt and pepper

1 Mix together the crabmeat, (bell) pepper, Chinese leaves (cabbage), bean sprouts, soy sauce and lime juice. Season and leave to stand for 15 minutes.

2 Spread out the wonton wrappers on a work surface (counter). Spoon a little of the crabmeat mixture into the centre of each wrapper. Brush the edges with egg and fold in half, pushing out any air. Press the edges together to seal.

3 Heat the peanut oil in a preheated wok or frying pan (skillet). Fry the ravioli, in batches, for 3–4 minutes, turning, until browned. Remove with a slotted spoon and drain on kitchen paper (paper towels).

4 Heat any remaining filling in the wok or frying pan (skillet) over a gentle heat until hot. Serve the ravioli with the hot filling and sprinkled with sesame oil.

COOK'S TIP

Make sure that the edges of the ravioli are sealed well and that all of the air is pressed out to prevent them from opening during cooking.

Pork Sesame Toasts

This classic Chinese appetizer is also a great nibble for serving at parties – but be sure to make plenty!

NUTRITIONAL INFORMATION

Calories . . . . . . .674 Sugars 2g
Protein . . . . .33g Fat 46g
Carbohydrate . . .33g Saturates 7g

 5 MINS   🕐 35 MINS

SERVES 4

I N G R E D I E N T S

250 g/9 oz lean pork

250 g/9 oz/⅔ cup uncooked peeled prawns (shrimp), deveined

4 spring onions (scallions), trimmed

1 garlic clove, crushed

1 tbsp chopped fresh coriander (cilantro) leaves and stems

1 tbsp fish sauce

1 egg

8–10 slices of thick-cut white bread

3 tbsp sesame seeds

150 ml/¼ pint/⅔ cup vegetable oil

salt and pepper

TO GARNISH

sprigs of fresh coriander (cilantro)

red (bell) pepper, sliced finely

1 Put the pork, prawns (shrimp), spring onions (scallions), garlic, coriander (cilantro), fish sauce, egg and seasoning into a food processor or blender. Process for a few seconds until the ingredients are finely chopped. Transfer the mixture to a bowl. Alternatively, chop the pork, prawns (shrimp) and spring onions (scallions) very finely, and mix with the garlic, coriander (cilantro), fish sauce, beaten egg and seasoning until all the ingredients are well combined.

2 Spread the pork and prawn (shrimp) mixture thickly over the bread so that it reaches right up to the edges. Cut off the crusts and slice each piece of bread into 4 squares or triangles.

3 Sprinkle the topping liberally with sesame seeds.

4 Heat the oil in a wok or frying pan (skillet). Fry a few pieces of the bread,

topping side down first so that it sets the egg, for about 2 minutes or until golden brown. Turn the pieces over to cook on the other side, about 1 minute.

5 Drain the pork and prawn (shrimp) toasts and place them on kitchen paper (paper towels). Fry the remaining pieces. Serve garnished with sprigs of fresh coriander (cilantro) and strips of red (bell) pepper.

Seven Spice Aubergines

This is a really simple dish which is perfect served with a chilli dip.

NUTRITIONAL INFORMATION

Calories 169	Sugars 2g
Protein 2g	Fat 12g
Carbohydrate ...15g	Saturates 1g

 35 MINS   20 MINS

SERVES 4

INGREDIENTS

450 g/1 lb aubergines (eggplants), wiped

1 egg white

50 g/1¾ oz/3½ tbsp cornflour (cornstarch)

1 tsp salt

1 tbsp seven spice seasoning

oil, for deep-frying

1 Using a sharp knife, thinly slice the aubergines (eggplants). Place the aubergine (eggplant) in a colander, sprinkle with salt and leave to stand for 30 minutes. This will remove all the bitter juices.

2 Rinse the aubergine (eggplant) thoroughly and pat dry with absorbent kitchen paper (paper towels).

3 Place the egg white in a small bowl and whip until light and foamy.

4 Using a spoon, mix together the cornflour (cornstarch), salt and seven spice powder on a large plate.

5 Heat the oil for deep-frying in a large preheated wok or heavy-based frying pan (skillet).

6 Dip the aubergines (eggplants) into the egg white, and then into the cornflour (cornstarch) and seven spice mixture to coat evenly.

7 Deep-fry the coated aubergine (eggplant) slices, in batches, for 5 minutes, or until pale golden and crispy.

8 Transfer the aubergines (eggplants) to absorbent kitchen paper (paper towels) and leave to drain. Transfer the seven spice aubergines (eggplants) to serving plates and serve hot.

COOK'S TIP

The best oil to use for deep-frying is groundnut oil which has a high smoke point and mild flavour, so it will neither burn or taint the food. About 600 ml/1 pint oil is sufficient.

Chinese Potato Sticks

These potato sticks are a variation of the great Western favourite, being flavoured with soy sauce and chilli.

NUTRITIONAL INFORMATION

Calories 326	Sugars 1g
Protein 4g	Fat 22g
Carbohydrate . . .29g	Saturates 3g

 10 MINS | 15 MINS

SERVES 4

I N G R E D I E N T S

650 g/1 lb 7 oz medium-size potatoes

8 tbsp vegetable oil

1 fresh red chilli, halved

1 small onion, quartered

2 garlic cloves, halved

2 tbsp soy sauce

pinch of salt

1 tsp wine vinegar

1 tbsp coarse sea salt

pinch of chilli powder

1 Peel the potatoes and cut into thin slices along their length. Cut the slices into matchsticks.

2 Bring a saucepan of water to the boil and blanch the potato sticks for 2 minutes, drain, rinse under cold water and drain well again. Pat the potato sticks thoroughly dry with absorbent kitchen paper (paper towels).

3 Heat the oil in a preheated wok until it is almost smoking. Add the chilli, onion and garlic and stir-fry for 30 seconds. Remove and discard the chilli, onion and garlic.

4 Add the potato sticks to the oil and fry for 3–4 minutes, or until golden.

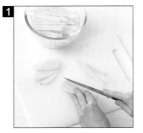

5 Add the soy sauce, salt and vinegar to the wok, reduce the heat and fry for 1 minute, or until the potatoes are crisp.

6 Remove the potatoes with a slotted spoon and leave to drain on absorbent kitchen paper (paper towels).

7 Transfer the potato sticks to a serving dish, sprinkle with the sea salt and chilli powder and serve.

VARIATION

Sprinkle other flavourings over the cooked potato sticks, such as curry powder, or serve with a chilli dip.

Rice Cubes with Sauce

Plain rice cubes are a good foil to any piquant dipping sauce, and they are often served with satay, to complement the dipping sauce.

NUTRITIONAL INFORMATION

Calories 317	Sugars 3g	
Protein 10g	Fat 10g	
Carbohydrate . . .49g	Saturates 2g	

8¼ HOURS   25 MINS

SERVES 4

INGREDIENTS

300 g/10½ oz/1½ cups jasmine rice

1.3 litres/2¼ pints/5 cups water

CORIANDER (CILANTRO) DIPPING SAUCE

1 garlic clove

2 tsp salt

1 tbsp black peppercorns

60 g/2 oz/1 cup washed coriander (cilantro), including roots and stem

3 tbsp lemon juice

175 ml/6 fl oz/¾ cup coconut milk

2 tbsp peanut butter

2 spring onions (scallions), chopped roughly

1 red chilli, deseeded and sliced

1 Grease and line a 20 x 10 x 2.5 cm/ 8 x 4 x 1 inch tin.

2 To make the sauce, grind together the garlic, salt, peppercorns, coriander (cilantro) and lemon juice in a pestle and mortar or blender.

3 Add the coconut milk, peanut butter, spring onions (scallions) and chilli. Grind finely. Transfer to a saucepan and bring to the boil. Leave to cool.

4 To cook the rice, do not rinse. Bring the water to the boil and add the rice.

Stir and return to a medium boil. Cook, uncovered, for 14–16 minutes until very soft. Drain thoroughly.

5 Put 125 g/4½ oz/⅔ cup of the cooked rice in a blender and purée until smooth. Alternatively, grind to a paste in a pestle and mortar.

6 Stir into the remaining cooked rice and spoon into the lined tin (pan). Level

the surface and cover with cling film (plastic wrap). Compress the rice by using either a smaller-sized tin (pan) or a small piece of board, and weigh this down with cans. Chill in the refrigerator for at least 8 hours or preferably overnight.

7 Invert the tin (pan) on to a board. Cut the rice into cubes with a wet knife. Serve with the Coriander (Cilantro) Dipping Sauce.

Sweet & Sour Prawns

Prawns (shrimp) are marinated in a soy sauce mixture then coated in a light batter, fried and served with a delicious sweet-and-sour dip.

NUTRITIONAL INFORMATION

Calories 294   Sugars 11g
Protein . . . . .14g   Fat 12g
Carbohydrate . . .34g   Saturates 2g

40 MINS   20 MINS

SERVES 4

INGREDIENTS

16 large raw prawns (shrimp), peeled

1 tsp grated fresh root ginger

1 garlic clove, crushed

2 spring onions (scallions), sliced

2 tbsp dry sherry

2 tsp sesame oil

1 tbsp light soy sauce

vegetable oil, for deep-frying

shredded spring onion (scallion),
    to garnish

BATTER

4 egg whites

4 tbsp cornflour (cornstarch)

2 tbsp plain (all-purpose) flour

SAUCE

2 tbsp tomato purée (paste)

3 tbsp white wine vinegar

4 tsp light soy sauce

2 tbsp lemon juice

3 tbsp light brown sugar

1 green (bell) pepper, seeded and cut into
    thin matchsticks

½ tsp chilli sauce

300 ml/½ pint/1¼ cups vegetable stock

2 tsp cornflour (cornstarch)

1 Using tweezers, devein the prawns (shrimp), then flatten them with a large knife.

2 Place the prawns (shrimp) in a dish and add the ginger, garlic, spring onions (scallions), dry sherry, sesame oil and soy sauce. Cover with cling film (plastic wrap) and leave to marinate for 30 minutes.

3 Make the batter by beating the egg whites until thick. Fold in the cornflour (cornstarch) and plain (all-purpose) flour to form a light batter.

4 Place all of the sauce ingredients in a saucepan and bring to the boil. Reduce the heat and leave to simmer for 10 minutes.

5 Remove the prawns (shrimp) from the marinade and dip them into the batter to coat.

6 Heat the vegetable oil in a preheated wok or large frying pan (skillet) until almost smoking. Reduce the heat and fry the prawns (shrimp) for 3–4 minutes, until crisp and golden brown.

7 Garnish the prawns (shrimp) with shredded spring onion (scallion) and serve with the sauce.

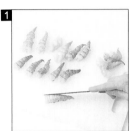

Salads & Pickles

Vegetables play an important part of the Chinese diet and although salads as we know them in the West do not feature greatly on the Chinese menu, many lightly cooked

vegetable dishes can be classified as salads when allowed to cool and are lightly tossed in dressing. The freshest vegetables and brief cooking ensure the necessary balance of texture and flavour, while dressings add a touch of sharpness and acidity. Pickled vegetables are very popular in China. They are often served as snacks and appetizers, and can also be served with cold meat dishes. Once made, they will keep in the refrigerator for up to 2 weeks.

Prawn (Shrimp) Salad

Noodles and bean sprouts form the basis of this refreshing salad which combines the flavours of fruit and prawns (shrimp).

NUTRITIONAL INFORMATION

Calories	....	.359
Protein	....	.31g
Carbohydrate	...	25g

Sugars	....	.4g
Fat	....	.15g
Saturates	....	.2g

 15 MINS   5 MINS

SERVES 4

I N G R E D I E N T S

250 g/9 oz fine egg noodles

3 tbsp sunflower oil

1 tbsp sesame oil

1 tbsp sesame seeds

150 g/5½ oz/1½ cups bean sprouts

1 ripe mango, sliced

6 spring onions (scallions), sliced

75 g/2¾ oz radish, sliced

350 g/12 oz peeled cooked prawns (shrimp)

2 tbsp light soy sauce

1 tbsp sherry

1 Place the egg noodles in a large bowl and pour over enough boiling water to cover. Leave to stand for 10 minutes.

2 Drain the noodles thoroughly and pat dry with kitchen paper (paper towels).

COOK'S TIP

If fresh mango is unavailable, use canned mango slices, rinsed and drained, instead.

3 Heat the sunflower oil in a large wok or frying pan (skillet) and stir-fry the noodles for 5 minutes. tossing frequently.

4 Remove the wok from the heat and add the sesame oil, sesame seeds and bean sprouts, tossing to mix well.

5 In a separate bowl, mix together the sliced mango, spring onions (scallions), radish and prawns (shrimp). Stir in the light soy sauce and sherry and mix until thoroughly combined.

6 Toss the prawn (shrimp) mixture with the noodles and transfer to a serving dish. Alternatively, arrange the noodles around the edge of a serving plate and pile the prawn (shrimp) mixture into the centre. Serve immediately as this salad is best eaten warm.

Sweet & Sour Tofu Salad

Tofu (bean curd) is a delicious, healthy alternative to meat. Mixed with crisp stir-fried vegetables it makes an ideal light meal or starter.

NUTRITIONAL INFORMATION

Calories	262	Sugars	........15g
Protein	........16g	Fat	..........14g
Carbohydrate	...19g	Saturates	.......2g

🥘 10 MINS   🕐 15 MINS

SERVES 4

I N G R E D I E N T S

2 tbsp vegetable oil

1 garlic clove, crushed

500 g/1 lb 2 oz tofu (bean curd), cubed

1 onion, sliced

1 carrot, cut into julienne strips

1 stick celery, sliced

2 small red (bell) peppers, cored, seeded and sliced

250 g/9 oz mangetout (snow peas), trimmed and halved

125 g/4½ oz broccoli, trimmed and divided into florets

125g/4½ oz thin green beans, halved

2 tbsp oyster sauce

1 tbsp tamarind concentrate

1 tbsp fish sauce

1 tbsp tomato purée (paste)

1 tbsp light soy sauce

1 tbsp chilli sauce

2 tbsp sugar

1 tbsp white vinegar

pinch of ground star anise

1 tsp cornflour (cornstarch)

300 ml/½ pint/1¼ cups water

1 Heat the vegetable oil in a large, heavy-based frying pan (skillet) or wok until hot.

2 Add the crushed garlic to the wok or pan and cook for a few seconds.

3 Add the tofu (bean curd), in batches, and stir-fry over a gentle heat, until golden on all sides. Remove with a slotted spoon and keep warm.

4 Add the onion, carrot, celery, red (bell) pepper, mangetout (snow peas), broccoli and green beans to the pan and stir-fry for about 2-3 minutes or until tender-crisp.

5 Add the oyster sauce, tamarind concentrate, fish sauce, tomato purée (paste), soy sauce, chilli sauce, sugar, vinegar and star anise, mixing well to blend. Stir-fry for a further 2 minutes.

6 Mix the cornflour (cornstarch) with the water and add to the pan with the fried tofu (bean curd). Stir-fry gently until the sauce boils and thickens slightly.

7 Transfer the sweet and sour tofu (bean curd) salad to warm serving plates and serve immediately.

Chicken & Paw-paw Salad

Try this recipe with a selection of different fruits for an equally tasty salad.

NUTRITIONAL INFORMATION

Calories	408	Sugars	.........8g
Protein	........30g	Fat	..........28g
Carbohydrate	...10g	Saturates	.......5g

5 MINS   15 MINS

SERVES 4

INGREDIENTS

4 skinless, boneless chicken
  breasts

1 red chilli, deseeded and chopped

30 ml/1 fl oz/1⅔ tbsp red wine
  vinegar

75 ml/3 fl oz/⅓ cup olive oil

1 paw-paw (papaya), peeled

1 avocado, peeled

125 g/4½ oz alfalfa sprouts

125 g/4½ oz bean sprouts

salt and pepper

TO GARNISH

diced red (bell) pepper

diced cucumber

VARIATION

Try this recipe with
peaches or nectarines
instead of paw-paw (papaya).

1 Poach the chicken breasts in boiling water for about 15 minutes or until cooked through.

2 Remove the chicken with a slotted spoon and set aside to cool.

3 To make the dressing, combine the chilli, red wine vinegar and olive oil, season well with salt and pepper and set aside.

4 Place the chicken breasts on a chopping board. Using a very sharp knife, cut the chicken breasts across the grain into thin diagonal slices. Set aside.

5 Slice the paw-paw (papaya) and avocado to the same thickness as the chicken.

6 Arrange the slices of paw-paw (papaya) and avocado, together with the chicken, in an alternating pattern on four serving plates.

7 Arrange the alfalfa sprouts and bean sprouts on the serving plates and garnish with the diced red (bell) pepper and cucumber. Serve the salad with the dressing.

Hot and Sour Duck Salad

This is a lovely tangy salad, drizzled with a lime juice and fish sauce dressing. It makes a splendid starter or light main course dish.

NUTRITIONAL INFORMATION

Calories ....236 Sugars 3g
Protein ....27g Fat 10g
Carbohydrate ...10g Saturates 3g

40 MINS   5 MINS

SERVES 4

I N G R E D I E N T S

2 heads crisp salad lettuce, washed and separated into leaves

2 shallots, thinly sliced

4 spring onions (scallions), chopped

1 celery stick, finely sliced into julienne strips

5 cm/2 in piece cucumber, cut into julienne strips

125 g/4½ oz bean sprouts

1 x 200 g/7 oz can water chestnuts, drained and sliced

4 duck breast fillets, roasted and sliced (see page 183)

orange slices, to serve

D R E S S I N G

3 tbsp fish sauce

1½ tbsp lime juice

2 garlic cloves, crushed

1 red chilli pepper, seeded and very finely chopped

1 green chilli pepper, seeded and very finely chopped

1 tsp palm or demerara (brown crystal) sugar

1 Place the lettuce leaves into a large mixing bowl. Add the sliced shallots, chopped spring onions (scallions), celery strips, cucumber strips, bean sprouts and sliced water chestnuts. Toss well to mix. Place the mixture on a large serving platter.

2 Arrange the duck breast slices on top of the salad in an attractive overlapping pattern.

3 To make the dressing, put the fish sauce, lime juice, garlic, chillies and sugar into a small saucepan. Heat gently, stirring constantly. Taste and adjust the piquancy if liked by adding more lime juice, or add more fish sauce to reduce the sharpness.

4 Drizzle the warm salad dressing over the duck salad and serve immediately with orange slices.

Oriental Salad

This colourful crisp salad has a fresh orange dressing and is topped with crunchy vermicelli.

NUTRITIONAL INFORMATION

Calories 139   Sugars 8g
Protein . . . . .5g   Fat 7g
Carbohydrate . . .15g   Saturates 1g

10 MINS   5 MINS

SERVES 4

I N G R E D I E N T S

25 g/1 oz/¼ cup dried vermicelli

½ head Chinese leaves (cabbage)

125 g/4½ oz/2 cups bean sprouts

6 radishes

125 g/4½ oz mangetout (snow peas)

1 large carrot

125 g/4½ oz sprouting beans

D R E S S I N G

juice of 1 orange

1 tbsp sesame seeds, toasted

1 tsp honey

1 tsp sesame oil

1 tbsp hazelnut oil

1 Break the vermicelli into small strands. Heat a wok and dry-fry the vermicelli until lightly golden.

COOK'S TIP

Make your own sprouting beans by soaking mung and aduki beans overnight in cold water, drain and rinse. Place in a large jar covered with muslin to secure it. Lay the jar on its side and place in indirect light. For the next 3 days rinse the beans once each day in cold water until they are ready to eat.

2 Remove from the pan with a slotted spoon and set aside until required.

3 Using a sharp knife or food processor, shred the Chinese leaves (cabbage) and wash with the bean sprouts. Drain thoroughly and place the leaves and bean sprouts in a large mixing bowl.

4 Thinly slice the radishes. Trim the mangetout (snow peas) and cut each

into 3 pieces. Cut the carrot into thin matchsticks. Add the sprouting beans and prepared vegetables to the bowl.

5 Place all the dressing ingredients in a screw-top jar and shake until well-blended. Pour over the salad and toss.

6 Transfer the salad to a serving bowl and sprinkle over the reserved vermicelli before serving.

Paw-paw Salad

Choose firm paw-paws – or papayas as they are sometimes called – for this delicious salad.

NUTRITIONAL INFORMATION

Calories 193   Sugars 11g
Protein ....3g   Fat 15g
Carbohydrate ...12g   Saturates 2g

10 MINS   0 MINS

SERVES 4

I N G R E D I E N T S

D R E S S I N G

4 tbsp olive oil

1 tbsp fish sauce or light soy sauce

2 tbsp lime or lemon juice

1 tbsp dark muscovado sugar

1 tsp finely chopped fresh red or
    green chilli

S A L A D

1 crisp lettuce

¼ small white cabbage

2 paw-paws (papayas)

2 tomatoes

25 g/1 oz/¼ cup roasted peanuts,
    chopped roughly

4 spring onions (scallions), trimmed
    and sliced thinly

basil leaves, to garnish

1 To make the dressing, whisk together the oil, fish sauce or soy sauce, lime or lemon juice, sugar and chilli. Set aside, stirring occasionally to dissolve the sugar.

2 Shred the lettuce and white cabbage, then toss together and arrange on a large serving plate.

3 Peel the paw-paws (papayas) and slice them in half. Scoop out the seeds, then slice the flesh thinly. Arrange on top of the lettuce and cabbage.

4 Soak the tomatoes in a bowl of boiling water for 1 minute, then lift out and peel. Remove the seeds and chop the flesh. Arrange on the salad leaves.

5 Scatter the peanuts and spring onions (scallions) over the top. Whisk the dressing and pour over the salad. Garnish with basil leaves and serve at once.

COOK'S TIP

Choose plain, unsalted peanuts and toast them under the grill (broiler) until golden to get the best flavour. Take care not to burn them, as they brown very quickly.

Chicken & Noodle Salad

Strips of chicken are coated in a delicious spicy mixture, then stir-fried with noodles and served on a bed of salad.

NUTRITIONAL INFORMATION

Calories 217   Sugars 1g
Protein . . . . .21g   Fat 11g
Carbohydrate . . . .9g   Saturates 2g

  10 MINS   🕐 10 MINS

SERVES 4

I N G R E D I E N T S

1 tsp finely grated fresh ginger root

½ tsp Chinese five-spice powder

1 tbsp plain (all-purpose) flour

½ tsp chilli powder

350 g/12 oz boned chicken breast, skinned and sliced thinly

60 g/2 oz rice noodles

125 g/4½ oz/1½ cups Chinese leaves (cabbage) or hard white cabbage, shredded finely

7 cm/3 inch piece of cucumber, sliced finely

1 large carrot, pared thinly

1 tbsp olive oil

2 tbsp lime or lemon juice

2 tbsp sesame oil

salt and pepper

TO GARNISH

lemon or lime slices

fresh coriander (cilantro) leaves

1 Mix together the ginger, five-spice powder, flour and chilli powder in a shallow mixing bowl. Season with salt and pepper. Add the strips of chicken and roll in the mixture until well coated.

2 Put the noodles into a large bowl and cover with warm water. Leave to soak for about 5 minutes, then drain them well.

3 Mix together the Chinese leaves (cabbage) or white cabbage, cucumber and carrot, and arrange in a salad bowl. Whisk together the olive oil and lime or lemon juice, season with a salt and pepper, and use to dress the salad.

4 Heat the sesame oil in a wok or frying pan (skillet) and add the chicken. Stir-fry for 5–6 minutes until well-browned and crispy on the outside. Remove from the wok or frying pan (skillet) with a perforated spoon and drain on absorbent kitchen paper (paper towels).

5 Add the noodles to the wok or frying pan (skillet) and stir-fry for 3–4 minutes until heated through. Remove from the wok, mix with the chicken and pile the mixture on top of the salad. Serve garnished with lime or lemon slices and coriander (cilantro) leaves.

Chinese Hot Salad

This salad can also be eaten cold – add 3-4 tablespoons French dressing as the vegetables cool, toss well and serve cold or chilled.

NUTRITIONAL INFORMATION

Calories 192   Sugars 13g
Protein . . . . .5g   Fat 9g
Carbohydrate . . .20g   Saturates 1g

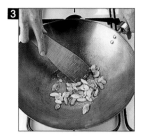

 5 MINS   10 MINS

SERVES 4

I N G R E D I E N T S

1 tbsp dark soy sauce

1½-2 tsp bottled sweet chilli sauce

2 tbsp sherry

1 tbsp brown sugar

1 tbsp wine vinegar

2 tbsp sunflower oil

1 garlic clove, crushed

4 spring onions (scallions), thinly sliced
   diagonally

250 g/9 oz courgettes (zucchini),
   cut into julienne strips about
   4 cm/1½ inches long

250 g/9 oz carrots, cut into julienne strips
   about 4 cm/1½ inches long

1 red or green (bell) pepper, cored, seeded
   and thinly sliced

1 x 400 g/14 ½oz can bean sprouts, well
   drained

125 g/4½ oz French (green) or fine beans,
   cut into 5 cm/2 inch lengths

1 tbsp sesame oil

salt and pepper

1-2 tsp sesame seeds, to garnish

1 Combine the soy sauce, chilli sauce, sherry, sugar, vinegar and seasoning.

2 Heat the 2 tablespoons of sunflower oil in a wok or large, heavy-based frying pan (skillet), swirling it around until it is really hot.

3 Add the garlic and spring onions (scallions) to the wok and stir-fry for 1-2 minutes.

4 Add the courgettes (zucchini), carrots and (bell) peppers and stir-fry for 1-2 minutes, then add the soy sauce mixture and bring to the boil.

5 Add the bean sprouts and French (green) beans and stir-fry for 1-2 minutes, making sure all the vegetables are thoroughly coated with the sauce.

6 Drizzle the sesame oil over the vegetables in the wok and stir-fry for about 30 seconds.

7 Serve the salad hot, sprinkled with sesame seeds.

Potato & Chicken Salad

The spicy peanut dressing served with this salad may be prepared in advance and left to chill a day before required.

NUTRITIONAL INFORMATION

Calories 802	Sugars 15g
Protein 35g	Fat 55g
Carbohydrate . . .45g	Saturates 10g

   5 MINS   15 MINS

SERVES 4

I N G R E D I E N T S

4 large waxy potatoes

300 g/10½ oz fresh pineapple, diced

2 carrots, grated

175 g/6 oz bean sprouts

1 bunch spring onions (scallions), sliced

1 large courgette (zucchini), cut into matchsticks

3 celery sticks, cut into matchsticks

175 g/6 oz unsalted peanuts

2 cooked chicken breast fillets, about 125 g/4½ oz each, sliced

D R E S S I N G

6 tbsp crunchy peanut butter

6 tbsp olive oil

2 tbsp light soy sauce

1 red chilli, chopped

2 tsp sesame oil

4 tsp lime juice

COOK'S TIP

Unsweetened canned pineapple may be used in place of the fresh pineapple for convenience. If only sweetened canned pineapple is available, drain it and rinse under cold running water before using.

1 Using a sharp knife, cut the potatoes into small dice. Bring a saucepan of water to the boil.

2 Cook the diced potatoes in a saucepan of boiling water for 10 minutes or until tender. Drain and leave to cool until required.

3 Transfer the cooled potatoes to a salad bowl.

4 Add the pineapple, carrots, bean sprouts, spring onions (scallions), courgette (zucchini), celery, peanuts and sliced chicken to the potatoes. Toss well to mix all the salad ingredients together.

5 To make the dressing, put the peanut butter in a small mixing bowl and gradually whisk in the olive oil and light soy sauce.

6 Stir in the chopped red chilli, sesame oil and lime juice. Mix until well combined.

7 Pour the spicy dressing over the salad and toss lightly to coat all of the ingredients. Serve the potato and chicken salad immediately.

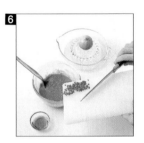

Gado Gado Salad

The vegetables in this salad can either be arranged in individual piles on the serving platter or mixed together.

NUTRITIONAL INFORMATION

Calories 450   Sugars 11g
Protein . . . . .19g   Fat 28g
Carbohydrate . . .29g   Saturates 6g

🍲 20 MINS   🕐 25 MINS

SERVES 4

I N G R E D I E N T S

250 g/9 oz new potatoes, scrubbed

125 g/4½ oz green beans

125 g/4½ oz cauliflower, broken into small florets

125 g/4½ oz/1½ cups white cabbage, shredded

1 carrot, cut into thin sticks

¼ cucumber, cut into chunks

125 g/4½ oz/2 cups bean sprouts

2 hard-boiled (hard-cooked) eggs, shelled

S A U C E

6 tbsp crunchy peanut butter

300 ml/½ pint/1¼ cups cold water

1 garlic clove, crushed

1 fresh red chilli, deseeded and finely chopped

2 tbsp soy sauce

1 tbsp dry sherry

2 tsp sugar

1 tbsp lemon juice

1 Halve the potatoes and place in a saucepan of lightly salted water. Bring to the boil and then simmer for 12–15 minutes, or until cooked through.

2 Drain and plunge into cold water to cool. Set aside until required.

3 Bring another pan of lightly salted water to the boil. Add the green beans, cauliflower and cabbage, and cook for 3 minutes. Drain and plunge the vegetables into cold water to cool and prevent any further cooking.

4 Drain the potatoes and other cooked vegetables. Arrange in piles on a large serving platter with the carrot, cucumber and bean sprouts.

5 Cut the hard-boiled (hard-cooked) eggs into quarters and arrange on the salad. Cover and set aside.

6 To make the sauce, place the peanut butter in a bowl and blend in the water gradually, followed by the remaining ingredients.

7 Uncover the salad and drizzle some sauce over each serving.

Beef & Peanut Salad

This recipe looks stunning if you arrange the ingredients rather than toss them together.

NUTRITIONAL INFORMATION

Calories ....194 Sugars 3g
Protein ....21g Fat 10g
Carbohydrate ....5g Saturates 3g

 10 MINS   10 MINS

SERVES 4

INGREDIENTS

½ head Chinese leaves (cabbage)

1 large carrot

115 g/4 oz radishes

100 g/3½ oz baby corn

1 tbsp groundnut oil

1 red chilli, deseeded and chopped finely

1 clove garlic, chopped finely

350 g/12 oz lean beef (such as fillet, sirloin or rump), trimmed and shredded finely

1 tbsp dark soy sauce

25 g/1 oz fresh peanuts (optional)

red chilli, sliced, to garnish

DRESSING

1 tbsp smooth peanut butter

1 tsp caster (superfine) sugar

2 tbsp light soy sauce

1 tbsp sherry vinegar

salt and pepper

VARIATION

If preferred, use chicken, turkey, lean pork or even strips of venison instead of beef in this recipe. Cut off all visible fat before you begin.

1 Finely shred the Chinese leaves (cabbage) and arrange on a platter.

2 Peel the carrot and cut into thin, matchstick-like strips. Wash, trim and quarter the radishes, and halve the baby corn lengthwise. Arrange these ingredients around the edge of the dish and set aside.

3 Heat the groundnut oil in a non-stick wok or large frying pan (skillet) until really hot.

4 Add the red chilli, garlic and beef to the wok or frying pan (skillet) and stir-fry for 5 minutes.

5 Add the dark soy sauce and stir-fry for a further 1–2 minutes until tender and cooked through.

6 Meanwhile, make the dressing. Place all of the ingredients in a small bowl and blend them together until smooth.

7 Place the hot cooked beef in the centre of the salad ingredients. Spoon over the dressing and sprinkle with a few peanuts, if using. Garnish with slices of red chilli and serve immediately.

Carrot and Coriander Salad

This tangy, crunchy salad makes an ideal accompaniments to Aubergine (Eggplant) and Mushroom Satay with Peanut Sauce (see page 112).

NUTRITIONAL INFORMATION

Calories 50	Sugars 4g
Protein 1g	Fat 3g
Carbohydrate 5g	Saturates 0.4g

 5 MINS   0 MINS

SERVES 4

I N G R E D I E N T S

4 large carrots

2 celery sticks, cut into matchsticks

2 tbsp roughly chopped fresh coriander (cilantro)

D R E S S I N G

1 tbsp sesame oil

1½ tbsp rice vinegar

½ tsp sugar

½ tsp salt

1 To create flower-shaped carrot slices, as shown, cut several grooves length-ways along each carrot before slicing it.

2 Slice each carrot into very thin slices, using the slicing cutter of a grater.

3 Combine the carrot, celery and coriander (cilantro) in a bowl.

4 To make the dressing, combine the sesame oil, rice vinegar, sugar and salt in a bowl.

5 Just before serving, toss the carrot, celery and coriander (cilantro) mixture in the dressing and transfer to a serving dish.

Noodle & Mango Salad

Fruit combines well with the peanut dressing, (bell) peppers and chilli in this delicous hot salad.

NUTRITIONAL INFORMATION

Calories . . . . . . .368 Sugars 11g
Protein . . . . .11g Fat 26g
Carbohydrate . . .24g Saturates 5g

15 MINS   5 MINS

SERVES 4

I N G R E D I E N T S

250 g/9 oz thread egg noodles

2 tbsp groundnut oil

4 shallots, sliced

2 cloves garlic, crushed

1 red chilli, deseeded and sliced

1 red (bell) pepper, deseeded and sliced

1 green (bell) pepper, deseeded and sliced

1 ripe mango, sliced into thin strips

25 g/1 oz/¼ cup salted peanuts, chopped

D R E S S I N G

4 tbsp peanut butter

100 ml/3½ fl oz/⅓ cup coconut milk

1 tbsp tomato purée (tomato paste)

1 Place the egg noodles in a large dish or bowl. Pour over enough boiling water to cover the noodles and leave to stand for 10 minutes.

COOK'S TIP

If preferred, gently heat the peanut dressing before pouring over the noodle salad.

2 Heat the groundnut oil in a large preheated wok or frying pan (skillet).

3 Add the shallots, crushed garlic, chilli and (bell) pepper slices to the wok or frying pan (skillet) and stir-fry for 2–3 minutes.

4 Drain the egg noodles thoroughly in a colander. Add the drained noodles and mango slices to the wok or frying pan

(skillet) and heat through for about 2 minutes.

5 Transfer the noodle and mango salad to warmed serving dishes and scatter with chopped peanuts.

6 To make the dressing, mix together the peanut butter, coconut milk and tomato purée (tomato paste) then spoon over the noodle salad. Serve immediately.

Duckling & Radish Salad

Juicy duckling breasts are coated with sesame seeds, then cooked, thinly sliced and served with a crisp salad.

NUTRITIONAL INFORMATION

Calories 328	Sugars 0.2g	
Protein 22g	Fat 24g	
Carbohydrate 7g	Saturates 4g	

 5 MINS   🕐 10 MINS

SERVES 4

INGREDIENTS

350 g/12 oz boneless duckling breasts, skinned

2 tbsp plain (all-purpose) flour

1 egg

2 tbsp water

2 tbsp sesame seeds

3 tbsp sesame oil

½ head Chinese leaves (cabbage), shredded

3 celery sticks, sliced finely

8 radishes, trimmed and halved

salt and pepper

fresh basil leaves, to garnish

DRESSING

finely grated rind of 1 lime

2 tbsp lime juice

2 tbsp olive oil

1 tbsp light soy sauce

1 tbsp chopped fresh basil

1 Put each duckling breast between sheets of greaseproof paper (baking parchment) or cling film (plastic wrap). Use a meat mallet or rolling pin to beat them out and flatten them slightly.

2 Sprinkle the flour on to a large plate and season with salt and pepper.

3 Beat the egg and water together in a shallow bowl, then sprinkle the sesame seeds on to a separate plate.

4 Dip the duckling breasts first into the seasoned flour, then into the egg mixture and finally into the sesame seeds, to coat the duckling evenly.

5 Heat the sesame oil in a preheated wok or large frying pan (skillet).

6 Fry the duckling breasts over a medium heat for about 8 minutes, turning once. To test whether they are cooked, insert a sharp knife into the thickest part – the juices should run clear. Lift them out and drain on kitchen paper (paper towels).

7 To make the dressing for the salad, whisk together the lime rind and juice, olive oil, soy sauce and chopped basil. Season with a little salt and pepper.

8 Arrange the Chinese leaves (cabbage), celery and radish on a serving plate. Slice the duckling breasts thinly and place on top of the salad.

9 Drizzle with the dressing and garnish with fresh basil leaves. Serve at once.

Cucumber Salad

This is a very refreshing accompaniment to any main dish and is an excellent 'cooler' for curries.

NUTRITIONAL INFORMATION

Calories 33	Sugars 8g
Protein 0.2g	Fat 0g
Carbohydrate 9g	Saturates 0g

 10 MINS   0 MINS

SERVES 4

I N G R E D I E N T S

½ cucumber

1 tbsp rice vinegar

2 tbsp sugar

½ tsp salt

2 tbsp hot water

1 small shallot

1 Wash the cucumber thoroughly and pat dry with absorbent kitchen paper (paper towels).

2 Peel the cucumber, halve it lengthways, and deseed it, using a teaspoon or a melon baller.

3 Using a sharp knife, slice the cucumber thinly.

4 Arrange the cucumber slices in an attractive pattern on a serving plate.

5 To make the dressing, mix together the rice vinegar, sugar and salt in a bowl. Pour on the hot water and stir until the sugar has dissolved. Leave the dressing to cool slightly.

6 Pour the dressing evenly over the cucumber slices.

7 Using a sharp knife, thinly slice the shallot and sprinkle over the cucumber.

8 Cover the cucumber salad with cling film (plastic wrap) and leave to chill in the refrigerator before serving. Serve as a cooling accompaniment to curries.

COOK'S TIP

Some people dislike the bitter taste that cucumbers can have – I find that peeling off the skin and deseeding the cucumber often eliminates this problem. Using a melon baller is the neatest method of deseeding a cucumber.

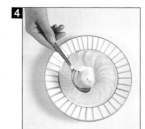

Hot & Sweet Salad

This salad is made by mixing fruit and vegetables with the sharp, sweet and fishy flavours of the dressing.

NUTRITIONAL INFORMATION

Calories 169	Sugars 8g
Protein 14g	Fat 8g
Carbohydrate 11g	Saturates 1g

🥗 15 MINS   🕐 0 MINS

SERVES 4

I N G R E D I E N T S

250 g/9 oz white cabbage, finely shredded

2 tomatoes, skinned, seeded and chopped

250 g/9 oz cooked green beans, halved if large

125 g/4½ oz peeled prawns (shrimp)

1 paw-paw (papaya), peeled, seeded and chopped

1-2 fresh red chillies, seeded and very finely sliced

60 g/2 oz/scant ⅓ cup roasted salted peanuts, crushed

handful of lettuce or baby spinach leaves, shredded or torn into small pieces

D R E S S I N G

4 tbsp lime juice

2 tbsp fish sauce

sugar, to taste

pepper

1 Mix the white cabbage with the tomatoes, green beans, prawns (shrimp), three-quarters of the paw-paw (papaya) and half the chillies in a large mixing bowl.

2 Stir in two-thirds of the crushed peanuts and mix well.

3 Line the rim of a large serving plate with the lettuce or spinach leaves and pile the salad mixture into the centre of the leaves.

4 To make the dressing, beat the lime juice with the fish sauce and add sugar and pepper to taste. Drizzle over the salad.

5 Scatter the top with the remaining paw-paw (papaya), chillies and crushed peanuts. Serve at once.

COOK'S TIP

To skin tomatoes, make a cross at the base with a very sharp knife, then immerse in a bowl of boiling water for a few minutes. Remove with a slotted spoon and peel off the skin.

Hot Rice Salad

Nutty brown rice combines well with peanuts and a sweet and sour mixture of fruit and vegetables in this tangy combination.

NUTRITIONAL INFORMATION

Calories	464	Sugars	........17g
Protein	........15g	Fat	..........24g
Carbohydrate	...52g	Saturates	.......4g

5 MINS   30 MINS

SERVES 4

INGREDIENTS

300 g/10½ oz/1½ cups brown rice

1 bunch spring onions (scallions)

1 red (bell) pepper

125 g/4½ oz radishes

425 g/15 oz can pineapple pieces in natural juice, drained

125 g/4½ oz/2 cups bean sprouts

90 g/3 oz/¾ cup dry-roasted peanuts

DRESSING

2 tbsp crunchy peanut butter

1 tbsp groundnut oil

2 tbsp light soy sauce

2 tbsp white wine vinegar

2 tsp clear honey

1 tsp chilli powder

½ tsp garlic salt

pepper

1 Put the rice in a pan and cover with water. Bring to the boil, then cover and simmer for 30 minutes until tender.

2 Meanwhile, chop the spring onions (scallions), using a sharp knife. Deseed and chop the red (bell) pepper and thinly slice the radishes.

3 To make the dressing. Place the crunchy peanut butter, groundnut oil, light soy sauce, white wine vinegar, honey, chilli powder, garlic salt and pepper in a small bowl and whisk for a few seconds until well combined.

4 Drain the rice thoroughly and place in a heatproof bowl.

5 Heat the dressing in a small saucepan for 1 minute and then toss into the rice and mix well.

6 Working quickly, stir the pineapple pieces, spring onions (scallions), (bell) pepper, bean sprouts and peanuts into the mixture in the bowl.

7 Pile the hot rice salad into a warmed serving dish.

8 Arrange the radish slices around the outside of the salad and serve immediately.

Oriental Chicken Salad

Mirin, soy sauce and sesame oil give an oriental flavour to this delicious salad.

NUTRITIONAL INFORMATION

Calories	361	Sugars	........2g
Protein	........34g	Fat	..........16g
Carbohydrate	...17g	Saturates	.......3g

 5 MINS   35 MINS

SERVES 4

INGREDIENTS

4 skinless, boneless chicken breasts

75 ml/3 fl oz/⅓ cup mirin or sweet sherry

75 ml/3 fl oz/⅓ cup light soy sauce

1 tbsp sesame oil

3 tbsp olive oil

1 tbsp red wine vinegar

1 tbsp Dijon mustard

250 g/9 oz egg noodles

250 g/9 oz bean sprouts

250 g/9 oz Chinese leaves (cabbage), shredded

2 spring onions (scallions), sliced

125 g/4½ oz mushrooms, sliced

1 fresh red chilli, finely sliced, to garnish

1 Pound the chicken breasts out to an even thickness between two sheets of cling film (plastic wrap) with a rolling pin or cleaver.

2 Put the chicken breasts in a roasting tin (pan). Combine the mirin and soy sauce and brush over the chicken.

3 Place the chicken in a preheated oven, 200°C/ 400°F/Gas Mark 6, for 20–30 minutes, basting often.

4 Remove the chicken from the oven and allow to cool slightly.

5 Combine the sesame oil, olive oil and red wine vinegar with the mustard.

6 Cook the noodles according to the instructions on the packet. Rinse under cold running water, then drain.

7 Toss the noodles in the dressing until the noodles are completely coated.

7 Toss the noodles in the dressing until the noodles are completely coated.

8 Toss the bean sprouts, Chinese leaves (cabbage), spring onions (scallions) and mushrooms with the noodles.

9 Slice the cooked chicken very thinly and stir into the noodles. Garnish the salad with the chilli slices and serve.

Mango Salad

This is an unusual combination but works well as long as the mango is very unripe. Paw-paw (papaya) can be used instead, if you prefer.

NUTRITIONAL INFORMATION

Calories	....	.26
Protein	....	1g
Carbohydrate	....	6g
Sugars	....	3g
Fat	....	0.2g
Saturates	....	0g

10 MINS   0 MINS

SERVES 4

I N G R E D I E N T S

1 large unripe mango, peeled and
 cut into long thin shreds

1 small red chilli, deseeded and
 chopped finely

2 shallots, chopped finely

2 tbsp lemon juice

1 tbsp light soy sauce

6 roasted canned chestnuts,
 quartered

1 melon, to serve

1 lollo biondo lettuce, or any crunchy
 lettuce

15 g/½ oz coriander (cilantro) leaves

1 Soak the mango briefly in cold water, in order to remove any syrup. Meanwhile, combine the chilli, shallots, lemon juice and soy sauce. Drain the mango and combine with the chestnuts.

2 To make the melon basket, stand the watermelon on one end on a level surface. Holding a knife level and in one place, turn the watermelon on its axis so that the knife marks an even line all around the middle. Mark a 2.5 cm/ 1 inch wide handle across the top and through the centre stem, joining the middle line at either end. (If you prefer a zigzag finish, mark the shape to be cut at this point before any cuts are made, to ensure even zigzags.)

3 Take a sharp knife and, following the marks made for the handle, make the first vertical cut. Then cut down the other side of the handle. Now follow the middle line and make your straight or zigzag cut, taking care that the knife is always pointing towards the centre of the watermelon, and is level with the work surface (counter), as this ensures that when you reach the handle cuts, the cut out piece of melon will pull away cleanly.

4 Hollow out the flesh with a spoon, leaving a clean edge and line with the lettuce and coriander (cilantro). Fill with the salad, pour over the dressing and serve.

COOK'S TIP

A relative of the onion, though less pungent, shallots come in round and elongated varieties. When buying shallots, choose firm, dry-skinned ones which show no signs of wrinkling. Fresh shallots can be stored in the refrigerator for up to a week.

Chinese Salad Nests

Crisp fried potato nests are perfect as an edible salad bowl and delicious when filled with a colourful Chinese-style salad of vegetables and fruit.

NUTRITIONAL INFORMATION

Calories 272   Sugars 11g
Protein . . . . .4g   Fat 4g
Carbohydrate . . .59g   Saturates 0.4g

  15 MINS   15 MINS

SERVES 4

I N G R E D I E N T S

POTATO NESTS

450 g/1 lb floury (mealy) potatoes, grated

125 g/4½ oz/1 cup cornflour (cornstarch)

vegetable oil, for frying

fresh chives, to garnish

SALAD

125 g/4½ oz pineapple, cubed

1 green (bell) pepper, cut into strips

1 carrot, cut into thin strips

50 g/1¾ oz mangetout (snowpeas), sliced thickly

4 baby sweetcorn cobs, halved lengthways

25 g/1 oz beansprouts

2 spring onions (scallions), sliced

DRESSING

1 tbsp clear honey

1 tsp light soy sauce

1 garlic clove, crushed

1 tsp lemon juice

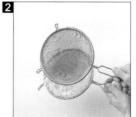

1 To make the nests, rinse the potatoes several times in cold water. Drain well on kitchen paper (paper towels) so they are completely dry. This is to prevent the potatoes spitting when they are cooked in the fat. Place the potatoes in a mixing bowl. Add the cornflour (cornstarch), mixing well to coat the potatoes.

2 Half fill a wok with vegetable oil and heat until smoking. Line a 15 cm/ 6 inch diameter wire sieve with a quarter of the potato mixture and press another sieve of the same size on top.

3 Lower the sieves into the oil and cook for 2 minutes until the potato nest is golden brown and crisp. Remove from the wok, allowing the excess oil to drain off.

4 Repeat 3 more times to use up all of the mixture and make a total of 4 nests. Leave to cool.

5 Mix the salad ingredients together then spoon into the potato baskets.

6 Mix the dressing ingredients together in a bowl. Pour the dressing over the salad, garnish with chives and serve immediately.

Bean Sprout Salad

This is a very light dish and is ideal on its own for a summer meal or as a starter.

NUTRITIONAL INFORMATION

Calories 70   Sugars 5g
Protein . . . . .4g   Fat 3g
Carbohydrate . . . .7g   Saturates 0.5g

 10 MINS   5 MINS

SERVES 4

INGREDIENTS

1 green (bell) pepper, seeded

1 carrot

1 celery stick

2 tomatoes, finely chopped

350 g/12 oz bean sprouts

1 small cucumber

1 garlic clove, crushed

dash of chilli sauce

2 tbsp light soy sauce

1 tsp wine vinegar

2 tsp sesame oil

16 fresh chives

1 Using a sharp knife, cut the green (bell) pepper, carrot and celery into matchsticks and finely chop the tomatoes.

2 Blanch the bean sprouts in boiling water for 1 minute. Drain well and rinse under cold water. Drain thoroughly again.

3 Cut the cucumber in half lengthways. Scoop out the seeds with a teaspoon and discard. Cut the flesh into matchsticks.

4 Mix the cucumber with the bean sprouts, green (bell) pepper, carrot, tomatoes and celery.

5 To make the dressing, mix together the garlic, chilli sauce, soy sauce, wine vinegar and sesame oil in a small bowl.

6 Pour the dressing over the vegetables, tossing well to coat.

7 Spoon the bean sprout salad into a serving dish or on to 4 individual serving plates. Garnish the salad with fresh chives and serve.

VARIATION

Substitute 350 g/12 oz cooked, cooled green beans or mangetout (snow peas) for the cucumber. Vary the bean sprouts for a different flavour. Try aduki (adzuki) bean or alfalfa sprouts, as well as the better-known mung and soya bean sprouts.

Chinese Chicken Salad

This is a refreshing dish suitable for a summer meal or light lunch.

NUTRITIONAL INFORMATION

Calories 162	Sugars 3g
Protein 15g	Fat 10g
Carbohydrate 5g	Saturates 2g

25 MINS   10 MINS

SERVES 4

INGREDIENTS

225 g/8 oz skinless, boneless chicken
   breasts

2 tsp light soy sauce

1 tsp sesame oil

1 tsp sesame seeds

2 tbsp vegetable oil

125 g/4½ oz bean sprouts

1 red (bell) pepper, seeded and thinly sliced

1 carrot, cut into matchsticks

3 baby corn cobs, sliced

snipped chives and carrot matchsticks,
   to garnish

SAUCE

2 tsp rice wine vinegar

1 tbsp light soy sauce

dash of chilli oil

1 Place the chicken breasts in a shallow glass dish.

2 Mix together the soy sauce and sesame oil and pour over the chicken. Sprinkle with the sesame seeds and let stand for 20 minutes, turning the chicken over occasionally.

3 Remove the chicken from the marinade and cut the meat into thin slices.

4 Heat the vegetable oil in a preheated wok or large frying pan (skillet). Add the chicken and fry for 4-5 minutes, until cooked through and golden brown on both sides. Remove the chicken from the wok with a slotted spoon, set aside and leave to cool.

5 Add the bean sprouts, (bell) pepper, carrot and baby corn cobs to the wok and stir-fry for 2-3 minutes. Remove from

the wok with a slotted spoon, set aside and leave to cool.

6 To make the sauce, mix together the rice wine vinegar, light soy sauce and chilli oil.

7 Arrange the chicken and vegetables together on a serving plate. Spoon the sauce over the salad, garnish with chives and carrot matchsticks and serve.

Sweet & Sour Fish Salad

This refreshing blend of pink and white fish mixed with fresh pineapple and (bell) peppers would make an interesting starter or a light meal.

NUTRITIONAL INFORMATION

Calories 168	Sugars 5g
Protein 24g	Fat 6g
Carbohydrate 5g	Saturates 1g

   25 MINS 10 MINS

SERVES 4

INGREDIENTS

225 g/8 oz trout fillets

225 g/8 oz white fish fillets (such as haddock or cod)

300 ml /½ pint/ 1¼ cups water

1 stalk lemon grass

2 lime leaves

1 large red chilli

1 bunch spring onions (scallions), trimmed and shredded

115 g/4 oz fresh pineapple flesh, diced

1 small red (bell) pepper, deseeded and diced

1 bunch watercress, washed and trimmed

fresh snipped chives, to garnish

DRESSING

1 tbsp sunflower oil

1 tbsp rice wine vinegar

pinch of chilli powder

1 tsp clear honey

salt and pepper

1 Rinse the fish, place in a frying pan (skillet) and pour over the water.

2 Bend the lemon grass in half to bruise it and add to the pan with the lime leaves. Prick the chilli with a fork and add to the pan. Bring to the boil and simmer for 7–8 minutes. Leave to cool.

3 Drain the fish, flake the flesh away from the skin and place in a bowl.

Gently stir in the spring onions (scallions), pineapple and (bell) pepper.

4 Arrange the washed watercress on 4 serving plates, spoon the cooked fish mixture on top and set aside.

5 To make the dressing, mix all the ingredients together and season well. Spoon over the fish and serve garnished with chives.

Broccoli & Almond Salad

This is a colourful, crunchy salad with a delicious dressing. It is better left overnight if possible for the flavours to mingle.

NUTRITIONAL INFORMATION

Calories 181   Sugars 7g
Protein . . . . .9g   Fat 12g
Carbohydrate . . . .9g   Saturates 2g

4¹/₂ HOURS   10 MINS

SERVES 4

INGREDIENTS

450 g/1 lb small broccoli florets

50 g/1¾ oz baby corn cobs, halved, lengthways

1 red (bell) pepper, seeded and cut into thin strips

50 g/1¾ oz blanched almonds

DRESSING

1 tbsp sesame seeds

1 tbsp peanut oil

2 garlic cloves, crushed

2 tbsp light soy sauce

1 tbsp clear honey

2 tsp lemon juice

pepper

lemon zest, to garnish (optional)

1 Blanch the broccoli and baby corn cobs in boiling water for 5 minutes. Drain well, rinse and drain again.

2 Transfer the broccoli and baby corn cobs to a large mixing bowl and add the (bell) pepper and almonds.

3 To make the dressing, heat a wok and add the sesame seeds. Dry-fry, stirring constantly, for about 1 minute, or until the sesame seeds are lightly browned and are giving off a delicious aroma.

4 Mix the peanut oil, garlic, soy sauce, honey, lemon juice and pepper to taste. Add the sesame seeds and mix well.

5 Pour the dressing over the salad, cover and set aside in the refrigerator for a minimum of 4 hours and preferably overnight.

6 Garnish the salad with lemon zest (if using) and serve.

COOK'S TIP

Take care when browning the sesame seeds, as they will quickly burn. Dry-fry over a low heat and stir constantly.

Pickled Cucumber

The pickling takes minutes rather than days – but the longer you leave it, the better the result.

NUTRITIONAL INFORMATION

Calories	29	Sugars	.........3g
Protein	........0.2g	Fat	..........2g
Carbohydrate	....3g	Saturates	.....0.3g

 35 MINS   0 MINS

SERVES 4

INGREDIENTS

1 slender cucumber, about 30 cm/
  12 inches long

1 tsp salt

2 tsp caster (superfine) sugar

1 tsp rice vinegar

1 tsp red chilli oil

a few drops sesame oil

1 Wash and halve the cucumber, leaving it unpeeled, lengthways.

2 Scrape out the seeds from the cucumber using a knife or a teaspoon and discard. Cut the cucumber across into thick chunks.

3 Sprinkle the cucumber chunks with the salt and mix well.

4 Leave the cucumber chunks to marinate for at least 20-30 minutes, longer if possible, then pour the juice away. Drain and rinse the cucumber, then pat dry.

5 Transfer the cucumber chunks to a serving dish.

6 Add the caster (superfine) sugar, rice vinegar and chilli oil to the cucumber chunks in the dish and mix thoroughly until the cucumber is completely coated in the mixture.

7 Sprinkle the pickled cucumber with the sesame oil just before serving.

8 Serve as a snack or appetizer or as an accompaniment to cold meat dishes.

COOK'S TIP

Pickled vegetables and fruits are very popular with the Chinese. Usually, the vegetables are allowed to stay in the marinade for 3-4 days. Once made, they will keep in the refrigerator for up to 2 weeks.

Green Sesame Salad

A very elegant and light salad which will complement rice and noodle dishes beautifully.

NUTRITIONAL INFORMATION

Calories ....78 Sugars 8g
Protein ....3g Fat 3g
Carbohydrate ....3g Saturates 0.5g

10 MINS   0 MINS

SERVES 4

I N G R E D I E N T S

125 g/4½ oz/2 cups bean sprouts

1½ tbsp chopped fresh coriander (cilantro)

3 tbsp fresh lime juice

½ tsp mild chilli powder

1 tsp sugar

½ tsp salt

3 celery sticks

1 large green (bell) pepper, deseeded

1 large Granny Smith apple

2 tbsp toasted sesame seeds, to garnish

1 Rinse the bean sprouts and drain thoroughly.

2 Pick over the bean sprouts, removing any that seem a little brown or limp – it is essential that they are fresh and crunchy for this recipe.

3 To make the dressing, combine the coriander (cilantro), lime juice, chilli powder, sugar and salt in a small bowl and mix thoroughly.

4 Using a sharp knife, cut the celery into 2.5 cm/1 inch pieces. Cut the (bell) pepper into small pieces and the Granny Smith apple into small chunks.

5 Place the chopped celery, (bell) pepper and apple into a large mixing bowl and stir gently to mix.

6 Just before serving, pour the dressing over the salad, tossing well to mix.

7 Garnish the green sesame salad with the toasted sesame seeds and serve with rice or noodle dishes.

COOK'S TIP

Keeping each ingredient as fresh and crunchy as possible will make all the difference to the appearance and taste of this elegant salad. To prevent the apples from going brown, soak the slices briefly in a little lemon juice and water as soon as you have cut them.

Sweet & Sour Cucumber

Chunks of cucumber are marinated in vinegar and sweetened with honey to make a sweet and sour appetizer.

NUTRITIONAL INFORMATION

Calories	45	Sugars	.........2g
Protein	.........1g	Fat	...........3g
Carbohydrate	....4g	Saturates	.....0.4g

 50 MINS 0 MINS

SERVES 4

INGREDIENTS

1 cucumber

1 tsp salt

2 tsp honey

2 tbsp rice vinegar

3 tbsp chopped fresh coriander (cilantro)

2 tsp sesame oil

¼ tsp crushed red peppercorns

strips of red and yellow (bell) pepper, to garnish

1 Peel thin strips off the cucumber, along the length, to give a pretty striped effect. Cut the cucumber in quarters lengthways and then into 2.5 cm/

1 inch long pieces. Place in a colander. Sprinkle with salt and leave to stand for 30 minutes to allow the salt to draw out the excess water from the cucumber.

2 Wash the cucumber thoroughly to remove the salt, drain and pat dry with kitchen paper (paper towels).

3 Place the cucumber pieces in a large mixing bowl.

4 Combine the honey with the vinegar and pour over the cucumber. Mix together and marinate for 15 minutes.

5 Stir in the chopped fresh coriander (cilantro) and sesame oil, and place in a serving bowl.

6 Sprinkle over the crushed red peppercorns. Serve garnished with strips of red and yellow (bell) pepper.

COOK'S TIP

Rice vinegar is a common Chinese cooking ingredient. White rice vinegar is made from rice wine, whereas red rice vinegar is made from fermented rice. Both have a distinctive flavour, but the white version tends to be used more often, as it will not colour the food.

Stir-Fried Chilli Cucumber

Warm cucumbers are absolutely delicious, especially when combined with the heat of chilli and the flavour of ginger.

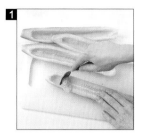

NUTRITIONAL INFORMATION

Calories 67   Sugars 4g
Protein ....1g   Fat 5g
Carbohydrate ....5g   Saturates 1g

30 MINS   5 MINS

SERVES 4

INGREDIENTS

2 medium cucumbers

2 tsp salt

1 tbsp vegetable oil

2 garlic cloves, crushed

1-cm/½-inch fresh root ginger, grated

2 fresh red chillies, chopped

2 spring onions (scallions), chopped

1 tsp yellow bean sauce

1 tbsp clear honey

125 ml/4 fl oz/½ cup water

1 tsp sesame oil

1 Peel the cucumbers and cut in half lengthways. Scrape the seeds from the centre with a teaspoon or melon baller and discard.

2 Cut the cucumber into strips and place on a plate. Sprinkle the salt over the cucumber strips and set aside for 20 minutes. Rinse well under cold running water and pat dry with absorbent kitchen paper (paper towels).

3 Heat the vegetable oil in a preheated wok or large frying pan (skillet) until it is almost smoking. Lower the heat slightly and add the garlic, ginger, chillies and spring onions (scallions) and stir-fry for 30 seconds.

4 Add the cucumbers to the wok, together with the yellow bean sauce and honey and stir-fry for 30 seconds.

5 Add the water and cook over a high heat until most of the water has evaporated.

6 Sprinkle the sesame oil over the stir-fry. Transfer to a warm serving dish and serve immediately.

COOK'S TIP

The cucumber is sprinkled with salt and left to stand in order to draw out the excess water, thus preventing a soggy meal!

Poultry

Second to pork, poultry is one of the most popular foods throughout China. It also plays an important symbolic role in Chinese cooking. The cock symbolizes the male, positiveness and aggression while the duck represents happiness and fidelity. Being uniformly tender, poultry is ideal for Chinese cooking methods which rely on the rapid

cooking of small, even-sized pieces of meat. Poultry can be cut into wafer-thin slices, thin matchstick strips or cubes, and can be quickly cooked without any loss of moisture or tenderness. This chapter contains dishes which are stir-fried, braised, steamed and roasted and contains old favourites such as Lemon Chicken and Aromatic & Crispy Duck, as well as more unusual dishes such as Duck with Lime & Kiwi Fruit and Honey & Soy Chicken.

Chicken Chop Suey

Chop suey is a well known and popular dish based on bean sprouts and soy sauce with a meat or vegetable flavouring.

NUTRITIONAL INFORMATION

Calories 337	Sugars 7g
Protein 32g	Fat 18g
Carbohydrate . . .14g	Saturates 3g

 25 MINS   15 MINS

SERVES 4

INGREDIENTS

4 tbsp light soy sauce

2 tsp light brown sugar

500 g/1 lb 2 oz skinless, boneless chicken breasts

3 tbsp vegetable oil

2 onions, quartered

2 garlic cloves, crushed

350 g/12 oz bean sprouts

3 tsp sesame oil

1 tbsp cornflour (cornstarch)

3 tbsp water

425 ml/¾ pint/2 cups chicken stock

shredded leek, to garnish

VARIATION

This recipe may be made with strips of lean steak, pork or with mixed vegetables. Change the type of stock accordingly.

1 Mix the soy sauce and sugar together, stirring until the sugar has dissolved.

2 Trim any fat from the chicken and cut into thin strips. Place the meat in a shallow dish and spoon the soy mixture over them, turning to coat. Marinate in the refrigerator for 20 minutes.

3 Heat the oil in a wok and stir-fry the chicken for 2–3 minutes, until golden brown. Add the onions and garlic and cook for a further 2 minutes. Add the bean sprouts, cook for 4–5 minutes, then add the sesame oil.

4 Mix the cornflour (cornstarch) and water to form a smooth paste. Pour the stock into the wok, add the cornflour (cornstarch) paste and bring to the boil, stirring until the sauce is thickened and clear. Serve, garnished with shredded leek.

Cashew Chicken

Yellow bean sauce is available from large supermarkets. Try to buy a chunky sauce rather than a smooth sauce for texture.

NUTRITIONAL INFORMATION

Calories	398	Sugars	.........2g
Protein	........31g	Fat	..........27g
Carbohydrate	....8g	Saturates	.......4g

 10 MINS   15 MINS

SERVES 4

INGREDIENTS

450 g/1 lb boneless chicken breasts

2 tbsp vegetable oil

1 red onion, sliced

175 g/6 oz/1½ cups flat mushrooms, sliced

100 g/3½ oz/⅓ cup cashew nuts

75 g/2¾ oz jar yellow bean sauce

fresh coriander (cilantro), to garnish

egg fried rice or plain boiled rice, to serve

1 Using a sharp knife, remove the excess skin from the chicken breasts, if desired. Cut the chicken into small, bite-sized chunks.

2 Heat the vegetable oil in a preheated wok or frying pan (skillet).

3 Add the chicken to the wok and stir-fry for 5 minutes.

4 Add the red onion and mushrooms to the wok and continue to stir-fry for a further 5 minutes.

5 Place the cashew nuts on a baking tray (cookie sheet) and toast under a preheated medium grill (broiler) until just browning – toasting nuts brings out their flavour.

6 Toss the toasted cashew nuts into the wok together with the yellow bean sauce and heat through.

7 Allow the sauce to bubble for 2–3 minutes.

8 Transfer the chop suey to warm serving bowls and garnish with fresh coriander (cilantro). Serve hot with egg fried rice or plain boiled rice.

VARIATION

Chicken thighs could be used instead of the chicken breasts for a more economical dish.

Lemon Chicken

This is on everyone's list of favourite Chinese dishes, and it is so simple to make. Serve with stir-fried vegetables for a truly delicious meal.

NUTRITIONAL INFORMATION

Calories 272   Sugars 1g
Protein ....36g   Fat 11g
Carbohydrate ....5g   Saturates 2g

 5 MINS   15 MINS

SERVES 4

INGREDIENTS

vegetable oil, for deep-frying

650 g/1 lb 7 oz skinless, boneless chicken, cut into strips

lemon slices and shredded spring onion (scallion), to garnish

SAUCE

1 tbsp cornflour (cornstarch)

6 tbsp cold water

3 tbsp fresh lemon juice

2 tbsp sweet sherry

½ tsp caster (superfine) sugar

1 Heat the oil for deep-frying in a preheated wok or frying pan (skillet) to 180°C/350°F or until a cube of bread browns in 30 seconds.

2 Reduce the heat and stir-fry the chicken strips for 3–4 minutes, until cooked through.

3 Remove the chicken with a slotted spoon, set aside and keep warm. Drain the oil from the wok.

4 To make the sauce, mix the cornflour (cornstarch) with 2 tablespoons of the water to form a paste.

5 Pour the lemon juice and remaining water into the mixture in the wok.

6 Add the sweet sherry and caster (superfine) sugar and bring to the boil, stirring until the sugar has completely dissolved.

7 Stir in the cornflour (cornstarch) mixture and return to the boil. Reduce the heat and simmer, stirring constantly, for 2-3 minutes, until the sauce is thickened and clear.

8 Transfer the chicken to a warm serving plate and pour the sauce over the top.

9 Garnish the chicken with the lemon slices and shredded spring onion (scallion) and serve immediately.

COOK'S TIP

If you would prefer to use chicken portions rather than strips, cook them in the oil, covered, over a low heat for about 30 minutes, or until cooked through.

Celery & Cashew Chicken

Stir-fry yellow bean sauce gives this quick and easy Chinese dish a really authentic taste. Pecan nuts can be used in place of the cashews.

NUTRITIONAL INFORMATION

Calories ....549 Sugars 24g
Protein ....41g Fat 31g
Carbohydrate ...28g Saturates 5g

 5 MINS   10 MINS

SERVES 4

INGREDIENTS

3-4 boneless, skinned chicken breasts, about 625g/1 lb 6 oz

2 tbsp sunflower or vegetable oil

125 g/4½ oz/1 cup cashew nuts (unsalted)

4-6 spring onions (scallions), thinly sliced diagonally

5-6 celery sticks, thinly sliced diagonally

1 x 175 g/6 oz jar stir-fry yellow bean sauce

salt and pepper

celery leaves, to garnish (optional)

plain boiled rice, to serve

1 Using a sharp knife or metal cleaver, cut the chicken into thin slices across the grain.

2 Heat the oil in a preheated wok or large frying pan (skillet), swirling it around until it is really hot.

3 Add the cashew nuts and stir-fry until they begin to brown but do not allow them to burn.

4 Add the chicken and stir-fry until well sealed and almost cooked through.

5 Add the spring onions (scallions) and celery and continue to stir-fry for 2-3 minutes, stirring the food well around the wok.

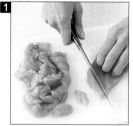  

6 Add the stir-fry yellow bean sauce to the wok or frying pan (skillet) and season lightly with salt and pepper.

7 Toss the mixture in the wok until the chicken and vegetables are thoroughly coated with the sauce and piping hot.

8 Serve at once with plain boiled rice, garnished with celery leaves, if liked.

VARIATION

This recipe can be adapted to use turkey fillets or steaks, or pork fillet or boneless steaks. Cut the turkey or pork lengthwise first, then slice thinly across the grain. Alternatively, cut into 2 cm/½ inch cubes.

Aromatic & Crispy Duck

As it is very time-consuming to make the pancakes, buy ready-made ones from Oriental stores, or use crisp lettuce leaves as the wrapper.

NUTRITIONAL INFORMATION

Calories ....169 Sugars 1g
Protein ....7g Fat 11g
Carbohydrate ....7g Saturates 3g

9¼ HOURS   3¼ HOURS

SERVES 4

INGREDIENTS

2 large duckling quarters

1 tsp salt

3-4 pieces star anise

1 tsp Szechuan red peppercorns

1 tsp cloves

2 cinnamon sticks, broken into pieces

2-3 spring onions (scallions), cut into short
sections

4-5 small slices ginger root

3-4 tbsp rice wine or dry sherry

vegetable oil, for deep-frying

TO SERVE

12 ready-made pancakes or 12 crisp
lettuce leaves

hoisin or plum sauce

¼ cucumber, thinly shredded

3-4 spring onions (scallions), thinly
shredded

1 Rub the duck with the salt and arrange the star anise, peppercorns, cloves and cinnamon on top. Sprinkle with the spring onions (scallions), ginger and wine and marinate for at least 3-4 hours.

2 Arrange the duck pieces on a plate that will fit inside a bamboo steamer. Pour some hot water into a wok, place the bamboo steamer on top, sitting on a trivet. Add the duck and cover with the bamboo lid. Steam the duck over a high heat for 2-3 hours, until tender and cooked through. Top up the hot water from time to time as required. Remove the duck and leave to cool for at least 4-5 hours so the duck becomes crispy.

3 Pour off the water and wipe the wok dry. Pour in the oil and heat until smoking. Deep-fry the duck pieces, skin-side down, for 4-5 minutes or until crisp and brown. Remove and drain.

4 To serve, scrape the meat off the bone, place about 1 teaspoon of hoisin or plum sauce on the centre of a pancake (or lettuce leaf), add a few pieces of cucumber and spring onion (scallion) with a portion of the duck meat. Wrap up to form a small parcel and eat with your fingers.

Stir-Fried Ginger Chicken

The oranges add colour and piquancy to this refreshing dish, which complements the chicken well.

NUTRITIONAL INFORMATION

Calories 289   Sugars 15g
Protein . . . . .20g   Fat 9g
Carbohydrate . . .17g   Saturates 2g

 5 MINS   20 MINS

SERVES 4

I N G R E D I E N T S

2 tbsp sunflower oil

1 onion, sliced

175 g/6 oz carrots, cut into thin sticks

1 clove garlic, crushed

350 g/12 oz boneless skinless chicken
    breasts

2 tbsp fresh ginger, peeled and grated

1 tsp ground ginger

4 tbsp sweet sherry

1 tbsp tomato purée (tomato paste)

1 tbsp demerara sugar

100 ml/3½ fl oz/⅓ cup orange juice

1 tsp cornflour (cornstarch)

1 orange, peeled and segmented

fresh snipped chives, to garnish

1 Heat the oil in a large preheated wok. Add the onion, carrots and garlic and stir-fry over a high heat for 3 minutes or until the vegetables begin to soften.

2 Slice the chicken into thin strips. Add to the wok with the fresh and ground ginger. Stir-fry for a further 10 minutes, or until the chicken is well cooked through and golden in colour.

3 Mix together the sherry, tomato purée (tomato paste), sugar, orange juice and cornflour (cornstarch) in a bowl. Stir the mixture into the wok and heat through until the mixture bubbles and the juices start to thicken.

4 Add the orange segments and carefully toss to mix.

5 Transfer the stir-fried chicken to warm serving bowls and garnish with freshly snipped chives. Serve immediately.

COOK'S TIP

Make sure that you do not continue cooking the dish once the orange segments have been added in step 4, otherwise they will break up.

Barbecued Chicken Legs

Just the thing to put on the barbecue – chicken legs, coated with a spicy, curry-like butter, then grilled until crispy and golden.

NUTRITIONAL INFORMATION

Calories 660	Sugars 4g	
Protein 34g	Fat 57g	
Carbohydrate 4g	Saturates 30g	

5 MINS   20 MINS

SERVES 4

I N G R E D I E N T S

12 chicken drumsticks

S P I C E D   B U T T E R

175 g/6 oz/¾ cup butter

2 garlic cloves, crushed

1 tsp grated ginger root

2 tsp ground turmeric

4 tsp cayenne pepper

2 tbsp lime juice

3 tbsp mango chutney

T O   S E R V E

crisp green seasonal salad

boiled rice

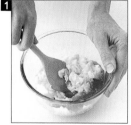  

1 To make the Spiced Butter mixture, beat the butter with the garlic, ginger, turmeric, cayenne pepper, lime juice and chutney until well blended.

2 Using a sharp knife, slash each chicken leg to the bone 3-4 times.

3 Cook the drumsticks over a moderate barbecue (grill) for about 12-15 minutes or until almost cooked.

Alternatively, grill (broil) the chicken for about 10-12 minutes until almost cooked, turning halfway through.

4 Spread the chicken legs liberally with the butter mixture and continue to cook for a further 5-6 minutes, turning and basting frequently with the butter until golden and crisp. Serve the chicken legs hot or cold with a crisp green salad and rice.

VARIATION

This spicy butter mixture would be equally effective on grilled chicken or turkey breast fillets. Skin before coating with the mixture.

Braised Chicken

This is a delicious way to cook a whole chicken. It has a wonderful glaze, which is served as a sauce.

NUTRITIONAL INFORMATION

Calories 294	Sugars 9g
Protein 31g	Fat 15g
Carbohydrate ...10g	Saturates 3g

🍲 5 MINS   🕐 1¼ HOURS

SERVES 4

I N G R E D I E N T S

1.5 kg/3 lb 5 oz chicken

3 tbsp vegetable oil

1 tbsp peanut oil

2 tbsp dark brown sugar

5 tbsp dark soy sauce

150 ml/¼ pint/⅔ cup water

2 garlic cloves, crushed

1 small onion, chopped

1 fresh red chilli, chopped

celery leaves and chives,
  to garnish

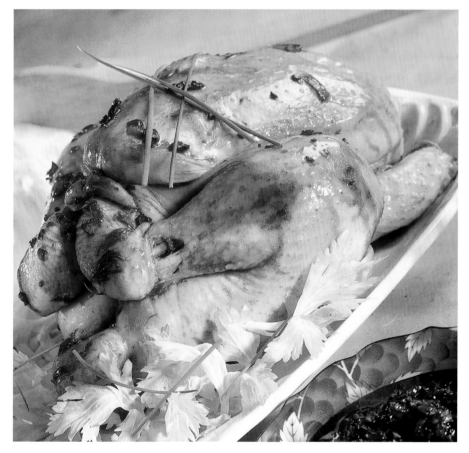

1 Preheat a large wok or large frying pan (skillet).

2 Clean the chicken inside and out with damp kitchen paper (paper towels).

3 Put the vegetable oil and peanut oil in the wok, add the dark brown sugar and heat gently until the sugar caramelizes.

4 Stir the soy sauce into the wok. Add the chicken and turn it in the mixture to coat thoroughly on all sides.

5 Add the water, garlic, onion and chilli. Cover and simmer, turning the chicken occasionally, for about 1 hour, or

until cooked through. Test by piercing a thigh with the point of a knife or a skewer – the juices will run clear when the chicken is cooked.

6 Remove the chicken from the wok and set aside. Increase the heat and reduce the sauce in the wok until thickened. Transfer the chicken to a serving plate, garnish with celery leaves and chives and serve with the sauce.

COOK'S TIP

For a spicier sauce, add 1 tbsp finely chopped fresh root ginger and 1 tbsp ground Szechuan peppercorns with the chilli in step 5.

Yellow Bean Chicken

Ready-made yellow bean sauce is available from large supermarkets and Chinese food stores. It is made from yellow soya beans and is quite salty.

NUTRITIONAL INFORMATION

Calories . . . . . . .234 Sugars 1g
Protein . . . . .26g Fat 12g
Carbohydrate . . . .6g Saturates 2g

25 MINS   10 MINS

SERVES 4

INGREDIENTS

450 g/1 lb skinless, boneless chicken
 breasts

1 egg white, beaten

1 tbsp cornflour (cornstarch)

1 tbsp rice wine vinegar

1 tbsp light soy sauce

1 tsp caster (superfine) sugar

3 tbsp vegetable oil

1 garlic clove, crushed

1-cm/½-inch piece fresh root
 ginger, grated

1 green (bell) pepper, seeded
 and diced

2 large mushrooms, sliced

3 tbsp yellow bean sauce

yellow or green (bell) pepper strips,
 to garnish

VARIATION

Black bean sauce would work equally well with this recipe. Although this would affect the appearance of the dish, as it is much darker in colour, the flavours would be compatible.

1 Trim any fat from the chicken and cut the meat into 2.5-cm/1-inch cubes.

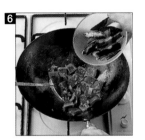

2 Mix the egg white and cornflour (cornstarch) in a shallow bowl. Add the chicken and turn in the mixture to coat. Set aside for 20 minutes.

3 Mix the rice wine vinegar, soy sauce and caster (superfine) sugar in a bowl.

4 Remove the chicken from the egg white mixture.

5 Heat the oil in a preheated wok, add the chicken and stir-fry for 3–4 minutes, until golden brown. Remove the chicken from the wok with a slotted spoon, set aside and keep warm.

6 Add the garlic, ginger, (bell) pepper and mushrooms to the wok and stir-fry for 1–2 minutes.

7 Add the yellow bean sauce and cook for 1 minute. Stir in the vinegar mixture and return the chicken to the wok. Cook for 1–2 minutes and serve hot, garnished with (bell) pepper strips.

Kung Po Chicken

In this recipe, cashew nuts are used but peanuts, walnuts or almonds can be substituted, if preferred.

NUTRITIONAL INFORMATION

Calories 294	Sugars 3g	
Protein 21g	Fat 18g	
Carbohydrate ...10g	Saturates 4g	

10 MINS   5 MINS

SERVES 4

INGREDIENTS

250-300 g/9-10½ oz chicken meat, boned and skinned

¼ tsp salt

⅓ egg white

1 tsp cornflour (cornstarch) paste (see page 31)

1 medium green (bell) pepper, cored and seeded

4 tbsp vegetable oil

1 spring onion (scallion), cut into short sections

a few small slices of ginger root

4-5 small dried red chillies, soaked, seeded and shredded

2 tbsp crushed yellow bean sauce

1 tsp rice wine or dry sherry

125 g/4½ oz roasted cashew nuts

a few drops of sesame oil

boiled rice, to serve

1 Cut the chicken into small cubes about the size of sugar lumps. Place the chicken in a small bowl and mix with a pinch of salt, the egg white and the cornflour (cornstarch) paste, in that order.

2 Cut the green (bell) pepper into cubes or triangles about the same size as the chicken pieces.

3 Heat the oil in a wok, add the chicken and stir-fry for 1 minute. Remove with a slotted spoon and keep warm.

4 Add the spring onion (scallion), ginger, chillies and green (bell) pepper. Stir-fry for 1 minute, then add the chicken with the yellow bean sauce and wine. Blend well and stir-fry for another minute. Finally stir in the cashew nuts and sesame oil. Serve hot with boiled rice.

VARIATION

Any nuts can be used in place of the cashew nuts, if preferred. The important point is the crunchy texture, which is very much a feature of Szechuan cooking.

Fruity Duck Stir-fry

The pineapple and plum sauce add a sweetness and fruity flavour to this colourful recipe which blends well with the duck.

NUTRITIONAL INFORMATION

Calories 241	Sugars 7g	
Protein 26g	Fat 8g	
Carbohydrate . . .16g	Saturates 2g	

5 MINS   25 MINS

SERVES 4

I N G R E D I E N T S

4 duck breasts

1 tsp Chinese five-spice powder

1 tbsp cornflour (cornstarch)

1 tbsp chilli oil

225 g/8 oz baby onions, peeled

2 cloves garlic, crushed

100 g/3½ oz/1 cup baby corn cobs

175 g/6 oz/1¼ cups canned pineapple chunks

6 spring onions (scallions), sliced

100 g/3½ oz/1 cup bean sprouts

2 tbsp plum sauce

1 Remove any skin from the duck breasts. Cut the duck into thin slices.

2 Mix the five-spice powder and the cornflour (cornstarch). Toss the duck in the mixture until well coated.

3 Heat the oil in a preheated wok. Stir-fry the duck for 10 minutes, or until just begining to crispen around the edges. Remove from the wok and set aside.

4 Add the onions and garlic to the wok and stir-fry for 5 minutes, or until softened. Add the baby corn cobs and stir-fry for a further 5 minutes. Add the pineapple, spring onions (scallions) and bean sprouts and stir-fry for 3–4 minutes. Stir in the plum sauce.

5 Return the cooked duck to the wok and toss until well mixed. Transfer to warm serving dishes and serve hot.

COOK'S TIP

Buy pineapple chunks in natural juice rather than syrup for a fresher flavour. If you can only obtain pineapple in syrup, rinse it in cold water and drain thoroughly before using.

Green Chicken Stir-Fry

Tender chicken is mixed with a selection of spring greens and flavoured with yellow bean sauce in this crunchy stir-fry.

NUTRITIONAL INFORMATION

Calories ....297 Sugars 5g
Protein ....30g Fat 16g
Carbohydrate ....8g Saturates 3g

  5 MINS   🕐 15 MINS

SERVES 4

I N G R E D I E N T S

2 tbsp sunflower oil

450 g/1 lb skinless, boneless chicken breasts

2 cloves garlic, crushed

1 green (bell) pepper

100 g/3½ oz/1½ cups mangetout (snow peas)

6 spring onions (scallions), sliced, plus extra to garnish

225 g/8 oz spring greens or cabbage, shredded

160 g/5¾ oz jar yellow bean sauce

50 g/1¾ oz/3 tbsp roasted cashew nuts

1 Heat the sunflower oil in a large preheated wok.

2 Slice the chicken into thin strips and add to the wok together with the garlic. Stir-fry for about 5 minutes or until the chicken is sealed on all sides and beginning to turn golden.

3 Using a sharp knife, deseed the green (bell) pepper and cut into thin strips.

4 Add the mangetout (snow peas), spring onions (scallions), green (bell) pepper strips and spring greens or cabbage to the wok. Stir-fry for a further 5 minutes or until the vegetables are just tender.

5 Stir in the yellow bean sauce and heat through for about 2 minutes or until the mixture starts to bubble.

6 Scatter the roasted cashew nuts into the wok.

7 Transfer the stir-fry to warm serving plates and garnish with extra spring onions (scallions), if desired. Serve the stir-fry immediately.

COOK'S TIP

Do not add salted cashew nuts to this dish otherwise the dish will be too salty.

Chicken with Bean Sprouts

This is the basic Chicken Chop Suey to be found in almost every Chinese restaurant and takeaway all over the world.

NUTRITIONAL INFORMATION

Calories	153	Sugars	........4g
Protein	.........9g	Fat	..........10g
Carbohydrate	....8g	Saturates	.......1g

 3¹/₂ HOURS 10 MINS

SERVES 4

INGREDIENTS

125 g/4½ oz chicken breast fillet, skinned

1 tsp salt

¼ egg white, lightly beaten

2 tsp cornflour (cornstarch) paste
   (see page 31)

about 300 ml/½ pint/1¼ cups vegetable oil

1 small onion, thinly shredded

1 small green (bell) pepper, cored, seeded
   and thinly shredded

1 small carrot, thinly shredded

125 g/4½ oz fresh beansprouts

½ tsp sugar

1 tbsp light soy sauce

1 tsp rice wine or dry sherry

2-3 tbsp Chinese Stock (see page 30)

a few drops of sesame oil

chilli sauce, to serve

COOK'S TIP

Chop Suey actually originated in San Francisco at the turn of the century when Chinese immigrants were first settling there, and was first devised as a handy dish for using up leftovers.

1 Using a sharp knife or meat cleaver, cut the chicken into thin shreds and place in a bowl.

2 Add a pinch of the salt, the egg white and cornflour (cornstarch) paste to the chicken and mix well.

3 Heat the vegetable oil in a preheated wok or large frying pan (skillet).

4 Add the chicken and stir-fry for about 1 minute, stirring to separate the shreds. Remove with a slotted spoon and drain on kitchen paper (paper towels).

5 Pour off the oil, leaving about 2 tablespoons in the wok. Add the onion, green (bell) pepper and carrot and stir-fry for about 2 minutes.

6 Add the bean sprouts and stir-fry for a few seconds.

7 Add the chicken with the remaining salt, sugar, soy sauce and rice wine or dry sherry, blend well and add the Chinese stock or water.

8 Sprinkle the stir-fry with the sesame oil and serve with the chilli sauce.

Chilli Coconut Chicken

This tasty dish combines the flavours of lime, peanut, coconut and chilli.
You'll find coconut cream in most supermarkets or delicatessens.

NUTRITIONAL INFORMATION

Calories 348	Sugars 2g	
Protein 36g	Fat 21g	
Carbohydrate 3g	Saturates 8g	

🍲 5 MINS   🕐 15 MINS

SERVES 4

I N G R E D I E N T S

150 ml/¼ pint/⅔ cup hot chicken stock

25 g/1 oz/⅓ cup coconut cream

1 tbsp sunflower oil

8 skinless, boneless chicken thighs,
    cut into long, thin strips

1 small red chilli, sliced thinly

4 spring onions (scallions),
    sliced thinly

4 tbsp smooth or crunchy peanut butter

finely grated rind and juice of 1 lime

1 fresh red chilli and spring onion (scallion)
    tassel, to garnish

boiled rice, to serve

1 Pour the chicken stock into a measuring jug or small bowl. Crumble the coconut cream into the chicken stock and stir the mixture until the coconut cream dissolves.

2 Heat the oil in a preheated wok or large heavy pan.

3 Add the chicken strips and cook, stirring, until the chicken turns a golden colour.

4 Stir in the chopped red chilli and spring onions (scallions) and cook gently for a few minutes.

5 Add the peanut butter, coconut cream and chicken stock mixture, lime rind, lime juice and simmer, uncovered, for about 5 minutes, stirring frequently to prevent the mixture sticking to the base of the wok or pan.

6 Transfer the chilli coconut chicken to a warm serving dish, garnish with the red chilli and spring onion (scallion) tassel and serve with boiled rice.

COOK'S TIP

Serve jasmine rice with this spicy dish. It has a fragrant aroma that is well-suited to the flavours in this dish.

Chicken with Black Bean Sauce

This tasty chicken stir-fry is quick and easy to make and is full of fresh flavours and crunchy vegetables.

NUTRITIONAL INFORMATION

Calories 205	Sugars 4g	
Protein 25g	Fat 9g	
Carbohydrate 6g	Saturates 2g	

40 MINS   10 MINS

SERVES 4

INGREDIENTS

425 g/15 oz chicken breasts, sliced thinly

pinch of salt

pinch of cornflour

2 tbsp oil

1 garlic clove, crushed

1 tbsp black bean sauce

1 each small red and green (bell) pepper, cut into strips

1 red chilli, chopped finely

75 g/2¾ oz/1 cup mushrooms, sliced

1 onion, chopped

6 spring onions (scallions), chopped

salt and pepper

SEASONING

½ tsp salt

½ tsp sugar

3 tbsp chicken stock

1 tbsp dark soy sauce

2 tbsp beef stock

2 tbsp rice wine

1 tsp cornflour (cornstarch), blended with a little rice wine

1 Put the chicken strips in a bowl. Add a pinch of salt and a pinch of cornflour and cover with water. Leave to stand for 30 minutes.

2 Heat 1 tablespoon of the oil in a wok or deep-sided frying pan (skillet) and stir-fry the chicken for 4 minutes.

3 Remove the chicken to a warm serving dish and clean the wok.

4 Add the remaining oil to the wok and add the garlic, black bean sauce, green and red (bell) peppers, chilli, mushrooms, onion and spring onions (scallions). Stir-fry for 2 minutes then return the chicken to the wok.

5 Add the seasoning ingredients, fry for 3 minutes and thicken with a little of the cornflour (cornstarch) blend. Serve with fresh noodles.

Duck with Ginger & Lime

Just the thing for a lazy summer day – roasted duck sliced and served with a dressing made of ginger, lime juice, sesame oil and fish sauce.

NUTRITIONAL INFORMATION

Calories 529   Sugars 3g
Protein ....38g   Fat 41g
Carbohydrate ....3g   Saturates 6g

20 MINS   25 MINS

SERVES 4

INGREDIENTS

3 boneless Barbary duck breasts, about 250 g/9 oz each

salt

DRESSING

125 ml/4 fl oz/½ cup olive oil

2 tsp sesame oil

2 tbsp lime juice

grated rind and juice of 1 orange

2 tsp fish sauce

1 tbsp grated ginger root

1 garlic clove, crushed

2 tsp light soy sauce

3 spring onions (scallions), finely chopped

1 tsp sugar

about 250 g/9 oz assorted salad leaves

orange slices, to garnish (optional)

1 Wash the duck breasts, dry on kitchen paper (paper towels), then cut in half. Prick the skin all over with a fork and season well with salt. Place the duck pieces, skin-side down, on a wire rack or trivet over a roasting tin (pan).

2 Cook the duck in a preheated oven for 10 minutes, then turn over and cook for a further 12-15 minutes, or until the duck is cooked, but still pink in the centre, and the skin is crisp.

3 To make the dressing, beat the olive oil and sesame oil with the lime juice, orange rind and juice, fish sauce, grated ginger root, garlic, light soy sauce, spring onions (scallions) and sugar until well blended.

4 Remove the duck from the oven, and allow to cool. Using a sharp knife, cut the duck into thick slices.

5 Add a little of the dressing to moisten and coat the duck.

6 To serve, arrange assorted salad leaves on a serving dish. Top with the sliced duck breasts and drizzle with the remaining salad dressing.

7 Garnish with orange slices, if using, then serve at once.

Red Chicken Curry

The chicken is cooked with a curry paste using red chillies. It is a fiery hot sauce – for a milder version, reduce the number of chillies used.

NUTRITIONAL INFORMATION

Calories 331   Sugars 5g
Protein . . . . .36g   Fat 17g
Carbohydrate . . . .7g   Saturates 3g

 10 MINS   🕐 10 MINS

SERVES 4

INGREDIENTS

4 tbsp vegetable oil

2 garlic cloves, crushed

400 ml/14 fl oz/1¾ cups coconut milk

6 chicken breast fillets, skinned and
   cut into bite-sized pieces

125 ml/4 fl oz/½ cup chicken stock

2 tbsp fish sauce

sliced red and green chillies,
   to garnish

boiled rice, to serve

RED CURRY PASTE

8 dried red chillies, seeded
   and chopped

2.5 cm/1 inch galangal or ginger root,
   peeled and sliced

3 stalks lemon grass, chopped

1 garlic clove, peeled

2 tsp shrimp paste

1 kaffir lime leaf, chopped

1 tsp ground coriander

¾ tsp ground cumin

1 tbsp chopped fresh coriander
   (cilantro)

1 tsp salt and black pepper

1 To make the red curry paste, place all the ingredients in a food processor or blender and process until smooth.

2 Heat the vegetable oil in a large, heavy-based pan or wok. Add the garlic and cook for 1 minute or until it turns golden.

3 Stir in the red curry paste and cook for 10-15 seconds.

4 Gradually add the coconut milk, stirring constantly (don't worry if the mixture starts to look curdled at this stage).

5 Add the chicken pieces and turn in the sauce mixture to coat. Cook gently for about 3-5 minutes or until almost tender.

6 Stir in the chicken stock and fish sauce, mixing well, then cook for a further 2 minutes.

7 Transfer the chicken curry to a warmed serving dish and garnish with sliced red and green chillies. Serve with rice.

Barbecued (Grilled) Duckling

The sweet, spicy marinade used in this recipe gives the duckling a subtle flavour of the Orient.

NUTRITIONAL INFORMATION

Calories 249   Sugars 20g
Protein . . . . .27g   Fat 6g
Carbohydrate . . .23g   Saturates 2g

6¼ HOURS   30 MINS

SERVES 4

I N G R E D I E N T S

3 cloves garlic, crushed

150 ml/5 fl oz/⅔ cup light soy sauce

5 tbsp light muscovado sugar

2.5 cm/1 inch piece root (fresh) ginger, grated

1 tbsp chopped, fresh coriander (cilantro)

1 tsp five-spice powder

4 duckling breasts

sprig of fresh coriander (cilantro), to garnish (optional)

1 To make the marinade, mix together the garlic, soy sauce, sugar, grated ginger, chopped coriander (cilantro) and five-spice powder in a small bowl until well combined.

2 Place the duckling breasts in a shallow, non-metallic dish and pour over the marinade. Carefully turn over the duckling so that it is fully coated with the marinade on both sides.

3 Cover the bowl with cling film (plastic wrap) and leave to marinate for 1-6 hours, turning the duckling once or twice so that the marinade is fully absorbed.

4 Remove the duckling from the marinade, reserving the marinade for basting.

  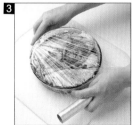

5 Barbecue (grill) the duckling breasts over hot coals for about 20–30 minutes, turning and basting frequently with the reserved marinade, using a pastry brush.

6 Cut the duckling into slices and transfer to warm serving plates. Serve the barbecued (grilled) duckling garnished with a sprig of fresh coriander (cilantro), if using.

COOK'S TIP

Duckling is quite a fatty meat so there is no need to add oil to the marinade. However, you must remember to oil the barbecue (grill) rack to prevent the duckling from sticking. Oil the barbecue (grill) rack well away from the barbecue (grill) to avoid any danger of a flare-up.

Garlic & Lime Chicken

Garlic and coriander (cilantro) flavour the chicken breasts which are served with a caramelised sauce, sharpened with lime juice.

NUTRITIONAL INFORMATION

Calories 280   Sugars 7g
Protein . . . . .26g   Fat 17g
Carbohydrate . . . .7g   Saturates 8g

10 MINS   25 MINS

SERVES 4

I N G R E D I E N T S

4 large skinless, boneless
   chicken breasts

50 g/1¾oz/3 tbsp garlic butter,
   softened

3 tbsp chopped fresh coriander
   (cilantro)

1 tbsp sunflower oil

finely grated zest and juice of 2 limes,
   plus extra zest, to garnish

25 g/1 oz/4 tbsp palm sugar or
   demerara (brown crystal) sugar

TO SERVE

boiled rice

lemon wedges

1 Place each chicken breast between 2 sheets of cling film (plastic wrap) and pound with a rolling pin until flattened to about 1 cm/½ inch thick.

2 Mix together the garlic butter and coriander (cilantro) and spread over each flattened chicken breast. Roll up like a Swiss roll and secure with a cocktail stick (toothpick).

3 Heat the sunflower oil in a preheated wok or heavy-based frying pan (skillet).

4 Add the chicken rolls to the wok or pan and cook, turning, for 15–20 minutes or until cooked through.

5 Remove the chicken from the wok and transfer to a board. Cut each chicken roll into slices.

6 Add the lime zest, juice and sugar to the wok and heat gently, stirring, until the sugar has dissolved. Raise the heat and allow to bubble for 2 minutes.

7 Arrange the chicken on warmed serving plates and spoon the pan juices over to serve.

8 Garnish the garlic and lime chicken with extra lime zest, if desired

COOK'S TIP

Be sure to check that the chicken is cooked through before slicing and serving. Cook over a gentle heat so as not to overcook the outside, while the inside remains raw.

Orange Chicken Stir-Fry

Chicken thighs are inexpensive, meaty portions which are readily available. Although not as tender as breast, it is perfect for stir-frying.

10 MINS   15 MINS

SERVES 4

INGREDIENTS

3 tbsp sunflower oil

350 g/12 oz boneless chicken thighs, skinned and cut into thin strips

1 onion, sliced

1 clove garlic, crushed

1 red (bell) pepper, deseeded and sliced

75 g/2¾ oz/1¼ cups mangetout (snow peas)

4 tbsp light soy sauce

4 tbsp sherry

1 tbsp tomato purée (tomato paste)

finely grated rind and juice of 1 orange

1 tsp cornflour (cornstarch)

2 oranges

100 g/3½ oz/1 cup bean sprouts

cooked rice or noodles, to serve

1 Heat the oil in a large preheated wok. Add the chicken and stir-fry for 2–3 minutes or until sealed on all sides.

2 Add the onion, garlic, (bell) pepper and mangetout (snow peas) to the wok. Stir-fry for a further 5 minutes, or until the vegetables are just tender and the chicken is completely cooked through.

3 Mix together the soy sauce, sherry, tomato purée (tomato paste), orange rind and juice and the cornflour (cornstarch). Add to the wok and cook, stirring, until the juices start to thicken.

4 Using a sharp knife, peel and segment the oranges. Add the segments to the mixture in the wok with the bean sprouts and heat through for a further 2 minutes.

5 Transfer the stir-fry to serving plates and serve at once with cooked rice or noodles.

COOK'S TIP

Bean sprouts are sprouting mung beans and are a regular ingredient in Chinese cooking. They require very little cooking and may even be eaten raw, if wished.

Sweet Mango Chicken

The sweet, scented flavour of mango gives this dish its characteristic sweetness.

NUTRITIONAL INFORMATION

Calories	244	Sugars 18g
Protein	. . . . .27g	Fat 7g
Carbohydrate	. . .2.1g	Saturates 2g

 10 MINS   15 MINS

SERVES 4

INGREDIENTS

1 tbsp sunflower oil

6 skinless, boneless chicken thighs

1 ripe mango

2 cloves garlic, crushed

225 g/8 oz leeks, shredded

100 g/3½ oz/1 cup bean sprouts

150 ml/¼ pint/⅔ cup mango juice

1 tbsp white wine vinegar

2 tbsp clear honey

2 tbsp tomato ketchup

1 tsp cornflour (cornstarch)

COOK'S TIP

Mango juice is avaialable in jars from most supermarkets and is quite thick and sweet. If it is unavailable, purée and sieve a ripe mango and add a little water to make up the required quantity.

1 Heat the sunflower oil in a large preheated wok.

2 Cut the chicken into bite-sized cubes, add to the wok and stir-fry over a high heat for 10 minutes, tossing frequently until the chicken is cooked through and golden in colour.

3 Peel and slice the mango and add to the wok with the garlic, leeks and bean sprouts. Stir-fry for a further 2–3 minutes, or until softened.

4 Mix together the mango juice, white wine vinegar, honey, tomato ketchup and cornflour (cornstarch). Pour into the wok and stir-fry for a further 2 minutes, or until the juices start to thicken.

5 Transfer to a warmed serving dish and serve immediately.

Peking Duck

No Chinese cookery book would be complete without this famous recipe in which crispy skinned duck is served with pancakes and a tangy sauce.

NUTRITIONAL INFORMATION

Calories	357	Sugars	.......48g
Protein	........20g	Fat	.........10g
Carbohydrate	...49g	Saturates	.......2g

6¼ HOURS   1½ HOURS

SERVES 4

INGREDIENTS

1.8 kg/4 lb duck

1.75 litres/3 pints/7½ cups boiling water

4 tbsp clear honey

2 tsp dark soy sauce

2 tbsp sesame oil

125 ml/4 fl oz/½ cup hoisin sauce

125 g/4½ oz/⅔ cup caster (superfine) sugar

125 ml/4 fl oz/½ cup water

carrot strips, to garnish

Chinese pancakes, cucumber matchsticks and spring onions (scallions), to serve

1 Place the duck on a rack set over a roasting tin (pan) and pour 1.2 litres/2 pints/5 cups of the boiling water over it.

2 Remove the duck and rack and discard the water. Pat dry with absorbent kitchen paper (paper towels), replace the duck and the rack and set aside for several hours.

3 In a small bowl, mix together the clear honey, remaining boiling water and dark soy sauce, until they are thoroughly combined.

4 Brush the mixture over the skin and inside the duck. Reserve the remaining glaze. Set the duck aside for 1 hour, until the glaze has dried.

5 Coat the duck with another layer of glaze. Let dry and repeat until all of the glaze is used.

6 Heat the sesame oil in a saucepan and add the hoisin sauce, caster (superfine) sugar and water. Simmer for 2–3 minutes, until thickened. Leave to cool and then refrigerate until required.

7 Cook the duck in a preheated oven, at 190°C/375°F/Gas Mark 5, for 30 minutes. Turn the duck over and cook for 20 minutes. Turn the duck again and cook for 20–30 minutes, or until cooked through and the skin is crisp.

8 Remove the duck from the oven and set aside for 10 minutes.

9 Meanwhile, heat the pancakes in a steamer for 5–7 minutes or according to the instructions on the packet. Cut the skin and duck meat into strips, garnish with the carrot strips and serve with the pancakes, sauce, cucumber and spring onions (scallions).

Szechuan Chilli Chicken

In China, the chicken pieces are chopped through the bone for this dish, but if you do not possess a cleaver, use filleted chicken meat.

NUTRITIONAL INFORMATION

Calories	.218	Sugars	.4g
Protein	.23g	Fat	.9g
Carbohydrate	..8g	Saturates	.2g

 4 HOURS   15 MINS

SERVES 4

INGREDIENTS

500 g/1 lb 2 oz chicken thighs

¼ tsp pepper

1 tbsp sugar

2 tsp light soy sauce

1 tsp dark soy sauce

1 tbsp rice wine or dry sherry

2 tsp cornflour (cornstarch)

2-3 tbsp vegetable oil

1-2 garlic cloves, crushed

2 spring onions (scallions), cut into
    short sections, with the green
    and white parts separated

4-6 small dried red chillies, soaked and
    seeded

2 tbsp crushed yellow bean sauce

about 150 ml/¼ pint/⅔ cup Chinese Stock
    (see page 30) or water

1 Cut or chop the chicken thighs into bite-sized pieces and marinate with the pepper, sugar, soy sauce, wine and cornflour (cornstarch) for 25-30 minutes.

2 Heat the oil in a pre-heated wok and stir-fry the chicken for about 1-2 minutes until lightly brown. Remove with a slotted spoon, transfer to a warm dish and reserve. Add the garlic, the white parts of the spring onions (scallions), the chillies and yellow bean sauce to the wok and stir-fry for about 30 seconds.

3 Return the chicken to the wok, stirring constantly for about 1-2 minutes, then add the stock or water, bring to the boil and cover. Braise over a medium heat for 5-6 minutes, stirring once or twice. Garnish with the green parts of the spring onions (scallions) and serve immediately.

COOK'S TIP

One of the striking features of Szechuan cooking is the quantity of chillies used. Food generally in this region is much hotter than elsewhere in China – people tend to keep a string of dry chillies hanging from the eaves of their houses.

Chicken with Mushrooms

Dried Chinese mushrooms (Shiitake) should be used for this dish – otherwise use black rather than white fresh mushrooms.

NUTRITIONAL INFORMATION

Calories ....125 Sugars 0.3g
Protein ....20g Fat 3g
Carbohydrates ....3g Saturates 1g

1¼ HOURS   20 MINS

SERVES 4

INGREDIENTS

300-350 g/10½-12 oz chicken, boned and skinned

½ tsp sugar

1 tbsp light soy sauce

1 tsp rice wine or dry sherry

2 tsp cornflour (cornstarch)

4-6 dried Chinese mushrooms, soaked in warm water

1 tbsp finely shredded ginger root

salt and pepper

a few drops of sesame oil

coriander (cilantro) leaves, to garnish

1 Using a sharp knife or meat cleaver, cut the chicken into small bite-sized pieces and place in a bowl.

2 Add the sugar, light soy sauce, wine or sherry and cornflour (cornstarch) to the chicken, toss to coat and leave to marinate for 25-30 minutes.

3 Drain the mushrooms and dry on absorbent kitchen paper (paper towels). Slice the mushrooms into thin shreds, discarding any hard pieces of stem.

4 Place the chicken pieces on a heat-proof dish that will fit inside a bamboo steamer. Arrange the mushroom slices and ginger shreds on top of the chicken and sprinkle with salt, pepper and sesame oil.

5 Place the dish on the rack inside a hot steamer or on a rack in a wok filled with hot water and steam over a high heat for 20 minutes.

6 Serve hot, garnished with coriander (cilantro) leaves.

COOK'S TIP

Do not throw away the soaking water from the dried Chinese mushrooms. It is very useful, as it can be added to soups and stocks to give extra flavour.

Chicken with Vegetables

Coconut adds a creamy texture and delicious flavour to this stir-fry, which is spiked with green chilli.

NUTRITIONAL INFORMATION

Calories	330	Sugars	.........4g
Protein	........23g	Fat	..........24g
Carbohydrate	....6g	Saturates	......10g

10 MINS   10 MINS

SERVES 4

INGREDIENTS

3 tbsp sesame oil

350 g/12 oz chicken breast, sliced thinly

8 shallots, sliced

2 garlic cloves, finely chopped

2.5 cm/1 inch piece fresh root ginger, grated

1 green chilli, finely chopped

1 each red and green (bell) pepper, sliced thinly

3 courgettes (zucchini), thinly sliced

2 tbsp ground almonds

1 tsp ground cinnamon

1 tbsp oyster sauce

50 g/1¾ oz/¼ cup creamed coconut, grated

salt and pepper

1 Heat the sesame oil in a preheated wok or large frying pan (skillet).

2 Add the chicken slices to the wok or frying pan (skillet), season with salt and pepper and stir fry for about 4 minutes.

3 Add the shallots, garlic, ginger and chilli and stir-fry for 2 minutes.

4 Add the red and green (bell) peppers and courgettes (zucchini) and cook for about 1 minute.

5 Finally, add the ground almonds, cinnamon, oyster sauce and coconut. Stir fry for 1 minute.

6 Transfer to a warm serving dish and serve immediately.

VARIATION

You can vary the vegetables in this dish according to seasonal availability or whatever you have at hand. Try broccoli florets or baby sweetcorn cobs.

Duck In Spicy Sauce

Chinese five-spice powder gives a lovely flavour to this sliced duck, and the chilli adds a little subtle heat.

NUTRITIONAL INFORMATION

Calories	162	Sugars	.........2g
Protein	........20g	Fat	..........7g
Carbohydrate	....3g	Saturates	.......2g

5 MINS   25 MINS

SERVES 4

INGREDIENTS

1 tbsp vegetable oil

1 tsp grated fresh root ginger

1 garlic clove, crushed

1 fresh red chilli, chopped

350 g/12 oz skinless, boneless duck meat, cut into strips

125 g/4½ oz cauliflower, cut into florets

60 g/2 oz mangetout (snow peas)

60 g/2 oz baby corn cobs, halved lengthways

300 ml/½ pint/1¼ cups chicken stock

1 tsp Chinese five-spice powder

2 tsp Chinese rice wine or dry sherry

1 tsp cornflour (cornstarch)

2 tsp water

1 tsp sesame oil

1 Heat the oil in a wok. Lower the heat slightly, add the ginger, garlic, chilli and duck and stir-fry for 2–3 minutes. Remove from the wok and set aside.

2 Add the vegetables to the wok and stir-fry for 2–3 minutes. Pour off any excess oil from the wok and push the vegetables to one side.

3 Return the duck to the wok and pour in the stock. Sprinkle the Chinese five-spice powder over the top, stir in the wine or sherry and cook over a low heat for 15 minutes, or until the duck is tender.

4 Blend the cornflour (cornstarch) with the water to form a paste and stir into the wok with the sesame oil. Bring to the boil, stirring until the sauce has thickened and cleared. Transfer the duck and spicy sauce to a warm serving dish and serve immediately.

COOK'S TIP

Omit the chilli for a milder dish, or deseed the chilli before adding it to remove some of the heat.

Cumin-spiced Chicken

Cumin seeds are more frequently associated with Indian cooking, but they are used in this Chinese recipe for their earthy flavour.

NUTRITIONAL INFORMATION

Calories	245	Sugars	.........9g
Protein	........28g	Fat	..........10g
Carbohydrate	....11g	Saturates	.......2g

5 MINS   15 MINS

SERVES 4

INGREDIENTS

450 g/1 lb boneless, skinless chicken breasts

2 tbsp sunflower oil

1 clove garlic, crushed

1 tbsp cumin seeds

1 tbsp grated fresh ginger root

1 red chilli, deseeded and sliced

1 red (bell) pepper, deseeded and sliced

1 green (bell) pepper, deseeded and sliced

1 yellow (bell) pepper, deseeded and sliced

100 g/3½ oz/1 cup bean sprouts

350 g/12 oz pak choi or other green leaves

2 tbsp sweet chilli sauce

3 tbsp light soy sauce

deep-fried crispy ginger, to garnish (see Cook's Tip)

COOK'S TIP

To make the deep-fried ginger garnish, peel and thinly slice a large piece of root ginger. Carefully lower the slices of ginger into a wok or small pan of hot oil and cook for about 30 seconds. Transfer to kitchen paper and leave to drain thoroughly.

1 Using a sharp knife, slice the chicken breasts into thin strips.

2 Heat the oil in a large preheated wok.

3 Add the chicken to the wok and stir-fry for 5 minutes.

4 Add the garlic, cumin seeds, ginger and chilli to the wok, stirring to mix.

5 Add all the (bell) peppers to the wok and stir-fry for a further 5 minutes.

6 Toss in the bean sprouts and pak choi together with the sweet chilli sauce and soy sauce and continue to cook until the pak choi leaves start to wilt.

7 Transfer to warm serving bowls and garnish with deep-fried ginger (see Cook's Tip).

Spicy Peanut Chicken

This quick dish has many variations, but this version includes the classic combination of peanuts, chicken and chillies.

NUTRITIONAL INFORMATION

Calories	342	Sugars	.........3g
Protein	........25g	Fat	..........24g
Carbohydrate	....6g	Saturates	.......5g

5 MINS   10 MINS

SERVES 4

I N G R E D I E N T S

300 g/10½ oz skinless, boneless
   chicken breast

2 tbsp peanut oil

125 g/4½ oz/1 cup shelled peanuts

1 fresh red chilli, sliced

1 green (bell) pepper, seeded and
   cut into strips

fried rice, to serve

S A U C E

150 ml/¼ pint/⅔ cup chicken stock

1 tbsp Chinese rice wine or
   dry sherry

1 tbsp light soy sauce

1½ tsp light brown sugar

2 garlic cloves, crushed

1 tsp grated fresh root ginger

1 tsp rice wine vinegar

1 tsp sesame oil

1 Trim any fat from the chicken and cut the meat into 2.5-cm/1-inch cubes. Set aside until required.

2 Heat the peanut oil in a preheated wok or frying pan (skillet).

3 Add the peanuts to the wok and stir-fry for 1 minute. Remove the peanuts with a slotted spoon and set aside.

4 Add the chicken to the wok and cook for 1–2 minutes.

5 Stir in the chilli and green (bell) pepper and cook for 1 minute. Remove from the wok with a slotted spoon and set aside.

6 Put half of the peanuts in a food processor and process until almost smooth. If necessary, add a little stock to form a softer paste. Alternatively, place them in a plastic bag and crush them with a rolling pin.

7 To make the sauce, add the chicken stock, Chinese rice wine or dry sherry, light soy sauce, light brown sugar, crushed garlic cloves, grated fresh root ginger and rice wine vinegar to the wok.

8 Heat the sauce without boiling and stir in the peanut purée, remaining peanuts, chicken, sliced red chilli and green (bell) pepper strips. Mix well until all the ingredients are thoroughly combined.

9 Sprinkle the sesame oil into the wok, stir and cook for 1 minute. Transfer the spicy peanut chicken to a warm serving dish and serve hot with fried rice.

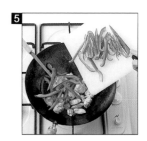

Duck with Leek & Cabbage

Duck is a strongly-flavoured meat which benefits from the added citrus peel to counteract this rich taste.

NUTRITIONAL INFORMATION

Calories . . . . . . .192 Sugars 5g
Protein . . . . .26g Fat 7g
Carbohydrate . . . .6g Saturates 2g

10 MINS   40 MINS

SERVES 4

I N G R E D I E N T S

4 duck breasts

350 g/12 oz green cabbage, thinly shredded

225 g/8 oz leeks, sliced

finely grated zest of 1 orange

6 tbsp oyster sauce

1 tsp toasted sesame seeds, to serve

1 Heat a large wok and dry-fry the duck breasts, with the skin on, for about 5 minutes on each side (you may need to do this in 2 batches).

2 Remove the duck breasts from the wok and transfer to a clean board.

3 Using a sharp knife, cut the duck breasts into thin slices.

4 Remove all but 1 tablespoon of the fat from the duck left in the wok; discard the rest.

5 Using a sharp knife, thinly shred the green cabbage.

6 Add the leeks, green cabbage and orange zest to the wok and stir-fry for about 5 minutes, or until the vegetables have softened.

7 Return the duck to the wok and heat through for 2–3 minutes.

8 Drizzle the oyster sauce over the mixture in the wok, toss well until all the ingredients are combined and then heat through.

9 Scatter the stir-fry with toasted sesame seeds, transfer to a warm serving dish and serve hot.

VARIATION

Use Chinese leaves (cabbage) for a lighter, sweeter flavour instead of the green cabbage, if you prefer.

Peppered Chicken

Crushed mixed peppercorns coat tender, thin strips of chicken which are cooked with green and red (bell) peppers for a really colourful dish.

NUTRITIONAL INFORMATION

Calories 219	Sugars 6g
Protein 22g	Fat 10g
Carbohydrate 11g	Saturates 2g

5 MINS   15 MINS

SERVES 4

INGREDIENTS

2 tbsp tomato ketchup

2 tbsp soy sauce

450 g/1 lb boneless, skinless chicken breasts

2 tbsp crushed mixed peppercorns

2 tbsp sunflower oil

1 red (bell) pepper

1 green (bell) pepper

175 g/6 oz/2½ cups sugar snap peas

2 tbsp oyster sauce

1 Mix the tomato ketchup with the soy sauce in a bowl.

2 Using a sharp knife, slice the chicken into thin strips.

3 Toss the chicken in the tomato ketchup and soy sauce mixture until the chicken is well coated.

4 Sprinkle the crushed peppercorns on to a plate. Dip the coated chicken in the peppercorns until evenly coated.

5 Heat the sunflower oil in a preheated wok or large frying pan (skillet), until the oil is smoking.

6 Add the chicken to the wok and stir-fry for 5 minutes.

7 Using a sharp knife, deseed and slice the (bell) peppers.

8 Add the (bell) peppers to the wok together with the sugar snap peas and stir-fry for a further 5 minutes.

9 Add the oyster sauce and allow to bubble for 2 minutes. Transfer the peppered chicken to serving bowls and serve immediately.

VARIATION

Use mangetout (snow peas) instead of the sugar snap peas, if you prefer.

Turkey with Cranberry Glaze

Traditional Christmas ingredients are given a Chinese twist in this stir-fry which containing cranberries, ginger, chestnuts and soy sauce!

NUTRITIONAL INFORMATION

Calories 167	Sugars 11g	
Protein 8g	Fat 7g	
Carbohydrate ...20g	Saturates 1g	

  5 MINS   15 MINS

SERVES 4

I N G R E D I E N T S

1 turkey breast

2 tbsp sunflower oil

15 g/½oz/2 tbsp stem ginger

50 g/1¾ oz/½ cup fresh or frozen cranberries

100 g/3½ oz/¼ cup canned chestnuts

4 tbsp cranberry sauce

3 tbsp light soy sauce

salt and pepper

1 Remove any skin from the turkey breast. Using a sharp knife, thinly slice the turkey breast.

2 Heat the sunflower oil in a large preheated wok or heavy-based frying pan (skillet).

3 Add the turkey to the wok and stir-fry for 5 minutes, or until cooked through.

4 Using a sharp knife, finely chop the stem ginger.

5 Add the ginger and the cranberries to the wok or frying pan (skillet) and stir-fry for 2–3 minutes or until the cranberries have softened.

6 Add the chestnuts, cranberry sauce and soy sauce, season to taste with salt and pepper and allow to bubble for 2–3 minutes.

7 Transfer the turkey stir-fry to warm serving dishes and serve immediately.

COOK'S TIP

It is very important that the wok is very hot before you stir-fry. Test by by holding your hand flat about 7.5 cm/3 inches above the base of the interior – you should be able to feel the heat radiating from it.

Chicken & Corn Sauté

This quick and healthy dish is stir-fried, which means you need use only the minimum of fat.

NUTRITIONAL INFORMATION

Calories	280	Sugars	.........7g
Protein	........31g	Fat	...........11g
Carbohydrate	....9g	Saturates	.......2g

 5 MINS   10 MINS

SERVES 4

INGREDIENTS

4 skinless, boneless chicken breasts

250 g/9 oz/1⅓ cups baby sweetcorn (corn-on-the-cob)

250 g/9 oz mangetout (snow peas)

2 tbsp sunflower oil

1 tbsp sherry vinegar

1 tbsp honey

1 tbsp light soy sauce

1 tbsp sunflower seeds

pepper

rice or Chinese egg noodles, to serve

1 Using a sharp knife, slice the chicken breasts into long, thin strips.

2 Cut the baby sweetcorn in half lengthways and top and tail the mangetout (snow peas).

3 Heat the sunflower oil in a preheated wok or a wide frying pan (skillet).

4 Add the chicken and fry over a fairly high heat, stirring, for 1 minute.

5 Add the baby sweetcorn and mangetout (snow peas) and stir-fry over a moderate heat for 5–8 minutes, until evenly cooked. The vegetables should still be slightly crunchy.

6 Mix together the sherry vinegar, honey and soy sauce in a small bowl.

7 Stir the vinegar mixture into the pan with the sunflower seeds.

8 Season well with pepper. Cook, stirring, for 1 minute.

9 Serve the chicken & corn sauté hot with rice or Chinese egg noodles.

VARIATION

Rice vinegar or balsamic vinegar makes a good substitute for the sherry vinegar.

Duck with Lime & Kiwi Fruit

Tender breasts of duck served in thin slices, with a sweet but very tangy lime and wine sauce, full of pieces of kiwi fruit.

NUTRITIONAL INFORMATION

Calories	264	Sugars	.......20g
Protein	........20g	Fat	..........10g
Carbohydrate	...21g	Saturates	.......2g

1¼ HOURS   15 MINS

SERVES 4

INGREDIENTS

4 boneless or part-boned
   duck breasts

grated rind and juice of 2 large limes

2 tbsp sunflower oil

4 spring onions (scallions), thinly
   sliced diagonally

125 g/4½ oz carrots, cut into
   matchsticks

6 tbsp dry white wine

60 g/2 oz/¼ cup white sugar

2 kiwi fruit, peeled, halved and sliced

salt and pepper

parsley sprigs and lime halves in knots
   (see Cook's Tip), to garnish

COOK'S TIP

To make the garnish, trim a piece off the base of each lime half so they stand upright. Pare off a thin strip of rind from the top of the lime halves, about 5 mm/¼ inch thick, but do not detach it. Tie the strip into a knot with the end bending over the cut surface of the lime.

1 Trim any fat from the duck, then prick the skin all over with a fork and lay in a shallow dish. Add half the grated lime and half the juice to the duck breasts, rubbing in thoroughly. Leave to stand in a cool place for at least 1 hour, turning the breasts at least once.

2 Drain the duck breasts, reserving the marinade. Heat 1 tbsp of oil in a wok. Add the duck and fry quickly to seal all over then lower the heat and continue to cook for about 5 minutes, turning several times until just cooked through and well browned all over. Remove and keep warm.

3 Wipe the wok clean with kitchen paper (paper towels) and heat the remaining oil. Add the spring onions (scallions) and carrots and stir-fry for 1 minute, then add the remaining lime marinade, wine and sugar. Bring to the boil and simmer for 2–3 minutes until slightly syrupy.

4 Add the duck breasts to the sauce, season and add the kiwi fruit. Stir-fry for a minute or until really hot and both the duck and kiwi fruit are well coated in the sauce.

5 Cut each duck breast into slices, leaving a 'hinge' at one end, open out into a fan shape and arrange on plates. Spoon the sauce over the duck, sprinkle with the remaining pieces of lime peel, garnish and serve.

Chicken with (Bell) Peppers

Red (bell) pepper or celery can also be used in this recipe, the method is the same.

 5 MINS 5 MINS

SERVES 4

INGREDIENTS

300 g/10½ oz boned, skinned chicken breast

1 tsp salt

½ egg white

2 tsp cornflour (cornstarch) paste (see page 31)

1 medium green (bell) pepper, cored and seeded

300 ml/½ pint/1¼ cups vegetable oil

1 spring onion (scallion), finely shredded

a few strips of ginger root, thinly shredded

1-2 red chillies, seeded and thinly shredded

½ tsp sugar

1 tbsp rice wine or dry sherry

a few drops of sesame oil

1 Cut the chicken breast into strips. Mix the chicken with a pinch of the salt, the egg white and cornflour (cornstarch).

2 Cut the green (bell) pepper into fairly thin shreds.

3 Heat the oil in a preheated wok, and deep-fry the chicken strips in batches for about 1 minute, or until the chicken changes colour. Remove the chicken strips with a slotted spoon, pat dry on kitchen paper (paper towels) and keep warm.

4 Pour off the excess oil from the wok, leaving about 1 tablespoon. Add the spring onion (scallion), ginger, chillies and green (bell) pepper and stir-fry for 1 minute.

5 Return the chicken to the wok with the remaining salt, the sugar and wine or sherry. Stir-fry for another minute, sprinkle with sesame oil and serve immediately.

COOK'S TIP

Rice wine is used everywhere in China for both cooking and drinking. Made from glutinous rice, it is known as 'yellow wine' because of its rich amber colour. Sherry is the best substitute as a cooking ingredient.

Duck with Broccoli & Peppers

This is a colourful dish using different coloured (bell) peppers and broccoli to make it both tasty and appealing to the eye.

NUTRITIONAL INFORMATION

Calories	261	Sugars	.........3g
Protein	........26g	Fat	..........13g
Carbohydrate	....11g	Saturates	.......2g

 35 MINS   🕐 15 MINS

SERVES 4

INGREDIENTS

1 egg white

2 tbsp cornflour (cornstarch)

450 g/1 lb skinless, boneless duck meat

vegetable oil, for deep-frying

1 red (bell) pepper, seeded and diced

1 yellow (bell) pepper, seeded and diced

125 g/4½ oz small broccoli florets

1 garlic clove, crushed

2 tbsp light soy sauce

2 tsp Chinese rice wine or dry sherry

1 tsp light brown sugar

125 ml/4 fl oz/½ cup chicken stock

2 tsp sesame seeds

1   In a mixing bowl, beat together the egg white and cornflour (cornstarch).

2   Using a sharp knife, cut the duck into 2.5-cm/1-inch cubes and stir into the egg white mixture. Leave to stand for 30 minutes.

3   Heat the oil for deep-frying in a preheated wok or heavy-based frying pan (skillet) until almost smoking.

4   Remove the duck from the egg white mixture, add to the wok and fry in the oil for 4–5 minutes, until crisp. Remove the duck from the oil with a slotted spoon and drain on kitchen paper (paper towels).

5   Add the (bell) peppers and broccoli to the wok and fry for 2–3 minutes. Remove with a slotted spoon and drain on kitchen paper (paper towels).

6   Pour all but 2 tablespoons of the oil from the wok and return to the heat. Add the garlic and stir-fry for 30 seconds.

Stir in the soy sauce, Chinese rice wine or sherry, sugar and chicken stock and bring to the boil.

7   Stir in the duck and reserved vegetables and cook for 1–2 minutes.

8   Carefully spoon the duck and vegetables on to a warmed serving dish and sprinkle with the sesame seeds. Serve immediately.

Honey & Soy Chicken

Clear honey is often added to Chinese recipes for sweetness. It combines well with the saltiness of the soy sauce.

NUTRITIONAL INFORMATION

Calories 279	Sugars 10g
Protein 38g	Fat 8g
Carbohydrate ...12g	Saturates 2g

35 MINS   25 MINS

SERVES 4

INGREDIENTS

2 tbsp clear honey

3 tbsp light soy sauce

1 tsp Chinese five-spice powder

1 tbsp sweet sherry

1 clove garlic, crushed

8 chicken thighs

1 tbsp sunflower oil

1 red chilli

100 g/3½ oz/1¼ cups baby corn cobs, halved

8 spring onions (scallions), sliced

150 g/5½ oz/1½ cups bean sprouts

1 Mix together the honey, soy sauce, Chinese five-spice powder, sherry and garlic in a large bowl.

2 Using a sharp knife, make 3 slashes in the skin of each chicken thigh. Brush the honey and soy marinade over the chicken thighs, cover and leave to stand for at least 30 minutes.

3 Heat the oil in a large preheated wok. Add the chicken and cook over a fairly high heat for 12–15 minutes, or until the chicken browns and the skin begins to crispen. Remove the chicken with a slotted spoon and keep warm until required.

4 Using a sharp knife, deseed and very finely chop the chilli.

5 Add the chilli, corn cobs, spring onions (scallions) and bean sprouts to the wok and stir-fry for 5 minutes.

6 Return the chicken to the wok and mix all of the ingredients together until completely heated through. Transfer to serving plates and serve immediately.

COOK'S TIP

Chinese five-spice powder is found in most large supermarkets and is a blend of star anise, fennel seeds, cloves, cinnamon bark and Szechuan pepper.

Roast Baby Chickens

Poussins are stuffed with lemon grass and lime leaves, coated with a spicy marinade, then roasted until crisp and golden.

NUTRITIONAL INFORMATION

Calories 183   Sugars 1g
Protein ....30g   Fat 7g
Carbohydrate ....1g   Saturates 2g

🍲 10 MINS   🕐 55 MINS

SERVES 4

I N G R E D I E N T S

4 small poussins, weighing about
 350-500 g/12 oz-1 lb 2 oz each

coriander (cilantro) leaves and lime
 wedges, to garnish

a mixture of wild rice and Basmati rice,
 to serve

M A R I N A D E

4 garlic cloves, peeled

2 fresh coriander roots

1 tbsp light soy sauce

salt and pepper

S T U F F I N G

4 blades lemon grass

4 kaffir lime leaves

4 slices ginger root

about 6 tbsp coconut milk, to brush

1 Wash the chickens and dry on kitchen paper (paper towels).

2 Place all the ingredients for the marinade in a small blender and purée until smooth. Alternatively, grind to a paste in a pestle and mortar. Season to taste with salt and pepper.

3 Rub this marinade mixture into the skin of the chickens, using the back of a spoon to spread it evenly over the skins.

4 Place a blade of lemon grass, a lime leaf and a piece of ginger in the cavity of each chicken.

5 Place the chickens in a roasting pan and brush lightly with the coconut milk. Roast for about 30 minutes in a preheated oven.

6 Remove from the oven, brush again with coconut milk, return to the oven and cook for a further 15-25 minutes, until golden and cooked through, depending upon the size of the chickens. The chickens are cooked when the juices from the thigh run clear and are not tinged at all with pink.

7 Serve the baby chickens with the pan juices poured over. Garnish with coriander (cilantro) leaves and lime wedges and serve with rice.

Duck With Mangoes

Use fresh mangoes in this recipe for a terrific flavour and colour. If they are unavailable, use canned mangoes and rinse them before using.

NUTRITIONAL INFORMATION

Calories 235   Sugars 6g
Protein ....23g   Fat 14g
Carbohydrate ....6g   Saturates 2g

 5 MINS   35 MINS

SERVES 4

INGREDIENTS

2 medium-size ripe mangoes

300 ml/½ pint/1¼ cups chicken stock

2 garlic cloves, crushed

1 tsp grated fresh root ginger

3 tbsp vegetable oil

2 large skinless duck breasts, about
    225 g/8 oz each

1 tsp wine vinegar

1 tsp light soy sauce

1 leek, sliced

freshly chopped parsley, to garnish

1 Peel the mangoes and cut the flesh from each side of the stones (pits). Cut the flesh into strips.

2 Put half of the mango pieces and the chicken stock in a food processor and process until smooth. Alternatively, press half of the mangoes through a fine sieve and mix with the stock.

3 Rub the garlic and ginger over the duck. Heat the vegetable oil in a preheated wok and cook the duck breasts, turning, until sealed. Reserve the oil in the wok and remove the duck.

4 Place the duck on a rack set over a roasting tin (pan) and cook in a preheated oven, at 220°C/425°F/Gas Mark 7, for 20 minutes, until the duck is cooked through.

5 Meanwhile, place the mango and stock mixture in a saucepan and add the wine vinegar and light soy sauce.

6 Bring the mixture in the saucepan to the boil and cook over a high heat, stirring, until reduced by half.

7 Heat the oil reserved in the wok and stir-fry the sliced leek and remaining mango for 1 minute. Remove from the wok, transfer to a serving dish and keep warm until required.

8 Slice the cooked duck breasts and arrange the slices on top of the leek and mango mixture. Pour the sauce over the duck slices, garnish and serve.

Chicken & Vegetables

This is a popular dish in Chinese restaurants in the West, although nothing beats making it yourself.

NUTRITIONAL INFORMATION

Calories 298	Sugars 4g
Protein 22g	Fat 19g
Carbohydrate 11g	Saturates 4g

🥗 30 MINS   🕐 15 MINS

SERVES 4

I N G R E D I E N T S

300 g/10½ oz boneless, skinless chicken breasts

1 tbsp cornflour (cornstarch)

1 tsp sesame oil

1 tbsp hoisin sauce

1 tsp light soy sauce

3 garlic cloves, crushed

2 tbsp vegetable oil

75 g/2¾ oz/¾ cup unsalted cashew nuts

25 g/1 oz mangetout (snow peas)

1 celery stick, sliced

1 onion, cut into 8 pieces

60 g/2 oz bean sprouts

1 red (bell) pepper, seeded and diced

S A U C E

2 tsp cornflour (cornstarch)

2 tbsp hoisin sauce

200 ml/7 fl oz/⅞ cup chicken stock

1 Trim any fat from the chicken breasts and cut the meat into thin strips. Place the chicken in a mixing bowl. Sprinkle with the cornflour (cornstarch) and toss to coat the chicken, shaking off any excess. Mix together the sesame oil, hoisin sauce, soy sauce and 1 garlic clove. Pour this mixture over the chicken, turning to coat. Leave to marinate for 20 minutes.

2 Heat half of the vegetable oil in a preheated wok. Add the cashew nuts and stir-fry for 1 minute, until browned.

3 Add the mangetout (snow peas), celery, the remaining garlic, the onion, bean sprouts and red (bell) pepper and cook, stirring occasionally, for 2–3 minutes. Remove the vegetables from the wok with a slotted spoon, set aside and keep warm.

4 Heat the remaining oil in the wok. Remove the chicken from the marinade and stir-fry for 3–4 minutes. Return the vegetables to the wok.

5 To make the sauce, mix the cornflour (cornstarch), hoisin sauce and chicken stock together and pour into the wok. Bring to the boil, stirring until thickened and clear. Tranfer the stir-fry to a warm serving dish and serve.

Peanut Sesame Chicken

Sesame seeds and peanuts give extra crunch and flavour to this stir-fry and the fruit juice glaze gives a lovely shiny coating to the sauce.

NUTRITIONAL INFORMATION

Calories ....435 Sugars 10g
Protein ....38g Fat 26g
Carbohydrate ...14g Saturates 4g

10 MINS · 15 MINS

SERVES 4

INGREDIENTS

2 tbsp vegetable oil

2 tbsp sesame oil

500 g/1 lb 2 oz boneless, skinned chicken breasts, sliced into strips

250 g/9 oz broccoli, divided into small florets

250 g/9 oz baby or dwarf corn, halved if large

1 small red (bell) pepper, cored, seeded and sliced

2 tbsp soy sauce

250 ml/9 fl oz/1 cup orange juice

2 tsp cornflour (cornstarch)

2 tbsp toasted sesame seeds

60 g/2 oz/⅓ cup roasted, shelled, unsalted peanuts

rice or noodles, to serve

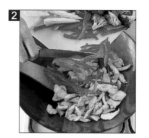

1 Heat the vegetable oil and sesame oil in a large, heavy-based frying pan (skillet) or wok until smoking. Add the chicken strips and stir-fry until browned, about 4-5 minutes.

2 Add the broccoli, corn and red (bell) pepper and stir-fry for a further 1-2 minutes.

3 Meanwhile, mix the soy sauce with the orange juice and cornflour (cornstarch). Stir into the chicken and vegetable mixture, stirring constantly until the sauce has slightly thickened and a glaze develops.

4 Stir in the sesame seeds and peanuts, mixing well. Heat the stir-fry for a further 3-4 minutes.

5 Transfer the stir-fry to a warm serving dish and serve with rice or noodles.

COOK'S TIP

Make sure you use the unsalted variety of peanuts or the dish will be too salty, as the soy sauce adds saltiness.

Chicken Fu-Yung

Although commonly described as an omelette, a foo-yung ('white lotus petals') should use egg whites only to create a very delicate texture.

NUTRITIONAL INFORMATION

Calories 220   Sugars 1g
Protein . . . . .16g   Fat 14g
Carbohydrate . . . .7g   Saturates 3g

 5 MINS   5 MINS

SERVES 4

I N G R E D I E N T S

175 g/6 oz chicken breast fillet, skinned

½ tsp salt

pepper

1 tsp rice wine or dry sherry

1 tbsp cornflour (cornstarch)

3 eggs

½ tsp finely chopped spring onions
    (scallions)

3 tbsp vegetable oil

125 g/4½ oz green peas

1 tsp light soy sauce

salt

few drops of sesame oil

1 Cut the chicken across the grain into very small, paper-thin slices, using a cleaver. Place the chicken slices in a shallow dish.

2 In a small bowl, mix together ½ teaspoon salt, pepper, rice wine or dry sherry and cornflour (cornstarch).

3 Pour the mixture over the chicken slices in the dish, turning the chicken until well coated.

4 Beat the eggs in a small bowl with a pinch of salt and the spring onions (scallions).

5 Heat the vegetable oil in a preheated wok, add the chicken slices and stir-fry for about 1 minute, making sure that the slices are kept separated.

6 Pour the beaten eggs over the chicken, and lightly scramble until set. Do not stir too vigorously, or the mixture will break up in the oil. Stir the oil from the bottom of the wok so that the foo-yung rises to the surface.

7 Add the peas, light soy sauce and salt to taste and blend well. Transfer to warm serving dishes, sprinkle with sesame oil and serve.

COOK'S TIP

If available, chicken *goujons* can be used for this dish: these are small, delicate strips of chicken which require no further cutting and are very tender.

Coconut Chicken Curry

Okra or ladies fingers are slightly bitter in flavour. The pineapple and coconut in this recipe offsets them in both colour and flavour.

NUTRITIONAL INFORMATION

Calories . . . . . . .456 Sugars 21g
Protein . . . . .29g Fat 29g
Carbohydrate . . .22g Saturates 17g

 5 MINS   45 MINS

SERVES 4

I N G R E D I E N T S

2 tbsp sunflower oil

450 g/1 lb boneless, skinless chicken thighs or breasts

150 g/5½ oz/1 cup okra

1 large onion, sliced

2 cloves garlic, crushed

3 tbsp mild curry paste

300 ml/½ pint/2¼ cups chicken stock

1 tbsp fresh lemon juice

100 g/3½ oz/½ cup creamed coconut, coarsely grated

175 g/6 oz/1¼ cups fresh or canned pineapple, cubed

150 ml/¼ pint/⅔ cup thick, natural (unsweetened) yogurt

2 tbsp chopped fresh coriander (cilantro)

freshly boiled rice, to serve

TO GARNISH

lemon wedges

fresh coriander (cilantro) sprigs

1 Heat the oil in a wok. Cut the chicken into bite-sized pieces, add to the wok and stir-fry until evenly browned.

2 Using a sharp knife, trim the okra. Add the onion, garlic and okra to the wok and cook for a further 2–3 minutes, stirring constantly.

3 Mix the curry paste with the chicken stock and lemon juice and pour into the wok. Bring to the boil, cover and leave to simmer for 30 minutes.

4 Stir the grated coconut into the curry and cook for about 5 minutes.

5 Add the pineapple, yogurt and coriander (cilantro) and cook for 2 minutes, stirring. Garnish and serve.

COOK'S TIP

Score around the top of the okra with a knife before cooking to release the sticky glue-like substance which is bitter in taste.

Crispy Chicken

In this recipe, the chicken is brushed with a syrup and deep-fried until golden. It is a little time consuming, but well worth the effort.

NUTRITIONAL INFORMATION

Calories	283	Sugars	.........8g
Protein	........29g	Fat	..........15g
Carbohydrate	....8g	Saturates	.......3g

15 HOURS   35 MINS

SERVES 4

INGREDIENTS

1.5 kg/3 lb 5 oz oven-ready chicken

2 tbsp clear honey

2 tsp Chinese five-spice powder

2 tbsp rice wine vinegar

850 ml/1½ pints/3¾ cups vegetable oil,
   for deep-frying

chilli sauce, to serve

1 Rinse the chicken inside and out under cold running water and pat dry with kitchen paper (paper towels).

2 Bring a large saucepan of water to the boil and remove from the heat. Place the chicken in the water, cover and set aside for 20 minutes.

3 Remove the chicken from the water and pat dry with absorbent kitchen

paper (paper towels). Cool and leave to chill in the refrigerator overnight.

4 To make the glaze, mix the honey, Chinese five-spice powder and rice wine vinegar.

5 Brush some of the glaze all over the chicken and return to the refrigerator for 20 minutes.

6 Repeat this process of glazing and refrigerating the chicken until all of the glaze has been used up. Return the chicken to the refrigerator for at least 2 hours after the final coating.

7 Using a cleaver or heavy kitchen knife, open the chicken out by splitting it through the centre through the breast and then cut each half into 4 pieces.

8 Heat the oil for deep-frying in a wok until almost smoking. Reduce the heat and fry each piece of chicken for 5–7 minutes, until golden and cooked through. Remove from the oil with a slotted spoon and drain on absorbent kitchen paper (paper towels).

9 Transfer to a serving dish and serve hot with a little chilli sauce.

COOK'S TIP

If it is easier, use chicken portions instead of a whole chicken. You could also use chicken legs for this recipe, if you prefer.

Duck with Pineapple

For best results, use ready-cooked duck meat, widely available from Chinese restaurants and takeaways.

NUTRITIONAL INFORMATION

Calories ....187 Sugars 7g
Protein ....10g Fat 12g
Carbohydrate ....11g Saturates 2g

 25 MINS   10 MINS

SERVES 4

INGREDIENTS

125-175 g/4½-6 oz cooked duck meat

3 tbsp vegetable oil

1 small onion, thinly shredded

2-3 slices ginger root, thinly shredded

1 spring onion (scallion), thinly shredded

1 small carrot, thinly shredded

125 g/4½ oz canned pineapple, cut into
  small slices

½ tsp salt

1 tbsp red rice vinegar

2 tbsp syrup from the pineapple

1 tbsp cornflour (cornstarch) paste (see
  page 31)

black bean sauce, to serve (optional)

1 Using a sharp knife or metal cleaver, cut the cooked duck meat into thin even-sized strips and set aside until required.

2 Heat the oil in a preheated wok or large heavy-based frying pan (skillet).

3 Add the shredded onion and stir-fry until the shreds are opaque.

4 Add the slices of ginger root, spring onion (scallion) shreds and carrot shreds to the wok and stir-fry for about 1 minute.

5 Add the duck shreds and pineapple to the wok together with the salt, rice vinegar and the pineapple syrup. Stir until the mixture is well blended.

6 Add the cornflour (cornstarch) paste and stir for 1-2 minutes until the sauce has thickened.

7 Transfer to a serving dish and serve with black bean sauce, if desired.

COOK'S TIP

Red rice vinegar is made from fermented rice. It has a distinctive dark colour and depth of flavour. If unavailable, use red wine vinegar, which is similar in flavour.

Red Chicken with Tomatoes

This is a really colourful dish, the red of the tomatoes perfectly complementing the orange sweet potato.

NUTRITIONAL INFORMATION

Calories	316	Sugars	.........5g
Protein	........28g	Fat	..........19g
Carbohydrate	....8g	Saturates	.......3g

 5 MINS 35 MINS

SERVES 4

I N G R E D I E N T S

1 tbsp sunflower oil

450 g/1 lb boneless, skinless chicken

2 cloves garlic, crushed

2 tbsp red curry paste

2 tbsp fresh grated galangal or
    root ginger

1 tbsp tamarind paste

4 lime leaves

225 g/8 oz sweet potato

600 ml/1 pint/2½ cups coconut milk

225 g/8 oz cherry tomatoes, halved

3 tbsp chopped fresh coriander (cilantro)

cooked jasmine or fragrant rice,
    to serve

1 Heat the sunflower oil in a large preheated wok or heavy-based frying pan (skillet).

COOK'S TIP

Fresh root galangal is a spice very similar to ginger but not as pungent. It can be bought fresh from Oriental food stores but is also available dried and as a powder. The fresh root needs to be peeled before slicing to use.

2 Using a sharp knife, thinly slice the chicken. Add the chicken to the wok or frying pan (skillet) and stir-fry for 5 minutes until lightly browned.

3 Add the garlic, curry paste, galangal or root ginger, tamarind paste and lime leaves to the wok and stir-fry for 1 minute.

4 Using a sharp knife, peel and dice the sweet potato.

5 Add the coconut milk and sweet potato to the mixture in the wok and bring to the boil. Allow to bubble over a medium heat for 20 minutes, or until the juices start to thicken and reduce.

6 Add the cherry tomatoes and coriander (cilantro) to the curry and cook for a further 5 minutes, stirring occasionally. Transfer to serving plates and serve hot with cooked jasmine or fragrant rice.

Chilli Chicken

This is quite a hot dish, using fresh chillies. If you prefer a milder dish, halve the number of chillies used.

NUTRITIONAL INFORMATION

Calories 265   Sugars 3g
Protein . . . . .21g   Fat 14g
Carbohydrate . . . .11g   Saturates 2g

10 MINS   10 MINS

SERVES 4

I N G R E D I E N T S

350 g/12 oz skinless, boneless
   lean chicken

½ tsp salt

1 egg white, lightly beaten

2 tbsp cornflour (cornstarch)

4 tbsp vegetable oil

2 garlic cloves, crushed

1-cm/½-inch piece fresh root ginger,
   grated

1 red (bell) pepper, seeded and diced

1 green (bell) pepper, seeded and diced

2 fresh red chillies, chopped

2 tbsp light soy sauce

1 tbsp dry sherry or Chinese rice wine

1 tbsp wine vinegar

1 Cut the chicken into cubes and place in a mixing bowl.

2 Mix together the salt, egg white, cornflour (cornstarch) and 1 tablespoon of the oil and pour over the chicken. Turn the chicken in the mixture to coat thoroughly.

3 Heat the remaining oil in a preheated wok or large frying pan (skillet).

4 Add the garlic and ginger and stir-fry for 30 seconds.

5 Add the chicken pieces to the wok and stir-fry for 2–3 minutes, or until browned.

6 Stir in the red and green (bell) peppers, chillies, soy sauce, sherry or Chinese rice wine and wine vinegar and cook for a further 2–3 minutes, until the chicken is cooked through. Transfer the chilli chicken to a warm serving dish and serve immediately.

COOK'S TIP

When preparing chillies, wear rubber gloves to prevent the juices from burning and irritating your hands. Be careful not to touch your face, especially your lips or eyes, until you have washed your hands.

Lemon & Sesame Chicken

Sesame seeds have a strong flavour which adds nuttiness to recipes. They are perfect for coating these thin chicken strips.

NUTRITIONAL INFORMATION

Calories .... .273	Sugars 5g
Protein 29g	Fat .... .13g
Carbohydrate 11g	Saturates 3g

10 MINS   10 MINS

SERVES 4

INGREDIENTS

4 boneless, skinless chicken breasts

1 egg white

25 g/1 oz/2 tbsp sesame seeds

2 tbsp vegetable oil

1 onion, sliced

1 tbsp demerara (brown crystal) sugar

finely grated zest and juice of 1 lemon

3 tbsp lemon curd

200 g/7 oz can water chestnuts, drained

lemon zest, to garnish

COOK'S TIP

Water chestnuts are commonly added to Chinese recipes for their crunchy texture as they do not have a great deal of flavour.

1 Place the chicken breasts between 2 sheets of cling film (plastic wrap) and pound with a rolling pin to flatten. Slice the chicken into thin strips.

2 Whisk the egg white until light and foamy. Dip the chicken strips into the egg white, then coat in the sesame seeds.

3 Heat the oil in a wok and stir-fry the onion for 2 minutes until softened.

4 Add the chicken to the wok and stir-fry for 5 minutes, or until the chicken turns golden.

5 Mix the sugar, lemon zest, lemon juice and lemon curd and add to the wok. Allow it to bubble slightly.

6 Slice the water chestnuts thinly, add to the wok and cook for 2 minutes. Garnish with lemon zest and serve hot.

Honey-glazed Duck

The honey and soy glaze gives a wonderful sheen and flavour to the duck skin. Such a simple recipe, yet the result is unutterably delicious.

NUTRITIONAL INFORMATION

Calories 176	Sugars 8g	
Protein 22g	Fat 5g	
Carbohydrate ...10g	Saturates 1g	

2¼ HOURS 30 MINS

SERVES 4

INGREDIENTS

1 tsp dark soy sauce

2 tbsp clear honey

1 tsp garlic vinegar

2 garlic cloves, crushed

1 tsp ground star anise

2 tsp cornflour (cornstarch)

2 tsp water

2 large boneless duck breasts, about
    225g/8 oz each

celery leaves, cucumber wedges and
    snipped chives, to garnish

1 Mix together the soy sauce, honey, garlic vinegar, garlic and star anise.

2 Blend the cornflour (cornstarch) with the water to form a smooth paste and stir it into the soy sauce mixture.

3 Place the duck breasts in a shallow ovenproof dish. Brush with the soy marinade, turning to coat them completely. Cover and leave to marinate in the refrigerator for at least 2 hours, or overnight if possible.

4 Remove the duck from the marinade and cook in a preheated oven, at 220°C/425°F/Gas Mark 7, for 20–25 minutes, basting frequently with the glaze.

5 Remove the duck from the oven and transfer to a preheated grill (broiler). Grill (broil) for about 3–4 minutes to caramelize the top.

6 Remove the duck from the grill (broiler) pan and cut into thin slices. Arrange the duck slices in a warm serving dish, garnish with celery leaves, cucumber wedges and snipped chives and serve immediately.

COOK'S TIP

If the duck begins to burn slightly while it is cooking in the oven, cover with foil. Check that the duck breasts are cooked through by inserting the point of a sharp knife into the thickest part of the flesh – the juices should run clear.

Chicken with Peanut Sauce

A tangy stir-fry with a strong peanut flavour. Serve with freshly boiled rice or noodles.

NUTRITIONAL INFORMATION

Calories . . . . .538 Sugars 5g
Protein . . . . .45g Fat 36g
Carbohydrate . . .10g Saturates 16g

 10 MINS   10 MINS

SERVES 4

INGREDIENTS

4 boneless, skinned chicken breasts, about 625 g/1 lb 6 oz

4 tbsp soy sauce

4 tbsp sherry

3 tbsp crunchy peanut butter

350 g/12 oz courgettes (zucchini), trimmed

2 tbsp sunflower oil

4–6 spring onions (scallions), thinly sliced diagonally

1 x 250 g/9 oz can bamboo shoots, well drained and sliced

salt and pepper

4 tbsp desiccated (shredded) coconut, toasted

1 Cut the chicken into thin strips across the grain and season lightly with salt and pepper.

2 Stir the soy sauce in a bowl with the sherry and peanut butter until smooth and well blended.

3 Cut the courgettes (zucchini) into 5 cm/2 inch lengths and then cut into sticks about 5mm/¼ inch thick.

4 Heat the oil in a preheated wok, swirling it around until it is really hot.

5 Add the spring onions (scallions) and stir-fry for a minute or so then add the chicken strips and stir-fry for 3–4 minutes until well sealed and almost cooked.

6 Add the courgettes (zucchini) and bamboo shoots and continue to stir-fry for 1–2 minutes.

7 Add the peanut butter mixture and heat thoroughly, stirring all the time so everything is coated in the sauce as it thickens.

8 Adjust the seasoning to taste and serve the chicken very hot, sprinkled with toasted coconut.

VARIATION

This dish can also be made with turkey fillet or pork fillet.

For coconut lovers dissolve 25 g/1 oz creamed coconut in 2–3 tablespoons boiling water and add to the soy sauce mixture before adding to the wok

Chicken with Chilli & Basil

Chicken drumsticks are cooked in a delicious sauce and served with deep-fried basil for colour and flavour.

NUTRITIONAL INFORMATION

Calories 196   Sugars 2g
Protein . . . . .23g   Fat 10g
Carbohydrate . . . .3g   Saturates 2g

5 MINS   30 MINS

SERVES 4

INGREDIENTS

8 chicken drumsticks

2 tbsp soy sauce

1 tbsp sunflower oil

1 red chilli

100 g/3½ oz carrots, cut into thin sticks

6 celery stalks, cut into sticks

3 tbsp sweet chilli sauce

oil, for frying

about 50 fresh basil leaves

1 Remove the skin from the chicken drumsticks if desired. Make 3 slashes in each drumstick. Brush the drumsticks with the soy sauce.

2 Heat the sunflower oil in a preheated wok and fry the drumsticks for 20 minutes, turning frequently, until they are cooked through.

3 Deseed and finely chop the chilli. Add the chilli, carrots and celery to the wok and cook for a further 5 minutes. Stir in the chilli sauce, cover and allow to bubble gently whilst preparing the basil leaves.

4 Heat a little oil in a heavy based pan. Carefully add the basil leaves – stand well away from the pan and protect

your hand with a tea towel (dish cloth) as they may spit a little. Cook the basil leaves for about 30 seconds or until they begin to curl up but not brown. Leave the leaves to drain on absorbent kitchen paper (paper towels).

5 Arrange the cooked chicken, vegetables and pan juices on to a warm serving plate, garnish with the deep-fried crispy basil leaves and serve immediately.

COOK'S TIP

Basil has a very strong flavour which is perfect with chicken and Chinese flavourings. You could use baby spinach instead of the basil, if you prefer.

Meat

Pork is the most popular meat in China because it is tender and suitable for all Chinese cooking methods. Lamb is popular in northern China where religious laws forbid the eating of pork. Beef, although it is used in some dishes, is less popular than pork. This is partly because of economic and religious reasons, but also because it is less versatile in

cooking. One of the favourite cooking methods in China is stir-frying because it is a simple and easy way of preparing meat, as well as being healthy and economical. Stir-frying gives a dry, chewy texture, whereas braising and steaming, which are other popular cooking methods, ensure a tender result. This is also true of double-cooking in which the meat is first tenderized by long, slow simmering in water, following by a quick crisping or stir-frying in a sauce.

Beef & Broccoli Stir-fry

This is a great combination of ingredients in terms of colour and flavour, and it is so simple to prepare.

NUTRITIONAL INFORMATION

Calories 232	Sugars 1g	
Protein 12g	Fat 19g	
Carbohydrate 4g	Saturates 6g	

4¼ HOURS   15 MINS

SERVES 4

INGREDIENTS

225 g/8 oz lean steak, trimmed

2 garlic cloves, crushed

dash of chilli oil

1-cm/½-inch piece fresh root ginger, grated

½ tsp Chinese five-spice powder

2 tbsp dark soy sauce

2 tbsp vegetable oil

150 g/5½ oz broccoli florets

1 tbsp light soy sauce

150 ml/¼ pint/⅔ cup beef stock

2 tsp cornflour (cornstarch)

4 tsp water

carrot strips, to garnish

1 Using a sharp knife, cut the steak into thin strips and place in a shallow glass dish.

2 Mix together the garlic, chilli oil, grated ginger, Chinese five-spice powder and dark soy sauce in a small bowl and pour over the beef, tossing to coat the strips evenly.

3 Cover the bowl and leave the meat to marinate in the refrigerator for several hours to allow the flavours to develop fully.

4 Heat 1 tablespoon of the vegetable oil in a preheated wok or large frying pan (skillet). Add the broccoli and stir-fry over a medium heat for 4–5 minutes. Remove from the wok with a slotted spoon and set aside until required.

5 Heat the remaining oil in the wok. Add the steak together with the marinade, and stir-fry for 2-3 minutes, until the steak is browned and sealed.

6 Return the broccoli to the wok and stir in the light soy sauce and stock.

7 Blend the cornflour (cornstarch) with the water to form a smooth paste and stir into the wok. Bring to the boil, stirring, until thickened and clear. Cook for 1 minute. Transfer the beef & broccoli stir-fry to a warm serving dish, arrange the carrot strips in a lattice on top and serve immediately.

Pork with Mooli

Pork and mooli (white radish) are a perfect combination, especially with the added heat of the sweet chilli sauce.

NUTRITIONAL INFORMATION

Calories 280   Sugars 1g
Protein ....25g   Fat 19g
Carbohydrate ....2g   Saturates 4g

 10 MINS   15 MINS

SERVES 4

I N G R E D I E N T S

4 tbsp vegetable oil

450 g/1 lb pork tenderloin

1 aubergine (eggplant)

225 g/8 oz mooli (white radish)

2 cloves garlic, crushed

3 tbsp soy sauce

2 tbsp sweet chilli sauce

boiled rice or noodles, to serve

1 Heat 2 tablespoons of the vegetable oil in a large preheated wok or frying pan (skillet).

2 Using a sharp knife, thinly slice the pork into even-size pieces.

3 Add the slices of pork to the wok or frying pan (skillet) and stir-fry for about 5 minutes.

4 Using a sharp knife, trim and dice the aubergine (eggplant). Peel and slice the mooli (white radish).

5 Add the remaining vegetable oil to the wok.

6 Add the diced aubergine (eggplant) to the wok or frying pan (skillet) together with the garlic and stir-fry for 5 minutes.

7 Add the mooli (white radish) to the wok and stir-fry for about 2 minutes.

8 Stir the soy sauce and sweet chilli sauce into the mixture in the wok and cook until heated through.

9 Transfer the pork and mooli (white radish) to warm serving bowls and serve immediately with boiled rice or noodles.

COOK'S TIP

Mooli (white radish) are long white vegetables common in Chinese cooking. Usually grated, they have a milder flavour than red radish. They are generally available in most large supermarkets.

Beef with Bamboo Shoots

Tender beef, marinated in a soy and tomato sauce, is stir-fried with crisp bamboo shoots and mangetout (snow peas) in this simple recipe.

NUTRITIONAL INFORMATION

Calories	275	Sugars	.........3g
Protein	........21g	Fat	..........19g
Carbohydrate	....6g	Saturates	.......6g

1¼ HOURS   10 MINS

SERVES 4

INGREDIENTS

350 g/12 oz rump steak

3 tbsp dark soy sauce

1 tbsp tomato ketchup

2 cloves garlic, crushed

1 tbsp fresh lemon juice

1 tsp ground coriander

2 tbsp vegetable oil

175 g/6 oz/2¾ cups mangetout (snow peas)

200 g/7 oz can bamboo shoots

1 tsp sesame oil

COOK'S TIP

Leave the meat to marinate for at least 1 hour in order for the flavours to penetrate and increase the tenderness of the meat. If possible, leave for a little longer for a fuller flavour to develop.

1 Thinly slice the meat and place in a non metallic dish together with the dark soy sauce, tomato ketchup, garlic, lemon juice and ground coriander. Mix well so that all of the meat is coated in the marinade, cover and leave for at least 1 hour.

2 Heat the vegetable oil in a preheated wok. Add the meat to the wok and stir-fry for 2–4 minutes (depending on how well cooked you like your meat) or until cooked through.

3 Add the mangetout (snow peas) and bamboo shoots to the mixture in the wok and stir-fry over a high heat, tossing frequently, for a further 5 minutes.

4 Drizzle with the sesame oil and toss well to combine. Transfer to serving dishes and serve hot.

Lamb with Garlic Sauce

This dish contains Szechuan pepper which is quite hot and may be replaced with black pepper, if preferred.

NUTRITIONAL INFORMATION

Calories ....320 Sugars 2g
Protein ....25g Fat 21g
Carbohydrate ....4g Saturates 6g

35 MINS   10 MINS

SERVES 4

INGREDIENTS

450 g/1 lb lamb fillet or loin

2 tbsp dark soy sauce

2 tsp sesame oil

2 tbsp Chinese rice wine or dry sherry

½ tsp Szechuan pepper

4 tbsp vegetable oil

4 garlic cloves, crushed

60 g/2 oz water chestnuts, quartered

1 green (bell) pepper, seeded and sliced

1 tbsp wine vinegar

1 tbsp sesame oil

rice or noodles, to serve

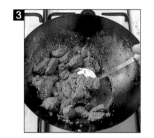

1 Cut the lamb into 2.5-cm/1-inch pieces and place in a shallow dish.

2 Mix together 1 tablespoon of the soy sauce, the sesame oil, Chinese rice wine or sherry and Szechuan pepper. Pour the mixture over the lamb, turning to coat, and leave to marinate for 30 minutes.

3 Heat the vegetable oil in a preheated wok. Remove the lamb from the marinade and add to the wok, together with the garlic. Stir-fry for 2–3 minutes.

4 Add the water chestnuts and (bell) pepper to the wok and stir-fry for 1 minute.

5 Add the remaining soy sauce and the wine vinegar, mixing together well.

6 Add the sesame oil and cook, stirring constantly, for 1–2 minutes, or until the lamb is cooked through.

7 Transfer the lamb and garlic sauce to a warm serving dish and serve immediately with rice or noodles.

COOK'S TIP

Chinese chives, also known as garlic chives, would make an appropriate garnish for this dish.

Sesame oil is used as a flavouring, rather than for frying, as it burns readily, hence it is added at the end of cooking.

Pork with Vegetables

This is a basic 'meat and veg' recipe – the meat can be pork, chicken, beef or lamb, and the vegetables can be varied according to the season.

NUTRITIONAL INFORMATION

Calories 227	Sugars 4g
Protein 15g	Fat 16g
Carbohydrate 7g	Saturates 3g

3³/₄ HOURS   10 MINS

SERVES 4

INGREDIENTS

250 g/9 oz pork fillet

1 tsp sugar

1 tbsp light soy sauce

1 tsp rice wine or dry sherry

1 tsp cornflour (cornstarch) paste (see page 29)

1 small carrot

1 small green (bell) pepper, cored and seeded

about 175 g/6 oz Chinese leaves (cabbage)

4 tbsp vegetable oil

1 spring onion (scallion), cut into short sections

a few small slices of peeled ginger root

1 tsp salt

2-3 tbsp Chinese Stock (see page 30) or water

a few drops of sesame oil

VARIATION

This dish can be made with other meats, as mentioned in the introduction. If using chicken strips, reduce the initial cooking time in the wok.

1 Thinly slice the pork fillet into small pieces and place in a shallow dish.

2 In a small bowl, mix together half the sugar and the soy sauce, the wine or sherry and cornflour (cornstarch) paste. Pour the mixture over the pork, stir well to coat the meat and leave in the refrigerator to marinate for 10-15 minutes.

3 Cut the carrot, green (bell) pepper and Chinese leaves (cabbage) into thin slices roughly the same length and width as the pork pieces.

4 Heat the oil in a preheated wok and stir-fry the pork for about 1 minute to seal in the flavour. Remove with a slotted spoon and keep warm.

5 Add the carrot, (bell) pepper, Chinese leaves (cabbage), spring onion (scallion) and ginger and stir-fry for about 2 minutes.

6 Add the salt and remaining sugar, followed by the pork and remaining soy sauce, and the Chinese stock or water. Blend well and stir for another 1-2 minutes until hot. Sprinkle the stir-fry with the sesame oil and serve immediately.

Twice-cooked Pork

Twice-cooked is a popular way of cooking meat in China. The meat is first boiled to tenderize it, then cut into strips or slices and stir-fried.

NUTRITIONAL INFORMATION

Calories 199	Sugars 3g
Protein 15g	Fat 13g
Carbohydrate 4g	Saturates 3g

3¼ HOURS   30 MINS

SERVES 4

INGREDIENTS

250-300 g/9-10½ oz shoulder or leg of pork, in one piece

1 small green (bell) pepper, cored and seeded

1 small red (bell) pepper, cored and seeded

125 g/4½ oz canned sliced bamboo shoots, rinsed and drained

3 tbsp vegetable oil

1 spring onion (scallion), cut into short sections

1 tsp salt

½ tsp sugar

1 tbsp light soy sauce

1 tsp chilli bean sauce or freshly minced chilli

1 tsp rice wine or dry sherry

a few drops of sesame oil

1 Immerse the pork in a pot of boiling water to cover. Return to the boil and skim the surface. Reduce the heat, cover and simmer for 15-20 minutes. Turn off the heat and leave the pork in the water to cool for at least 2-3 hours.

2 Remove the pork and drain well. Trim off any excess fat, then cut into small, thin slices. Cut the (bell) peppers into pieces about the same size as the pork and the sliced bamboo shoots.

3 Heat the vegetable oil in a preheated wok and add the vegetables together with the spring onion (scallion). Stir-fry for about 1 minute.

4 Add the pork, followed by the salt, sugar, light soy sauce, chilli bean sauce and wine or sherry. Blend well and continue stirring for another minute. Transfer the stir-fry to a warm serving dish, sprinkle with sesame oil and serve.

COOK'S TIP

For ease of handling, buy a boned piece of meat, and roll into a compact shape. Tie securely with string before placing in the boiling water.

Hot Lamb

This is quite a spicy dish, using 2 chillies in the sauce. Halve the number of chillies to reduce the heat or seed the chillies before using if desired.

NUTRITIONAL INFORMATION

Calories 323	Sugars 4g	
Protein 26g	Fat 22g	
Carbohydrate 5g	Saturates 7g	

25 MINS   15 MINS

SERVES 4

I N G R E D I E N T S

450 g/1 lb lean, boneless lamb

2 tbsp hoisin sauce

1 tbsp dark soy sauce

1 garlic clove, crushed

2 tsp grated fresh root ginger

2 tbsp vegetable oil

2 onions, sliced

1 fennel bulb, sliced

4 tbsp water

S A U C E

1 large fresh red chilli, cut into thin strips

1 fresh green chilli, cut into thin strips

2 tbsp rice wine vinegar

2 tsp light brown sugar

2 tbsp peanut oil

1 tsp sesame oil

VARIATION

Use beef, pork or duck instead of the lamb and vary the vegetables, using leeks or celery instead of the onion and fennel.

 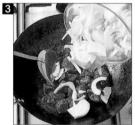 

1 Cut the lamb into 2.5-cm/1-inch cubes and place in a glass dish.

2 Mix together the hoisin sauce, soy sauce, garlic and ginger and pour over the lamb, turning to coat well. Leave to marinate for 20 minutes.

3 Heat the oil in a preheated wok and stir-fry the lamb for 1–2 minutes. Add the onions and fennel and cook for a further 2 minutes, or until they are just beginning to brown. Stir in the water, cover and cook for 2–3 minutes.

4 To make the sauce, place all the ingredients in a pan and cook over a low heat for 3-4 minutes, stirring.

5 Transfer the lamb and onions to a serving dish, toss lightly in the sauce and serve immediately.

Lamb with Satay Sauce

This recipe demonstrates the classic serving of lamb satay – lamb marinated in chilli and coconut and threaded on to wooden skewers.

NUTRITIONAL INFORMATION

Calories 501	Sugars 6g	
Protein 34g	Fat 37g	
Carbohydrate 9g	Saturates 10g	

35 MINS   25 MINS

SERVES 4

INGREDIENTS

450 g/1 lb lamb loin fillet

1 tbsp mild curry paste

150 ml/5 fl oz/⅔ cup coconut milk

2 cloves garlic, crushed

½ tsp chilli powder

½ tsp cumin

SATAY SAUCE

1 tbsp corn oil

1 onion, diced

6 tbsp crunchy peanut butter

1 tsp tomato purée (paste)

1 tsp fresh lime juice

100 ml/3½ fl oz/1⅓ cup cold water

1 Using a sharp knife, thinly slice the lamb and place in a large dish.

2 Mix together the curry paste, coconut milk, garlic, chilli powder and cumin in a bowl. Pour over the lamb, toss well, cover and marinate for 30 minutes.

3 To make the satay sauce. Heat the oil in a large wok and stir-fry the onion for 5 minutes, then reduce the heat and cook for 5 minutes.

4 Stir in the peanut butter, tomato purée (paste), lime juice and water.

5 Thread the lamb on to wooden skewers, reserving the marinade.

6 Grill (broil) the lamb skewers under a hot grill (broiler) for 6–8 minutes, turning once.

7 Add the reserved marinade to the wok, bring to the boil and cook for 5 minutes. Serve the lamb skewers with the satay sauce.

COOK'S TIP

Soak the wooden skewers in cold water for 30 minutes before grilling (broiling) to prevent the skewers from burning.

Stir-Fried Beef & Vegetables

Fillet of beef is perfect for stir-frying as it is so tender and lends itself to quick cooking.

NUTRITIONAL INFORMATION

Calories	.521	Sugars	.7g
Protein	.31g	Fat	.35g
Carbohydrate	...18g	Saturates	.8g

10 MINS   20 MINS

SERVES 4

INGREDIENTS

2 tbsp sunflower oil

350 g/12 oz fillet of beef, sliced

1 red onion, sliced

175 g/6 oz courgettes (zucchini)

175 g/6 oz carrots, thinly sliced

1 red (bell) pepper, deseeded and sliced

1 small head Chinese leaves (cabbage), shredded

150 g/5½ oz/1½ cups bean sprouts

225 g/8 oz can bamboo shoots, drained

150 g/5½ oz/½ cup cashew nuts, toasted

SAUCE

3 tbsp medium sherry

3 tbsp light soy sauce

1 tsp ground ginger

1 clove garlic, crushed

1 tsp cornflour (cornstarch)

1 tbsp tomato purée (paste)

1 Heat the sunflower oil in a large preheated wok. Add the sliced beef and red onion to the wok and stir-fry for about 4–5 minutes or until the onion begins to soften and the meat is just browning.

2 Trim the courgettes (zucchini) and slice diagonally.

3 Add the carrots, (bell) pepper, and courgettes (zucchini) and stir-fry for 5 minutes.

4 Toss in the Chinese leaves (cabbage), bean sprouts and bamboo shoots and heat through for 2–3 minutes, or until the leaves are just beginning to wilt.

5 Scatter the cashews nuts over the stir-fry and toss well to mix.

6 To make the sauce, mix together the sherry, soy sauce, ground ginger, garlic, cornflour (cornstarch) and tomato purée (tomato paste) until well combined.

7 Pour the sauce over the stir-fry and toss to mix. Allow the sauce to bubble for 2–3 minutes or until the juices thicken.

8 Transfer to warm serving dishes and serve at once.

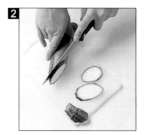

Crispy Shredded Beef

A very popular Szechuan dish served in most Chinese restaurants all over the world.

NUTRITIONAL INFORMATION

Calories . . . . .341 Sugars 17g
Protein . . . . .20g Fat 17g
Carbohydrate . . .29g Saturates 4g

  3½ HOURS   15 MINS

SERVES 4

INGREDIENTS

300-350 g/10½-12 oz beef steak (such as topside or rump)

2 eggs

¼ tsp salt

4-5 tbsp plain (all-purpose) flour

vegetable oil, for deep-frying

2 medium carrots, finely shredded

2 spring onions (scallions), thinly shredded

1 garlic clove, finely chopped

2-3 small fresh green or red chillies, seeded and thinly shredded

4 tbsp sugar

3 tbsp rice vinegar

1 tbsp light soy sauce

2-3 tbsp Chinese Stock (see page 30) or water

1 tsp cornflour (cornstarch) paste (see page 31)

1 Cut the steak across the grain into thin strips. Beat the eggs in a bowl with the salt and flour, adding a little water if necessary. Add the beef strips to the batter and mix well until coated.

2 Heat the oil in a preheated wok until smoking. Add the beef strips and deep-fry for 4-5 minutes, stirring to separate the shreds. Remove with a slotted spoon and drain on absorbent kitchen paper (paper towels)

3 Add the carrots to the wok and deep-fry for about 1-1½ minutes, then remove with a slotted spoon and drain.

4 Pour off the excess oil, leaving about 1 tablespoon in the wok. Add the spring onions (scallions), garlic, chillies and carrots and stir-fry for 1 minute.

5 Add the sugar, rice vinegar, light soy sauce and Chinese stock or water to the wok, blend well and bring to the boil.

6 Stir in the cornflour (cornstarch) paste and simmer for a few minutes to thicken the sauce.

7 Return the beef to the wok and stir until the shreds of meat are well coated with the sauce. Serve hot.

Sweet & Sour Pork

In this classic Chinese dish, tender pork pieces are fried and served in a crunchy sauce. This dish is perfect served with plain rice.

NUTRITIONAL INFORMATION

Calories 357	Sugars 25g	
Protein 28g	Fat 14g	
Carbohydrate ...30g	Saturates 4g	

10 MINS   20 MINS

SERVES 4

INGREDIENTS

450 g/1 lb pork tenderloin

2 tbsp sunflower oil

225 g/8 oz courgettes (zucchini)

1 red onion, cut into thin wedges

2 cloves garlic, crushed

225 g/8 oz carrots, cut into thin sticks

1 red (bell) pepper, deseeded and sliced

100 g/3½ oz/1 cup baby corn corbs

100 g/3½ oz button mushrooms, halved

175 g/6 oz/1¼ cups fresh pineapple, cubed

100 g/3½ oz/1 cup bean sprouts

150 ml/¼ pint/⅔ cup pineapple juice

1 tbsp cornflour (cornstarch)

2 tbsp soy sauce

3 tbsp tomato ketchup

1 tbsp white wine vinegar

1 tbsp clear honey

COOK'S TIP

If you prefer a crisper coating, toss the pork in a mixture of cornflour (cornstarch) and egg white and deep fry in the wok in step 2.

1 Using a sharp knife, thinly slice the pork tenderloin into even-size pieces.

2 Heat the sunflower oil in a large preheated wok. Add the pork to the wok and stir-fry for 10 minutes, or until the pork is completely cooked through and beginning to turn crispy at the edges.

3 Meanwhile, cut the courgettes (zucchini) into thin sticks.

4 Add the onion, garlic, carrots, courgettes (zucchini), (bell) pepper, corn cobs and mushrooms to the wok and stir-fry for a further 5 minutes.

5 Add the pineapple cubes and bean sprouts to the wok and stir-fry for 2 minutes.

6 Mix together the pineapple juice, cornflour (cornstarch), soy sauce, tomato ketchup, white wine vinegar and honey.

7 Pour the sweet and sour mixture into the wok and cook over a high heat, tossing frequently, until the juices thicken. Transfer the sweet and sour pork to serving bowls and serve hot.

Beef & Beans

The green of the beans complements the dark colour of the beef, served in a rich sauce.

NUTRITIONAL INFORMATION

Calories	.381	Sugars	.3g
Protein	.25g	Fat	.27g
Carbohydrate	.10g	Saturates	.8g

  35 MINS   15 MINS

SERVES 4

INGREDIENTS

450 g/1 lb rump or fillet steak, cut into 2.5-cm/1-inch pieces

MARINADE

2 tsp cornflour (cornstarch)

2 tbsp dark soy sauce

2 tsp peanut oil

SAUCE

2 tbsp vegetable oil

3 garlic cloves, crushed

1 small onion, cut into 8

225 g/8 oz thin green beans, halved

25 g/1 oz/¼ cup unsalted cashews

25 g/1 oz canned bamboo shoots, drained and rinsed

2 tsp dark soy sauce

2 tsp Chinese rice wine or dry sherry

125 ml/4 fl oz/½ cup beef stock

2 tsp cornflour (cornstarch)

4 tsp water

salt and pepper

1 To make the marinade, mix together the cornflour (cornstarch), soy sauce and peanut oil.

2 Place the steak in a shallow glass bowl. Pour the marinade over the steak, turn to coat thoroughly, cover and leave to marinate in the refrigerator for at least 30 minutes.

3 To make the sauce, heat the oil in a preheated wok. Add the garlic, onion, beans, cashews and bamboo shoots and stir-fry for 2–3 minutes.

4 Remove the steak from the marinade, drain, add to the wok and stir-fry for 3–4 minutes.

5 Mix the soy sauce, Chinese rice wine or sherry and beef stock together. Blend the cornflour (cornstarch) with the water and add to the soy sauce mixture, mixing to combine.

6 Stir the mixture into the wok and bring the sauce to the boil, stirring until thickened and clear. Reduce the heat and leave to simmer for 2–3 minutes. Season to taste and serve immediately.

Pork with Plums

Plum sauce is often used in Chinese cooking with duck or rich, fattier meat to counteract the flavour

NUTRITIONAL INFORMATION

Calories . . . . .281 Sugars 6g
Protein . . . . .25g Fat 14g
Carbohydrate . . .10g Saturates 4g

 35 MINS   25 MINS

SERVES 4

INGREDIENTS

450 g/1 lb pork fillet (tenderloin)

1 tbsp cornflour (cornstarch)

2 tbsp light soy sauce

2 tbsp Chinese rice wine

4 tsp light brown sugar

pinch of ground cinnamon

5 tsp vegetable oil

2 garlic cloves, crushed

2 spring onions (scallions), chopped

4 tbsp plum sauce

1 tbsp hoisin sauce

150 ml/¼ pint/ ⅔ cup water

dash of chilli sauce

fried plum quarters and spring onions
   (scallions), to garnish

1 Cut the pork fillet (tenderloin) into thin slices.

2 Combine the cornflour (cornstarch), soy sauce, rice wine, sugar and cinnamon in a small bowl.

3 Place the pork in a shallow dish and pour the cornflour (cornstarch) mixture over it. Toss the meat in the marinade until it .is completely coated. Cover and leave to marinate for at least 30 minutes.

4 Remove the pork from the dish, reserving the marinade.

5 Heat the oil in a preheated wok or large frying pan (skillet). Add the pork and stir-fry for 3–4 minutes, until a light golden colour.

6 Stir in the garlic, spring onions (scallions), plum sauce, hoisin sauce, water and chilli sauce. Bring the sauce to

the boil. Reduce the heat, cover and leave to simmer for 8–10 minutes, or until the pork is cooked through and tender.

7 Stir in the reserved marinade and cook, stirring, for about 5 minutes.

8 Transfer the pork stir-fry to a warm serving dish and garnish with fried plum quarters and spring onions (scallions). Serve immediately.

Deep-fried Pork Fritters

Small pieces of pork are coated in a light batter and deep-fried in this recipe – they are delicious dipped in a soy and honey sauce.

NUTRITIONAL INFORMATION

Calories	528	Sugars	........12g
Protein	........32g	Fat	..........22g
Carbohydrate	...52g	Saturates	.......6g

 10 MINS   15 MINS

SERVES 4

INGREDIENTS

450 g/1 lb pork fillet (tenderloin)

2 tbsp peanut oil

200 g/7 oz/1¾ cups plain (all-purpose) flour

2 tsp baking powder

1 egg, beaten

225 ml/8 fl oz/1 cup milk

pinch of chilli powder

vegetable oil, for deep-frying

SAUCE

2 tbsp dark soy sauce

3 tbsp clear honey

1 tbsp wine vinegar

1 tbsp chopped chives

1 tbsp tomato purée (paste)

chives, to garnish

1 Using a sharp knife, cut the pork into 2.5-cm/1-inch cubes.

2 Heat the peanut oil in a preheated wok. Add the pork to the wok and stir-fry for 2-3 minutes, until sealed.

3 Remove the pork with a slotted spoon and set aside until required.

4 Sift the flour and baking powder into a mixing bowl and make a well in the centre. Gradually beat in the egg, milk and chilli powder to make a thick batter.

5 Heat the oil for deep-frying in a wok until almost smoking, then reduce the heat slightly.

6 Toss the pork pieces in the batter to coat thoroughly. Add the pork to the wok and deep-fry until golden brown and cooked through. Remove with a slotted spoon and drain well on absorbent kitchen paper (paper towels).

7 Meanwhile, mix together the soy sauce, honey, wine vinegar, chives and tomato purée (paste) and spoon into a small serving bowl.

8 Transfer the pork fritters to serving dishes, garnish with chives and serve with the sauce.

Lamb with Mushroom Sauce

Use a lean cut of lamb, such as fillet, for this recipe for both flavour and tenderness.

NUTRITIONAL INFORMATION

Calories	.219	Sugars	.1g
Protein	.21g	Fat	.14g
Carbohydrate	.4g	Saturates	.4g

 5 MINS 10 MINS

SERVES 4

I N G R E D I E N T S

350 g/12 oz lean boneless lamb, such as fillet or loin

2 tbsp vegetable oil

3 garlic cloves, crushed

1 leek, sliced

175 g/6 oz large mushrooms, sliced

½ tsp sesame oil

fresh red chillies, to garnish

S A U C E

1 tsp cornflour (cornstarch)

4 tbsp light soy sauce

3 tbsp Chinese rice wine or dry sherry

3 tbsp water

½ tsp chilli sauce

1 Using a sharp knife or meat cleaver, cut the lamb into thin strips.

2 Heat the vegetable oil in a preheated wok or large frying pan (skillet).

3 Add the lamb strips, garlic and leek and stir-fry for about 2-3 minutes.

4 To make the sauce, mix together the cornflour (cornstarch), soy sauce, Chinese rice wine or dry sherry, water and chilli sauce and set aside.

5 Add the sliced mushrooms to the wok and stir-fry for 1 minute.

6 Stir in the prepared sauce and cook for 2–3 minutes, or until the lamb is cooked through and tender.

7 Sprinkle the sesame oil over the top and transfer the lamb and mushrooms to a warm serving dish. Garnish with red chillies and serve immediately.

VARIATION

The lamb can be replaced with lean steak or pork fillet (tenderloin) in this classic recipe from Beijing. You could also use 2-3 spring onions (scallions), 1 shallot or 1 small onion instead of the leek, if you prefer.

Sesame Lamb Stir-Fry

This is a very simple, but delicious dish, in which lean pieces of lamb are cooked in sugar and soy sauce and then sprinkled with sesame seeds.

NUTRITIONAL INFORMATION

Calories . . . . . . .276 Sugars 4g
Protein . . . . .25g Fat 18g
Carbohydrate . . . .5g Saturates 6g

 5 MINS   🕐 10 MINS

SERVES 4

INGREDIENTS

450 g/1 lb boneless lean lamb

2 tbsp peanut oil

2 leeks, sliced

1 carrot, cut into matchsticks

2 garlic cloves, crushed

85 ml/3 fl oz/⅓ cup lamb or vegetable stock

2 tsp light brown sugar

1 tbsp dark soy sauce

4½ tsp sesame seeds

1 Using a sharp knife, cut the lamb into thin strips.

2 Heat the peanut oil in a preheated wok or large frying pan (skillet) until it is really hot.

3 Add the lamb and stir-fry for 2–3 minutes. Remove the lamb from the wok with a slotted spoon and set aside until required.

4 Add the leeks, carrot and garlic to the wok or frying pan (skillet) and stir-fry in the remaining oil for 1–2 minutes.

5 Remove the vegetables from the wok with a slotted spoon and set aside.

6 Drain any remaining oil from the wok. Place the lamb or vegetable stock,

light brown sugar and dark soy sauce in the wok and add the lamb. Cook, stirring constantly to coat the lamb, for 2–3 minutes.

7 Sprinkle the sesame seeds over the top, turning the lamb to coat.

8 Spoon the leek, carrot and garlic mixture on to a warm serving dish and top with the lamb. Serve immediately.

COOK'S TIP

Be careful not to burn the sugar in the wok when heating and coating the meat, otherwise the flavour of the dish will be spoiled.

Beef & Bok Choy

In this recipe, a colourful selection of vegetables is stir-fried with tender strips of steak.

NUTRITIONAL INFORMATION

Calories	369	Sugars	.........9g
Protein	........29g	Fat	..........23g
Carbohydrate	...12g	Saturates	.......8g

🍲 15 MINS   🕐 5 MINS

SERVES 4

INGREDIENTS

1 large head of bok choy, about 250-275 g/9-9½ oz, torn into large pieces

2 tbsp vegetable oil

2 garlic cloves, crushed

500 g/1 lb 2 oz rump or fillet steak, cut into thin strips

150 g/5½ oz mangetout (snow peas), trimmed

150 g/5½ oz baby or dwarf corn

6 spring onions (scallions), chopped

2 red (bell) peppers, cored, seeded and thinly sliced

2 tbsp oyster sauce

1 tbsp fish sauce

1 tbsp sugar

rice or noodles, to serve

COOK'S TIP

Bok choy is one of the most important ingredients in this dish. If unavailable, use Chinese leaves (cabbage), kai choy (mustard leaves) or pak choy.

1 Steam the bok choy over boiling water until just tender. Keep warm.

2 Heat the oil in a large, heavy-based frying pan (skillet) or wok, add the garlic and steak strips and stir-fry until just browned, about 1-2 minutes.

3 Add the mangetout (snow peas), baby corn, spring onions (scallions), red (bell) pepper, oyster sauce, fish sauce and sugar to the pan, mixing well. Stir-fry for a further 2-3 minutes until the vegetables are just tender, but still crisp.

4 Arrange the bok choy leaves in the base of a heated serving dish and spoon the beef and vegetable mixture into the centre.

5 Serve the stir-fry immediately, with rice or noodles.

Lamb with Lime Leaves

Groundnut oil is used here for flavour – it is a common oil used for stir-frying.

NUTRITIONAL INFORMATION

Calories 302   Sugars 15g
Protein . . . . .24g   Fat 16g
Carbohydrate . . .17g   Saturates 6g

5 MINS   35 MINS

SERVES 4

I N G R E D I E N T S

2 red chillies

2 tbsp groundnut oil

2 cloves garlic, crushed

4 shallots, chopped

2 stalks lemon grass, sliced

6 lime leaves

1 tbsp tamarind paste

25 g/1 oz/2 tbsp palm sugar

450 g/1 lb lean lamb (leg or loin fillet)

600 ml/1 pint/2½ cups coconut milk

175 g/6 oz cherry tomatoes, halved

1 tbsp chopped fresh coriander
   (cilantro)

fragrant rice, to serve

1 Using a sharp knife, deseed and very finely chop the red chillies.

2 Heat the oil in a large preheated wok or frying pan (skillet).

3 Add the garlic, shallots, lemon grass, lime leaves, tamarind paste, palm sugar and chillies to the wok and stir-fry for about 2 minutes.

4 Using a sharp knife, cut the lamb into thin strips or cubes. Add the lamb to the wok or frying pan (skillet) and stir-fry for about 5 minutes, tossing well so that the lamb is evenly coated in the spice mixture.

5 Pour the coconut milk into the wok and bring to the boil. Reduce the heat and leave to simmer for 20 minutes.

6 Add the tomatoes and coriander (cilantro) to the wok and leave to simmer for 5 minutes. Transfer to serving plates and serve hot with fragrant rice.

COOK'S TIP

When buying fresh coriander (cilantro), look for bright green, unwilted leaves. To store it, wash and dry the leaves, leaving them on the stem. Wrap the leaves in damp kitchen paper (paper towels) and keep them in a plastic bag in the refrigerator.

Beef & Black Bean Sauce

It is not necessary to use the expensive cuts of beef steak for this recipe: the meat will be tender as it is cut into small thin slices and marinated.

NUTRITIONAL INFORMATION

Calories ...... .392	Sugars 2g	
Protein 13g	Fat .... .36g	
Carbohydrate 3g	Saturates 7g	

 3¹/₄ HOURS   10 MINS

SERVES 4

INGREDIENTS

250-300 g/9-10½ oz beef steak (such as rump)

1 small onion

1 small green (bell) pepper, cored and seeded

about 300 ml/½ pint/1¼ cups vegetable oil

1 spring onion (scallion), cut into short sections

a few small slices of ginger root

1-2 small green or red chillies, seeded and sliced

2 tbsp crushed black bean sauce

MARINADE

½ tsp bicarbonate of soda (baking soda) or baking powder

½ tsp sugar

1 tbsp light soy sauce

2 tsp rice wine or dry sherry

2 tsp cornflour (cornstarch) paste (see page 31)

2 tsp sesame oil

1 Using a sharp knife or meat cleaver, cut the beef into small, thin strips.

2 To make the marinade, mix together all the ingredients in a shallow dish. Add the beef strips, turn to coat and leave to marinate for at least 2-3 hours.

3 Cut the onion and green (bell) pepper into small cubes.

4 Heat the vegetable oil in a pre-heated wok or large frying pan (skillet). Add the beef strips and stir-fry for about 1 minute, or until the colour changes. Remove the beef strips with a slotted spoon and drain on absorbent kitchen paper (paper towels). Keep warm and set aside until required.

5 Pour off the excess oil, leaving about 1 tablespoon in the wok. Add the spring onion (scallion), ginger, chillies, onion and green (bell) pepper and stir-fry for about 1 minute.

6 Add the black bean sauce and stir until smooth. Return the beef strips to the wok, blend well and stir-fry for another minute. Transfer the stir-fry to a warm serving dish and serve hot.

Spicy Pork & Rice

Pork is coated in a spicy mixture before being fried until crisp in this recipe and then stirred into a delicious egg rice for a very filling meal.

Calories ....599 Sugars 11g
Protein ....30g Fat 22g
Carbohydrate ...76g Saturates 7g

10 MINS   35 MINS

SERVES 4

I N G R E D I E N T S

275 g/9½ oz/1¼ cups long-grain white rice

600 ml/1 pint/2½ cups cold water

350 g/12 oz pork tenderloin

2 tsp Chinese five-spice powder

25 g/1 oz/4 tbsp cornflour (cornstarch)

3 large eggs, beaten

25 g/1 oz/2 tbsp demerara (brown crystal) sugar

2 tbsp sunflower oil

1 onion

2 cloves garlic, crushed

100 g/3½ oz carrots, diced

1 red (bell) pepper, deseeded and diced

100 g/3½ oz/¾ cup peas

15 g/½ oz/2 tbsp butter

salt and pepper

1 Rinse the rice under cold running water. Place the rice in a large saucepan, add the cold water and a pinch of salt. Bring to the boil, cover, then reduce the heat and leave to simmer for about 9 minutes, or until all of the liquid has been absorbed and the rice is tender.

2 Meanwhile, slice the pork tenderloin into very thin even-sized pieces, using

a sharp knife or meat cleaver. Set the pork strips aside until required.

3 Whisk together the Chinese five-spice powder, cornflour (cornstarch), 1 egg and the demerara (brown crystal) sugar. Toss the pork in the mixture until coated.

4 Heat the sunflower oil in a large wok or frying pan (skillet). Add the pork and cook over a high heat until the pork is cooked through and crispy. Remove the pork from the wok with a slotted spoon and set aside until required.

5 Using a sharp knife, cut the onion into dice.

6 Add the onion, garlic, carrots, (bell) pepper and peas to the wok and stir-fry for 5 minutes.

7 Return the pork to the wok together with the cooked rice and stir-fry for 5 minutes.

8 Heat the butter in a frying pan (skillet). Add the remaining beaten eggs and cook until set. Turn out on to a clean board and slice thinly. Toss the strips of egg into the rice mixture and serve immediately.

Fish-flavoured Pork

'Fish-flavoured' is a Szechuan cookery term meaning that the dish is prepared with seasonings normally used in fish dishes.

NUTRITIONAL INFORMATION

Calories	183	Sugars	.......0.2g
Protein	........14g	Fat	..........13g
Carbohydrate	....3g	Saturates	.......3g

25 MINS   10 MINS

SERVES 4

INGREDIENTS

about 2 tbsp dried wood ears

250-300 g/9-10½ oz pork fillet

1 tsp salt

2 tsp cornflour (cornstarch) paste
(see page 31)

3 tbsp vegetable oil

1 garlic clove, finely chopped

½ tsp finely chopped ginger root

2 spring onions (scallions), finely chopped,
with the white and green parts separated

2 celery stalks, thinly sliced

½ tsp sugar

1 tbsp light soy sauce

1 tbsp chilli bean sauce

2 tsp rice vinegar

1 tsp rice wine or dry sherry

a few drops of sesame oil

COOK'S TIP

Also known as cloud ears, wood ears are a dried grey-black fungus widely used in Szechuan cooking. They are always soaked in warm water before using. Wood ears have a crunchy texture and a mild flavour.

1 Soak the wood ears in warm water for about 20 minutes, then rinse in cold water until the water is clear. Drain well, then cut into thin shreds.

2 Cut the pork into thin shreds, then mix in a bowl with a pinch of salt and about half the cornflour (cornstarch) paste until well coated.

3 Heat 1 tablespoon of vegetable oil in a preheated wok. Add the pork strips and stir-fry for about 1 minute, or until the colour changes, then remove with a slotted spoon and set aside until required.

4 Heat the remaining oil in the wok. Add the garlic, ginger, the white parts of the spring onions (scallions), the wood ears and celery and stir-fry for about 1 minute.

5 Return the pork strips together with the salt, sugar, soy sauce, chilli bean sauce, vinegar and wine or sherry. Blend well and continue stirring for another minute.

6 Finally add the green parts of the spring onions (scallions) and blend in the remaining cornflour (cornstarch) paste and sesame oil. Stir until the sauce has thickened. Transfer the fish-flavoured pork to a warm serving dish and serve immediately.

Oyster Sauce Beef

Like Pork with Vegetables (see page 224), the vegetables used in this recipe can be varied as you wish.

NUTRITIONAL INFORMATION

Calories	462	Sugars	.........2g
Protein	........16g	Fat	..........42g
Carbohydrate	....4g	Saturates	.......8g

  4 HOURS   10 MINS

SERVES 4

I N G R E D I E N T S

300 g/10½ oz beef steak

1 tsp sugar

1 tbsp light soy sauce

1 tsp rice wine or dry sherry

1 tsp cornflour (cornstarch) paste
(see page 31)

½ small carrot

60 g/2 oz mangetout (snow peas)

60 g/2 oz canned bamboo shoots

60 g/2 oz canned straw mushrooms

about 300 ml/½ pint/1¼ cups vegetable oil

1 spring onion (scallion), cut into short
sections

2-3 small slices ginger root

½ tsp salt

2 tbsp oyster sauce

2-3 tbsp Chinese Stock (see page 30) or
water

1 Cut the beef into small, thin slices. Place in a shallow dish with the sugar, soy sauce, wine and cornflour (cornstarch) paste and leave to marinate for 25-30 minutes.

2 Slice the carrot, mangetout (snow peas), bamboo shoots and straw mushrooms into roughly the same size pieces as each other.

3 Heat the oil in a wok and add the beef slices. Stir-fry for 1 minute, then remove and keep warm.

4 Pour off the oil, leaving about 1 tablespoon in the wok. Add the sliced vegetables with the spring onion (scallion) and ginger and stir-fry for about 2 minutes. Add the salt, beef and oyster sauce with stock or water. Blend well until heated through and serve.

VARIATION

You can use whatever vegetables are available for this dish, but it is important to get a good contrast of colour – don't use all red or all green for example.

Spicy Pork Balls

These small meatballs are packed with flavour and cooked in a crunchy tomato sauce for a very quick dish.

NUTRITIONAL INFORMATION

Calories	299	Sugars	.........3g
Protein	........28g	Fat	..........15g
Carbohydrate	...14g	Saturates	.......4g

10 MINS   40 MINS

SERVES 4

I N G R E D I E N T S

450 g/1 lb minced (ground) pork

2 shallots, finely chopped

2 cloves garlic, crushed

1 tsp cumin seeds

½ tsp chilli powder

25 g/1 oz/½ cup wholemeal
  breadcrumbs

1 egg, beaten

2 tbsp sunflower oil

400 g/14 oz can chopped tomatoes,
  flavoured with chilli

2 tbsp soy sauce

200 g/7 oz can water chestnuts,
  drained

3 tbsp chopped fresh coriander (cilantro)

COOK'S TIP

Add a few teaspoons of chilli
sauce to a tin of chopped
tomatoes, if you can't find the
flavoured variety.

1 Place the minced (ground) pork in a large mixing bowl. Add the shallots, garlic, cumin seeds, chilli powder, breadcrumbs and beaten egg and mix together well.

2 Form the mixture into balls between the palms of your hands.

3 Heat the oil in a large preheated wok. Add the pork balls and stir-fry, in batches, over a high heat for about 5 minutes or until sealed on all sides.

4 Add the tomatoes, soy sauce and water chestnuts and bring to the boil. Return the pork balls to the wok, reduce the heat and leave to simmer for 15 minutes.

5 Scatter with chopped fresh coriander (cilantro) and serve hot.

Pork with (Bell) Peppers

This is a really simple yet colourful dish, the trio of (bell) peppers offsetting the pork and sauce wonderfully.

NUTRITIONAL INFORMATION

Calories 459	Sugars 5g	
Protein 19g	Fat 39g	
Carbohydrate 8g	Saturates 13g	

  30 MINS   25 MINS

SERVES 4

I N G R E D I E N T S

15 g/½ oz Chinese dried mushrooms

450 g/1 lb pork leg steaks

2 tbsp vegetable oil

1 onion, sliced

1 red (bell) pepper, deseeded and diced

1 green (bell) pepper, deseeded and diced

1 yellow (bell) pepper, deseeded and diced

4 tbsp oyster sauce

1 Place the mushrooms in a large bowl. Pour over enough boiling water to cover and leave to stand for 20 minutes.

2 Using a sharp knife, trim any excess fat from the pork steaks. Cut the pork into thin strips.

3 Bring a large saucepan of water to the boil. Add the pork to the boiling water and cook for 5 minutes.

4 Remove the pork from the pan with a slotted spoon and leave to drain thoroughly.

5 Heat the oil in a large preheated wok. Add the pork to the wok and stir-fry for about 5 minutes.

6 Remove the mushrooms from the water and leave to drain thoroughly. Roughly chop the mushrooms.

7 Add the mushrooms, onion and the (bell) peppers to the wok and stir-fry for 5 minutes.

8 Stir in the oyster sauce and cook for 2-3 minutes. Serve immediately.

COOK'S TIP

Use open-cap mushrooms, sliced, instead of Chinese mushrooms, if you prefer.

Spare Ribs with Chilli

For best results, chop the spare ribs into small bite-size pieces.

NUTRITIONAL INFORMATION

Calories ....497 Sugars 3g
Protein ....13g Fat 47g
Carbohydrate ....4g Saturates 11g

  4¼ HOURS   20 MINS

SERVES 4

I N G R E D I E N T S

500 g/1 lb 2 oz pork spare ribs

1 tsp sugar

1 tbsp light soy sauce

1 tsp rice wine or dry sherry

1 tsp cornflour (cornstarch)

about 600 ml/1 pint/2½ cups vegetable oil

1 garlic clove, finely chopped

1 spring onion (scallion), cut into short
    sections

1 small hot chilli pepper (green or red),
    thinly sliced

2 tbsp black bean sauce

about 150 ml/¼ pint/⅔ cup Chinese Stock
    (see page 30) or water

1 small onion, diced

1 medium green (bell) pepper, cored,
    seeded and diced

COOK'S TIP

Be very careful when handling
and cutting chilli peppers as their
juice can cause irritation of the
skin. Be sure to wash your hands
after handling, and keep well away
from face and eyes. The seeds of the
chilli are the hottest part – remove
seeds if you want a milder dish.

1 Trim any excess fat from the ribs. Using a sharp knife
or meat cleaver, chop each rib into 3-4 bite-sized
piecess and place in a shallow dish.

2 Mix together the sugar, soy sauce, wine and cornflour
(cornstarch) and pour the mixture over the pork ribs.
Leave to marinate for 35-45 minutes.

3 Heat the vegetable oil in a large preheated wok or
frying pan (skillet).

4 Add the spare ribs to the wok and deep-fry for 2-3
minutes until light brown. Remove with a slotted
spoon and drain on absorbent kitchen paper (paper towels).

5 Pour off the oil, leaving about 1 tablespoon in the wok.
Add the garlic, spring onion (scallion), chilli pepper and
black bean sauce and stir-fry for 30-40 seconds.

6 Add the spare ribs, blend well, then add the stock or
water. Bring to the boil, then reduce the heat, cover
and braise for 8-10 minutes, stirring once or twice.

7 Add the onion and green (bell) pepper, increase the
heat to high, and stir uncovered for about 2 minutes to
reduce the sauce a little. Serve hot.

Stir-Fried Lamb with Orange

Oranges and lamb are a great combination because the citrus flavour offsets the fattier, fuller flavour of the lamb.

NUTRITIONAL INFORMATION

Calories	209	Sugars 4g
Protein	........25g	Fat 10g
Carbohydrate	....5g	Saturates 5g

 5 MINS   🕐 30 MINS

SERVES 4

I N G R E D I E N T S

450 g/1 lb minced (ground) lamb

2 cloves garlic, crushed

1 tsp cumin seeds

1 tsp ground coriander

1 red onion, sliced

finely grated zest and juice of
   1 orange

2 tbsp soy sauce

1 orange, peeled and segmented

salt and pepper

snipped fresh chives, to garnish

1 Heat a wok or large, heavy-based frying pan (skillet), without adding any oil.

2 Add the minced (ground) lamb to the wok. Dry fry the minced (ground) lamb for 5 minutes, or until the lamb is evenly browned. Drain away any excess fat from the wok.

3 Add the garlic, cumin seeds, coriander and red onion to the wok and stir-fry for a further 5 minutes.

4 Stir in the finely grated orange zest and juice and the soy sauce, mixing until thoroughly combined. Cover, reduce the heat and leave to simmer, stirring occasionally, for 15 minutes.

5 Remove the lid, increase the heat and add the orange segments. Stir to mix.

6 Season with salt and pepper to taste and heat through for a further 2–3 minutes.

7 Transfer the stir-fry to warm serving plates and garnish with snipped fresh chives. Serve immediately.

COOK'S TIP

If you wish to serve wine with your meal, try light, dry white wines and lighter Burgundy-style red wines as they blend well with Oriental food.

Lamb & Ginger Stir-fry

Slices of lamb cooked with garlic, ginger and shiitake mushrooms make a quick and easy supper. It is best served with Chinese egg noodles.

NUTRITIONAL INFORMATION

Calories 347	Sugars 2g	
Protein 31g	Fat 21g	
Carbohydrate 7g	Saturates 7g	

 10 MINS   5 MINS

SERVES 4

INGREDIENTS

500 g/1 lb 2 oz lamb fillet (tenderloin)

2 tbsp sunflower oil

1 tbsp chopped ginger root

2 garlic cloves, chopped

6 spring onions (scallions), white and
   green parts diagonally sliced

175 g/6 oz shiitake mushrooms, sliced

175 g/6 oz sugar snap peas

1 tsp cornflour (cornstarch)

2 tbsp dry sherry

1 tbsp light soy sauce

1 tsp sesame oil

1 tbsp sesame seeds, toasted

Chinese egg noodles to serve

1 Using a sharp knife or meat cleaver, cut the lamb into 5 mm/½ inch slices.

2 Heat the sunflower oil in a large preheated wok or frying pan (skillet).

3 Add the lamb to the wok or frying pan (skillet) and stir-fry for 2 minutes.

4 Add the chopped ginger root, chopped garlic cloves, sliced spring onions (scallions), mushrooms and sugar snap peas and stir-fry for 2 minutes.

5 Blend the cornflour (cornstarch) with the sherry and stir into the wok.

6 Add the light soy sauce and sesame oil and cook, stirring, for 1 minute until thickened.

7 Sprinkle over the sesame seeds, transfer the lamb and ginger stir-fry to a warm serving dish and serve the stir-fry with Chinese egg noodles.

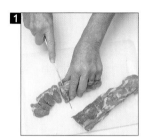

COOK'S TIP

Shiitake mushrooms are much used in Chinese cooking. They have a slightly meaty flavour and can be bought both fresh and dried. Their powerful flavour will permeate more bland mushrooms. Cook them briefly or they begin to toughen.

Pork Ribs with Plum Sauce

Pork ribs are always very popular at barbecues (grills), and you can flavour them with a number of spicy bastes.

NUTRITIONAL INFORMATION

Calories 590	Sugars 1g	
Protein 26g	Fat 51g	
Carbohydrate 3g	Saturates 17g	

35 MINS   45 MINS

SERVES 4

INGREDIENTS

900 g/2 lb pork spare ribs

2 tbsp sunflower oil

1 tsp sesame oil

2 cloves garlic, crushed

2.5 cm/1 inch piece root (fresh) ginger, grated

150 ml/¼ pint/⅔ cup plum sauce

2 tbsp dry sherry

2 tbsp hoisin sauce

2 tbsp soy sauce

4–6 spring onions (scallions), to garnish (optional)

1 To prepare the garnish, trim the spring onions (scallions) to about 7.5 cm/ 3 inches long. Slice both ends into thin strips, leaving the onion intact in the centre.

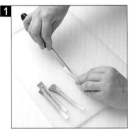

2 Put the spring onions (scallions) into a bowl of iced water for at least 30 minutes until the ends start to curl up. Leave them in the water and set aside until required.

3 If you buy the spare ribs in a single piece, cut them into individual ribs. Bring a large pan of water to the boil and add the ribs. Cook for 5 minutes, then drain thoroughly.

4 Heat the oils in a pan, add the garlic and ginger and cook gently for 1–2 minutes. Stir in the plum sauce, sherry, hoisin and soy sauce and heat through.

5 Brush the sauce over the pork ribs. Barbecue (grill) over hot coals for 5–10 minutes, then move to a cooler part of the barbecue (grill) for a further 15–20 minutes, basting with the remaining sauce. Garnish and serve hot.

COOK'S TIP

Par-cooking the ribs in boiling water removes excess fat, which helps prevent the ribs from spitting during cooking. Do not be put off by the large quantity – there is only a little meat on each, but they are quite cheap to buy.

Pork Satay Stir-Fry

Satay sauce is easy to make and is one of the best known and loved sauces in Oriental cooking. It is perfect with beef, chicken or pork.

NUTRITIONAL INFORMATION

Calories	506	Sugars	........11g
Protein	........31g	Fat	..........36g
Carbohydrate	...15g	Saturates	.......8g

10 MINS   15 MINS

SERVES 4

INGREDIENTS

150 g/5½ oz carrots

2 tbsp sunflower oil

350 g/12 oz pork neck fillet, thinly sliced

1 onion, sliced

2 cloves garlic, crushed

1 yellow (bell) pepper, deseeded and sliced

150 g/5½ oz/2⅓ cups mangetout (snow peas)

75 g/2¾ oz/1½ cups fine asparagus

chopped salted peanuts, to serve

SATAY SAUCE

6 tbsp crunchy peanut butter

6 tbsp coconut milk

1 tsp chilli flakes

1 clove garlic, crushed

1 tsp tomato purée (paste)

COOK'S TIP

Cook the sauce just before serving as it tends to thicken very quickly and will not be spoonable if you cook it too far in advance.

1 Using a sharp knife, slice the carrots into thin sticks.

2 Heat the oil in a large, preheated wok. Add the pork, onion and garlic and stir-fry for 5 minutes or until the lamb is cooked through.

3 Add the carrots, (bell) pepper, mangetout (snow peas) and asparagus to the wok and stir-fry for 5 minutes.

4 To make the satay sauce, place the peanut butter, coconut milk, chilli flakes, garlic and tomato purée (paste) in a small pan and heat gently, stirring, until well combined. Be careful not to let the sauce stick to the bottom of the pan.

5 Transfer the stir-fry to warm serving plates. Spoon the satay sauce over the stir-fry and scatter with chopped peanuts. Serve immediately.

Marinated Beef

This dish is quick to cook, but benefits from lengthy marinating, as this tenderizes and flavours the meat.

1¼ HOURS   10 MINS

SERVES 4

INGREDIENTS

225 g/8 oz lean steak

1 tbsp light soy sauce

1 tsp sesame oil

2 tsp Chinese rice wine or dry sherry

1 tsp caster (superfine) sugar

2 tsp hoisin sauce

1 garlic clove, crushed

½ tsp cornflour (cornstarch)

green (bell) pepper slices, to garnish

rice or noodles, to serve

SAUCE

2 tbsp dark soy sauce

1 tsp caster (superfine) sugar

½ tsp cornflour (cornstarch)

3 tbsp oyster sauce

8 tbsp water

2 tbsp vegetable oil

3 garlic cloves, crushed

1-cm/½-inch piece fresh root ginger, grated

8 baby corn cobs, halved lengthways

½ green (bell) pepper, seeded and thinly sliced

25 g/1 oz bamboo shoots, drained and rinsed

1 Using a sharp knife or meat cleaver, cut the steak into 2.5-cm/1-inch cubes and place in a shallow dish.

2 Mix together the soy sauce, sesame oil, Chinese rice wine or sherry, caster (superfine) sugar, hoisin sauce, garlic and cornflour (cornstarch) and pour over the steak, turning it to coat completely. Cover and marinate for at least 1 hour, or preferably overnight in the refrigerator for a fuller flavour.

3 Meanwhile, make the sauce. Mix together the dark soy sauce with the caster (superfine) sugar, cornflour (cornstarch), oyster sauce and water.

4 Heat the oil in a preheated wok. Add the steak, together with the marinade, and stir-fry for 2–3 minutes, until sealed and lightly browned.

5 Add the garlic, ginger, baby corn cobs, (bell) pepper and bamboo shoots. Stir in the oyster sauce mixture and bring to the boil. Reduce the heat and cook for 2–3 minutes.

6 Transfer to a warm serving dish, garnish with green (bell) pepper slices and serve immediately with rice or noodles.

Peppered Beef Cashew

A simple but stunning dish of tender strips of beef mixed with crunchy cashew nuts, coated in a hot sauce. Serve with rice noodles.

NUTRITIONAL INFORMATION

Calories 403   Sugars 7g
Protein . . . . .26g   Fat 29g
Carbohydrate . . . .11g   Saturates 9g

 10 MINS   10 MINS

SERVES 4

INGREDIENTS

1 tbsp groundnut or sunflower oil

1 tbsp sesame oil

1 onion, sliced

1 garlic clove, crushed

1 tbsp grated ginger root

500 g/1 lb 2 oz fillet or rump steak, cut into thin strips

2 tsp palm sugar

2 tbsp light soy sauce

1 small yellow (bell) pepper, cored, seeded and sliced

1 red (bell) pepper, cored, seeded and sliced

4 spring onions (scallions), chopped

2 celery sticks, chopped

4 large open-cap mushrooms, sliced

4 tbsp roasted cashew nuts

3 tbsp stock or white wine

1 Heat the oils in a large, heavy-based frying pan (skillet) or wok. Add the onion, garlic and ginger and stir-fry for about 2 minutes until softened.

2 Add the steak strips and stir-fry for a further 2-3 minutes, until the meat has browned.

3 Add the sugar and soy sauce, stirring to mix well.

4 Add the (bell) peppers, spring onions (scallions), celery, mushrooms and cashews, mixing well.

5 Add the stock or white wine and stir-fry for 2-3 minutes until the beef is cooked through and the vegetables are tender-crisp.

6 Serve the stir-fry immediately with rice noodles.

COOK'S TIP

Palm sugar is a thick brown sugar with a slightly caramel taste. It is sold in cakes, or in small containers. If not available, use soft dark brown or demerara (brown crystal) sugar.

Beef Teriyaki

This Japanese-style teriyaki sauce complements barbecued (grilled) beef, but it can also be used to accompany chicken or salmon.

NUTRITIONAL INFORMATION

Calories ....184 Sugars 6g
Protein ....24g Fat 5g
Carbohydrate ....8g Saturates 2g

2¼ HOURS   15 MINS

SERVES 4

INGREDIENTS

450 g/1 lb extra thin lean beef steaks

8 spring onions (scallions), trimmed and cut into short lengths

1 yellow (bell) pepper, deseeded and cut into chunks

green salad, to serve

SAUCE

1 tsp cornflour (cornstarch)

2 tbsp dry sherry

2 tbsp white wine vinegar

3 tbsp soy sauce

1 tbsp dark muscovado sugar

1 clove garlic, crushed

½ tsp ground cinnamon

½ tsp ground ginger

1 Place the meat in a shallow, non-metallic dish.

2 To make the sauce, combine the cornflour (cornstarch) with the sherry, then stir in the remaining sauce ingredients. Pour the sauce over the meat and leave to marinate for at least 2 hours.

3 Remove the meat from the sauce. Pour the sauce into a small saucepan.

4 Cut the meat into thin strips and thread these, concertina-style, on to pre-soaked wooden skewers, alternating each strip of meat with the prepared pieces of spring onion (scallion) and (bell) pepper,

5 Gently heat the sauce until it is just simmering, stirring occasionally.

6 Barbecue (grill) the kebabs (kabobs) over hot coals for 5–8 minutes, turning and basting the beef and vegetables occasionally with the reserved teriyaki sauce.

7 Arrange the skewers on serving plates and pour the remaining sauce over the kebabs. Serve with a green salad.

Lamb Meatballs

These small meatballs are made with minced (ground) lamb and flavoured with chilli, garlic, parsley and Chinese curry powder.

NUTRITIONAL INFORMATION

Calories 320	Sugars 1g	
Protein 28g	Fat 20g	
Carbohydrate 8g	Saturates 6g	

 5 MINS   20 MINS

SERVES 4

INGREDIENTS

450 g/1 lb minced (ground) lamb

3 garlic cloves, crushed

2 spring onions (scallions), finely chopped

½ tsp chilli powder

1 tsp Chinese curry powder

1 tbsp chopped fresh parsley

25 g/1 oz/½ cup fresh white breadcrumbs

1 egg, beaten

3 tbsp vegetable oil

125 g/4½ oz Chinese leaves (cabbage), shredded

1 leek, sliced

1 tbsp cornflour (cornstarch)

2 tbsp water

300 ml/½ pint/1¼ cups lamb stock

1 tbsp dark soy sauce

shredded leek, to garnish

VARIATION

Use minced (ground) pork or beef instead of the lamb as an alternative.

1 Mix the lamb, garlic, spring onions (scallions), chilli powder, Chinese curry powder, parsley and breadcrumbs together in a bowl. Work the egg into the mixture, bringing it together to form a firm mixture. Roll into 16 small, even-sized balls.

2 Heat the oil in a preheated wok. Add the Chinese leaves (cabbage) and leek and stir-fry for 1 minute. Remove from the wok with a slotted spoon and set aside.

3 Add the meatballs to the wok and fry in batches, turning gently, for 3-4 minutes, or until golden brown all over.

4 Mix the cornflour (cornstarch) and water together to form a smooth paste and set aside. Pour the lamb stock and soy sauce into the wok and cook for 2–3 minutes. Stir in the cornflour (cornstarch) paste. Bring to the boil and cook, stirring constantly, until the sauce is thickened and clear.

5 Return the Chinese leaves (cabbage) and leek to the wok and cook for 1 minute, until heated through. Arrange the Chinese leaves (cabbage) and leek on a warm serving dish, top with the meatballs, garnish with shredded leek and serve immediately.

Pork Fry with Vegetables

This is a very simple dish which lends itself to almost any combination of vegetables that you have to hand.

NUTRITIONAL INFORMATION

Calories 216   Sugars 3g
Protein . . . . .19g   Fat 12g
Carbohydrate . . . .5g   Saturates 3g

 5 MINS   15 MINS

SERVES 4

I N G R E D I E N T S

350 g/12 oz lean pork fillet (tenderloin)

2 tbsp vegetable oil

2 garlic cloves, crushed

1-cm/½-inch piece fresh root ginger, cut into slivers

1 carrot, cut into thin strips

1 red (bell) pepper, seeded and diced

1 fennel bulb, sliced

25 g/1 oz water chestnuts, halved

75 g/2 ¾ oz bean sprouts

2 tbsp Chinese rice wine

300 ml/½ pint/1¼ cups pork or chicken stock

pinch of dark brown sugar

1 tsp cornflour (cornstarch)

2 tsp water

1 Cut the pork into thin slices. Heat the oil in a preheated wok. Add the garlic, ginger and pork and stir-fry for 1–2 minutes, until the meat is sealed.

2 Add the carrot, (bell) pepper, fennel and water chestnuts to the wok and stir-fry for about 2–3 minutes.

3 Add the bean sprouts and stir-fry for 1 minute. Remove the pork and vegetables from the wok and keep warm.

4 Add the Chinese rice wine, pork or chicken stock and sugar to the wok. Blend the cornflour (cornstarch) to a smooth paste with the water and stir it into the sauce. Bring to the boil, stirring constantly until thickened and clear.

5 Return the meat and vegetables to the wok and cook for 1–2 minutes, until heated through and coated with the sauce. Serve immediately.

VARIATION

Use dry sherry instead of the Chinese rice wine if you have difficulty obtaining it.

Garlic Lamb with Soy Sauce

The long marinating time allows the garlic to really penetrate the meat, creating a much more flavourful dish.

NUTRITIONAL INFORMATION

Calories	309	Sugars	.......0.2g
Protein	........25g	Fat	..........21g
Carbohydrate	....3g	Saturates	.......9g

1¼ HOURS   15 MINS

SERVES 4

INGREDIENTS

450 g/1 lb lamb loin fillet

2 cloves garlic

2 tbsp groundnut oil

3 tbsp dry sherry or rice wine

3 tbsp dark soy sauce

1 tsp cornflour (cornstarch)

2 tbsp cold water

25 g/1 oz/2 tbsp butter

1 Using a sharp knife, make small slits in the flesh of the lamb.

2 Carefully peel the cloves of garlic and cut them into slices, using a sharp knife.

3 Push the slices of garlic into the slits in the lamb. Place the garlic-infused lamb in a shallow dish.

4 In a small bowl, mix together 1 tablespoon each of the groundnut oil, dry sherry or rice wine and dark soy sauce. Drizzle this mixture over the lamb, cover with cling film (plastic wrap) and leave to marinate for at least 1 hour, preferably overnight.

5 Using a sharp knife or meat cleaver, thinly slice the marinated lamb.

6 Heat the remaining oil in a preheated wok or large frying pan (skillet). Add the marinated lamb and stir-fry for 5 minutes.

7 Add the marinade juices and the remaining sherry and soy sauce to the wok and allow the juices to bubble for 5 minutes.

8 Blend the cornflour (cornstarch) to a smooth paste with the cold water. Add the cornflour (cornstarch) mixture to the wok and cook, stirring occasionally, until the juices start to thicken.

9 Cut the butter into small pieces. Add the butter to the wok or frying pan (skillet) and stir until the butter melts. Transfer the lamb to serving dishes and serve immediately.

COOK'S TIP

Adding the butter at the end of the recipe gives a glossy, rich sauce which is ideal with the lamb.

Soy & Sesame Beef

Soy sauce and sesame seeds are classic ingredients in Chinese cookery.
Use a dark soy sauce for fuller flavour and richness.

NUTRITIONAL INFORMATION

Calories	324	Sugars 2g
Protein	........25g	Fat 22g
Carbohydrate	....3g	Saturates 6g

5 MINS   10 MINS

SERVES 4

INGREDIENTS

25 g/1 oz/2 tbsp sesame seeds

450 g/1 lb beef fillet

2 tbsp vegetable oil

1 green (bell) pepper, deseeded and thinly sliced

4 cloves garlic, crushed

2 tbsp dry sherry

4 tbsp soy sauce

6 spring onions (scallions), sliced

noodles, to serve

1 Heat a large wok or heavy-based frying pan (skillet) until it is very hot.

2 Add the sesame seeds to the wok or frying pan (skillet) and dry fry, stirring, for 1–2 minutes or until they just begin to brown. Remove the sesame seeds from the wok and set aside until required.

3 Using a sharp knife or meat cleaver, thinly slice the beef.

4 Heat the vegetable oil in the wok or frying pan (skillet). Add the beef and stir-fry for 2–3 minutes or until sealed on all sides.

5 Add the sliced (bell) pepper and crushed garlic to the wok and continue stir-frying for 2 minutes.

6 Add the dry sherry and soy sauce to the wok together with the spring onions (scallions). Allow the mixture in the wok to bubble, stirring occasionally, for about 1 minute, but do not let the mixture burn.

7 Transfer the garlic beef stir-fry to warm serving bowls and scatter with the dry-fried sesame seeds. Serve hot with boiled noodles.

COOK'S TIP

You can spread the sesame seeds out on a baking tray (cookie sheet) and toast them under a preheated grill (broiler) until browned all over, if you prefer.

Five-spice Lamb

Chinese five-spice powder is a blend of cinnamon, fennel, star anise, ginger and cloves, all finely ground together.

NUTRITIONAL INFORMATION

Calories 361	Sugars 3g
Protein 35g	Fat 22g
Carbohydrate 5g	Saturates 8g

1¼ HOURS   10 MINS

SERVES 4

INGREDIENTS

625 g/1 lb 6 oz lean boneless lamb (leg or fillet)

2 tsp Chinese five-spice powder

3 tbsp sunflower oil

1 red (bell) pepper, cored, seeded and thinly sliced

1 green (bell) pepper, cored, seeded and thinly sliced

1 yellow or orange (bell) pepper, cored, seeded and thinly sliced

4-6 spring onions (scallions), thinly sliced diagonally

175 g/6 oz French (green) or fine beans, cut into 4 cm/1½ inch lengths

2 tbsp soy sauce

4 tbsp sherry

salt and pepper

Chinese noodles, to serve

TO GARNISH

strips of red and yellow (bell) pepper

fresh coriander (cilantro) leaves

1 Cut the lamb into narrow strips, about 4 cm/1½ inches long, across the grain. Place in a bowl, add the five-spice powder and ¼ teaspoon salt, mix well and leave to marinate, covered, in a cool place for at least an hour and up to 24 hours.

2 Heat half the oil in the wok, swirling it around until really hot. Add the lamb and stir-fry briskly for 3-4 minutes until almost cooked through. Remove from the pan and set aside.

3 Add the remaining oil to the wok and when hot add the (bell) peppers and spring onions (scallions). Stir-fry for 2-3 minutes, then add the beans and stir for a minute or so.

4 Add the soy sauce and sherry to the wok and when hot return the lamb and any juices to the wok. Stir-fry for 1-2 minutes until the lamb is really hot again and thoroughly coated in the sauce. Season to taste.

5 Serve the Five-spice Lamb with Chinese noodles, garnished with strips of red and green (bell) pepper and fresh coriander (cilantro).

Sweet & Sour Pork

This dish is a popular choice in Western diets, and must be one of the best known of Chinese recipes.

NUTRITIONAL INFORMATION

Calories 471   Sugars 47g
Protein . . . . .16g   Fat 13g
Carbohydrate . . .77g   Saturates 2g

10 MINS   20 MINS

SERVES 4

INGREDIENTS

150 ml/¼ pint/⅔ cup vegetable oil, for deep-frying

225 g/8 oz pork fillet (tenderloin), cut into 1-cm/½-inch cubes

1 onion, sliced

1 green (bell) pepper, seeded and sliced

225 g/8 oz pineapple pieces

1 small carrot, cut into thin strips

25 g/1 oz canned bamboo shoots, drained, rinsed and halved

rice or noodles, to serve

BATTER

125 g/4½ oz/1 cup plain (all-purpose) flour

1 tbsp cornflour (cornstarch)

1½ tsp baking powder

1 tbsp vegetable oil

SAUCE

125 g/4½ oz/⅔ cup light brown sugar

2 tbsp cornflour (cornstarch)

125 ml/4 fl oz/½ cup white wine vinegar

2 garlic cloves, crushed

4 tbsp tomato purée (paste)

6 tbsp pineapple juice

1 To make the batter, sift the plain (all-purpose) flour into a mixing bowl, together with the cornflour (cornstarch) and baking powder. Add the vegetable oil and stir in enough water to make a thick, smooth batter (about 175 ml/6 fl oz/ ¾ cup).

2 Pour the vegetable oil into a preheated wok and heat until almost smoking.

3 Dip the cubes of pork into the batter, and cook in the hot oil, in batches, until the pork is cooked through. Remove the pork from the wok with a slotted spoon and drain on absorbent kitchen paper (paper towels). Set aside and keep warm until required.

4 Drain all but 1 tablespoon of oil from the wok and return it to the heat. Add the onion, (bell) pepper, pineapple pieces, carrot and bamboo shoots and stir-fry for 1–2 minutes. Remove from the wok with a slotted spoon and set aside.

5 Mix all of the sauce ingredients together and pour into the wok. Bring to the boil, stirring until thickened and clear. Cook for 1 minute, then return the pork and vegetables to the wok. Cook for a further 1–2 minutes, then transfer to a serving plate and serve with rice or noodles.

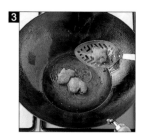

Sweet Potato & Coconut Beef

This is a truly aromatic dish, blending the heat of red curry paste with the aroma and flavour of the lime leaves and coconut.

NUTRITIONAL INFORMATION

Calories 322	Sugars 9g
Protein 18g	Fat 18g
Carbohydrate . . .24g	Saturates 6g

 10 MINS   25 MINS

SERVES 4

I N G R E D I E N T S

2 tbsp vegetable oil

2 cloves garlic

1 onion

350 g/12 oz rump steak

350 g/12 oz sweet potato

2 tbsp red curry paste

300 ml/½ pint/1¼ cups coconut milk

3 limes leaves

cooked jasmine rice, to serve

1 Heat the vegetable oil in a large preheated wok or large heavy-based frying pan (skillet).

2 Peel the garlic cloves and crush them in a pestle and mortar. Thinly slice the onions.

3 Using a sharp knife, thinly slice the beef. Add the beef to the wok and stir-fry for about 2 minutes or until sealed on all sides.

4 Add the garlic and the onion to the wok and stir-fry for a further 2 minutes.

5 Using a sharp knife, peel and dice the sweet potato.

6 Add the sweet potato to the wok with the red curry paste, coconut milk and lime leaves and bring to a rapid boil. Reduce the heat, cover and leave to simmer for about 15 minutes or until the potatoes are tender.

7 Remove and discard the lime leaves and transfer the stir-fry to warm serving bowls. Serve hot with cooked jasmine rice.

VARIATION

If you cannot obtain lime leaves, use grated lime zest instead.

Oyster Sauce Lamb

This really is a speedy dish, lamb leg steaks being perfect for the short cooking time.

NUTRITIONAL INFORMATION

Calories 243   Sugars 0.4g
Protein ....26g   Fat 14
Carbohydrate ....3g   Saturates 5g

 5 MINS   10 MINS

SERVES 4

INGREDIENTS

450 g/1 lb lamb leg steaks

1 tsp ground Szechuan peppercorns

1 tbsp groundnut oil

2 cloves garlic, crushed

8 spring onions (scallions), sliced

2 tbsp dark soy sauce

6 tbsp oyster sauce

175 g/6 oz Chinese leaves (cabbage)

prawn (shrimp) crackers, to serve (optional)

1 Using a sharp knife, remove any excess fat from the lamb. Slice the lamb thinly.

2 Sprinkle the ground Szechuan peppercorns over the meat and toss together until well combined.

3 Heat the groundnut oil in a preheated wok or large heavy-based frying pan (skillet).

4 Add the lamb to the wok or frying pan (skillet) and stir-fry for about 5 minutes.

5 Meanwhile, crush the garlic cloves in a pestle and mortar and slice the spring onions (scallions). Add the garlic

and spring onions (scallions) to the wok together with the dark soy sauce and stir-fry for 2 minutes.

6 Add the oyster sauce and Chinese leaves (cabbage) and stir-fry for a further 2 minutes, or until the leaves have wilted and the juices are bubbling.

7 Transfer the stir-fry to warm serving bowls and serve hot with prawn (shrimp) crackers (if using).

COOK'S TIP

Oyster sauce is made from oysters which are cooked in brine and soy sauce. Sold in bottles, it will keep in the refrigerator for months.

Red Spiced Beef

A spicy stir-fry flavoured with paprika, chilli and tomato, with a crisp bite to it from the celery strips.

NUTRITIONAL INFORMATION

Calories 431	Sugars 0g
Protein 32g	Fat 28g
Carbohydrate . . .14g	Saturates 10g

40 MINS   10 MINS

SERVES 4

INGREDIENTS

625 g/1 lb 6 oz sirloin or rump steak

2 tbsp paprika

2-3 tsp mild chilli powder

½ tsp salt

6 celery sticks

4 tomatoes, peeled, seeded and sliced

6 tbsp stock or water

2 tbsp tomato purée (paste)

2 tbsp clear honey

3 tbsp wine vinegar

1 tbsp Worcestershire sauce

2 tbsp sunflower oil

4 spring onions (scallions), thinly sliced diagonally

1-2 garlic cloves, crushed

Chinese noodles, to serve

celery leaves, to garnish (optional)

1 Using a sharp knife or meat cleaver, cut the steak across the grain into narrow strips 1 cm/½ inch thick and place in a bowl.

2 Combine the paprika, chilli powder and salt, add to the beef and mix thoroughly until the meat strips are evenly coated with the spices. Leave the beef to marinate in a cool place for at least 30 minutes.

3 Cut the celery into 5 cm/2 inch lengths, then cut the lengths into strips about 5 mm/¼ inches thick.

4 Combine the stock, tomato purée (paste), honey, wine vinegar and Worcestershire sauce and set aside.

5 Heat the oil in the wok until really hot. Add the spring onion (scallions), celery and garlic and stir-fry for about 1 minute until the vegetables are beginning to soften, then add the steak strips. Stir-fry over a high heat for 3-4 minutes until the meat is well sealed.

6 Add the sauce to the wok and continue to stir-fry briskly until thoroughly coated and sizzling.

7 Serve with noodles and garnish with celery leaves, if liked.

Pork Balls with Mint Sauce

Made with lean minced pork the balls are first stir-fried, then braised in the wok with stock and pickled walnuts to give a tangy flavour.

NUTRITIONAL INFORMATION

Calories 318   Sugars 2g
Protein . . . . .30g   Fat 20g
Carbohydrate . . . .6g   Saturates 5g

    5 MINS   25 MINS

SERVES 4

I N G R E D I E N T S

500 g/1 lb 2 oz lean minced
   (ground) pork

40 g/1½ oz/¾ cup fine fresh white
   breadcrumbs

½ tsp ground allspice

1 garlic clove, crushed

2 tbsp freshly chopped mint

1 egg, beaten

2 tbsp sunflower oil

1 red (bell) pepper, cored, seeded
   and thinly sliced

250 ml/9 fl oz/1 cup chicken stock

4 pickled walnuts, sliced

salt and pepper

rice or Chinese noodles, to serve

fresh mint, to garnish

1 Mix together the minced (ground) pork, breadcrumbs, seasoning, allspice, garlic and half the chopped mint in a mixing bowl, then bind together with the beaten egg.

2 Shape the meat mixture into 20 small balls with your hands, damping your hands if it is easier for shaping.

3 Heat the sunflower oil in the a wok or heavy-based frying pan (skillet),

swirling the oil around until really hot, then stir-fry the pork balls for about 4-5 minutes, or until browned all over.

4 Remove the pork balls from the wok with a slotted spoon as they are ready and drain on absorbent kitchen paper (paper towels).

5 Pour off all but 1 tablespoon of fat and oil from the wok or frying pan (skillet) then add the red (bell) pepper slices and stir-fry for 2-3 minutes, or until they begin to soften, but not colour.

6 Add the chicken stock and bring to the boil. Season well with salt and pepper and return the pork balls to the wok, stirring well to coat in the sauce. Simmer for 7-10 minutes, turning the pork balls from time to time.

7 Add the remaining chopped mint and the pickled walnuts to the wok and continue to simmer for 2-3 minutes, turning the pork balls regularly to coat them in the sauce.

8 Adjust the seasoning and serve the pork balls with rice or Chinese noodles, or with a stir-fried vegetable dish, garnished with sprigs of fresh mint.

Meatballs in Peanut Sauce

Choose very lean minced (ground) beef to make these meatballs – or better still, buy some lean beef and mince (grind) it yourself.

NUTRITIONAL INFORMATION

Calories 553	Sugars 10g
Protein 32g	Fat 43g
Carbohydrate ...21g	Saturates 12g

5 MINS   30 MINS

SERVES 4

INGREDIENTS

500 g/1 lb 2 oz/2 cups lean minced (ground) beef

2 tsp finely grated fresh ginger root

1 small red chilli, deseeded and chopped finely

1 tbsp chopped fresh basil or coriander (cilantro)

1 tbsp sesame oil

1 tbsp vegetable oil

salt and pepper

SAUCE

2 tbsp red curry paste

300 ml/½ pint/1¼ cups coconut milk

125 g/4½ oz/1 cup ground peanuts

1 tbsp fish sauce

TO GARNISH

chopped fresh basil

sprigs of fresh basil or coriander (cilantro)

VARIATION

Minced (ground) lamb makes a delicious alternative to beef. If you do use lamb, try substituting ground almonds for the peanuts and fresh mint for the basil.

1 Put the beef, ginger, chilli and basil or coriander (cilantro) into a food processor or blender. Add ¹/₂ teaspoon of salt and plenty of pepper. Process for about 10–15 seconds until finely chopped. Alternatively, chop the ingredients finely and mix together.

2 Form the beef mixture into about 12 balls. Heat the sesame oil and vegetable oil in a wok or frying pan (skillet) and fry the meatballs over a medium-high heat until well browned on all sides, about 10 minutes. Lift them out and drain on kitchen paper (paper towels).

3 To make the sauce, stir-fry the red curry paste in the wok or frying pan (skillet) for 1 minute. Add the coconut milk, peanuts and fish sauce. Heat, stirring, until just simmering.

4 Return the meatballs to the wok or frying pan (skillet) and cook gently in the sauce for 10–15 minutes. If the sauce begins to get too thick, add a little extra coconut milk or water. Season with a little salt and pepper, according to taste.

5 Serve garnished with chopped fresh basil and sprigs of fresh basil or coriander (cilantro).

Roast Red Pork

Pork fillet (tenderloin) is given a marvellous flavour and distinctive red colour in this excellent recipe.

NUTRITIONAL INFORMATION

Calories	305	Sugars	.........4g
Protein	........40g	Fat	..........13g
Carbohydrate	....5g	Saturates	.......5g

 12¼ HOURS 40 MINS

SERVES 4

INGREDIENTS

750 g/1 lb 10 oz pork fillet (tenderloin)

1 tsp red food colouring

4 garlic cloves, crushed

1 tsp Chinese five-spice powder

1 tbsp light soy sauce

1 tbsp fish sauce

1 tbsp dry sherry

1 tbsp dark muscovado sugar

1 tbsp sesame oil

1 tbsp finely grated fresh ginger root

TO GARNISH

lettuce

spring onions (scallions), finely sliced

1 Rinse the pork and trim off any fat. Place in a large clear plastic food bag or freezer bag and add the red food colouring. Roll the pork around in the bag to coat it in the colouring.

2 Mix all the remaining ingredients together and add the mixture to the pork in the plastic bag. Secure the opening and chill overnight, or for at least 12 hours, turning the bag over occasionally.

3 Place the pork on a rack over a roasting tin (pan). Cook in a preheated oven at 220°C/425°F/Gas Mark 7 for 15 minutes. Remove from the oven and baste with the remaining marinade.

4 Reduce the oven temperature to 180°C/350°F/Gas Mark 4 and roast the pork for a further 25 minutes, basting with any remaining marinade. Leave to cool for at least 10 minutes before slicing.

5 Slice thinly, arrange on a serving platter, garnish and serve.

COOK'S TIP

Putting the pork in a plastic bag helps to prevent your hands from turning red from the food colouring.

Lamb with Black Bean Sauce

Red onions add great colour to recipes and are perfect in this dish, combining with the colours of the (bell) peppers.

NUTRITIONAL INFORMATION

Calories	328	Sugars	.........5g
Protein	........26g	Fat	..........20g
Carbohydrate	...12g	Saturates	.......6g

  10 MINS   15 MINS

SERVES 4

I N G R E D I E N T S

450 g/1 lb lamb neck fillet or boneless leg of lamb chops

1 egg white, lightly beaten

25 g/1 oz/4 tbsp cornflour (cornstarch)

1 tsp Chinese five spice powder

3 tbsp sunflower oil

1 red onion

1 red (bell) pepper, deseeded and sliced

1 green (bell) pepper, deseeded and sliced

1 yellow or orange (bell) pepper, deseeded and sliced

5 tbsp black bean sauce

boiled rice or noodles, to serve

1 Using a sharp knife, slice the lamb into very thin strips.

2 Mix together the egg white, cornflour (cornstarch) and Chinese five-spice powder. Toss the lamb strips in the mixture until evenly coated.

3 Heat the oil in a wok and stir-fry the lamb over a high heat for 5 minutes or until it crispens around the edges.

4 Slice the red onion. Add the onion and (bell) pepper slices to the wok and stir-fry for 5–6 minutes, or until the vegetables just begin to soften.

5 Stir the black bean sauce into the mixture in the wok and heat through.

6 Transfer the lamb and sauce to warm serving plates and serve hot with freshly boiled rice or noodles.

COOK'S TIP

Take care when frying the lamb as the cornflour (cornstarch) mixture may cause it to stick to the wok. Move the lamb around the wok constantly during stir-frying.

Caramelised Beef

Palm sugar or brown sugar is used in this recipe to give the beef a slightly caramelised flavour.

NUTRITIONAL INFORMATION

Calories . . . . . . .335 Sugars 8g
Protein . . . . .23g Fat 21g
Carbohydrate . . .14g Saturates 7g

1¼ HOURS   10 MINS

SERVES 4

I N G R E D I E N T S

450 g/1 lb fillet beef

2 tbsp soy sauce

1 tsp chilli oil

1 tbsp tamarind paste

2 tbsp palm sugar or demerara (brown crystal) sugar

2 cloves garlic, crushed

2 tbsp sunflower oil

225 g/8 oz baby onions

2 tbsp chopped fresh coriander (cilantro), to garnish

1 Using a sharp knife or meat cleaver, thinly slice the beef.

2 Place the slices of beef in a large, shallow non-metallic dish.

3 Mix together the soy sauce, chilli oil, tamarind paste, palm or demerara (brown crystal) sugar and garlic in a mixing bowl.

4 Spoon the sugar mixture over the beef. Toss well to coat the beef in the mixture, cover with cling film (plastic wrap) and leave to marinate for at least 1 hour, the longer the better.

5 Heat the oil in a preheated wok or large frying pan (skillet).

6 Peel the onions and cut them in half. Add the onion pieces to the wok and stir-fry for 2–3 minutes, or until just browning.

7 Add the beef and marinade juices to the wok and stir-fry over a high heat for about 5 minutes.

8 Scatter with chopped fresh coriander (cilantro) and serve at once.

COOK'S TIP

Use the chilli oil carefully as it is very hot and could easily spoil the dish if too much is added.

Curried Lamb with Potatoes

This dish is very filling, only requiring a simple vegetable accompaniment or bread.

NUTRITIONAL INFORMATION

Calories	375	Sugars	.........6g
Protein	........26g	Fat	..........19g
Carbohydrate	...27g	Saturates	.......6g

10 MINS   1 HOUR

SERVES 4

I N G R E D I E N T S

450 g/1 lb potatoes, diced

450 g/1 lb lean lamb, cubed

2 tbsp medium hot curry paste

3 tbsp sunflower oil

1 onion, sliced

1 aubergine (eggplant), diced

2 cloves garlic, crushed

1 tbsp grated fresh root ginger

150 ml/5 fl oz/⅔ cup lamb or beef stock

salt

2 tbsp chopped fresh coriander (cilantro), to garnish

1 Bring a large saucepan of lightly salted water to the boil. Add the potatoes and cook for 10 minutes. Remove the potatoes from the saucepan with a slotted spoon and drain thoroughly.

COOK'S TIP

The wok is an ancient Chinese invention, the name coming from the Cantonese, meaning a 'cooking vessel'.

2 Meanwhile, place the lamb cubes in a large mixing bowl. Add the curry paste and mix well until the lamb is evenly coated in the paste.

3 Heat the sunflower oil in a large preheated wok.

4 Add the onion, aubergine (eggplant), garlic and ginger to the wok and stir-fry for about 5 minutes.

5 Add the lamb to the wok and stir-fry for a further 5 minutes.

6 Add the stock and cooked potatoes to the wok, bring to the boil and leave to simmer for 30 minutes, or until the lamb is tender and cooked through.

7 Transfer the stir-fry to warm serving dishes and scatter with chopped fresh coriander (cilantro). Serve immediately.

Spicy Beef

In this recipe beef is marinated in a five-spice and chilli marinade for a spicy flavour.

NUTRITIONAL INFORMATION

Calories 246	Sugars 2g
Protein 21g	Fat 13g
Carbohydrate ...10g	Saturates 3g

1¼ HOURS   10 MINS

SERVES 4

INGREDIENTS

225 g/8 oz fillet steak

2 garlic cloves, crushed

1 tsp powdered star anise

1 tbsp dark soy sauce

spring onion (scallion) tassels, to garnish

SAUCE

2 tbsp vegetable oil

1 bunch spring onions (scallions), halved
   lengthways

1 tbsp dark soy sauce

1 tbsp dry sherry

¼ tsp chilli sauce

150 ml/¼ pint/⅔ cup water

2 tsp cornflour (cornstarch)

4 tsp water

1 Cut the steak into thin strips and place in a shallow dish.

2 Mix together the garlic, star anise and dark soy sauce in a bowl.

3 Pour the sauce mixture over the steak strips, turning them to coat thoroughly. Cover and leave to marinate in the refrigerator for at least 1 hour.

4 To make the sauce, heat the oil in a preheated wok or large frying pan (skillet). Reduce the heat and stir-fry the spring onions (scallions) for 1-2 minutes.

5 Remove the spring onions (scallions) from the wok with a slotted spoon, drain on absorbent kitchen paper (paper towels) and set aside until required.

6 Add the beef to the wok, together with the marinade, and stir-fry for 3-4 minutes. Return the spring onions (scallions) to the wok and add the soy sauce, sherry, chilli sauce and two thirds of the water.

7 Blend the cornflour (cornstarch) with the remaining water and stir into the wok. Bring to the boil, stirring until the sauce thickens and clears.

8 Transfer to a warm serving dish, garnish and serve immediately.

Beef with Green Peas

This recipe is the perfect example of quick stir-frying ingredients for a delicious, crisp, colourful dish.

NUTRITIONAL INFORMATION

Calories 325   Sugars 2g
Protein . . . . .26g   Fat 22g
Carbohydrate . . . .8g   Saturates 7g

 5 MINS   10 MINS

SERVES 4

INGREDIENTS

450 g/1 lb rump steak

2 tbsp sunflower oil

1 onion

2 cloves garlic

150 g/5½oz/1 cup fresh or
    frozen peas

160 g/5¾oz jar black bean sauce

150 g/5½ oz Chinese leaves
    (cabbage), shredded

1 Using a sharp knife, trim away any fat from the beef. Cut the beef into thin slices.

2 Heat the sunflower oil in a large preheated wok.

3 Add the beef to the wok and stir-fry for 2 minutes.

4 Using a sharp knife, peel and slice the onion and crush the garlic cloves in a pestle and mortar.

5 Add the onion, garlic and peas to the wok and stir-fry for 5 minutes.

6 Add the black bean sauce and Chinese leaves (cabbage) to the wok.

7 Heat the mixture in the wok for a further 2 minutes until the Chinese leaves (cabbage) have wilted.

8 Transfer to warm serving bowls then serve immediately.

COOK'S TIP

Buy a chunky black bean sauce if you can for the best texture and flavour.

Chinese leaves (cabbage) are now widely available. They look like a pale, elongated head of lettuce with light green, tightly packed crinkly leaves.

Stir-fried Pork & Cabbage

Rustle up this quick dish in a matter of moments. Assemble all your ingredients first, then everything is ready to hand as you start to stir-fry.

NUTRITIONAL INFORMATION

Calories ....226 Sugars 2g
Protein ....21g Fat 12g
Carbohydrate ....4g Saturates 3g

  5 MINS 10 MINS

SERVES 4

INGREDIENTS

375 g/13 oz pork fillet (tenderloin)

8 spring onions (scallions), trimmed

½ small white cabbage

½ cucumber

2 tsp finely grated fresh ginger root

1 tbsp fish sauce or light soy sauce

2 tbsp dry sherry

2 tbsp water

2 tsp cornflour (cornstarch)

1 tbsp chopped fresh mint or coriander
 (cilantro)

2 tbsp sesame oil

salt and pepper

TO GARNISH

sprigs of fresh mint or coriander (cilantro)

1 chilli flower (see Cook's Tip, right)

1 Slice the pork very thinly. Shred the spring onions (scallions) and cabbage, and cut the cucumber into matchsticks.

2 Mix together the ginger, fish sauce or soy sauce, sherry, water, cornflour (cornstarch) and chopped mint or coriander (cilantro) until blended.

3 Heat the sesame oil in a wok and add the pork. Stir-fry briskly over a high heat until browned, about 4–5 minutes.

4 Add the spring onions (scallions), cabbage and cucumber and stir-fry for a further 2 minutes. Add the cornflour (cornstarch) mixture and continue to cook for about 1 minute, until slightly thickened. Season to taste.

5 Transfer the stir-fry to a warmed dish and serve at once, garnished with sprigs of fresh mint or coriander (cilantro) and a chilli flower.

COOK'S TIP

To make chilli flowers, hold the stem of the chilli and cut down its length several times with a sharp knife. Place in a bowl of chilled water and chill so that the 'petals' turn out. Remove the chilli seeds when the 'petals' have opened.

Fish & Seafood

China's many miles of coastline, rivers and lakes offer an enormous variety of fresh and salt-water fish and seafood. Among the most popular are carp, bass, bream, clams, crab,

crawfish and prawns (shrimp). Dishes which include shark's fins, abalone, squid and edible seaweed are also common. When buying fish and seafood for Chinese cooking, freshness is imperative to flavour so be sure to buy it and use it as soon as possible, preferably the same day. Chinese chefs buy live fish which are kept alive until just before cooking. Favourite cooking methods for fish are steaming and quick poaching in boiling water or broth.

(Small) Shrimp Fu Yong

The classic ingredients of this popular dish are eggs, carrots and (small) shrimps. Add extra ingredients such as peas or crabmeat, if desired.

NUTRITIONAL INFORMATION

Calories	240	Sugars	.........1g
Protein	........22g	Fat	..........16g
Carbohydrate	....1g	Saturates	.......3g

5 MINS   10 MINS

SERVES 4

INGREDIENTS

2 tbsp vegetable oil

1 carrot, grated

5 eggs, beaten

225 g/8 oz raw (small) shrimp, peeled

1 tbsp light soy sauce

pinch of Chinese five-spice powder

2 spring onions (scallions), chopped

2 tsp sesame seeds

1 tsp sesame oil

COOK'S TIP

If only cooked prawns (shrimp) are available, add them just before the end of cooking, but make sure they are fully incorporated into the fu yong. They require only heating through. Overcooking will make them chewy and tasteless.

1 Heat the vegetable oil in a preheated wok or frying pan (skillet), swirling it around until the oil is really hot.

2 Add the grated carrot and stir-fry for 1–2 minutes.

3 Push the carrot to one side of the wok or frying pan (skillet) and add the beaten eggs. Cook, stirring gently, for 1–2 minutes.

4 Stir the (small) shrimp, light soy sauce and five-spice powder into the mixture in the wok. Stir-fry the mixture for 2–3 minutes, or until the (small) shrimps change colour and the mixture is almost dry.

5 Turn the (small) shrimp fu yong out on to a warm plate and sprinkle the spring onions (scallions), sesame seeds and sesame oil on top. Serve immediately.

Fried Prawns with Cashews

Cashew nuts are delicious as part of a stir-fry with almost any other ingredient. Use the unsalted variety in cooking.

NUTRITIONAL INFORMATION

Calories 406   Sugar 3g
Protein . . . . .31g   Fat 25g
Carbohydrate . . .13g   Saturates 4g

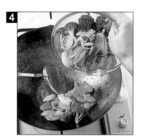

5 MINS   5 MINS

SERVES 4

INGREDIENTS

2 garlic cloves, crushed

1 tbsp cornflour (cornstarch)

pinch of caster (superfine) sugar

450 g/1 lb raw tiger prawns
(jumbo shrimp)

4 tbsp vegetable oil

1 leek, sliced

125 g/4½ oz broccoli florets

1 orange (bell) pepper, seeded
and diced

75 g/2¾ oz/¾ cup unsalted
cashew nuts

SAUCE

175 ml/6 fl oz/¾ cup fish stock

1 tbsp cornflour (cornstarch)

dash of chilli sauce

2 tsp sesame oil

1 tbsp Chinese rice wine

1 Mix together the garlic, cornflour (cornstarch) and sugar in a bowl.

2 Peel and devein the prawns (shrimp). Stir the prawns (shrimp) into the mixture to coat thoroughly.

3 Heat the vegetable oil in a preheated wok and add the prawn (shrimp) mixture. Stir-fry over a high heat for 20–30 seconds until the prawns (shrimp) turn pink. Remove the prawns (shrimp) from the wok with a slotted spoon, drain on absorbent kitchen paper (paper towels) and set aside until required.

4 Add the leek, broccoli and (bell) pepper to the wok and stir-fry for 2 minutes.

5 To make the sauce, place the fish stock, cornflour (cornstarch), chilli sauce to taste, the sesame oil and Chinese rice wine in a small bowl. Mix until thoroughly

6 Add the sauce to the wok, together with the cashew nuts. Return the prawns (shrimp) to the wok and cook for 1 minute to heat through.

7 Transfer the prawn (shrimp) stir-fry to a warm serving dish and serve immediately.

Szechuan White Fish

Szechuan pepper is quite hot and should be used sparingly to avoid making the dish unbearably spicy.

NUTRITIONAL INFORMATION

Calories	225	Sugars	.........3g
Protein	........20g	Fat	...........8g
Carbohydrate	...17g	Saturates	.......1g

5 MINS   20 MINS

SERVES 4

INGREDIENTS

350 g/12 oz white fish fillets

1 small egg, beaten

3 tbsp plain (all-purpose) flour

4 tbsp dry white wine

3 tbsp light soy sauce

vegetable oil, for frying

1 garlic clove, cut into slivers

1-cm/½-inch piece fresh root ginger, finely chopped

1 onion, finely chopped

1 celery stick, chopped

1 fresh red chilli, chopped

3 spring onions (scallions), chopped

1 tsp rice wine vinegar

½ tsp ground Szechuan pepper

175 ml/6 fl oz/¾ cup fish stock

1 tsp caster (superfine) sugar

1 tsp cornflour (cornstarch)

2 tsp water

1 Cut the fish into 4-cm/1½-inch cubes. Beat together the egg, flour, wine and 1 tablespoon of soy sauce to make a batter. Dip the cubes of fish into the batter to coat well.

2 Heat the oil in a wok, reduce the heat slightly and cook the fish, in batches, for 2–3 minutes, until golden brown. Remove with a slotted spoon, drain on kitchen paper (paper towels), set aside and keep warm.

3 Pour all but 1 tablespoon of oil from the wok and return to the heat. Add the garlic, ginger, onion, celery, chilli and spring onions (scallions) and stir-fry for 1–2 minutes. Stir in the remaining soy sauce and the vinegar.

4 Add the Szechuan pepper, fish stock and caster (superfine) sugar to the wok. Mix the cornflour (cornstarch) with the water to form a smooth paste and stir it into the stock. Bring to the boil and cook, stirring, for 1 minute, until the sauce thickens and clears.

5 Return the fish cubes to the wok and cook for 1–2 minutes. Serve immediately.

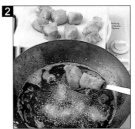

Fish with Black Bean Sauce

Steaming is one of the preferred methods of cooking whole fish in China as it maintains both the flavour and the texture.

NUTRITIONAL INFORMATION

Calories	292	Sugars	.........3g
Protein	........44g	Fat	...........7g
Carbohydrate	....6g	Saturates	.....0.4g

 10 MINS   10 MINS

SERVES 4

I N G R E D I E N T S

900 g/2 lb whole snapper, cleaned and scaled

3 garlic cloves, crushed

2 tbsp black bean sauce

1 tsp cornflour (cornstarch)

2 tsp sesame oil

2 tbsp light soy sauce

2 tsp caster (superfine) sugar

2 tbsp dry sherry

1 small leek, shredded

1 small red (bell) pepper, seeded and cut into thin strips

shredded leek and lemon wedges, to garnish

boiled rice or noodles, to serve

1 Rinse the fish inside and out with cold running water and pat dry with kitchen paper (paper towels).

2 Make 2-3 diagonal slashes in the flesh on each side of the fish, using a sharp knife. Rub the garlic into the fish.

3 Mix together the black bean sauce, cornflour (cornstarch), sesame oil, light soy sauce, sugar and dry sherry.

4 Place the fish in a shallow heatproof dish and pour the sauce mixture over the top. Sprinkle the shredded leek and (bell) pepper strips on top of the sauce.

5 Place the dish in the top of a steamer, cover and steam for 10 minutes, or until the fish is cooked through.

6 Transfer the fish to a serving dish, garnish with shredded leek and lemon wedges and serve with boiled rice or noodles.

COOK'S TIP

Insert the point of a sharp knife into the fish to test if it is cooked. The fish is cooked through if the knife goes into the flesh easily.

Stir-fried Salmon with Leeks

Salmon is marinated in a deliciously rich, sweet sauce, stir-fried and served on a bed of crispy leeks.

NUTRITIONAL INFORMATION

Calories . . . . . . .360 Sugars 9g
Protein . . . . .24g Fat 25
Carbohydrate . . . .11g Saturates 4g

 35 MINS   15 MINS

SERVES 4

INGREDIENTS

450 g/1 lb salmon fillet, skinned

2 tbsp sweet soy sauce

2 tbsp tomato ketchup

1 tsp rice wine vinegar

1 tbsp demerara (brown crystal)
    sugar

1 clove garlic, crushed

4 tbsp corn oil

450 g/1 lb leeks, thinly shredded

finely chopped red chillies,
    to garnish

1 Using a sharp knife, cut the salmon into slices. Place the slices of salmon in a shallow non-metallic dish.

2 Mix together the soy sauce, tomato ketchup, rice wine vinegar, sugar and garlic.

3 Pour the mixture over the salmon, toss well and leave to marinate for about 30 minutes.

4 Meanwhile, heat 3 tablespoons of the corn oil in a large preheated wok.

5 Add the leeks to the wok and stir-fry over a medium-high heat for about 10 minutes, or until the leeks become crispy and tender.

6 Using a slotted spoon, carefully remove the leeks from the wok and transfer to warmed serving plates.

7 Add the remaining oil to the wok. Add the salmon and the marinade to the wok and cook for 2 minutes.

8 Remove the salmon from the wok and spoon over the leeks, garnish with finely chopped red chillies and serve immediately.

VARIATION

You can use a fillet of beef instead of the salmon, if you prefer.

Sweet & Sour Prawns

Use raw prawns (shrimp) if possible. Omit steps 1 and 2 if ready-cooked ones are used.

NUTRITIONAL INFORMATION

Calories ....373 Sugars 11g
Protein ....13g Fat 26g
Carbohydrate ...19g Saturates 3g

3½ HOURS   10 MINS

SERVES 4

INGREDIENTS

175-250 g/6-9 oz peeled raw tiger prawns

pinch of salt

1 tsp egg white

1 tsp cornflour (cornstarch) paste (see page 31)

300 ml/½ pint/1¼ cups vegetable oil

SAUCE

1 tbsp vegetable oil

½ small green (bell) pepper, cored, seeded and thinly sliced

½ small carrot, thinly sliced

125 g/4½ oz canned water chestnuts, drained and sliced

½ tsp salt

1 tbsp light soy sauce

2 tbsp sugar

3 tbsp rice or sherry vinegar

1 tsp rice wine or dry sherry

1 tbsp tomato sauce

½ tsp chilli sauce

3-4 tbsp Chinese Stock (see page 30) or water

2 tsp cornflour (cornstarch) paste (see page 31)

a few drops sesame oil

1 Mix together the prawns (shrimp) with the salt, egg white and cornflour (cornstarch) paste.

2 Heat the oil in a preheated wok and stir-fry the prawns (shrimp) for 30-40 seconds only. Remove and drain on kitchen paper (paper towels).

3 Pour off the oil and wipe the wok clean with kitchen paper (paper towels). To make the sauce, first heat the tablespoon of oil. Add the vegetables and stir-fry for about 1 minute, then add the seasonings with the stock or water and bring to the boil.

4 Add the prawns (shrimp) and stir until blended well. Thicken the sauce with the cornflour (cornstarch) paste and stir until smooth. Sprinkle with sesame oil and serve hot.

Fried Squid Flowers

The addition of green (bell) pepper and black bean sauce to the squid makes a colourful and delicious dish from the Cantonese school.

NUTRITIONAL INFORMATION

Calories 172   Sugars 1g
Protein ....13g   Fat 13g
Carbohydrate ....2g   Saturates 1g

 10 MINS   5 MINS

SERVES 4

INGREDIENTS

350-400 g/12-14 oz prepared and cleaned squid (see Cook's Tip, below)

1 medium green (bell) pepper, cored and seeded

3-4 tbsp vegetable oil

1 garlic clove, finely chopped

¼ tsp finely chopped ginger root

2 tsp finely chopped spring onions (scallions)

½ tsp salt

2 tbsp crushed black bean sauce

1 tsp Chinese rice wine or dry sherry

a few drops sesame oil

boiled rice, to serve

1 If ready-prepared squid is not available, prepare as instructed in the Cook's Tip, below.

2 Open up the squid and, using a meat cleaver or sharp knife, score the inside of the flesh in a criss-cross pattern.

3 Cut the squid into pieces about the size of an oblong postage stamp.

4 Blanch the squid pieces in a bowl of boiling water for a few seconds. Remove and drain; dry well on absorbent kitchen paper (paper towels).

5 Cut the (bell) pepper into small triangular pieces. Heat the oil in a preheated wok or large frying pan (skillet) and stir-fry the (bell) pepper for about 1 minute.

6 Add the garlic, ginger, spring onion (scallion), salt and squid. Continue stirring for another minute.

7 Finally add the black bean sauce and Chinese rice wine or dry sherry, and blend well.

8 Transfer the squid flowers to a serving dish, sprinkle with sesame oil and serve with boiled rice.

COOK'S TIP

Clean the squid by first cutting off the head. Cut off the tentacles and reserve. Remove the small soft bone at the base of the tentacles and the transparent backbone, as well as the ink bag. Peel off the thin skin, then wash and dry well.

Fish with Saffron Sauce

White fish cooked in a bamboo steamer over the wok and served with a light creamy saffron sauce with a real bite to it.

NUTRITIONAL INFORMATION

Calories	254	Sugars	.......0.5g
Protein	........30g	Fat	..........14g
Carbohydrate	....2g	Saturates	.......5g

 5 MINS   30 MINS

SERVES 4

I N G R E D I E N T S

625-750 g/1 lb 6 oz-1 lb 10 oz white fish fillets (cod, haddock, whiting etc)

pinch of Chinese five-spice powder

4 sprigs fresh thyme

large pinch saffron threads

250 ml/9 fl oz/1 cup boiling fish or vegetable stock

2 tbsp sunflower oil

125 g/4½ oz button mushrooms, thinly sliced

grated rind of ½ lemon

1 tbsp lemon juice

½ tsp freshly chopped thyme or ¼ tsp dried thyme

½ bunch watercress, chopped

1½ tsp cornflour (cornstarch)

3 tbsp single or double (heavy) cream

salt and pepper

1 Skin the fish and cut into 4 even-sized portions. Season with salt and pepper and five-spice powder. Arrange the fish on a plate and place in the bottom of a bamboo steamer, laying a sprig of thyme on each piece of fish.

2 Stand a low metal trivet in a wok and add water to come almost to the top of it. Bring to the boil, stand the bamboo steamer on the trivet and cover with the bamboo lid and then the lid of the wok or a piece of foil. Simmer for 20 minutes until the fish is tender, adding more boiling water to the wok if necessary. Meanwhile, soak the saffron threads in the boiling stock.

3 When the fish is tender, remove and keep warm. Empty the wok and wipe dry. Heat the oil in the wok and stir-fry the mushrooms for about 2 minutes. Add the saffron stock, lemon rind and juice and chopped thyme and bring to the boil. Add the watercress and simmer for 1-2 minutes.

4 Blend the cornflour (cornstarch) with the cream, add a little of the sauce from the wok, then return to the wok and heat gently until thickened. Serve the fish surrounded by the sauce.

Sesame Salmon with Cream

Salmon fillet holds its shape when tossed in sesame seeds and stir-fried. It is served in a creamy sauce of diced courgettes (zucchini).

NUTRITIONAL INFORMATION

Calories	550	Sugars	.........1g
Protein	........35g	Fat	..........45g
Carbohydrate	....2g	Saturates	......12g

5 MINS   10 MINS

SERVES 4

INGREDIENTS

625-750 g/1 lb 6 oz– 1 lb 10 oz
    salmon or pink trout fillets

2 tbsp light soy sauce

3 tbsp sesame seeds

3 tbsp sunflower oil

4 spring onions (scallions), thinly
    sliced diagonally

2 large courgettes (zucchini),
    diced, or 2.5-cm/5-inch piece
    cucumber, diced

grated rind of ½ lemon

1 tbsp lemon juice

½ tsp turmeric

6 tbsp fish stock or water

3 tbsp double (heavy) cream or fromage
    frais

salt and pepper

curly endive, to garnish

1 Skin the fish and cut into strips about 4 x 2 cm/1½ x ¾ inches. Pat dry on kitchen paper (paper towels). Season lightly, then brush with soy sauce and sprinkle all over with sesame seeds.

2 Heat 2 tablespoons of oil in the wok. Add the pieces of fish and stir-fry for 3-4 minutes until lightly browned all over. Remove with a fish slice, drain on kitchen paper (paper towels) and keep warm.

3 Heat the remaining oil in the wok and add the spring onions (scallions) and courgettes (zucchini) or cucumber and stir-fry for 1-2 minutes. Add the lemon rind and juice, turmeric, stock and seasoning and bring to the boil for 1 minute. Stir in the cream or fromage frais.

4 Return the fish pieces to the wok and toss gently in the sauce until they are really hot. Garnish and serve.

COOK'S TIP

Lay the fillet skin-side down. Insert a sharp, flexible knife at one end between the flesh and the skin. Hold the skin tightly at the end and push the knife along, keeping the knife blade as flat as possible against the skin.

Crispy Fish

This is a very hot dish – not for the faint hearted! It may be made without the chilli flavourings, if preferred.

NUTRITIONAL INFORMATION

Calories . . . . .281 Sugars 3g
Protein . . . . .25g Fat 12g
Carbohydrate . . .15g Saturates 2g

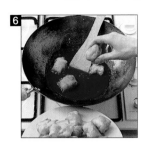

30 MINS   40 MINS

SERVES 4

INGREDIENTS

450 g/1 lb white fish fillets

BATTER

60 g/2 oz/½ cup plain (all-purpose) flour

1 egg, separated

1 tbsp peanut oil

4 tbsp milk

vegetable oil, for deep-frying

SAUCE

1 fresh red chilli, chopped

2 garlic cloves, crushed

pinch of chilli powder

3 tbsp tomato purée (paste)

1 tbsp rice wine vinegar

2 tbsp dark soy sauce

2 tbsp Chinese rice wine

2 tbsp water

pinch of caster (superfine) sugar

1 Cut the fish into 2.5-cm/1-inch cubes and set aside.

2 Sift the plain (all-purpose) flour into a mixing bowl and make a well in the centre. Add the egg yolk and peanut oil to the mixing bowl and gradually stir in the milk, incorporating the flour to form a smooth batter. Leave to stand for about 20 minutes.

3 Whisk the egg white until it forms peaks and fold into the batter until thoroughly incorporated.

4 Heat the vegetable oil in a preheated wok or large frying pan (skillet). Dip the fish into the batter and fry, in batches, for 8–10 minutes, until cooked through. Remove the fish from the wok with a slotted spoon, set aside and keep warm until required.

5 Pour off all but 1 tablespoon of oil from the wok and return to the heat. Add the chilli, garlic, chilli powder, tomato purée (paste), rice wine vinegar, soy sauce, Chinese rice wine, water and sugar and cook, stirring, for 3–4 minutes.

6 Return the fish to the wok and stir gently to coat it in the sauce. Cook for 2–3 minutes, until hot. Transfer to a serving dish and serve immediately.

Braised Fish Fillets

Any white fish, such as lemon sole or plaice, is ideal for this delicious dish.

NUTRITIONAL INFORMATION

Calories . . . . .107 Sugars 2g
Protein . . . . .17g Fat 2g
Carbohydrate . . . .6g Saturates 0.3g

 4 HOURS   10 MINS

SERVES 4

I N G R E D I E N T S

3-4 small Chinese dried mushrooms

300-350 g/10½-12 oz fish fillets

1 tsp salt

½ egg white, lightly beaten

1 tsp cornflour (cornstarch) paste
  (see page 31)

600 ml/1 pint/2½ cups vegetable oil

1 tsp finely chopped ginger root

2 spring onions (scallions),
  finely chopped

1 garlic clove, finely chopped

½ small green (bell) pepper, deseeded
  and cut into small cubes

½ small carrot, thinly sliced

60 g/2 oz/½ cup canned sliced bamboo
  shoots, rinsed and drained

½ tsp sugar

1 tbsp light soy sauce

1 tsp rice wine or dry sherry

1 tbsp chilli bean sauce

2-3 tbsp Chinese Stock (see page 30)
  or water

a few drops of sesame oil

1 Soak the dried mushrooms in a bowl of warm water for 30 minutes. Drain thoroughly on kitchen paper (paper towels), reserving the soaking water for stock or soup. Squeeze the mushrooms to extract all of the moisture, cut off and discard any hard stems and slice thinly.

2 Cut the fish into bite-sized pieces, then place in a shallow dish and mix with a pinch of salt, the egg white and cornflour (cornstarch) paste, turning the fish to coat well.

3 Heat the oil in a preheated wok. Add the fish pieces to the wok and deep-fry for about 1 minute. Remove the fish pieces with a slotted spoon and leave to drain on kitchen paper (paper towels).

4 Pour off the excess oil, leaving about 1 tablespoon in the wok. Add the ginger, spring onions (scallions) and garlic to flavour the oil for a few seconds, then add the (bell) pepper, carrots and bamboo shoots and stir-fry for about 1 minute.

5 Add the sugar, soy sauce, wine, chilli bean sauce, stock or water, and the remaining salt and bring to the boil. Add the fish pieces, stirring to coat with the sauce, and braise for 1 minute. Sprinkle with sesame oil and serve.

Baked Crab with Ginger

In Chinese restaurants, only live crabs are used, but ready-cooked ones can be used at home quite successfully.

NUTRITIONAL INFORMATION

Calories 261   Sugars 0.5g
Protein . . . . .18g   Fat 17g
Carbohydrate . . . .5g   Saturates 2g

 3³/₄ HOURS   10 MINS

SERVES 4

INGREDIENTS

1 large or 2 medium crabs, weighing about 750 g/1 lb 10 oz in total

2 tbsp Chinese rice wine or dry sherry

1 egg, lightly beaten

1 tbsp cornflour (cornstarch)

3-4 tbsp vegetable oil

1 tbsp finely chopped ginger root

3-4 spring onions (scallions), cut into sections

2 tbsp light soy sauce

1 tsp sugar

about 75 ml/5 tbsp/⅓ cup Chinese Stock (see page 30) or water

½ tsp sesame oil

coriander (cilantro) leaves, to garnish

1 Cut the crab in half from the underbelly. Break off the claws and crack them with the back of a cleaver or a large kitchen knife.

2 Discard the legs and crack the shell, breaking it into several pieces. Discard the feathery gills and the stomach sac. Place the crab meat in a bowl.

3 Mix together the wine or sherry, egg and cornflour (cornstarch). Pour the mixture over the crab and leave to marinate for 10-15 minutes.

  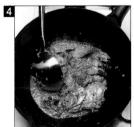

4 Heat the vegetable oil in a preheated wok and stir-fry the crab with the chopped ginger and spring onions (scallions) for 2-3 minutes.

5 Add the soy sauce, sugar and Chinese stock or water, blend well and bring to the boil. Cover and cook for 3-4 minutes, then remove the lid, sprinkle with sesame oil and serve, garnished with fresh coriander (cilantro) leaves.

COOK'S TIP

Crabs are almost always sold ready-cooked. The crab should feel heavy for its size, and when it is shaken, there should be no sound of water inside. A good medium-sized crab should yield about 500 g/1 lb 2 oz meat, enough for 3-4 people.

Stir-fried Prawns (Shrimp)

The (bell) peppers in this dish can be replaced by either mangetout (snow peas), or broccoli to maintain the attractive pink-green contrast.

NUTRITIONAL INFORMATION

Calories	116	Sugars	.........1g
Protein	........10g	Fat	...........6g
Carbohydrate	....4g	Saturates	.......1g

 5 MINS 10 MINS

SERVES 4

INGREDIENTS

170 g/6 oz raw prawns (shrimp), peeled

1 tsp salt

¼ tsp egg white

2 tsp cornflour (cornstarch) paste (see page 31)

300 ml/½ pint/1¼ cups vegetable oil

1 spring onion (scallion), cut into short sections

2.5-cm/1-inch piece ginger root, thinly sliced

1 small green (bell) pepper, cored, seeded and cubed

½ tsp sugar

1 tbsp light soy sauce

1 tsp rice wine or dry sherry

a few drops sesame oil

VARIATION

1-2 small green or red hot chillies, sliced, can be added with the green (bell) pepper to create a more spicy dish. Leave the chillies unseeded for a very hot dish.

1 Mix the prawns (shrimp) with a pinch of the salt, the egg white and cornflour (cornstarch) paste until well coated.

2 Heat the oil in a preheated wok and stir-fry the prawns (shrimp) for 30-40 seconds only. Remove and drain on kitchen paper (paper towels).

3 Pour off the oil, leaving about 1 tablespoon in the wok. Add the spring onion (scallion) and ginger to flavour the oil for a few seconds, then add the green (bell) pepper and stir-fry for about 1 minute.

4 Add the remaining salt and the sugar followed by the prawns (shrimp). Continue stirring for another minute or so, then add the soy sauce and wine and blend well. Sprinkle with sesame oil and serve immediately.

Steamed Stuffed Snapper

Red mullet may be used instead of the snapper, although they are a little more difficult to stuff because of their size. Use one mullet per person.

NUTRITIONAL INFORMATION

Calories 406	Sugar 4g
Protein 68g	Fat 9g
Carbohydrate 9g	Saturates 0g

🍲 20 MINS   🕐 10 MINS

SERVES 4

I N G R E D I E N T S

1.4 kg/3 lb whole snapper, cleaned and scaled

175 g/6 oz spinach

orange slices and shredded spring onion (scallion), to garnish

S T U F F I N G

60 g/2 oz/2 cups cooked long-grain rice

1 tsp grated fresh root ginger

2 spring onions (scallions), finely chopped

2 tsp light soy sauce

1 tsp sesame oil

½ tsp ground star anise

1 orange, segmented and chopped

1 Rinse the fish inside and out under cold running water and pat dry with kitchen paper (paper towels).

2 Blanch the spinach for 40 seconds, rinse in cold water and drain well, pressing out as much moisture as possible.

3 Arrange the spinach on a heatproof plate and place the fish on top.

4 To make the stuffing, mix together the cooked rice, grated ginger, spring onions (scallions), soy sauce, sesame oil, star anise and orange in a bowl.

5 Spoon the stuffing into the body cavity of the fish, pressing it in well with a spoon.

6 Cover the plate and cook in a steamer for 10 minutes, or until the fish is cooked through.

7 Transfer the fish to a warmed serving dish, garnish with orange slices and shredded spring onion (scallion) and serve.

COOK'S TIP

The name snapper covers a family of tropical and subtropical fish that vary in colour. They may be red, orange, pink, grey or blue-green. Some are striped or spotted and they range in size from about 15 cm/ 6 inches to 90 cm/3 ft.

Octopus & Squid with Chilli

Try to buy cleaned squid tubes for this dish; if they are not available, see page 278 for instructions on preparing squid.

NUTRITIONAL INFORMATION

Calories 319	Sugars 2g	
Protein 40g	Fat 13g	
Carbohydrate 4g	Saturates 1g	

8½ HOURS   10 MINS

SERVES 6

INGREDIENTS

150 ml/¼ pint/⅔ cup rice vinegar

50 ml/2 fl oz/¼ cup dry sherry

2 red chillies, chopped

1 tsp sugar

4 tbsp oil

12 baby octopus

12 small squid tubes, cleaned

2 spring onions (scallions), sliced

1 garlic clove, crushed

2.5 cm/1 inch piece ginger, grated

4 tbsp sweet chilli sauce

salt

1 Combine the vinegar, dry sherry, red chillies, sugar, 2 tbsp of the oil and a pinch of salt in a large bowl.

2 Wash each octopus under cold running water and drain. Lay each on its side on a chopping board. Find the 'neck' and cut through. The 'beak' of the octopus should be left in the head; if it is not, make a cut nearer the tentacles and check again. Discard the head and beak, and put the tentacles, which should all be in one piece, into the vinegar mixture.

3 Put the squid tubes into the vinegar mixture and turn to coat well. Cover and chill for 8 hours or overnight.

4 Heat the remaining oil in a wok and stir-fry the spring onions (scallions), garlic and ginger for 1 minute over a very hot barbecue. Remove from the heat and add the chilli sauce. Set aside.

5 Drain the fish from the marinade. Cut the pointed bottom end off each squid tube, so the tubes are of even width. Open out the squid so that it is flat. Score the squid to create a lattice pattern.

6 Cook the octopus and squid over the hottest part of the barbecue for 4–5 minutes, turning them constantly. The octopus tentacles will curl up, and are cooked when the flesh is no longer translucent. The squid tubes will curl back on themselves, revealing the lattice cuts.

7 When cooked, toss them into the pan with the chilli sauce to coat completely and serve immediately.

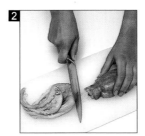

Tuna & Vegetable Stir-Fry

Fresh tuna is a dark, meaty fish and is now widely available at fresh fish counters. It lends itself perfectly to the rich flavours in this recipe.

NUTRITIONAL INFORMATION

Calories 245   Sugars 11g
Protein ....30g   Fat 7g
Carbohydrate ...14g   Saturates 1g

10 MINS   10 MINS

SERVES 4

INGREDIENTS

225 g/8 oz carrots

1 onion

175 g/6 oz/1¾ cups baby corn cobs

2 tbsp corn oil

175 g/6 oz/2½ cups mangetout (snow peas)

450 g/1 lb fresh tuna

2 tbsp fish sauce

15 g/½ oz/1 tbsp palm sugar

finely grated zest and juice of 1 orange

2 tbsp sherry

1 tsp cornflour (cornstarch)

rice or noodles, to serve

1 Using a sharp knife, cut the carrots into thin sticks, slice the onion and halve the baby corn cobs.

2 Heat the corn oil in a large preheated wok or frying pan (skillet).

3 Add the onion, carrots, mangetout (snow peas) and baby corn cobs to the wok or frying pan (skillet) and stir-fry for 5 minutes.

4 Using a sharp knife, thinly slice the fresh tuna.

5 Add the tuna slices to the wok or frying pan (skillet) and stir-fry for

about 2–3 minutes, or until the tuna turns opaque.

6 Mix together the fish sauce, palm sugar, orange zest and juice, sherry and cornflour (cornstarch).

7 Pour the mixture over the tuna and vegetables and cook for 2 minutes, or until the juices thicken. Serve the stir-fry with rice or noodles.

VARIATION

Try using swordfish steaks instead of the tuna. Swordfish steaks are now widely available and are similar in texture to tuna

Mullet with Ginger

Ginger is used widely in Chinese cooking for its strong, pungent flavour. Although fresh ginger is best, ground ginger may be used instead.

NUTRITIONAL INFORMATION

Calories ....195 Sugars 6g
Protein ....31g Fat 3g
Carbohydrate ....9g Saturates 0g

 10 MINS   15 MINS

SERVES 4

INGREDIENTS

1 whole mullet, cleaned and scaled

2 spring onions (scallions), chopped

1 tsp grated fresh root ginger

125 ml/4 fl oz/½ cup garlic wine vinegar

125 ml/4 fl oz/½ cup light soy sauce

3 tsp caster (superfine) sugar

dash of chilli sauce

125 ml/4 fl oz/½ cup fish stock

1 green (bell) pepper, seeded and thinly sliced

1 large tomato, skinned, seeded and cut into thin strips

salt and pepper

sliced tomato, to garnish

1 Rinse the fish inside and out and pat dry with kitchen paper (paper towels).

2 Make 3 diagonal slits in the flesh on each side of the fish. Season the fish with salt and pepper inside and out, according to taste.

3 Place the fish on a heatproof plate and scatter the chopped spring onions (scallions) and grated ginger over the top. Cover and steam for 10 minutes, or until the fish is cooked through.

4 Meanwhile, place the garlic wine vinegar, light soy sauce, caster (superfine) sugar, chilli sauce, fish stock, (bell) pepper and tomato in a saucepan and bring to the boil, stirring occasionally.

5 Cook the sauce over a high heat until the sauce has slightly reduced and thickened.

6 Remove the fish from the steamer and transfer to a warm serving dish. Pour the sauce over the fish, garnish with tomato slices and serve immediately.

VARIATION

Use fillets of fish for this recipe if preferred, and reduce the cooking time to 5–7 minutes.

Squid With Oyster Sauce

Squid is a delicious fish, which if prepared and cooked correctly, is a quick cooking, attractive and tasty ingredient.

NUTRITIONAL INFORMATION

Calories .... 320 Sugars 1g
Protein .... 18g Fat 26g
Carbohydrate .... 2g Saturates 3g

5 MINS   15 MINS

SERVES 4

INGREDIENTS

450 g/1 lb squid

150 ml/¼ pint/⅔ cup vegetable oil

1-cm/½-inch piece fresh root ginger, grated

60 g/2 oz mangetout (snow peas)

5 tbsp hot fish stock

red (bell) pepper triangles, to garnish

SAUCE

1 tbsp oyster sauce

1 tbsp light soy sauce

pinch of caster (superfine) sugar

1 garlic clove, crushed

1 To prepare the squid, cut down the centre of the body lengthways. Flatten the squid out, inside uppermost, and score a lattice design deep into the flesh, using a sharp knife.

2 To make the sauce, combine the oyster sauce, soy sauce, sugar and garlic in a small bowl. Stir to dissolve the sugar and set aside until required.

3 Heat the oil in a preheated wok until almost smoking. Lower the heat slightly, add the squid and stir-fry until they curl up. Remove with a slotted spoon and drain thoroughly on kitchen paper (paper towels).

4 Pour off all but 2 tablespoons of the oil and return the wok to the heat. Add the ginger and mangetout (snow peas) and stir-fry for 1 minute.

5 Return the squid to the wok and pour in the sauce and hot fish stock. Leave to simmer for 3 minutes until thickened. Transfer to a warm serving dish, garnish with (bell) pepper triangles and serve immediately.

COOK'S TIP

Take care not to overcook the squid, otherwise it will be rubbery and unappetizing.

Prawn (Shrimp) Omelette

This really is a meal in minutes, combining many Chinese ingredients for a truly tasty dish.

NUTRITIONAL INFORMATION

Calories	.270	Sugars	.1g
Protein	.30g	Fat	.15g
Carbohydrate	.3g	Saturates	.3g

5 MINS   10 MINS

SERVES 4

INGREDIENTS

2 tbsp sunflower oil

4 spring onions (scallions)

350 g/12 oz peeled prawns (shrimp)

100 g/3½ oz/1 cup bean sprouts

1 tsp cornflour (cornstarch)

1 tbsp light soy sauce

6 eggs

3 tbsp cold water

1 Heat the sunflower oil in a large preheated wok or frying pan (skillet).

2 Using a sharp knife, trim the spring onions (scallions) and cut into slices.

3 Add the prawns (shrimp), spring onions (scallions) and bean sprouts to the wok and stir-fry for 2 minutes.

4 In a small bowl, mix together the cornflour (cornstarch) and soy sauce until well combined.

5 In a separate bowl, beat the eggs with the water, using a metal fork, and then blend with the cornflour (cornstarch) and soy mixture.

6 Add the egg mixture to the wok and cook for 5–6 minutes, or until the mixture sets.

7 Transfer the omelette to a warm serving plate and cut into quarters to serve.

COOK'S TIP

It is important to use fresh bean sprouts for this dish as the canned ones don't have the crunchy texture necessary.

Trout with Pineapple

Pineapple is widely used in Chinese cooking. The tartness of fresh pineapple complements fish particularly well.

NUTRITIONAL INFORMATION

Calories ....243 Sugars 4g
Protein ....30g Fat 11g
Carbohydrate ....6g Saturates 2g

 5 MINS   15 MINS

SERVES 4

INGREDIENTS

4 trout fillets, skinned

2 tbsp vegetable oil

2 garlic cloves, cut into slivers

4 slices fresh pineapple, peeled and diced

1 celery stick, sliced

1 tbsp light soy sauce

50 ml/2 fl oz/¼ cup fresh or unsweetened
    pineapple juice

150 ml/¼ pint/⅔ cup fish stock

1 tsp cornflour (cornstarch)

2 tsp water

shredded celery leaves and fresh red chilli
    slices, to garnish

1 Cut the trout fillets into strips. Heat 1 tablespoon of the vegetable oil in a preheated wok until almost smoking. Reduce the heat slightly, add the fish and sauté for 2 minutes. Remove from the wok and set aside.

2 Add the remaining oil to the wok, reduce the heat and add the garlic, diced pineapple and celery. Stir-fry for 1–2 minutes.

3 Add the soy sauce, pineapple juice and fish stock to the wok. Bring to the boil and cook, stirring, for 2–3 minutes, or until the sauce has reduced.

4 Blend the cornflour (cornstarch) with the water to form a paste and stir it into the wok. Bring the sauce to the boil and cook, stirring constantly, until the sauce thickens and clears.

5 Return the fish to the wok, and cook, stirring gently, until heated through. Transfer to a warmed serving dish and serve, garnished with shredded celery leaves and red chilli slices.

VARIATION

Use canned pineapple instead of fresh pineapple if you wish, choosing slices in unsweetened, natural juice in preference to a syrup.

Szechuan Prawns (Shrimp)

Raw prawns (shrimp) should be used if possible, otherwise add the ready-cooked prawns (shrimp) at the beginning of step 3.

NUTRITIONAL INFORMATION

Calories 315	Sugars 1g
Protein 16g	Fat 27g
Carbohydrate 3g	Saturates 3g

3½ HOURS   10 MINS

SERVES 4

I N G R E D I E N T S

250-300 g/9-10½ oz raw tiger prawns (jumbo shrimp)

pinch of salt

½ egg white, lightly beaten

1 tsp cornflour (cornstarch) paste (see page 29)

600 ml/1 pint/2½ cups vegetable oil

fresh coriander (cilantro) leaves, to garnish

S A U C E

1 tsp finely chopped ginger root

2 spring onions (scallions), finely chopped

1 garlic clove, finely chopped

3-4 small dried red chillies, seeded and chopped

1 tbsp light soy sauce

1 tsp rice wine or dry sherry

1 tbsp tomato purée (paste)

1 tbsp oyster sauce

2-3 tbsp Chinese Stock (see page 28) or water

a few drops sesame oil

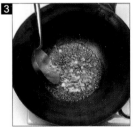

1 Peel the raw prawns (shrimp), then mix with the salt, egg white and cornflour (cornstarch) paste until the prawns (shrimp) are well coated.

2 Heat the oil in a preheated wok or large frying pan (skillet) until it is smoking, then deep-fry the prawns (shrimp) in hot oil for about 1 minute. Remove with a slotted spoon and drain on kitchen paper (paper towels).

3 Pour off the oil, leaving about 1 tablespoon in the wok. Add all the ingredients for the sauce, in the order listed, bring to the boil and stir until smooth and well blended.

4 Add the prawns (shrimp) to the sauce and stir until blended well.

5 Serve the prawns (shrimp) garnished with fresh coriander (cilantro) leaves.

Spiced Scallops

Scallops are available both fresh and frozen. Make sure they are completely defrosted before cooking.

10 MINS   10 MINS

SERVES 4

INGREDIENTS

12 large scallops with coral attached, defrosted if frozen, or 350 g/ 12 oz small scallops without coral, defrosted

4 tbsp sunflower oil

4-6 spring onions (scallions), thinly sliced diagonally

1 garlic clove, crushed

2.5 cm/1 inch ginger root, finely chopped

250 g/9 oz mangetout (snow peas)

125 g/4½ oz button or closed cup mushrooms, sliced

2 tbsp sherry

2 tbsp soy sauce

1 tbsp clear honey

¼ tsp ground allspice

salt and pepper

1 tbsp sesame seeds, toasted

1 Wash and dry the scallops, discarding any black pieces and detach the corals, if using.

2 Slice each scallop into 3-4 pieces and if the corals are large halve them.

3 Heat 2 tablespoons of the sunflower oil in a preheated wok or large,

heavy-based frying pan (skillet), swirling it around until really hot.

4 Add the spring onions (scallions), garlic and ginger to the wok or frying pan (skillet) and stir-fry for about 1 minute.

5 Add the mangetout (snow peas) to the wok and continue to cook for a further 2-3 minutes, stirring continuously. Remove to a bowl and set aside.

6 Add the remaining sunflower oil to the wok and when really hot add the scallops and corals and stir-fry for a couple of minutes.

7 Add the mushrooms and continue to cook for a further minute or so.

8 Add the sherry, soy sauce, honey and allspice to the wok, with salt and pepper to taste. Mix thoroughly, then return the mangetout (snow peas) mixture to the wok.

9 Season well with salt and pepper and toss together over a high heat for a minute or so until piping hot. Serve the scallops and vegetables immediately, sprinkled with sesame seeds.

Seafood Medley

Use any combination of fish and seafood in this delicious dish of coated fish served in a wine sauce.

NUTRITIONAL INFORMATION

Calories ....168 Sugars 2g
Protein ....29g Fat 3g
Carbohydrate ....4g Saturates 1g

  5 MINS   15 MINS

SERVES 4

I N G R E D I E N T S

2 tbsp dry white wine

1 egg white, lightly beaten

½ tsp Chinese five-spice powder

1 tsp cornflour (cornstarch)

300 g/10½ oz raw prawns (shrimp),
    peeled and deveined

125 g/4½ oz prepared squid,
    cut into rings

125 g/4½ oz white fish fillets,
    cut into strips

vegetable oil, for deep-frying

1 green (bell) pepper, seeded and
    cut into thin strips

1 carrot, cut into thin strips

4 baby corn cobs, halved lengthways

1 Mix the wine, egg white, five-spice powder and cornflour (cornstarch) in a large bowl. Add the prawns (shrimp), squid rings and fish fillets and stir to coat evenly. Remove the fish and seafood with a slotted spoon, reserving any leftover cornflour (cornstarch) mixture.

2 Heat the oil in a preheated wok and deep-fry the prawns (shrimp), squid and fish for 2–3 minutes. Remove the seafood mixture from the wok with a slotted spoon and set aside.

3 Pour off all but 1 tablespoon of oil from the wok and return to the heat. Add the (bell) pepper, carrot and corn cobs and stir-fry for 4–5 minutes.

4 Return the seafood to the wok with any remaining cornflour (cornstarch) mixture. Heat through, stirring, and serve.

COOK'S TIP

Open up the squid rings and using a sharp knife, score a lattice pattern on the flesh to make them look attractive.

Salmon with Pineapple

Presentation plays a major part in Chinese cooking and this dish demonstrates this perfectly with the wonderful combination of colours.

NUTRITIONAL INFORMATION

Calories ....347 Sugars 12g
Protein ....24g Fat 20g
Carbohydrate ...16g Saturates 3g

10 MINS   15 MINS

SERVES 4

INGREDIENTS

2 tbsp sunflower oil

1 red onion, sliced

1 orange (bell) pepper, deseeded and sliced

1 green (bell) pepper, deseeded and sliced

100 g/3½ oz/1 cup baby corn cobs

450 g/1 lb salmon fillet, skin removed

1 tbsp paprika

225 g/8 oz can cubed pineapple, drained

100 g/3½ oz/1 cup bean sprouts

2 tbsp tomato ketchup

2 tbsp soy sauce

2 tbsp medium sherry

1 tsp cornflour (cornstarch)

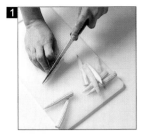

1 Cut each baby corn in half. Heat the oil in a large preheated wok. Add the onion, (bell) peppers and baby corn cobs to the wok and stir-fry for 5 minutes.

2 Rinse the salmon fillet under cold running water and pat dry with absorbent kitchen paper (paper towels).

3 Cut the salmon flesh into thin strips and place in a large bowl. Sprinkle with the paprika and toss well to coat.

4 Add the salmon to the wok together with the pineapple and stir-fry for a further 2–3 minutes or until the fish is tender.

5 Add the bean sprouts to the wok and toss well.

6 Mix together the tomato ketchup, soy sauce, sherry and cornflour (cornstarch). Add to the wok and cook until the juices start to thicken. Transfer to warm serving plates and serve immediately.

VARIATION

You can use trout fillets instead of the salmon as an alternative, if you prefer.

Crab in Ginger Sauce

In this recipe, the crabs are served in the shell for ease and visual effect and coated in a glossy ginger sauce.

NUTRITIONAL INFORMATION

Calories . . . . . . .125 Sugars 2g
Protein . . . . .8g Fat 8g
Carbohydrate . . . .5g Saturates 1g

10 MINS   10 MINS

SERVES 4

I N G R E D I E N T S

2 small cooked crabs

2 tbsp vegetable oil

9-cm/3-inch piece fresh root ginger, grated

2 garlic cloves, thinly sliced

1 green (bell) pepper, seeded and cut into thin strips

6 spring onions (scallions), cut into 2.5-cm/1-inch lengths

2 tbsp dry sherry

½ tsp sesame oil

150 ml/¼ pint/⅔ cup fish stock

1 tsp light brown sugar

2 tsp cornflour (cornstarch)

150 ml/¼ pint/⅔ cup water

1 Rinse the crabs and gently loosen around the shell at the top. Using a sharp knife, cut away the grey tissue and discard. Rinse the crabs again.

2 Twist off the legs and claws from the crabs. Using a pair of crab claw crackers or a cleaver, gently crack the claws to break through the shell to expose the flesh. Remove and discard any loose pieces of shell.

3 Separate the body and discard the inedible lungs and sac. Cut down the centre of each crab to separate the body into two pieces and then cut each of these in half again.

4 Heat the oil in a preheated wok. Add the ginger and garlic and stir-fry for 1 minute. Add the crab pieces and stir-fry for a further minute.

5 Stir in the (bell) pepper, spring onions (scallions), sherry, sesame oil, stock and sugar. Bring to the boil, reduce the heat, cover and simmer for 3–4 minutes.

6 Blend the cornflour (cornstarch) with the water and stir into the wok. Bring to the boil, stirring, until the sauce is thickened and clear. Transfer to a warm serving dish and serve immediately.

VARIATION

If preferred, remove the crabmeat from the shells prior to stir-frying and add to the wok with the (bell) pepper.

Squid with Black Bean Sauce

Squid really is wonderful if quickly cooked as in this recipe, and contrary to popular belief it is not tough and rubbery unless it is overcooked.

NUTRITIONAL INFORMATION

Calories 180   Sugars 2g
Protein ....19g   Fat 7g
Carbohydrate ...10g   Saturates 1g

5 MINS   20 MINS

SERVES 4

I N G R E D I E N T S

450 g/1 lb squid rings

2 tbsp plain (all-purpose) flour

½ tsp salt

1 green (bell) pepper

2 tbsp groundnut oil

1 red onion, sliced

160 g/5¾ oz jar black bean sauce

1 Rinse the squid rings under cold running water and pat dry thoroughly with absorbent kitchen paper (paper towels).

2 Place the plain (all-purpose) flour and salt in a bowl and mix together. Add the squid rings and toss until they are evenly coated.

3 Using a sharp knife, deseed the (bell) pepper. Slice the (bell) pepper into thin strips.

4 Heat the groundnut oil in a large preheated wok or heavy-based frying pan (skillet), swirling the oil around the base of the wok until it is really hot.

5 Add the (bell) pepper slices and red onion to the wok or frying pan (skillet) and stir-fry for about 2 minutes, or until the vegetables are just beginning to soften.

6 Add the squid rings to the wok or frying pan (skillet) and cook for a further 5 minutes, or until the squid is cooked through. Be careful not to overcook the squid.

7 Add the black bean sauce to the wok and heat through until the juices are bubbling. Transfer the squid stir-fry to warm serving bowls and serve immediately.

COOK'S TIP

Serve this recipe with fried rice or noodles tossed in soy sauce, if you wish.

Seared Scallops

Scallops have a terrific, subtle flavour which is complemented in this dish by the buttery sauce.

 5 MINS   10 MINS

SERVES 4

INGREDIENTS

450 g/1 lb fresh scallops, without roe, or
the same amount of frozen scallops,
defrosted thoroughly

6 spring onions (scallions)

2 tbsp vegetable oil

1 green chilli, deseeded and sliced

3 tbsp sweet soy sauce

50 g/1¾ oz/1½ tbsp butter, cubed

1 Rinse the scallops thoroughly under cold running water, drain and pat the scallops dry with absorbent kitchen paper (paper towels).

2 Using a sharp knife, slice each scallop in half horizontally.

COOK'S TIP

If you buy scallops on the shell, slide a knife underneath the membrane to loosen it and cut off the tough muscle that holds the scallop to the shell. Discard the black stomach sac and intestinal vein.

3 Using a sharp knife, trim and slice the spring onions (scallions).

4 Heat the vegetable oil in a large preheated wok or heavy-based frying pan (skillet), swirling the oil around the base of the wok until it is really hot.

5 Add the sliced green chilli, spring onions (scallions) and scallops to the wok and stir-fry over a high heat for

4–5 minutes, or until the scallops are just cooked through. If using frozen scallops, be sure not to overcook them as they will easily disintegrate.

6 Add the soy sauce and butter to the scallop stir-fry and heat through until the butter melts.

7 Transfer to warm serving bowls and serve hot.

Fish in Szechuan Hot Sauce

This is a classic Szechuan recipe. When served in a restaurant, the fish head and tail are removed before cooking.

NUTRITIONAL INFORMATION

Calories . . . . .470 Sugar . . . .∴.3g
Protein . . . . .45g Fat 29g
Carbohydrate . . . .7g Saturates 4g

3³/₄ HOURS   15 MINS

SERVES 4

I N G R E D I E N T S

1 carp, bream, sea bass, trout,
   grouper or grey mullet, about
   750g/1 lb 10 oz, gutted

1 tbsp light soy sauce

1 tbsp Chinese rice wine or dry sherry

vegetable oil, for deep-frying

flat-leaf parsley or coriander (cilatnro)
   sprigs, to garnish

S A U C E

2 garlic cloves, finely chopped

2-3 spring onions (scallions),
   finely chopped

1 tsp finely chopped ginger root

2 tbsp chilli bean sauce

1 tbsp tomato purée (paste)

2 tsp sugar

1 tbsp rice vinegar

125 ml/4 fl oz/½ cup Chinese Stock
   (see page 30) or water

1 tbsp cornflour (cornstarch) paste
   (see page 31)

½ tsp sesame oil

1 Wash the fish and dry well on kitchen
   paper absorbent (paper towels).

2 Score both sides of the fish to the
   bone with a sharp knife, making
   diagonal cuts at intervals of 2.5 cm/1 inch.

3 Rub the fish with the soy sauce and rice wine or sherry
   on both sides. Transfer the fish to a plate, cover with
   cling film (plastic wrap) and leave to marinate in the
   refrigerator for 10-15 minutes.

4 Heat the oil in a preheated wok or large frying pan
   (skillet) until smoking.

5 Deep-fry the fish in the hot oil for about 3-4 minutes
   on both sides, or until golden brown.

6 Pour off the oil, leaving about 1 tablespoon in the wok.
   Push the fish to one side of the wok and add the garlic,
   white parts of the spring onions (scallions), ginger, chilli
   bean sauce, tomato purée (paste), sugar, vinegar and
   Chinese stock or water.

7 Bring the mixture in the wok to the boil and braise the
   fish in the sauce for 4-5 minutes, turning it over once.

8 Add the green parts of the spring onions (scallions)
   and stir in the cornflour (cornstarch) paste to thicken
   the sauce.

9 Sprinkle with sesame oil and serve immediately,
   garnished with fresh parsley or coriander (cilantro).

Prawns with Vegetables

This colourful and delicious dish is cooked with vegetables: vary them according to seasonal availability.

NUTRITIONAL INFORMATION

Calories 298   Sugars 1g
Protein . . . . .13g   Fat 26g
Carbohydrate . . . .3g   Saturates 3g

 5 MINS   10 MINS

SERVES 4

INGREDIENTS

60 g/2 oz mangetout (snow peas)

½ small carrot

60 g/2 oz baby sweetcorn

60 g/2 oz straw mushrooms

175-250 g/6-9 oz raw tiger prawns (jumbo shrimp), peeled

1 tsp salt

½ egg white, lightly beaten

1 tsp cornflour (cornstarch) paste (see page 31)

about 300 ml/½ pint/1¼ cups vegetable oil

1 spring onion (scallion), cut into short sections

4 slices ginger root, peeled and finely chopped

½ tsp sugar

1 tbsp light soy sauce

1 tsp Chinese rice wine or dry sherry

a few drops sesame oil

lemon slices and chopped fresh chives, to garnish

1 Using a sharp knife, top and tail the mangetout (snow peas); cut the carrot into the same size as the mangetout (snow peas); halve the baby sweetcorn and straw mushrooms.

2 Mix the prawns (shrimp) with a pinch of the salt, the egg white and cornflour (cornstarch) paste until the prawns (shrimp) are evenly coated.

3 Preheat a wok over a high heat for 2-3 minutes, then add the vegetable oil and heat to medium-hot.

4 Add the prawns (shrimp) to the wok, stirring to separate them. Remove the prawns (shrimp) with a slotted spoon as soon as the colour changes.

5 Pour off the oil, leaving about 1 tablespoon in the wok. Add the mangetout (snow peas), carrot, sweetcorn, mushrooms and spring onions (scallions).

6 Add the prawns (shrimp) together with the ginger, sugar, soy sauce and wine or sherry, blending well.

7 Sprinkle with the sesame oil and serve hot, garnished with lemon slices and chopped fresh chives.

Fish & Ginger Stir-fry

This delicious and spicy recipe is a really quick fish dish, ideal for midweek family meals or light lunches at weekends.

NUTRITIONAL INFORMATION

Calories ....280 Sugars 2g
Protein ....31g Fat 10g
Carbohydrate ...17g Saturates 2g

5 MINS   15 MINS

SERVES 4

INGREDIENTS

4 tbsp cornflour (cornstarch)

½ tsp ground ginger

675 g/1½ lb firm white fish fillets, skinned and cubed

3 tbsp peanut oil

2.5-cm/1-inch fresh ginger root, grated

1 leek, thinly sliced

1 tbsp white wine vinegar

2 tbsp Chinese rice wine or dry sherry

3 tbsp dark soy sauce

1 tsp caster (superfine) sugar

2 tbsp lemon juice

finely shredded leek, to garnish

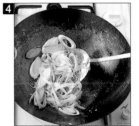
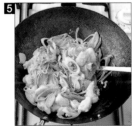

1 Mix the cornflour (cornstarch) and ground ginger in a bowl.

2 Add the cubes of fish, in batches, to the cornflour (cornstarch) mixture, turning to coat the fish thoroughly in the mixture.

3 Heat the peanut oil in a preheated wok or large, heavy-based frying pan (skillet), swirling the oil around the base of the wok until it is really hot.

4 Add the grated fresh ginger and sliced leek to the wok or frying pan (skillet) and stir-fry for 1 minute.

5 Add the coated fish to the wok and cook for a further 5 minutes, until browned, stirring to prevent the fish from sticking to the base of the wok.

6 Add the remaining ingredients and cook over a low heat for 3–4 minutes, until the fish is cooked through.

7 Transfer the fish and ginger stir-fry to a serving dish and serve immediately.

VARIATION

Use any firm white fish which will hold its shape, such as cod, haddock or monkfish.

Stir-Fried Cod with Mango

Fish and fruit are a classic combination, and in this recipe a tropical flavour is added which gives a great scented taste to the dish.

NUTRITIONAL INFORMATION

Calories	200	Sugars	........12g
Protein	........21g	Fat	..........7g
Carbohydrate	...14g	Saturates	.......1g

10 MINS   15 MINS

SERVES 4

INGREDIENTS

175 g/6 oz carrots

2 tbsp vegetable oil

1 red onion, sliced

1 red (bell) pepper, deseeded
   and sliced

1 green (bell) pepper, deseeded
   and sliced

450 g/1 lb skinless cod fillet

1 ripe mango

1 tsp cornflour (cornstarch)

1 tbsp soy sauce

100 ml/3½ fl oz/1⅓ cups tropical
   fruit juice

1 tbsp lime juice

1 tbsp chopped fresh coriander (cilantro),
   to garnish

1 Using a sharp knife, slice the carrots into thin sticks.

2 Heat the oil in a preheated wok and stir-fry the onion, carrots and (bell) peppers for 5 minutes.

3 Using a sharp knife, cut the cod into small cubes. Peel the mango, then carefully remove the flesh from the centre stone. Cut the flesh into thin slices.

4 Add the cod and mango to the wok and stir-fry for a further 4–5 minutes, or until the fish is cooked through. Be careful not to break the fish up.

5 Mix together the cornflour (cornstarch), soy sauce, fruit juice and lime juice. Pour the mixture into the wok and stir until the mixture bubbles and the juices thicken. Scatter with coriander (cilantro) and serve immediately.

VARIATION

You can use paw-paw (papaya) as an alternative to the mango, if you prefer.

Fish with Coconut & Basil

Fish curries are sensational and this is no exception. Red curry and coconut are fantastic flavours with the fried fish.

NUTRITIONAL INFORMATION

Calories 209   Sugars 10g
Protein . . . . .21g   Fat 8g
Carbohydrate . . .15g   Saturates 1g

5 MINS   15 MINS

SERVES 4

INGREDIENTS

2 tbsp vegetable oil

450 g/1 lb skinless cod fillet

25 g/1 oz/¼ cup seasoned flour

1 clove garlic, crushed

2 tbsp red curry paste

1 tbsp fish sauce

300 ml/½ pint/1¼ cups coconut milk

175 g/6 oz cherry tomatoes, halved

20 fresh basil leaves

fragrant rice, to serve

1 Heat the vegetable oil in a large preheated wok.

2 Using a sharp knife, cut the fish into large cubes, removing any bones with a pair of clean tweezers.

3 Place the seasoned flour in a bowl. Add the cubes of fish and mix until well coated.

4 Add the coated fish to the wok and stir-fry over a high heat for 3–4 minutes, or until the fish just begins to brown at the edges.

5 In a small bowl, mix together the garlic, curry paste, fish sauce and coconut milk. Pour the mixture over the fish and bring to the boil.

6 Add the tomatoes to the mixture in the wok and leave to simmer for 5 minutes.

7 Roughly chop or tear the fresh basil leaves. Add the basil to the wok, stir carefully to combine, taking care not to break up the cubes of fish.

8 Transfer to serving plates and serve hot with fragrant rice.

COOK'S TIP

Take care not to overcook the dish once the tomatoes are added, otherwise they will break down and the skins will come away.

Scallop Pancakes

Scallops, like most shellfish require very little cooking, and this original dish is a perfect example of how to use shellfish to its full potential.

NUTRITIONAL INFORMATION

Calories	240	Sugars	.........1g
Protein	........29g	Fat	..........9g
Carbohydrate	....11g	Saturates	.......1g

5 MINS   30 MINS

SERVES 4

I N G R E D I E N T S

100 g/3½ oz fine green beans

1 red chilli

450 g/1 lb scallops, without roe

1 egg

3 spring onions (scallions), sliced

50 g/1¾ oz/½ cup rice flour

1 tbsp fish sauce

oil, for frying

salt

sweet chilli dip, to serve

1 Using a sharp knife, trim the green beans and slice them very thinly.

2 Using a sharp knife, deseed and very finely chop the red chilli.

3 Bring a small saucepan of lightly salted water to the boil. Add the green beans to the pan and cook for 3–4 minutes or until just softened.

4 Roughly chop the scallops and place them in a large bowl. Add the cooked beans to the scallops.

5 Mix the egg with the spring onions (scallions), rice flour, fish sauce and chilli until well combined. Add to the scallops and mix well.

6 Heat about 2.5 cm/1 inch of oil in a large preheated wok. Add a ladleful of the mixture to the wok and cook for 5 minutes until golden and set.

7 Remove the pancake from the wok and leave to drain on absorbent kitchen paper (paper towels). Keep warm while cooking the remaining pancake mixture. Serve the pancakes hot with a sweet chilli dip.

VARIATION

You could use prawns (shrimp) or shelled clams instead of the scallops, if you prefer.

Shrimp & Sweetcorn Patties

Chopped (small) shrimps and sweetcorn are combined in a light batter, which is dropped in spoonfuls into hot fat to make these tasty patties.

NUTRITIONAL INFORMATION

Calories 250   Sugars 1g
Protein ....17g   Fat 9g
Carbohydrate ...26g   Saturates 2g

35 MINS   20 MINS

SERVES 4

INGREDIENTS

125 g/4½ oz/1 cup plain (all-purpose) flour

1½ tsp baking powder

2 eggs

about 250 ml/9 fl oz/1 cup cold water

1 garlic clove, very finely chopped

3 spring onions (scallions), trimmed and very finely chopped

250 g/9 oz/1 cup peeled (small) shrimps, chopped

125 g/4½ oz/½ cup canned sweetcorn, drained

vegetable oil for frying

salt and pepper

TO GARNISH

spring onion (scallion) brushes (see Cook's Tip, right)

lime slices

1 chilli flower (see Cook's Tip, page 269)

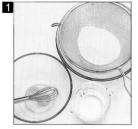  

1 Sift the flour, baking powder and ½ tsp salt into a bowl. Add the eggs and half the water and beat to make a smooth batter, adding extra water to give the consistency of double (heavy) cream. Add the garlic and spring onions (scallions). Cover and leave for 30 minutes.

2 Stir the (small) shrimps and corn into the batter. Season with pepper.

3 Heat 2–3 tablespoons of oil in a wok. Drop tablespoonfuls of the batter into the wok and cook over a medium heat until bubbles rise and the surface just sets. Flip the patties over and cook the other side until golden brown. Drain on kitchen paper (paper towels).

4 Cook the remaining batter in the same way, adding more oil to the wok if required. Garnish and serve at once.

COOK'S TIP

Make a spring onion (scallion) brush by trimming off the tips of the leaves and making several fine cuts from the leaf tips to the top of the bulb. Place in iced water to make the leaves curl.

Crispy Fried Squid

Squid tubes are classically used in Chinese cooking and are most attractive when presented as in the following recipe.

NUTRITIONAL INFORMATION

Calories 156   Sugars 0g
Protein ....17g   Fat 6g
Carbohydrate ....7g   Saturates 8g

 10 MINS   10 MINS

SERVES 4

INGREDIENTS

450 g/1 lb squid, cleaned

25 g/1 oz/4 tbsp cornflour (cornstarch)

1 tsp salt

1 tsp freshly ground black pepper

1 tsp chilli flakes

groundnut oil, for frying

dipping sauce, to serve

1 Using a sharp knife, remove the tentacles from the squid and trim. Slice the bodies down one side and open out to give a flat piece.

2 Score the flat pieces with a criss-cross pattern then cut each piece into 4.

3 Mix together the cornflour (cornstarch), salt, pepper and chilli flakes.

4 Place the salt and pepper mixture in a large polythene bag. Add the squid pieces and shake the bag thoroughly to coat the squid in the flour mixture.

5 Heat about 5 cm/2 inches of groundnut oil in a large preheated wok.

6 Add the squid pieces to the wok and stir-fry, in batches, for about 2 minutes, or until the squid pieces start to curl up. Do not overcook or the squid will become tough.

7 Remove the squid pieces with a slotted spoon, transfer to absorbent kitchen paper (paper towels) and leave to drain thoroughly.

8 Transfer the fried squid pieces to serving plates and serve immediately with a dipping sauce.

COOK'S TIP

Squid tubes may be purchased frozen if they are not available fresh. They are usually ready-cleaned and are easy to use. Ensure that they are completely defrosted before cooking.

Cantonese Prawns (Shrimp)

This prawn (shrimp) dish is very simple and is ideal for supper or lunch when time is short.

NUTRITIONAL INFORMATION

Calories 460	Sugar 3g
Protein 53g	Fat 24
Carbohydrate 6g	Saturates 5g

  10 MINS   20 MINS

SERVES 4

I N G R E D I E N T S

5 tbsp vegetable oil

4 garlic cloves, crushed

675 g/1½ lb raw prawns (shrimp), shelled and deveined

5-cm/2-inch piece fresh root ginger, chopped

175 g/6 oz lean pork, diced

1 leek, sliced

3 eggs, beaten

shredded leek and red (bell) pepper matchsticks, to garnish

rice, to serve

S A U C E

2 tbsp Chinese rice wine or dry sherry

2 tbsp light soy sauce

2 tsp caster (superfine) sugar

150 ml/¼ pint/⅔ cup fish stock

4½ tsp cornflour (cornstarch)

3 tbsp water

1 Heat 2 tablespoons of the vegetable oil in a preheated wok.

2 Add the garlic to the wok and stir-fry for 30 seconds.

3 Add the prawns (shrimp) to the wok and stir-fry for 5 minutes, or until

they change colour. Remove the prawns (shrimp) from the wok or frying pan (skillet) with a slotted spoon, set aside and keep warm.

4 Add the remaining oil to the wok and heat, swirling the oil around the base of the wok until it is really hot.

5 Add the ginger, diced pork and leek to the wok and stir-fry over a medium heat for 4-5 minutes, or until the pork is lightly coloured and sealed.

6 To make the sauce, add the rice wine or sherry, soy sauce, caster (superfine) sugar and fish stock to the wok and stir to blend.

7 In a small bowl, blend the cornflour (cornstarch) with the water to form a smooth paste and stir it into the wok. Cook, stirring, until the sauce thickens and clears.

8 Return the prawns (shrimp) to the wok and add the beaten eggs. Cook for 5–6 minutes, gently stirring occasionally, until the eggs set.

9 Transfer to a warm serving dish, garnish with shredded leek and (bell) pepper matchsticks and serve immediately with rice.

Scallops In Ginger Sauce

Scallops are both attractive and delicious. Cooked with ginger and orange, this dish is perfect served with plain rice.

NUTRITIONAL INFORMATION

Calories 216   Sugars 4g
Protein . . . . .30g   Fat 8g
Carbohydrate . . . .8g   Saturates 1g

5 MINS   10 MINS

SERVES 4

INGREDIENTS

2 tbsp vegetable oil

450 g/1 lb scallops, cleaned and halved

2.5-cm/1-inch piece fresh root ginger, finely chopped

3 garlic cloves, crushed

2 leeks, shredded

75 g/2¾ oz/¾ cup shelled peas

125 g/4½ oz canned bamboo shoots, drained and rinsed

2 tbsp light soy sauce

2 tbsp unsweetened orange juice

1 tsp caster (superfine) sugar

orange zest, to garnish

1 Heat the vegetable oil in a preheated wok or large frying pan (skillet). Add the scallops and stir-fry for 1–2 minutes. Remove the scallops from the wok with a slotted spoon, keep warm and set aside until required.

2 Add the ginger and garlic to the wok and stir-fry for 30 seconds. Stir in the leeks and peas and cook, stirring, for a further 2 minutes.

3 Add the bamboo shoots and return the scallops to the wok. Stir gently to mix without breaking up the scallops.

4 Stir in the soy sauce, orange juice and caster (superfine) sugar and cook for 1–2 minutes.

5 Transfer the stir-fry to a serving dish, garnish with the orange zest and serve immediately.

COOK'S TIP

The edible parts of a scallop are the round white muscle and the orange and white coral or roe. The frilly skirt surrounding the muscle – the gills and mantle – may be used for making shellfish stock. All other parts should be discarded.

Mussels with Lettuce

Mussels require careful preparation but very little cooking. They are available fresh or in vacuum packs when out of season.

NUTRITIONAL INFORMATION

Calories 205	Sugars 0.3g	
Protein 31g	Fat 9g	
Carbohydrate 1g	Saturates 4g	

 15 MINS   5 MINS

SERVES 4

I N G R E D I E N T S

1 kg/2 lb 4 oz mussels in their shells, scrubbed

2 stalks lemon grass

1 Iceberg lettuce

2 tbsp lemon juice

100 ml/3½ fl oz/⅓ cup water

25 g/1 oz/2 tbsp butter

finely grated zest of 1 lemon

2 tbsp oyster sauce

1 Place the scrubbed mussels in a large saucepan.

2 Using a sharp knife, thinly slice the lemon grass and shred the lettuce.

3 Add the lemon grass, lemon juice and water to the pan of mussels, cover with a tight-fitting lid and cook for 5 minutes or until the mussels have opened. Discard any mussels that do not open.

4 Carefully remove the cooked mussels from their shells, using a fork and set aside until required.

5 Heat the butter in a large preheated wok or frying pan (skillet). Add the lettuce and finely grated lemon zest to the wok or fying pan (skillet) and stir-fry for 2 minutes, or until the lettuce begins to wilt.

6 Add the oyster sauce to the mixture in the wok and heat through, stirring well until the sauce is thoroughly incorporated in the mixture.

7 Transfer the mixture in the wok to a warm serving dish and serve immediately.

COOK'S TIP

When using fresh mussels, be sure to discard any opened mussels before scrubbing and any unopened mussels after cooking.

Gingered Monkfish

This dish is a real treat and is perfect for special occasions. Monkfish has a tender flavour which is ideal with asparagus, chilli and ginger.

NUTRITIONAL INFORMATION

Calories ....133 Sugars 0g
Protein ....21g Fat 5g
Carbohydrate ....1g Saturates 1g

5 MINS

10 MINS

SERVES 4

INGREDIENTS

450 g/1 lb monkfish

1 tbsp freshly grated root ginger

2 tbsp sweet chilli sauce

1 tbsp corn oil

100 g/3½ oz/1 cup fine asparagus

3 spring onions (scallions), sliced

1 tsp sesame oil

1 Using a sharp knife, slice the monkfish into thin flat rounds. Set aside until required.

2 Mix together the freshly grated root ginger and the sweet chilli sauce in a small bowl until thoroughly blended. Brush the ginger and chilli sauce mixture over the monkfish pieces, using a pastry brush.

3 Heat the corn oil in a large preheated wok or heavy-based frying pan (skillet).

4 Add the monkfish pieces, asparagus and chopped spring onions (scallions) to the wok or frying pan (skillet) and cook for about 5 minutes, stirring gently so the fish pieces do not break up.

5 Remove the wok or frying pan (skillet) from the heat, drizzle the sesame oil over the stir-fry and toss well to combine.

6 Transfer the stir-fried gingered monkfish to warm serving plates and serve immediately.

COOK'S TIP

Monkfish is quite expensive, but it is well worth using as it has a wonderful flavour and texture. At a push you could use cubes of chunky cod fillet instead.

Mussels with Lemon Grass

Give fresh mussels a Far Eastern flavour by using some Kaffir lime leaves, garlic and lemon grass in the stock used for steaming them.

NUTRITIONAL INFORMATION

Calories ....194 Sugar 0g
Protein ....33g Fat 7g
Carbohydrate ....1g Saturates 1g

 10 MINS   10 MINS

SERVES 4

INGREDIENTS

750 g/1 lb 10 oz live mussels

1 tbsp sesame oil

3 shallots, chopped finely

2 garlic cloves, chopped finely

1 stalk lemon grass

2 Kaffir lime leaves

2 tbsp chopped fresh coriander (cilantro)

finely grated rind of 1 lime

2 tbsp lime juice

300 ml/½ pint/1¼ cups hot vegetable stock

crusty bread, to serve

fresh coriander (cilantro), to garnish

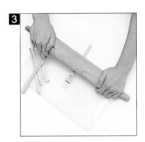

1 Using a small sharp knife, scrape the beards off the mussels under cold running water. Scrub them well, discarding any that are damaged or remain open when tapped. Keep rinsing until there is no trace of sand.

2 Heat the sesame oil in a large saucepan and fry the shallots and garlic gently until softened, about 2 minutes.

3 Bruise the lemon grass, using a meat mallet or rolling pin, and add to the pan with the Kaffir lime leaves, coriander (cilantro), lime rind and juice, mussels and stock. Put the lid on the saucepan and cook over a moderate heat for 3–5 minutes. Shake the pan from time to time.

4 Lift the mussels out into 4 warmed soup plates, discarding any that remain shut. Boil the remaining liquid rapidly to reduce slightly. Remove the lemon grass and lime leaves, then pour the liquid over the mussels.

5 Garnish with coriander (cilantro) and lime wedges, and serve at once.

COOK'S TIP

Mussels are now farmed, so they should be available from good fishmongers throughout the year.

Seafood Omelette

This delicious omelette is filled with a mixture of fresh vegetables, sliced squid and prawns (shrimp).

NUTRITIONAL INFORMATION

Calories	216	Sugars	. . . . .2g
Protein	. . . . .20g	Fat	. . . . .13g
Carbohydrate	. . . .4g	Saturates	. . . . . . .4g

  5 MINS 10 MINS

SERVES 4

INGREDIENTS

4 eggs

3 tbsp milk

1 tbsp fish sauce or light soy sauce

1 tbsp sesame oil

3 shallots, sliced finely

1 small red (bell) pepper, cored, deseeded and sliced very finely

1 small leek, trimmed and cut into matchstick pieces

125 g/4½ oz squid rings

125 g/4½ oz/⅔ cup cooked peeled prawns (shrimp)

1 tbsp chopped fresh basil

15 g/½ oz/1 tbsp butter

salt and pepper

sprigs of fresh basil, to garnish

VARIATION

Chopped, cooked chicken makes a delicious alternative to the squid.

Use fresh coriander (cilantro) instead of the basil, if desired.

1 Beat the eggs, milk and fish sauce or soy sauce together.

2 Heat the sesame oil in a wok or large frying pan (skillet) and add the shallots, (bell) pepper and leek. Stir-fry briskly for 2–3 minutes.

3 Add the squid rings, prawns (shrimp) and chopped basil to the wok or frying pan (skillet). Stir-fry for a further 2–3 minutes, until the squid looks opaque.

4 Season the mixture in the wok with salt and pepper to taste. Transfer to a warmed plate and keep warm until required.

5 Melt the butter in a large omelette pan or frying pan (skillet) and add the beaten egg mixture. Cook over a medium-high heat until just set.

6 Spoon the vegetable and seafood mixture in a line down the middle of the omelette, then fold each side of the omelette over.

7 Transfer the omelette to a warmed serving dish and cut into 4 portions. Garnish with sprigs of fresh basil and serve at once.

Prawns (Shrimp) with Ginger

Crispy ginger is a wonderful garnish which offsets the spicy prawns (shrimp) both visually and in flavour.

NUTRITIONAL INFORMATION

Calories 229   Sugars 7g
Protein ....29g   Fat 8g
Carbohydrate ...10g   Saturates 1g

10 MINS   15 MINS

SERVES 4

I N G R E D I E N T S

5 cm/2 inch piece fresh root ginger

oil, for frying

1 onion, diced

225 g/8 oz carrots, diced

100 g/3½ oz/½ cup frozen peas

100 g/3½ oz/1 cup bean sprouts

450 g/1 lb peeled king prawns (shrimp)

1 tsp Chinese five-spice powder

1 tbsp tomato purée (paste)

1 tbsp soy sauce

1 Using a sharp knife, peel the ginger and slice it into very thin sticks.

2 Heat about 2.5 cm/1 inch of oil in a large preheated wok. Add the ginger and stir-fry for 1 minute or until the ginger is crispy. Remove the ginger with a slotted spoon and leave to drain on absorbent kitchen paper (paper towels).

3 Drain all of the oil from the wok except for about 2 tablespoons. Add the onions and carrots to the wok and stir-fry for 5 minutes. Add the peas and bean sprouts and stir-fry for 2 minutes.

4 Rinse the prawns (shrimp) under cold running water and pat dry with absorbent kitchen paper (paper towels).

5 Combine the five-spice, tomato purée (paste) and soy sauce. Brush the mixture over the prawns (shrimp).

6 Add the prawns (shrimp) to the wok and stir-fry for a further 2 minutes, or until the prawns (shrimp) are completely cooked through. Transfer the prawn (shrimp) mixture to a warm serving bowl and top with the reserved crispy ginger. Serve immediately.

VARIATION

Use slices of white fish instead of the prawns (shrimp) as an alternative, if you wish.

Mussels in Black Bean Sauce

This dish looks so impressive, the combination of colours making it look almost too good to eat!

NUTRITIONAL INFORMATION

Calories 174	Sugars 4g
Protein 19g	Fat 8g
Carbohydrate 6g	Saturates 1g

5 MINS   10 MINS

SERVES 4

INGREDIENTS

350 g/12 oz leeks

350 g/12 oz cooked green-lipped mussels (shelled)

1 tsp cumin seeds

2 tbsp vegetable oil

2 cloves garlic, crushed

1 red (bell) pepper, deseeded and sliced

50 g/1¾ oz/¾ cup canned bamboo shoots, drained

175 g/6 oz baby spinach

160 g/5¾ oz jar black bean sauce

1 Using a sharp knife, trim the leeks and shred them.

2 Place the cooked green-lipped mussels in a large bowl, sprinkle with the cumin seeds and toss well to coat all over. Set aside until required.

3 Heat the vegetable oil in a preheated wok, swirling the oil around the base of the wok until it is really hot.

4 Add the shredded leeks, garlic and sliced red (bell) pepper to the wok and stir-fry for 5 minutes, or until the vegetables are tender.

5 Add the bamboo shoots, baby spinach leaves and cooked green-lipped

mussels to the wok and stir-fry for about 2 minutes.

6 Pour the black bean sauce over the ingredients in the wok, toss well to coat all the ingredients in the sauce and leave to simmer for a few seconds, stirring occasionally.

7 Transfer the stir-fry to warm serving bowls and serve immediately.

COOK'S TIP

If the green-lipped mussels are not available they can be bought shelled in cans and jars from most large supermarkets.

Fish with Ginger Butter

Whole mackerel or trout are stuffed with herbs, wrapped in foil, baked and then drizzled with a fresh ginger butter.

NUTRITIONAL INFORMATION

Calories 328   Sugar 0g
Protein ....24g   Fat 25g
Carbohydrate ....1g   Saturates 13g

10 MINS

30 MINS

SERVES 4

INGREDIENTS

4 x 250 g/9 oz whole trout or mackerel, gutted

4 tbsp chopped fresh coriander (cilantro)

5 garlic cloves, crushed

2 tsp grated lemon or lime zest

2 tsp vegetable oil

banana leaves, for wrapping (optional)

90 g/3 oz/6 tbsp butter

1 tbsp grated ginger root

1 tbsp light soy sauce

salt and pepper

coriander (cilantro) sprigs and lemon or lime wedges, to garnish

1 Wash and dry the fish. Mix the coriander (cilantro) with the garlic, lemon or lime zest and salt and pepper to taste. Spoon into the fish cavities.

2 Brush the fish with a little oil, season well and place each fish on a double thickness sheet of baking parchment or foil and wrap up well to enclose. Alternatively, wrap in banana leaves (see right).

3 Place on a baking tray (cookie sheet) and bake in a preheated oven for about 25 minutes or until the flesh will flake easily.

4 Meanwhile, melt the butter in a small pan. Add the ginger and mix well.

5 Stir the light soy sauce into the saucepan.

6 To serve, unwrap the fish parcels, drizzle over the ginger butter and garnish with coriander (cilantro) and lemon or lime wedges.

COOK'S TIP

For a really authentic touch, wrap the fish in banana leaves, which can be ordered from specialist oriental supermarkets. They are not edible, but impart a delicate flavour to the fish.

Chilli Prawns (Shrimp)

Large prawns (shrimp) are marinated in a chilli mixture then stir-fried with cashews. Serve with a fluffy rice and braised vegetables.

NUTRITIONAL INFORMATION

Calories	435	Sugars	.........2g
Protein	........4.2g	Fat	23
Carbohydrate	...10g	Saturates	.......4g

 2¹/₄ HOURS   5 MINS

SERVES 4

I N G R E D I E N T S

5 tbsp soy sauce

5 tbsp dry sherry

3 dried red chillies, seeded and chopped

2 garlic cloves, crushed

2 tsp grated ginger root

5 tbsp water

625 g/1 lb 6 oz shelled tiger prawns (jumbo shrimp)

1 large bunch spring onions (scallions), chopped

90 g/3 oz/⅔ cup salted cashew nuts

3 tbsp vegetable oil

2 tsp cornflour (cornstarch)

1 Mix the soy sauce, sherry, chillies, garlic, ginger and water in a bowl.

2 Add the tiger prawns (jumbo shrimp), spring onions (scallions) and cashews and mix well. Cover tightly and leave to marinate for at least 2 hours, stirring occasionally.

3 Heat the oil in a large wok. Remove the prawns (shrimp), spring onions (scallions) and cashews from the marinade with a slotted spoon and add to the wok, reserving the marinade. Stir-fry over a high heat for 1-2 minutes.

4 Mix the reserved marinade with the cornflour (cornstarch), add to the wok and stir-fry for about 30 seconds, until the marinade forms a slightly thickened shiny glaze over the prawn (shrimp) mixture. Serve immediately.

COOK'S TIP

For an attractive presentation serve this dish on mixed wild rice and basmati rice. Start cooking the wild rice in boiling water. After 10 minutes, add the basmati rice or other rice and continue boiling until all grains are tender. Drain well and adjust the seasoning.

Prawn (Shrimp) Stir-fry

A very quick and tasty stir-fry using prawns (shrimp) and cucumber, cooked with lemon grass, chilli and ginger.

NUTRITIONAL INFORMATION

Calories 178   Sugars 1g
Protein ....22g   Fat 7g
Carbohydrate ....3g   Saturates 1g

5 MINS   5 MINS

SERVES 4

INGREDIENTS

½ cucumber

2 tbsp sunflower oil

6 spring onions (scallions), halved
   lengthways and cut into 4 cm/
   1½ inch lengths

1 stalk lemon grass, sliced thinly

1 garlic clove, chopped

1 tsp chopped fresh red chilli

125 g/4½ oz oyster mushrooms

1 tsp chopped ginger root

350 g/12 oz cooked peeled prawns (shrimp)

2 tsp cornflour (cornstarch)

2 tbsp water

1 tbsp dark soy sauce

½ tsp fish sauce

2 tbsp dry sherry or rice wine

boiled rice, to serve

1 Cut the cucumber into strips about 5 mm x 4 cm/¼ x 1¾ inches.

2 Heat the sunflower oil in a wok or large frying pan (skillet).

3 Add the spring onions (scallions), cucumber, lemon grass, garlic, chilli, oyster mushrooms and ginger to the wok or frying pan (skillet) and stir-fry for 2 minutes.

4 Add the prawns (shrimp) and stir-fry for a further minute.

5 Mix together the cornflour (cornstarch), water, soy sauce and fish sauce until smooth.

6 Stir the cornflour (cornstarch) mixture and sherry or wine into the wok and heat through, stirring, until the sauce has thickened. Serve with rice.

COOK'S TIP

The white part of the lemon grass stem can be thinly sliced and left in the cooked dish. If using the whole stem, remove it before serving. You can buy lemon grass chopped and dried, or preserved in jars, but neither has the fragrance or delicacy of the fresh variety.

Prawns with Vegetables

In this recipe, a light Chinese omelette is shredded and tossed back into the dish before serving.

NUTRITIONAL INFORMATION

Calories	258	Sugars	.........7g
Protein	........21g	Fat	..........15g
Carbohydrate	...10g	Saturates	.......3g

 10 MINS   15 MINS

SERVES 4

I N G R E D I E N T S

225 g/8 oz courgettes (zucchini)

3 tbsp vegetable oil

2 eggs

2 tbsp cold water

225 g/8 oz carrots, grated

1 onion, sliced

150 g/5½ oz/1½ cups bean sprouts

225 g/8 oz peeled prawns (shrimp)

2 tbsp soy sauce

pinch of Chinese five-spice powder

25 g/1 oz/¼ cup peanuts, chopped

2 tbsp fresh chopped coriander
   (cilantro)

1 Finely grate the courgettes (zucchini).

2 Heat 1 tablespoon of the vegetable oil in a large preheated wok.

3 Beat the eggs with the water and pour the mixture into the wok and cook for 2–3 minutes or until the egg sets.

4 Remove the omelette from the wok and transfer to a clean board. Fold the omelette, cut it into thin strips and set aside until required.

5 Add the remaining oil to the wok. Add the carrots, onion and courgettes (zucchini) and stir-fry for 5 minutes.

6 Add the bean sprouts and prawns (shrimp) to the wok and cook for a further 2 minutes, or until the prawns (shrimp) are heated through.

7 Add the soy sauce, Chinese five-spice powder and peanuts to the wok, together with the strips of omelette and heat through. Garnish with chopped fresh coriander (cilantro) and serve.

COOK'S TIP

The water is mixed with the egg in step 3 for a lighter, less rubbery omelette.

Crab with Chinese Leaves

The delicate flavour of Chinese leaves (cabbage) and crab meat are enhanced by the coconut milk in this recipe.

NUTRITIONAL INFORMATION

Calories 109	Sugars 1g
Protein 11g	Fat 6g
Carbohydrate 2g	Saturates 1g

🍲 5 MINS   🕐 10 MINS

SERVES 4

I N G R E D I E N T S

225 g/8 oz shiitake mushrooms

2 tbsp vegetable oil

2 cloves garlic, crushed

6 spring onions (scallions), sliced

1 head Chinese leaves (cabbage), shredded

1 tbsp mild curry paste

6 tbsp coconut milk

200 g/7 oz can white crab meat, drained

1 tsp chilli flakes

1 Using a sharp knife, cut the mushrooms into slices.

2 Heat the vegetable oil in a large preheated wok or heavy-based frying pan (skillet).

3 Add the mushrooms and garlic to the wok or frying pan (skillet) and stir-fry for 3 minutes or until the mushrooms have softened.

4 Add the spring onions (scallions) and shredded Chinese leaves (cabbage) to the wok and stir-fry until the leaves have wilted.

5 Mix together the mild curry paste and coconut milk in a small bowl.

6 Add the curry paste and coconut milk mixture to the wok, together with the crab meat and chilli flakes. Mix together until well combined.

7 Heat the mixture in the wok until the juices start to bubble.

8 Transfer the crab and vegetable stir-fry to warm serving bowls and serve immediately.

COOK'S TIP

Shiitake mushrooms are now readily available in the fresh vegetable section of most large supermarkets.

Hot & Sweet Prawns (Shrimp)

Uncooked prawns (shrimp) are speared on skewers, brushed with a sesame oil, lime juice and coriander (cilantro) baste and then grilled.

NUTRITIONAL INFORMATION

Calories	239	Sugars	.........8g
Protein	........28g	Fat	...........11g
Carbohydrate	....8g	Saturates	.......2g

1 HOUR   10 MINS

SERVES 4

I N G R E D I E N T S

wooden skewers soaked in warm water for 20 minutes

500 g/1 lb 2 oz/2½ cups uncooked prawns (shrimp)

3 tbsp sesame oil

2 tbsp lime juice

1 tbsp chopped fresh coriander (cilantro)

S A U C E

4 tbsp light malt vinegar

2 tbsp fish sauce or light soy sauce

2 tbsp water

2 tbsp light muscovado sugar

2 garlic cloves, crushed

2 tsp grated fresh ginger root

1 red chilli, deseeded and chopped finely

2 tbsp chopped fresh coriander (cilantro)

salt

1 Peel the prawns (shrimp), leaving the tails intact. Remove the black vein that runs along the back of each one, then skewer the prawns (shrimp) on to the wooden skewers.

2 Mix together the sesame oil, lime juice and chopped coriander (cilantro) in a shallow bowl. Lay the skewered prawns (shrimp) in this mixture. Cover and chill in the refrigerator for 30 minutes, turning once, so that the prawns (shrimp) absorb the marinade.

3 Meanwhile, make the sauce. Heat the vinegar, fish sauce or soy sauce, water, sugar and salt to taste until boiling. Remove from the heat and leave to cool.

4 Mix together the crushed garlic, grated ginger, red chilli and coriander (cilantro) in a small serving bowl. Add the cooled vinegar mixture and stir until well combined.

5 Place the prawns (shrimp) on a foil-lined grill (broiler) pan under a preheated grill (broiler) for about 6 minutes, turning once and basting often with the marinade, until cooked.

6 Transfer to a warmed serving platter and serve with the dipping sauce.

Crab Claws with Chilli

Crab claws are frequently used in Chinese cooking, and look sensational. They are perfect with this delicious chilli sauce.

NUTRITIONAL INFORMATION

Calories	154	Sugar	.........3g
Protein	........16g	Fat	..........7g
Carbohydrate	....8g	Saturates	.......1g

5 MINS   10 MINS

SERVES 4

INGREDIENTS

700 g/1 lb 9 oz crab claws

1 tbsp corn oil

2 cloves garlic, crushed

1 tbsp grated fresh root ginger

3 red chillies, deseeded and finely chopped

2 tbsp sweet chilli sauce

3 tbsp tomato ketchup

300 ml/½ pint/1¼ cups cooled fish stock

1 tbsp cornflour (cornstarch)

salt and pepper

1 tbsp fresh chives, snipped

1 Gently crack the crab claws with a nut cracker. This process will allow the flavours of the chilli, garlic and ginger to fully penetrate the crab meat.

2 Heat the corn oil in a large preheated wok.

3 Add the crab claws to the wok and stir-fry for about 5 minutes.

4 Add the garlic, ginger and chillies to the wok and stir-fry for 1 minute, tossing the crab claws to coat all over.

5 Mix together the sweet chilli sauce, tomato ketchup, fish stock and cornflour (cornstarch) in a small bowl. Add this mixture to the wok and cook, stirring occasionally, until the sauce starts to thicken.

6 Season the mixture in the wok with salt and pepper to taste.

7 Transfer the crab claws and chilli sauce to warm serving dishes, garnish with snipped fresh chives and serve.

COOK'S TIP

If crab claws are not easily available, use a whole crab, cut into eight pieces, instead.

Coconut Prawns (Shrimp)

Fan-tail prawns (shrimp) make any meal a special occasion, especially when cooked in such a delicious crispy coating.

NUTRITIONAL INFORMATION

Calories 236   Sugars 1g
Protein ....27g   Fat 13g
Carbohydrate ....3g   Saturates 7g

 5 MINS   10 MINS

SERVES 4

I N G R E D I E N T S

50 g/1¾ oz/½ cup desiccated (shredded) coconut

25 g/1 oz/½ cup fresh white breadcrumbs

1 tsp Chinese five-spice powder

½ tsp salt

finely grated zest of 1 lime

1 egg white

450 g/1 lb fan-tail prawns (shrimp)

sunflower or corn oil, for frying

lemon wedges, to garnish

soy or chilli sauce, to serve

1 Mix together the dessicated (shredded) coconut, white breadcrumbs, Chinese five-spice powder, salt and finely grated lime zest in a bowl.

2 Lightly whisk the egg white in a separate bowl.

3 Rinse the prawns (shrimp) under cold running water, and pat dry with kitchen paper (paper towels).

4 Dip the prawns (shrimp) into the egg white then into the coconut and breadcrumb mixture, so that they are evenly coated.

5 Heat about 5 cm/2 inches of sunflower or corn oil in a large preheated wok.

6 Add the prawns (shrimp) to the wok and stir-fry for about 5 minutes or until golden and crispy.

7 Remove the prawns (shrimp) with a slotted spoon and leave to drain on kitchen paper (paper towels).

8 Transfer the coconut prawns (shrimp) to warm serving dishes and garnish with lemon wedges. Serve immediately with a soy or chilli sauce.

COOK'S TIP

Chinese five-spice powder is a mixture of star anise, fennel seeds, cloves, cinnamon bark and Szechuan pepper. It is very pungent, so should be used sparingly. It will keep indefinitely in an airtight container

Crab Meat Cakes

Make these tasty crab-meat cakes to serve as a snack or starter, or as an accompaniment to a main meal.

NUTRITIONAL INFORMATION

Calories	262	Sugars	.........4g
Protein	........13g	Fat	..........17g
Carbohydrate	...14g	Saturates	.......3g

20 MINS   55 MINS

SERVES 4

INGREDIENTS

90 g/3 oz/generous 1 cup long-grain rice

1 tbsp sesame oil

1 small onion, chopped finely

1 large garlic clove, crushed

2 tbsp chopped fresh coriander (cilantro)

200 g/7 oz can of crab meat, drained

1 tbsp fish sauce or light soy sauce

250 ml/9 fl oz/1 cup coconut milk

2 eggs

4 tbsp vegetable oil

salt and pepper

sliced spring onions (scallions), to garnish

1 Cook the rice in plenty of boiling, lightly salted water until just tender, about 12 minutes. Rinse with cold water and drain well.

2 Heat the sesame oil in a small frying pan (skillet) and fry the onion and garlic gently for about 5 minutes, until softened and golden brown.

3 Combine the rice, onion, garlic, coriander (cilantro), crab meat, fish sauce or soy sauce and coconut milk. Season. Beat the eggs and add to the mixture. Divide the mixture between 8 greased ramekin dishes or teacups and

place them in a baking dish or roasting tin (pan) with enough warm water to come halfway up their sides. Place in a preheated oven at 180°C/ 350°F/Gas Mark 4 for 25 minutes, until set. Leave to cool.

4 Turn the crab cakes out of the ramekin dishes . Heat the oil in a wok or frying pan (skillet) and fry the crab cakes in the oil until golden brown. Drain on kitchen paper (paper towels), garnish and serve.

COOK'S TIP

If you want, you can prepare these crab cakes up to the point where they have been baked. Cool them, then cover and chill, ready for frying when needed.

Vegetables

The Chinese eat far more vegetables than meat or poultry. This is partly because of widespread poverty which means that many people cannot afford meat, and also because of religious reasons. Vegetables are used extensively in all meals; even meat and poultry dishes include some kind of vegetable as a supplementary ingredient in order to give

the dish a harmonious balance of colour, aroma, flavour and texture. The Chinese like their vegetables crisp so they are cooked for only a very short time, thus preserving their bright colours as well as valuable nutrients. As with most ingredients in Chinese cooking, it is important to choose the freshest vegetables available to ensure maximum flavour and crispness. As well as side dishes, this chapter also contains deliciously filling main meals.

Green Bean Stir-fry

These beans are simply cooked in a spicy, hot sauce for a tasty and very easy recipe.

NUTRITIONAL INFORMATION

Calories 86   Sugars 4g
Protein ....2g   Fat 6g
Carbohydrates ....6g   Saturates 1g

5 MINS   5 MINS

SERVES 4

I N G R E D I E N T S

450 g/1 lb thin green beans

2 fresh red chillies

2 tbsp peanut oil

½ tsp ground star anise

1 garlic clove, crushed

2 tbsp light soy sauce

2 tsp clear honey

½ tsp sesame oil

1 Using a sharp knife, cut the green beans in half.

2 Slice the fresh chillies, removing the seeds first if you prefer a milder dish.

3 Heat the oil in a preheated wok or large frying pan (skillet) until the oil is almost smoking.

4 Lower the heat slightly, add the halved green beans to the wok and stir-fry for 1 minute.

5 Add the sliced red chillies, star anise and garlic to the wok and stir-fry for a further 30 seconds.

6 Mix together the soy sauce, honey and sesame oil in a small bowl.

7 Stir the sauce mixture into the wok. Cook for 2 minutes, tossing the beans to ensure that they are thoroughly coated in the sauce.

8 Transfer the mixture in the wok or pan to a warm serving dish and serve immediately.

VARIATION

This recipe is surprisingly delicious made with Brussels sprouts instead of green beans. Trim the sprouts, then shred them finely. Stir-fry the sprouts in hot oil for 2 minutes, then proceed with the recipe from step 4.

Bean Sprouts & Vegetables

This dish is served cold as a salad or appetizer and is very easy to make. It is a form of cold *chop suey*.

NUTRITIONAL INFORMATION

Calories	56	Sugars 5g
Protein	.........4g	Fat 1g
Carbohydrate	....9g	Saturates 0.2g

 3¹/₄ HOURS 0 MINS

SERVES 4

INGREDIENTS

450 g/1 lb bean sprouts

2 fresh red chillies, seeded and finely chopped

1 red (bell) pepper, seeded and thinly sliced

1 green (bell) pepper, seeded and thinly sliced

60 g/2 oz water chestnuts, quartered

1 celery stick, sliced

Chinese roasted meats and noodles, to serve

MARINADE

3 tbsp rice wine vinegar

2 tbsp light soy sauce

2 tbsp chopped chives

1 garlic clove, crushed

pinch of Chinese curry powder

1 Place the bean sprouts, chopped red chillies, red and green (bell) peppers, water chestnuts and celery in a large bowl and mix well to combine all the ingredients.

2 To make the marinade, mix together the rice wine vinegar, light soy sauce, chopped chives, crushed garlic and Chinese curry powder in a bowl.

3 Pour the marinade over the prepared vegetables. Toss to mix the vegetables thoroughly in the marinade.

4 Cover the salad with cling film (plastic wrap) and leave to chill in the refrigerator for at least 3 hours.

5 Drain the vegetables thoroughly, transfer to a serving dish and serve with Chinese roasted meats or noodles.

COOK'S TIP

There are hundreds of varieties of chillies and it is not always possible to tell how hot they are going to be. As a general rule, dark green chillies are hotter than light green and red chillies. Thin, pointed chillies are usually hotter than fatter, blunter chillies.

Honey-fried Chinese Leaves

Chinese leaves (cabbage) are rather similar to lettuce in that the leaves are delicate with a sweet flavour.

NUTRITIONAL INFORMATION

Calories	121	Sugars	.........6g
Protein	.........5g	Fat	...........7g
Carbohydrate	...10g	Saturates	.......1g

 5 MINS   10 MINS

SERVES 4

INGREDIENTS

450 g/1 lb Chinese leaves (cabbage)

1 tbsp peanut oil

1-cm/½-inch piece fresh root ginger, grated

2 garlic cloves, crushed

1 fresh red chilli, sliced

1 tbsp Chinese rice wine or dry sherry

4½ tsp light soy sauce

1 tbsp clear honey

125 ml/4 fl oz/½ cup orange juice

1 tbsp sesame oil

2 tsp sesame seeds

orange zest, to garnish

COOK'S TIP

Single-flower honey has a better, more individual flavour than blended honey. Acacia honey is typically Chinese, but you could also try clover, lemon blossom, lime flower or orange blossom.

1 Separate the Chinese leaves (cabbage) and shred them finely, using a sharp knife.

2 Heat the peanut oil in a preheated wok. Add the ginger, garlic and chilli to the wok and stir-fry the mixture for about 30 seconds.

3 Add the Chinese leaves (cabbage), Chinese rice wine or sherry, soy sauce,

honey and orange juice to the wok. Reduce the heat and leave to simmer for 5 minutes.

4 Add the sesame oil to the wok, sprinkle the sesame seeds on top and mix to combine.

5 Transfer to a warm serving dish, garnish with the orange zest and serve immediately.

Vegetable Sesame Stir-fry

Sesame seeds add a delicious flavour to any recipe and are particularly good with vegetables in this soy and rice wine or sherry sauce.

NUTRITIONAL INFORMATION

Calories 118   Sugars 2g
Protein . . . . .3g   Fat 9g
Carbohydrate . . . .5g   Saturates 1g

 5 MINS   10 MINS

SERVES 4

INGREDIENTS

2 tbsp vegetable oil

3 garlic cloves, crushed

1 tbsp sesame seeds,
   plus extra to garnish

2 celery sticks, sliced

2 baby corn cobs, sliced

60 g/2 oz button mushrooms

1 leek, sliced

1 courgette (zucchini), sliced

1 small red (bell) pepper, sliced

1 fresh green chilli, sliced

60 g/2 oz Chinese leaves (cabbage),
   shredded

rice or noodles, to serve

SAUCE

½ tsp Chinese curry powder

2 tbsp light soy sauce

1 tbsp Chinese rice wine or dry sherry

1 tsp sesame oil

1 tsp cornflour (cornstarch)

4 tbsp water

1 Heat the vegetable oil in a preheated wok or heavy-based frying pan (skillet), swirling the oil around the base of the wok until it is almost smoking.

2 Lower the heat slightly, add the garlic and sesame seeds and stir-fry for 30 seconds.

3 Add the celery, baby corn cobs, mushrooms, leek, courgette (zucchini), (bell) pepper, chilli and Chinese leaves (cabbage) and stir-fry for 4–5 minutes, until the vegetables are beginning to soften.

4 To make the sauce, mix together the Chinese curry powder, light soy sauce, Chinese rice wine or dry sherry, sesame oil, cornflour (cornstarch) and water.

5 Stir the sauce mixture into the wok until well combined with the other ingredients.

6 Bring to the boil and cook, stirring constantly, until the sauce thickens and clears.

7 Cook for 1 minute, spoon into a warm serving dish and garnish with sesame seeds. Serve the vegetable sesame stir-fry immediately with rice or noodles.

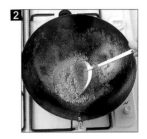

Pak Choi with Cashew Nuts

Plum sauce is readily available in jars and has a terrific, sweet flavour which complements the vegetables.

NUTRITIONAL INFORMATION

Calories 241	Sugars 7g
Protein 7g	Fat 19g
Carbohydrate 11g	Saturates 4g

 5 MINS   15 MINS

SERVES 4

I N G R E D I E N T S

2 red onions

175 g/6 oz red cabbage

2 tbsp groundnut oil

225 g/8 oz pak choi

2 tbsp plum sauce

100 g/3½ oz/⅓ cup roasted cashew nuts

1 Using a sharp knife, cut the red onions into thin wedges and thinly shred the red cabbage.

2 Heat the groundnut oil in a large preheated wok or heavy-based frying pan (skillet) until the oil is really hot.

3 Add the onion wedges to the wok or frying pan (skillet) and stir-fry for about 5 minutes or until the onions are just beginning to brown.

4 Add the red cabbage to the wok and stir-fry for a further 2–3 minutes.

5 Add the pak choi leaves to the wok or frying pan (skillet) and stir-fry for about 5 minutes, or until the leaves have just wilted.

6 Drizzle the plum sauce over the vegetables, toss together until well combined and heat until the liquid is bubbling.

7 Scatter with the roasted cashew nuts and transfer to warm serving bowls.

VARIATION

Use unsalted peanuts instead of the cashew nuts, if you prefer.

Bamboo with Cucumber

A simple stir-fried side dish of canned bamboo shoots and sliced cucumber is the perfect accompaniment to a Chinese main meal.

NUTRITIONAL INFORMATION

Calories 101   Sugars 0.2g
Protein . . . . .3g   Fat 7g
Carbohydrate . . . .7g   Saturates 1g

20 MINS   10 MINS

SERVES 4

INGREDIENTS

½ cucumber

2 tbsp sesame oil

4 shallots, chopped finely

1 garlic clove, sliced finely

350 g/12 oz can of bamboo shoots, drained

1 tbsp dry sherry

1 tbsp soy sauce

2 tsp cornflour (cornstarch)

1 tsp sesame seeds

salt

TO GARNISH

2 red chilli flowers (see page 269)

sliced spring onions (scallions)

1 Slice the cucumber thinly and sprinkle with salt. Leave for 10–15 minutes, then rinse with cold water. Prepare the chilli and spring onion (scallion) garnish.

2 Heat the sesame oil in a wok or frying pan (skillet) and add the shallots and garlic. Stir-fry for 2 minutes, until golden.

3 Add the bamboo shoots and cucumber to the wok or frying pan (skillet) and stir-fry for 2–3 minutes.

4 Blend together the dry sherry, soy sauce and cornflour (cornstarch). Add to the bamboo shoots and cucumber, stirring to combine.

5 Cook for 1–2 minutes to thicken slightly, then add the sesame seeds and stir through.

6 Transfer the vegetables to a warmed serving dish. Garnish with the chilli flowers and chopped spring onion (scallion). Serve at once.

COOK'S TIP

Salting the cucumber before it is stir-fried draws out some of its moisture so that it stays crisp.

Add some very finely sliced carrot to this dish to add some extra colour, if you like.

Shredded Vegetable Omelette

Cook this large omelette and then slice into four portions to serve as a side dish. If you like, double the quantities and serve it as a main course.

NUTRITIONAL INFORMATION

Calories 159   Sugars 3g
Protein ....8g   Fat 13g
Carbohydrate ....4g   Saturates 4g

5 MINS   10 MINS

SERVES 4

I N G R E D I E N T S

4 eggs

3 tbsp milk

1 tbsp fish sauce or light soy sauce

1 tbsp sesame oil

1 small red onion, very finely sliced

1 small courgette (zucchini),
   trimmed and cut into
   matchstick pieces

1 small leek, trimmed and cut into
   matchstick pieces

1 small carrot, trimmed and cut into
   matchstick pieces

5 cm/2 inch piece cucumber, cut into
   matchstick pieces

1 tbsp chopped fresh coriander
   (cilantro)

15 g/½ oz/1 tbsp butter

salt and pepper

TO GARNISH

sprigs of fresh basil

celery leaves

4 chilli flowers (see page 269)

1 Beat together the eggs, milk and fish sauce or soy sauce.

2 Heat the sesame oil in a wok or large frying pan (skillet), swirling the oil

around the base of the wok until it is really hot. Add all the vegetables and stir-fry them briskly for 3–4 minutes, then add the chopped fresh coriander (cilantro).

3 Season with salt and pepper to taste. Transfer the stir-fried vegetables to a warmed plate and keep warm.

4 Melt the butter in a large omelette pan or frying pan (skillet) and add the beaten egg mixture.

5 Cook the egg mixture over a medium-high heat until just set.

6 Tip the vegetable mixture along one side of the omelette, then roll up the omelette.

7 Slice into 4 portions and arrange on a warmed serving plate. Garnish with fresh basil, celery leaves and chilli flowers and serve at once.

Gingered Broccoli

Ginger and broccoli are a perfect combination of flavours and make an exceptionally tasty side dish.

NUTRITIONAL INFORMATION

Calories 118   Sugars 3g
Protein . . . . .8g   Fat 7g
Carbohydrate . . . .6g   Saturates 1g

5 MINS   15 MINS

SERVES 4

INGREDIENTS

5-cm/2-inch piece fresh root ginger

2 tbsp peanut oil

1 garlic clove, crushed

675 g/1½ lb broccoli florets

1 leek, sliced

75 g/2¾ oz water chestnuts, halved

½ tsp caster (superfine) sugar

125 ml/4 fl oz/½ cup vegetable stock

1 tsp dark soy sauce

1 tsp cornflour (cornstarch)

2 tsp water

1 Using a sharp knife, finely chop the ginger. (Alternatively, cut the ginger into larger strips, to be discarded later, for a slightly milder ginger flavour.)

2 Heat the peanut oil in a preheated wok. Add the garlic and ginger and stir-fry for 30 seconds.

3 Add the broccoli, leek and water chestnuts and stir-fry for a further 3–4 minutes.

4 Add the caster (superfine) sugar, vegetable stock and dark soy sauce to the wok, reduce the heat and simmer for 4–5 minutes, or until the broccoli is almost cooked.

5 Blend the cornflour (cornstarch) with the water to form a smooth paste and stir it into the wok. Bring to the boil and cook, stirring constantly, for 1 minute or until thickened.

6 If using larger strips of ginger, remove from the wok and discard.

7 Transfer the vegetables to a serving dish and serve immediately.

VARIATION

Use spinach instead of the broccoli, if you prefer. Trim the woody ends and cut the remainder into 5-cm/2-inch lengths, keeping the stalks and leaves separate. Add the stalks with the leek in step 3 and add the leaves 2 minutes later. Reduce the cooking time in step 4 to 3–4 minutes.

Stir-fried Bean Sprouts

Be sure to use fresh bean sprouts, rather than the canned variety, for this crunchy-textured dish.

NUTRITIONAL INFORMATION

Calories	98	Sugars 2g
Protein	.........2g	Fat 9g
Carbohydrate	....3g	Saturates 1g

 5 MINS   5 MINS

SERVES 4

INGREDIENTS

250 g/9 oz fresh bean sprouts

2-3 spring onions (scallions)

1 medium red chilli pepper (optional)

3 tbsp vegetable oil

½ tsp salt

½ tsp sugar

1 tbsp light soy sauce

a few drops sesame oil (optional)

1   Rinse the bean sprouts in cold water, discarding any husks or small pieces that float to the top.

2   Drain the bean sprouts well on kitchen paper (paper towels).

COOK'S TIP

The red chilli pepper gives a bite to this dish – leave the seeds in for an even hotter taste. If you prefer a milder, sweeter flavour use red (bell) pepper instead of the chilli pepper. Core, seed and cut into strips in the same way.

3   Using a sharp knife, cut the spring onions (scallions) into short sections.

4   Thinly shred the red chilli pepper, if using, discarding the seeds.

5   Heat the vegetable oil in a preheated wok, swirling the oil around the base of the wok until it is really hot.

6   Add the bean sprouts, spring onions (scallions) and chilli pepper, if using, to the wok and stir-fry the mixture for about 2 minutes.

7   Add the salt, sugar, soy sauce and sesame oil, if using, to the mixture in the wok. Stir well to blend. Serve the bean sprouts hot or cold.

Braised Chinese Leaves

White cabbage can be used instead of the Chinese leaves (cabbage) for this dish.

NUTRITIONAL INFORMATION

Calories	138	Sugars 4g
Protein	.........6g	Fat 9g
Carbohydrate	...10g	Saturates 1g

 5 MINS 5 MINS

SERVES 4

I N G R E D I E N T S

500 g/1 lb 2 oz Chinese leaves (cabbage) or white cabbage

3 tbsp vegetable oil

½ tsp Szechuan red peppercorns

5-6 small dried red chillies, seeded and chopped

½ tsp salt

1 tbsp sugar

1 tbsp light soy sauce

1 tbsp rice vinegar

a few drops sesame oil (optional)

1 Shred the Chinese leaves (cabbage) or white cabbage crosswise into thin pieces. (If Chinese leaves (cabbage) are unavailable, the best alternative to use in this recipe is a firm-packed white cabbage, not the dark green type of cabbage. Cut out the thick core of the cabbage with a sharp knife before shredding.)

2 Heat the vegetable oil in a preheated wok or large frying pan (skillet), add the Szechuan red peppercorns and dried red chillies and stir for a few seconds.

3 Add the Chinese leaves (cabbage) or shredded white cabbage to the peppercorns and chillies and stir-fry for about 1 minute.

4 Add the salt to the mixture in the wok or frying pan (skillet) and continue stirring for another minute.

5 Add the sugar, light soy sauce and rice vinegar, blend well and braise for one more minute.

6 Finally sprinkle on the sesame oil, if using. Serve the braised Chinese leaves (cabbage) hot or cold.

COOK'S TIP

Szechuan red peppercorns are not true (bell) peppers, but reddish brown dry berries with a pungent, aromatic odour which distinguishes them from the hotter black peppercorns. Roast them briefly in the oven or dry-fry them. Grind them in a blender and store in a jar until needed.

Bamboo with Spinach

In this recipe, spinach is fried with spices and then braised in a soy-flavoured sauce with bamboo shoots for a rich, delicious dish.

NUTRITIONAL INFORMATION

Calories 105   Sugars 1g
Protein . . . . .3g   Fat 9g
Carbohydrate . . . .3g   Saturates 2g

 5 MINS   10 MINS

SERVES 4

I N G R E D I E N T S

3 tbsp peanut oil

225 g/8 oz spinach, chopped

175 g/6 oz canned bamboo shoots, drained and rinsed

1 garlic clove, crushed

2 fresh red chillies, sliced

pinch of ground cinnamon

300 ml/½ pint/1¼ cups vegetable stock

pinch of sugar

pinch of salt

1 tbsp light soy sauce

COOK'S TIP

Fresh bamboo shoots are rarely available in the West and, in any case, are extremely time-consuming to prepare. Canned bamboo shoots are quite satisfactory, as they are used to provide a crunchy texture, rather than for their flavour, which is fairly insipid.

1 Heat the peanut oil in a preheated wok or large frying pan (skillet), swirling the oil around the base of the wok until it is really hot.

2 Add the spinach and bamboo shoots to the wok and stir-fry for 1 minute.

3 Add the garlic, chillies and cinnamon to the mixture in the wok and stir-fry for a further 30 seconds.

4 Stir in the stock, sugar, salt and light soy sauce, cover and cook over a medium heat for 5 minutes, or until the vegetables are cooked through and the sauce has reduced. If there is too much cooking liquid, blend a little cornflour (cornstarch) with double the quantity of cold water and stir into the sauce.

5 Transfer the bamboo shoots and spinach to a serving dish and serve.

Mushrooms in Coconut Milk

This filling and tasty main course dish, which comprises three varieties of mushroom, can be served over rice or noodles.

NUTRITIONAL INFORMATION

Calories 189   Sugars 6g
Protein . . . . .6g   Fat 15g
Carbohydrate . . . .7g   Saturates 2g

 10 MINS   10 MINS

SERVES 4

I N G R E D I E N T S

2 lemon grass stalks

2 green chillies

1 tbsp light soy sauce

2 garlic cloves, crushed

2 tbsp chopped fresh coriander
   (cilantro)

2 tbsp chopped fresh parsley

6 slices galangal, peeled

3 tbsp sunflower oil

1 aubergine (eggplant), cubed

60 g/2 oz/²⁄₃ cup oyster mushrooms

60 g/2 oz/²⁄₃ cup chestnut (crimini)
   mushrooms

60 g/2 oz/²⁄₃ cup field mushrooms,
   quartered if large

125 g/4½ oz French (green) beans,
   cut into 5 cm/2 inch lengths,
   blanched

300 ml/½ pint/1¼ cups coconut milk

1 tbsp lemon juice

fresh parsley or coriander (cilantro),
   to garnish

rice, to serve

1 Using a sharp knife, thinly slice the lemon grass. Deseed and finely chop the green chillies.

2 Grind together the lemon grass, chillies, light soy sauce, garlic, coriander (cilantro), parsley and galangal in a large pestle and mortar or a food processor. Set aside until required.

3 Heat the sunflower oil in a wok or large, heavy frying pan (skillet).

4 Add the aubergine (eggplant) to the wok or frying pan (skillet) and stir over a high heat for 3 minutes.

5 Stir in the three varieties of mushrooms and the French (green) beans. Cook for 3 minutes, stirring constantly.

6 Add the ground spice paste to the mixture in the wok or frying pan (skillet).

7 Add the coconut milk and lemon juice to the pan, bring to the boil and simmer for 2 minutes.

8 Transfer the mushrooms and their sauce to warm serving dishes half-filled with rice, garnish with fresh parsley or coriander (cilantro) and serve immediately.

Deep-fried Courgettes

These courgette (zucchini) fritters are irresistible and could be served as a starter or snack with a chilli dip.

NUTRITIONAL INFORMATION

Calories 117	Sugars 2g	
Protein 3g	Fat 6g	
Carbohydrate . . .14g	Saturates 1g	

 5 MINS   🕐 20 MINS

SERVES 4

I N G R E D I E N T S

450 g/1 lb courgettes (zucchini)

1 egg white

50 g/1¾ oz/⅓ cup cornflour (cornstarch)

1 tsp salt

1 tsp Chinese five-spice powder

oil, for deep-frying

chilli dip, to serve

1 Using a sharp knife, slice the courgettes (zucchini) into rings or chunky sticks.

2 Place the egg white in a small mixing bowl. Lightly whip the egg white until foamy, using a fork.

3 Mix the cornflour (cornstarch), salt and Chinese five-spice powder together and sprinkle on to a large plate.

4 Heat the oil for deep-frying in a large preheated wok or heavy-based frying pan (skillet).

5 Dip each piece of courgette (zucchini) into the beaten egg white then coat in the cornflour (cornstarch) and five-spice mixture.

6 Deep-fry the courgettes (zucchini), in batches, for about 5 minutes or until

pale golden and crispy. Repeat with the remaining courgettes (zucchini).

7 Remove the courgettes (zucchini) with a slotted spoon and leave to drain on absorbent kitchen paper (paper towels) while deep-frying the remainder.

8 Transfer the courgettes (zucchini) to serving plates and serve immediately with a chilli dip.

VARIATION

Alter the seasoning by using chilli powder or curry powder instead of the Chinese five-spice powder, if you prefer.

Stuffed Chinese Leaves

Mushrooms, spring onions (scallions), celery and rice are flavoured with five-spice powder and wrapped in Chinese leaves (cabbage).

NUTRITIONAL INFORMATION

Calories 166   Sugars 3g
Protein ....3g   Fat 13g
Carbohydrate ...10g   Saturates 8g

25 MINS   45 MINS

SERVES 4

I N G R E D I E N T S

8 large Chinese leaves (cabbage)

60 g/2 oz/⅓ cup long-grain rice

½ vegetable stock (bouillon) cube

60 g/2 oz/¼ cup butter

1 bunch spring onions (scallions), trimmed and chopped finely

1 celery stalk, chopped finely

125 g/4½ oz/1¼ cups button mushrooms, sliced

1 tsp Chinese five-spice powder

300 ml/½ pint/1¼ cups passata (sieved tomatoes)

salt and pepper

fresh chives, to garnish

1 Blanch the Chinese leaves (cabbage) in boiling water for 1 minute. Refresh them under cold running water and drain well. Be careful not to tear them.

2 Cook the rice in plenty of boiling water, with the stock (bouillon) cube, until just tender. Drain well and set aside until required.

3 Meanwhile, melt the butter in a frying pan (skillet) and fry the spring onions (scallions) and celery gently for 3–4 minutes until softened, but not browned.

4 Add the mushrooms to the wok or frying pan (skillet) and cook for a further 3–4 minutes, stirring frequently.

5 Add the cooked rice to the pan with the five-spice powder. Season with salt and pepper and stir well to combine the ingredients.

6 Lay out the Chinese leaves (cabbage) on a work surface (counter) and divide the rice mixture between them. Roll each leaf into a neat parcel (packet) to enclose the stuffing. Place them, seam-side down, in a greased ovenproof dish. Pour the passata over them and cover with foil. Bake in a preheated oven, 190°C/375°F/Gas Mark 5, for 25–30 minutes.

7 Serve the stuffed Chinese leaves (cabbage) immediately, garnished with fresh chives.

(Bell) Peppers with Chestnuts

This is a crisp and colourful recipe, topped with crisp, shredded leeks for both flavour and colour.

NUTRITIONAL INFORMATION

Calories	192	Sugars	.........5g
Protein	.........3g	Fat	..........14g
Carbohydrate	...13g	Saturates	......13g

5 MINS   15 MINS

SERVES 4

I N G R E D I E N T S

225 g/8 oz leeks

oil, for deep-frying

3 tbsp groundnut oil

1 yellow (bell) pepper, deseeded
  and diced

1 green (bell) pepper, deseeded
  and diced

1 red (bell) pepper, deseeded
  and diced

200 g/7 oz can water chestnuts,
  drained and sliced

2 cloves garlic, crushed

3 tbsp light soy sauce

1 To make the garnish, finely slice the leeks into thin strips, using a sharp knife.

2 Heat the oil for deep-frying in a wok or large, heavy-based frying pan (skillet)

3 Add the sliced leeks to the wok or frying pan (skillet) and cook for 2–3 minutes, or until crispy. Set aside until required.

4 Heat the 3 tablespoons of groundnut oil in the wok or frying pan (skillet).

5 Add the yellow, green and red (bell) peppers to the wok and stir-fry over a high heat for about 5 minutes, or until they are just beginning to brown at the edges and to soften.

6 Add the sliced water chestnuts, garlic and light soy sauce to the wok and stir-fry all of the vegetables for a further 2–3 minutes.

7 Spoon the (bell) pepper stir-fry on to warm serving plates, garnish with the crispy leeks and serve.

COOK'S TIP

Add 1 tbsp of hoisin sauce with the soy sauce in step 6 for extra flavour and spice.

Carrots with Coconut

Sliced carrots and chunks of parsnip are cooked in a creamy coconut sauce with ground almonds and served on a bed of spinach.

NUTRITIONAL INFORMATION

Calories 386   Sugars 14g
Protein . . . . .6g   Fat 32g
Carbohydrate . . .20g   Saturates 15g

10 MINS   35 MINS

SERVES 4

I N G R E D I E N T S

90 g/3 oz/⅓ cup creamed coconut

300 ml/½ pint/1¼ cups hot water

15 g/½ oz/2 tbsp flaked (slivered) almonds

4 tbsp vegetable oil

5 cardamom pods

4 thin slices ginger root

350 g/12 oz/2½ cups carrots, sliced

350 g/12 oz/2½ cups parsnips, cut into small chunks

¼ tsp five-spice powder

15 g/½ oz/2 tbsp ground almonds

200 g/7 oz/4 cups young spinach leaves

½ red onion, sliced thinly

1 garlic clove, sliced

salt

1 Crumble the creamed coconut into a bowl or jug, add the hot water and stir until dissolved.

2 Heat a saucepan and dry-fry the flaked (slivered) almonds until golden. Remove from the pan and set aside until required.

3 Heat half the oil in the saucepan. Lightly crush the cardamom pods (this helps to release their flavour) and add to the saucepan with the ginger root.

Fry for 30 seconds to flavour the oil. Add the chopped carrots and parsnips. Stir-fry for 2–3 minutes.

4 Stir in the five-spice powder and ground almonds, and pour in the coconut liquid. Bring to the boil and season with salt to taste. Cover and simmer for 12–15 minutes until the vegetables are tender. Stir occasionally, adding extra water if necessary.

5 Wash and drain the spinach. Remove any stalks. Heat the remaining oil in a wok and stir-fry the onion and garlic for 2 minutes. Add the spinach and stir-fry until it has just wilted. Drain off any excess liquid and season with salt.

6 Remove the cardamom pods and ginger from the carrots and parsnips, and adjust the seasoning. Serve on a bed of the spinach sprinkled with the almonds.

Cantonese Garden Vegetables

This dish tastes as fresh as it looks. Try to get hold of baby vegetables as they look and taste so much better in this dish.

NUTRITIONAL INFORMATION

Calories 130   Sugars 8g
Protein ....6g   Fat 8g
Carbohydrate ....8g   Saturates 1g

 5 MINS   10 MINS

SERVES 4

I N G R E D I E N T S

2 tbsp peanut oil

1 tsp Chinese five-spice powder

75 g/2¾ oz baby carrots, halved

2 celery sticks, sliced

2 baby leeks, sliced

50 g/1¾ oz mangetout (snow peas)

4 baby courgettes (zucchini), halved
   lengthwise

8 baby corn cobs

225 g/8 oz firm marinated tofu
   (bean curd), cubed

4 tbsp fresh orange juice

1 tbsp clear honey

celery leaves and orange zest,
   to garnish

cooked rice or noodles, to serve

VARIATION

Lemon juice would be
just as delicious as the
orange juice in this recipe,
but use 3 tablespoons instead
of 4 tablespoons.

1 Heat the peanut oil in a preheated wok or large frying pan (skillet) until almost smoking.

2 Add the Chinese five-spice powder, carrots, celery, leeks, mangetout (snow peas), courgettes (zucchini) and corn cobs and stir-fry for 3–4 minutes.

3 Add the tofu (bean curd) to the wok or frying pan (skillet) and cook for a further 2 minutes, stirring gently so the tofu (bean curd) does not break up.

4 Stir the fresh orange juice and clear honey into the wok or frying pan (skillet), reduce the heat and cook for 1–2 minutes.

5 Transfer the stir-fry to a serving dish, garnish with celery leaves and orange zest and serve with rice or noodles.

Stir-fried Greens

Eat your greens in this most delicious way – stir-fried so that they retain their colour, crunch and flavour.

NUTRITIONAL INFORMATION

Calories 116   Sugars 3g
Protein . . . . .5g   Fat 9g
Carbohydrate . . . .5g   Saturates 1g

5 MINS   10 MINS

SERVES 4

I N G R E D I E N T S

8 spring onions (scallions)

2 celery sticks

125 g/4½ oz white radish (mooli)

125 g/4½ oz sugar snap peas or mangetout (snow peas)

175 g/6 oz Chinese leaves (cabbage)

175 g/6 oz bok choy or spinach

2 tbsp vegetable oil

1 tbsp sesame oil

2 garlic cloves, chopped finely

1 tbsp fish sauce

2 tbsp oyster sauce

1 tsp finely grated fresh ginger root

pepper

1 Slice the spring onions (scallions) and celery finely. Cut the white radish (mooli) into matchstick strips. Trim the sugar snap peas or mangetout (snow peas). Shred the Chinese leaves (cabbage) and shred the bok choy or spinach.

2 Heat the vegetable oil and sesame oil together in a wok or large frying pan (skillet). Add the garlic and fry for about 1 minute.

3 Add the spring onions (scallions), celery, white radish (mooli) and sugar snap peas or mangetout (snow peas) to the wok or frying pan (skillet) and stir-fry for about 2 minutes.

4 Add the Chinese leaves (cabbage) and bok choy or spinach. Stir-fry for about 1 minute.

5 Stir the fish sauce and oyster sauce into the vegetables with the grated ginger. Cook for 1 minute. Season with pepper to taste, transfer to a warm serving dish and serve at once.

VARIATION

Any variety – and any amount – of fresh vegetables can be used in this dish. Just make sure that harder vegetables, such as carrots, are cut very finely so that they cook quickly.

Use light soy sauce as an alternative to the fish sauce, if you prefer.

Broccoli in Oyster Sauce

Some Cantonese restaurants use only the stalks of the broccoli for this dish, for the crunchy texture.

NUTRITIONAL INFORMATION

Calories 100   Sugars 1g
Protein . . . . .3g   Fat 9g
Carbohydrate . . . .2g   Saturates 1g

3¹/₂ HOURS   5 MINS

SERVES 4

I N G R E D I E N T S

250-300 g/9-10½ oz broccoli

3 tbsp vegetable oil

3-4 small slices ginger root

½ tsp salt

½ tsp sugar

3-4 tbsp Chinese Stock (see page 30) or water

1 tbsp oyster sauce

COOK'S TIP

The broccoli stalks have to be peeled and cut diagonally to ensure that they will cook evenly. If they are thin stalks, the pieces can be added to the wok at the same time as the florets, but otherwise add the stalks first, to ensure that they will be tender.

1 Using a sharp knife, cut the broccoli spears into small florets. Trim the stalks, peel off the rough skin, and cut the stalks diagonally into diamond-shaped chunks.

2 Heat the vegetable oil in a preheated wok until really hot.

3 Add the pieces of broccoli stalk and the slices of ginger root to the wok and stir-fry for half a minute, then add the florets and continue to stir-fry for another 2 minutes.

4 Add the salt, sugar and Chinese stock or water, and continue stirring for another minute or so.

5 Blend in the oyster sauce. Transfer the broccoli to a serving dish and serve hot or cold.

Eight Jewel Vegetables

This recipe, as the title suggests, is a colourful mixture of eight vegetables, cooked in a black bean and soy sauce.

NUTRITIONAL INFORMATION

Calories 110   Sugars 3g
Protein . . . . .4g   Fat 8g
Carbohydrate . . . .7g   Saturates 1g

🥘 5 MINS   ⏱ 10 MINS

SERVES 4

I N G R E D I E N T S

2 tbsp peanut oil

6 spring onions (scallions), sliced

3 garlic cloves, crushed

1 green (bell) pepper, seeded
  and diced

1 red (bell) pepper, seeded and diced

1 fresh red chilli, sliced

2 tbsp chopped water chestnuts

1 courgette (zucchini), chopped

125 g/4½ oz oyster mushrooms

3 tbsp black bean sauce

2 tsp Chinese rice wine or dry sherry

4 tbsp dark soy sauce

1 tsp dark brown sugar

2 tbsp water

1 tsp sesame oil

1 Heat the peanut oil in a preheated wok or large frying pan (skillet) until it is almost smoking.

2 Lower the heat slightly, add the spring onions (scallions) and garlic and stir-fry for about 30 seconds.

3 Add the red and green (bell) peppers, fresh red chilli, water chestnuts and courgette (zucchini) to the wok or frying pan (skillet) and stir-fry for 2–3 minutes,

or until the vegetables are just beginning to soften.

4 Add the oyster mushrooms, black bean sauce, Chinese rice wine or dry sherry, dark soy sauce, dark brown sugar and water to the wok and stir-fry for a further 4 minutes.

5 Sprinkle the stir-fry with sesame oil and serve immediately.

COOK'S TIP

Eight jewels or treasures form a traditional part of the Chinese New Year celebrations, which start in the last week of the old year. The Kitchen God, an important figure, is sent to give a report to heaven, returning on New Year's Eve in time for the feasting.

Spicy Mushrooms

A mixture of mushrooms, common in Western cooking, have been used in this recipe for a richly flavoured dish.

NUTRITIONAL INFORMATION

Calories 103	Sugars 4g
Protein 3g	Fat 8g
Carbohydrate 5g	Saturates 2g

5 MINS   10 MINS

SERVES 4

INGREDIENTS

2 tbsp peanut oil

2 garlic cloves, crushed

3 spring onions (scallions), chopped

300 g/10½ oz button mushrooms

2 large open-cap mushrooms, sliced

125 g/4½ oz oyster mushrooms

1 tsp chilli sauce

1 tbsp dark soy sauce

1 tbsp hoisin sauce

1 tbsp wine vinegar

½ tsp ground Szechuan pepper

1 tbsp dark brown sugar

1 tsp sesame oil

chopped parsley, to garnish

1 Heat the peanut oil in a preheated wok or large frying pan (skillet) until almost smoking.

2 Reduce the heat slightly, add the garlic and spring onions (scallions) to the wok or frying pan (skillet) and stir-fry for 30 seconds.

3 Add all the mushrooms to the wok, together with the chilli sauce, dark soy sauce, hoisin sauce, wine vinegar, ground Szechuan pepper and dark brown sugar and stir-fry for 4–5 minutes, or until the mushrooms are cooked through. Stir constantly to prevent the mixture sticking to the base of the wok.

4 Sprinkle the sesame oil on top of the mixture in the wok. Transfer to a warm serving dish, garnish with parsley and serve immediately.

COOK'S TIP

If Chinese dried mushrooms are available, add a small quantity to this dish for texture. Wood (tree) ears are widely used and are available dried from Chinese food stores. They should be rinsed, soaked in warm water for 20 minutes and rinsed again before use.

Golden Needles with Bamboo

Golden needles are the dried flower buds of the tiger lily and have a unique musky flavour. They are available, dried, from Chinese shops.

NUTRITIONAL INFORMATION

Calories 178   Sugars 3g
Protein ....4g   Fat 9g
Carbohydrate ...22g   Saturates 1g

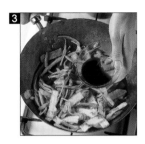

35 MINS   25 MINS

SERVES 4

INGREDIENTS

25 g/1 oz/¼ cup dried lily flowers

2 x 225 g/8 oz cans bamboo shoots, drained

60 g/2 oz/½ cup cornflour (cornstarch)

vegetable oil, for deep-frying

1 tbsp vegetable oil

450ml/¾ pint/scant 2 cups vegetable stock

1 tbsp dark soy sauce

1 tbsp dry sherry

1 tsp sugar

1 large garlic clove, sliced

½ red (bell) pepper

½ green (bell) pepper

½ yellow (bell) pepper

1 Soak the lily flowers in hot water for 30 minutes.

2 Coat the bamboo shoots in cornflour (cornstarch). Heat enough oil in a large heavy-based saucepan to deep-fry the bamboo shoots in batches until just beginning to colour. Remove with a perforated spoon and drain on absorbent kitchen paper (paper towels).

3 Drain the lily flowers and trim off the hard ends. Heat 1 tablespoon of oil in a wok or large frying pan (skillet). Add the lily flowers, bamboo shoots, stock, soy sauce, sherry, sugar and garlic.

4 Slice the (bell) peppers thinly and add to the wok or frying pan (skillet). Bring to the boil, stirring constantly, then reduce the heat and simmer for 5 minutes. Add extra water or stock if necessary.

5 Transfer the mixture in the wok to warm serving dishes and serve.

COOK'S TIP

To coat the bamboo shoots easily with cornflour (cornstarch), place the cornflour (cornstarch) in a plastic bag, add the bamboo shoots in batches and shake well.

Cauliflower with Greens

This is a delicious way to cook cauliflower – even without the greens.

NUTRITIONAL INFORMATION

Calories 49   Sugars 2g
Protein . . . . .2g   Fat 3g
Carbohydrate . . . .3g   Saturates 0.5g

 5 MINS   5 MINS

SERVES 4

INGREDIENTS

175 g/6 oz cauliflower, cut into
    florets

1 garlic clove

½ tsp turmeric

1 tbsp coriander (cilantro) root
    or stem

1 tbsp sunflower oil

2 spring onions (scallions), cut into
    2.5 cm/1 inch pieces

125 g/4½ oz oriental greens, such as
    bok choy or mustard greens,
    tough stalks removed

1 tsp yellow mustard seeds

1 Blanch the cauliflower, rinse in cold running water and drain. Set aside until required.

2 Grind together the garlic, turmeric and coriander (cilantro) root or stem together in a pestle and mortar or spice grinder.

3 Heat the sunflower oil in a wok or large, heavy frying pan (skillet).

4 Add the spring onions (scallions) to the wok or frying pan (skillet) and cook over a high heat for 2 minutes, stirring constantly.

5 Add the oriental greens and stir-fry for 1 minute. Keep warm and set aside until required.

6 Return the wok or frying pan (skillet) to the heat and add the mustard seeds. Stir until they start to pop, then add the turmeric and coriander (cilantro) mixture and the cauliflower, and stir until all the cauliflower is coated.

7 Serve the cauliflower with the greens on a warmed serving plate.

COOK'S TIP

Pestle and mortars are available in wood or stone. The stone mortar gives a finer grind than the wooden mortar. A coffee grinder can also be used , but will need a thorough clean afterwards, as some of the spices used in Chinese cooking can be quite pungent!

Sherry & Soy Vegetables

This is a simple, yet tasty side dish which is just as delicious as a snack or main course.

10 MINS   15 MINS

SERVES 4

INGREDIENTS

2 tbsp sunflower oil

1 red onion, sliced

175 g/6 oz carrots, thinly sliced

175 g/6 oz courgettes (zucchini), sliced diagonally

1 red (bell) pepper, deseeded and sliced

1 small head Chinese leaves (cabbage), shredded

150 g/5½ oz/3 cups bean sprouts

225 g/8 oz can bamboo shoots, drained

150 g/5½ oz/¼ cup cashew nuts, toasted

SAUCE

3 tbsp medium sherry

3 tbsp light soy sauce

1 tsp ground ginger

1 clove garlic, crushed

1 tsp cornflour (cornstarch)

1 tbsp tomato purée (paste)

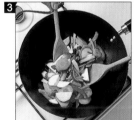

1 Heat the sunflower oil in a large preheated wok.

2 Add the red onion and stir-fry for 2–3 minutes or until softenened.

3 Add the carrots, courgettes (zucchini) and (bell) pepper slices to the wok and stir-fry for a further 5 minutes.

4 Add the Chinese leaves (cabbage), bean sprouts and bamboo shoots and heat through for 2–3 minutes, or until the leaves begin to wilt. Stir in the cashews.

5 Combine the sherry, soy sauce, ginger, garlic, cornflour (cornstarch) and tomato purée (paste). Pour over the vegetables and toss well. Leave to simmer for 2–3 minutes or until the juices start to thicken. Serve immediately.

VARIATION

Use any mixture of fresh vegetables that you have to hand in this very versatile dish.

Carrots with Pineapple

If you can use fresh pineapple the flavour is even better and the texture crisper.

NUTRITIONAL INFORMATION

Calories	125	Sugars	........17g
Protein	.........1g	Fat	...........6g
Carbohydrate	...18g	Saturates	.......1g

  5 MINS   15 MINS

SERVES 4

INGREDIENTS

1 tbsp sunflower oil

1 tbsp olive oil

1 small onion, finely sliced

2.5 cm/1 inch piece ginger root, peeled and grated

1-2 garlic cloves, crushed

500 g/1 lb 2 oz carrots, thinly sliced

1 x 200 g/7 oz can pineapple in natural juice, chopped, or 250 g/9 oz fresh pineapple, chopped

2-3 tbsp pineapple juice (from the can or fresh)

salt and coarsely ground black pepper

freshly chopped parsley or dill, to garnish

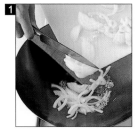  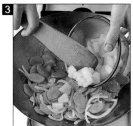

COOK'S TIP

If using canned pineapple make sure it is in natural juice, not syrup: the sweet taste of the syrup will ruin the fresh flavour of this dish. Most fruits can now be bought canned in natural juice, which gives a much fresher, lighter taste.

1 Heat the sunflower and olive oil in a wok. Add the onion, ginger and garlic and stir-fry briskly for 2-3 minutes.

2 Add the carrots and continue to stir-fry, lowering the heat a little, for about 5 minutes.

3 Add the pineapple and juice and plenty of seasoning and continue to stir-fry for 5-6 minutes, or until the carrots are tender-crisp and the liquid has almost evaporated.

4 Adjust the seasoning, adding plenty of black pepper and turn into a warmed serving dish. Sprinkle with chopped parsley or dill and serve as a vegetable accompaniment. Alternatively, you can allow the carrots to cool and serve as a salad, dressed with 2-4 tablespoons French dressing.

Fish Aubergine (Eggplant)

Like Fish-flavoured Shredded Pork (page 240), there is no fish involved in this dish, and the meat can be omitted without affecting the flavour.

NUTRITIONAL INFORMATION

Calories	130	Sugars	.........3g
Protein	.........8g	Fat	...........8g
Carbohydrate	....6g	Saturates	.......2g

35 MINS   15 MINS

SERVES 4

INGREDIENTS

500 g/1 lb 2 oz aubergine (eggplant)

vegetable oil, for deep-frying

1 garlic clove, finely chopped

½ tsp finely chopped ginger root

2 spring onions (scallions), finely chopped, with the white and green parts separated

125 g/4½ oz pork, thinly shredded (optional)

1 tbsp light soy sauce

2 tsp rice wine or dry sherry

1 tbsp chilli bean sauce

½ tsp sugar

1 tbsp rice vinegar

2 tsp cornflour (cornstarch) paste (see page 29)

a few drops sesame oil

salt

1 Using a sharp knife, cut the aubergine (eggplant) into rounds and then into thin strips about the size of potato chips – the skin can either be peeled or left on. Place the aubergine (eggplant) strips into a colander, sprinkle with salt and leave to stand for 30 minutes. Rinse thoroughly and pat dry on kitchen paper (paper towels). This process removes the bitter juices from the aubergine (eggplant).

2 Heat the vegetable oil in a preheated wok or large frying pan (skillet) until smoking.

3 Add the aubergine (eggplant) chips and deep-fry for about 3-4 minutes, or until soft. Remove and drain on absorbent kitchen paper (paper towels).

4 Pour off the hot oil, leaving about 1 tablespoon in the wok. Add the garlic, ginger and the white parts of the spring onions (scallions), followed by the pork (if using). Stir-fry for about 1 minute or until the colour of the meat changes, then add the light soy sauce, rice wine or dry sherry and chilli bean sauce, blending well.

5 Return the aubergine (eggplant) chips to the wok or frying pan (skillet) together with the sugar, ½ teaspoon salt and the rice vinegar.

6 Continue stirring the mixture in the wok for another minute or so, then add the cornflour (cornstarch) paste and stir until the sauce has thickened.

7 Add the green parts of the spring onions (scallions) to the wok and toss to combine. Sprinkle on the sesame oil and serve immediately.

Bamboo with (Bell) Peppers

This dish has a wonderfully strong ginger flavour which is integral to Chinese cooking. The mixed (bell) peppers give the dish a burst of colour.

 5 MINS   15 MINS

SERVES 4

I N G R E D I E N T S

2 tbsp peanut oil

225 g/8 oz canned bamboo shoots, drained and rinsed

2.5-cm/1-inch piece fresh root ginger, finely chopped

1 small red (bell) pepper, seeded and thinly sliced

1 small green (bell) pepper, seeded and thinly sliced

1 small yellow (bell) pepper, seeded and thinly sliced

1 leek, sliced

125 ml/4 fl oz/½ cup vegetable stock

1 tbsp light soy sauce

2 tsp light brown sugar

2 tsp Chinese rice wine or dry sherry

1 tsp cornflour (cornstarch)

2 tsp water

1 tsp sesame oil

1 Heat the peanut oil in a preheated wok or large frying pan (skillet), swirling the oil around the base of the wok or pan until it is really hot.

2 Add the bamboo shoots, ginger, (bell) peppers and leek to the wok and stir-fry for 2–3 minutes.

3 Stir in the vegetable stock, soy sauce, light brown sugar and Chinese rice wine or sherry and bring to the boil, stirring.

4 Reduce the heat and simmer for 4–5 minutes, or until the vegetables begin to soften.

5 Blend the cornflour (cornstarch) with the water to form a smooth paste.

6 Stir the cornflour (cornstarch) paste into the wok. Bring to the boil and cook, stirring constantly, until the sauce thickens and clears.

7 Sprinkle the sesame oil over the vegetables and cook for 1 minute. Transfer to a warm serving dish and serve immediately.

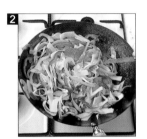

COOK'S TIP

Add a chopped fresh red chilli or a few drops of chilli sauce for a spicier dish.

Braised Vegetables

This colourful selection of braised vegetables makes a splendid accompaniment to a main dish.

NUTRITIONAL INFORMATION

Calories 170   Sugars 8g
Protein ....7g   Fat 10g
Carbohydrate ...14g   Saturates 1g

  10 MINS   10 MINS

SERVES 4

INGREDIENTS

3 tbsp sunflower oil

1 garlic clove, crushed

1 Chinese cabbage, thickly shredded

2 onions, peeled and cut into wedges

250 g/9 oz broccoli florets

2 large carrots, peeled and cut into thin julienne strips

12 baby or dwarf corn, halved if large

60 g/2 oz mangetout (snow peas), halved

90 g/3 oz Chinese or oyster mushrooms, sliced

1 tbsp grated ginger root

175 ml/6 fl oz/¾ cup vegetable stock

2 tbsp light soy sauce

1 tbsp cornflour (cornstarch)

salt and pepper

½ tsp sugar

1 Heat the oil in a wok. Add the garlic, cabbage, onions, broccoli, carrots, corn, mangetout (snow peas), mushrooms and ginger and stir-fry for 2 minutes.

2 Add the stock, cover and cook for a further 2-3 minutes.

3 Blend the soy sauce with the cornflour (cornstarch) and salt and pepper to taste.

4 Remove the braised vegetables from the pan with a slotted spoon and keep warm. Add the soy sauce mixture to the pan juices, mixing well. Bring to the boil, stirring constantly, until the mixture thickens slightly. Stir in the sugar.

5 Return the vegetables to the pan and toss in the slightly thickened sauce. Cook gently to just heat through then serve immediately.

COOK'S TIP

This dish also makes an ideal vegetarian main meal. Double the quantities, to serve 4-6, and serve with noodles or Green Rice (see page 423).

Vegetable & Tofu Pancakes

Chinese pancakes are made with hardly any fat – they are simply flattened white flour dough.

NUTRITIONAL INFORMATION

Calories	.312	Sugars	.5g
Protein	.13g	Fat	.19g
Carbohydrate	.25g	Saturates	.7g

5 MINS   15 MINS

SERVES 4

I N G R E D I E N T S

1 tbsp vegetable oil

1 garlic clove, crushed

2.5 cm/1 inch piece fresh root ginger, grated

1 bunch spring onions (scallions), trimmed and shredded lengthwise

100 g/3½ oz mangetout (snow peas), topped, tailed and shredded

225 g/8 oz tofu (bean curd), drained and cut into 1 cm/½ inch pieces

2 tbsp dark soy sauce, plus extra to serve

2 tbsp hoisin sauce, plus extra to serve

60 g/2 oz canned bamboo shoots, drained

60 g/2 oz canned water chestnuts, drained and sliced

100 g/3½ oz bean sprouts

1 small red chilli, deseeded and sliced thinly

1 small bunch fresh chives

12 soft Chinese pancakes

TO SERVE

shredded Chinese leaves (cabbage)

1 cucumber, sliced

strips of red chilli

1 Heat the oil in a frying pan (skillet) and stir-fry the garlic and ginger for 1 minute.

2 Add the spring onions (scallions), mangetout (snow peas), tofu (bean curd), soy sauce and hoisin sauce. Stir-fry for 2 minutes.

3 Add the bamboo shoots, water chestnuts, bean sprouts and chilli to the pan. Stir-fry gently for 2 minutes until the vegetables are just tender but still have bite. Snip the chives into 2.5 cm/ 1 inch lengths and stir into the pan.

4 Meanwhile, heat the pancakes according to the instructions on the packet. Divide the vegetables and tofu (bean curd) among the pancakes. Roll up the pancakes and serve with the Chinese leaves (cabbage) and extra sauce.

Spicy Aubergines (Eggplants)

Try to obtain the smaller Chinese aubergines (eggplants) for this dish, as they have a slightly sweeter taste.

NUTRITIONAL INFORMATION

Calories 120	Sugars 7g	
Protein 2g	Fat 9g	
Carbohydrate 9g	Saturates 1g	

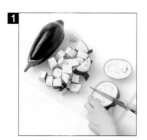

 35 MINS   20 MINS

SERVES 4

INGREDIENTS

450 g/1 lb aubergines (eggplants), rinsed

2 tsp salt

3 tbsp vegetable oil

2 garlic cloves, crushed

2.5-cm/1-inch piece fresh root ginger, chopped

1 onion, halved and sliced

1 fresh red chilli, sliced

2 tbsp dark soy sauce

1 tbsp hoisin sauce

½ tsp chilli sauce

1 tbsp dark brown sugar

1 tbsp wine vinegar

1 tsp ground Szechuan pepper

300 ml/½ pint/1¼ cups vegetable stock

1 Cut the aubergines (eggplants) into cubes if you are using the larger variety, or cut the smaller type in half. Place in a colander and sprinkle with the salt. Let stand for 30 minutes. Rinse under cold running water and pat dry with kitchen paper (paper towels).

2 Heat the oil in a preheated wok and add the garlic, ginger, onion and fresh chilli. Stir-fry for 30 seconds and add the aubergines (eggplants). Continue to cook for 1–2 minutes.

3 Add the soy sauce, hoisin sauce, chilli sauce, sugar, wine vinegar, Szechuan pepper and vegetable stock to the wok, reduce the heat and leave to simmer, uncovered, for 10 minutes, or until the aubergines (eggplants) are cooked.

4 Increase the heat and boil to reduce the sauce until thickened enough to coat the aubergines (eggplants). Serve immediately.

COOK'S TIP

Sprinkling the aubergines (eggplants) with salt and letting them stand removes the bitter juices, which would otherwise taint the flavour of the dish.

Stir-fried Seasonal Vegetables

When selecting different fresh vegetables for this dish, bear in mind that there should always be a contrast in colour as well as texture.

NUTRITIONAL INFORMATION

Calories 108   Sugars 3g
Protein . . . . .3g   Fat 9g
Carbohydrate . . . .4g   Saturates 1g

3¹/₂ HOURS   10 MINS

SERVES 4

I N G R E D I E N T S

1 medium red (bell) pepper, cored
    and seeded

125 g/4½ oz courgettes (zucchini)

125 g/4½ oz cauliflower

125 g/4½ oz French (green) beans

3 tbsp vegetable oil

a few small slices ginger root

½ tsp salt

½ tsp sugar

Chinese Stock (see page 30) or
    water

1 tbsp light soy sauce

a few drops of sesame oil (optional)

1 Using a sharp knife or cleaver, cut the red (bell) pepper into small squares. Thinly slice the courgettes (zucchini). Trim the cauliflower and divide into small florets, discarding any thick stems. Make sure the vegetables are cut into roughly similar shapes and sizes to ensure even cooking.

2 Top and tail the French (green) beans, then cut them in half.

3 Heat the vegetable oil in a pre-heated wok or large frying pan (skillet).

4 Add the prepared vegetables to the wok and stir-fry with the ginger for about 2 minutes.

5 Add the salt and sugar to the wok or frying pan (skillet), and continue to stir-fry for 1-2 minutes, adding a little Chinese stock or water if the vegetables appear to be too dry. Do not add liquid unless necessary.

6 Add the light soy sauce and sesame oil (if using) and stir well to lightly coat the vegetables.

7 Transfer the stir-fried vegetables to a warm serving dish and serve immediately.

VARIATION

Almost any vegetables could be used in this dish but make sure there is a good variety of colour, and always include several crisp vegetables such as carrots or mangetout (snow peas).

Vegetable Chop Suey

Make sure that the vegetables are all cut into pieces of a similar size in this recipe, so that they cook within the same amount of time.

NUTRITIONAL INFORMATION

Calories 155	Sugars 6g
Protein 4g	Fat 12g
Carbohydrate 9g	Saturates 2g

 5 MINS   ⊙ 5 MINS

SERVES 4

I N G R E D I E N T S

1 yellow (bell) pepper, seeded

1 red (bell) pepper, seeded

1 carrot

1 courgette (zucchini)

1 fennel bulb

1 onion

60 g/2 oz mangetout (snow peas)

2 tbsp peanut oil

3 garlic cloves, crushed

1 tsp grated fresh root ginger

125 g/4½ oz bean sprouts

2 tsp light brown sugar

2 tbsp light soy sauce

125 ml/4 fl oz/½ cup vegetable stock

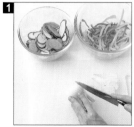

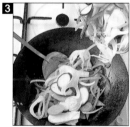

1 Cut the (bell) peppers, carrot, courgette (zucchini) and fennel into thin slices. Cut the onion into quarters and then cut each quarter in half. Slice the mangetout (snow peas) diagonally to create the maximum surface area.

2 Heat the oil in a preheated wok, add the garlic and ginger and stir-fry for 30 seconds. Add the onion and stir-fry for a further 30 seconds.

3 Add the (bell) peppers, carrot, courgette (zucchini), fennel and mangetout (snow peas) to the wok and stir-fry for 2 minutes.

4 Add the bean sprouts to the wok and stir in the sugar, soy sauce and stock. Reduce the heat to low and simmer for 1–2 minutes, until the vegetables are tender and coated in the sauce.

5 Transfer the vegetables and sauce to a serving dish and serve immediately.

VARIATION

Use any combination of colourful vegetables that you have to hand to make this versatile dish.

Caraway Cabbage

This makes a delicious vegetable accompaniment to all types of food: it can also be served as a vegetarian main dish.

NUTRITIONAL INFORMATION

Calories 223   Sugars 17g
Protein ....6g   Fat 14g
Carbohydrate ...18g   Saturates 1g

   5 MINS   🕐 10 MINS

SERVES 4

INGREDIENTS

500 g/1 lb 2 oz white cabbage

1 tbsp sunflower oil

4 spring onions (scallions), thinly sliced
   diagonally

60 g/2 oz/ 6 tbsp raisins

60 g/2 oz/½ cup walnut pieces or pecan
   nuts, roughly chopped

5 tbsp milk or vegetable stock

1 tbsp caraway seeds

1-2 tbsp freshly chopped mint

salt and pepper

mint sprigs, to garnish

1 Remove any outer leaves from the cabbage and cut out the stem, then shred the leaves very finely, either by hand or using the fine slicing blade on a food processor.

2 Heat the sunflower oil in a wok, swirling it around until it is really hot.

3 Add the spring onions (scallions) to the wok and stir-fry for a minute or so.

4 Add the shredded cabbage and stir-fry for 3-4 minutes, keeping the cabbage moving all the time and stirring from the outside to the centre of the wok. Make sure the cabbage does not stick to the wok or go brown.

5 Add the raisins, walnuts or pecans and milk or vegetable stock and continue to stir-fry for 3-4 minutes until the cabbage begins to soften slightly but is still crisp.

6 Season well with salt and pepper, add the caraway seeds and 1 tablespoon of the chopped mint and continue to stir-fry for a minute or so.

7 Serve sprinkled with the remaining chopped mint and garnish with sprigs of fresh mint.

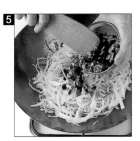

VARIATION

Red cabbage may be cooked in the same way in the wok, but substitute 2 tablespoons red or white wine vinegar and 3 tablespoons water for the milk and add 1 tablespoon brown sugar. Add a finely chopped dessert apple if liked.

Winter Vegetable Stir-fry

Ordinary winter vegetables are given extraordinary treatment in this lively stir-fry, just the thing for perking up jaded palates.

NUTRITIONAL INFORMATION

Calories 175	Sugars 7g
Protein 6g	Fat 13g
Carbohydrate 9g	Saturates 2g

 5 MINS 10 MINS

SERVES 4

INGREDIENTS

3 tbsp sesame oil

25 g/1 oz/¼ cup blanched almonds

1 large carrot, cut into thin strips

1 large turnip, cut into thin strips

1 onion, sliced finely

1 garlic clove, crushed

3 celery sticks, sliced finely

125 g/4½ oz Brussels sprouts, trimmed and halved

125 g/4½ oz cauliflower, broken into florets

125 g/4½ oz/2 cups white cabbage, shredded

2 tsp sesame seeds

1 tsp grated fresh root ginger

½ tsp medium chilli powder

1 tbsp chopped fresh coriander (cilantro)

1 tbsp light soy sauce

salt and pepper

sprigs of fresh coriander (cilantro), to garnish

1 Heat the oil in a wok or large frying pan (skillet). Stir-fry the almonds until lightly browned, then lift them out and drain on kitchen paper (paper towels).

2 Add all the vegetables to the wok or frying pan (skillet), except for the cabbage. Stir-fry the vegetables briskly for 3–4 minutes.

3 Add the cabbage, sesame seeds, ginger and chilli powder and cook, stirring, for 2 minutes. Season to taste.

4 Add the chopped coriander (cilantro), soy sauce and almonds, stirring gently to mix. Serve the vegetables, garnished with coriander (cilantro) sprigs.

COOK'S TIP

As well as adding protein, vitamins and useful fats to the diet, nuts and seeds add important flavour and texture to vegetarian meals. Sesame seeds are also a good source of vitamin E.

Lemon Chinese Leaves

These stir-fried Chinese leaves (cabbage) are served with a tangy sauce made of grated lemon rind, lemon juice and ginger.

NUTRITIONAL INFORMATION

Calories 120   Sugars 0g
Protein ....5g   Fat 8g
Carbohydrate ....8g   Saturates 1g

5 MINS   10 MINS

SERVES 4

INGREDIENTS

500 g/1 lb 2 oz Chinese leaves
   (cabbage)

3 tbsp vegetable oil

1 cm/½ inch piece ginger root, grated

1 tsp salt

1 tsp sugar

125 ml/4 fl oz/½ cup water or vegetable
   stock

1 tsp grated lemon rind

1 tbsp cornflour (cornstarch)

1 tbsp lemon juice

1 Separate the Chinese leaves (cabbage), wash and drain thoroughly. Pat dry with absorbent kitchen paper (paper towels).

2 Cut the Chinese leaves (cabbage) into 5 cm/2 inch wide slices.

COOK'S TIP

If Chinese leaves (cabbage) are unavailable, substitute slices of savoy cabbage. Cook for 1 extra minute to soften the leaves.

3 Heat the oil in a wok and add the grated ginger root followed by the Chinese leaves (cabbage), stir-fry for 2–3 minutes or until the leaves begin to wilt.

4 Add the salt and sugar, and mix well until the leaves soften. Remove the leaves with a slotted spoon and set aside.

5 Add the water or stock to the wok with the lemon rind. Bring to the boil.

6 Meanwhile, mix the cornflour (cornstarch) to a smooth paste with the lemon juice, then add to the wok. Simmer, stirring constantly, for about 1 minute to make a smooth sauce.

7 Return the cooked Chinese leaves (cabbage) to the pan and mix thoroughly to coat the leaves in the sauce. Arrange on a serving plate and serve immediately.

Potato Stir-Fry

In this sweet and sour dish, tender vegetables are simply stir-fried with spices and coconut milk, and flavoured with lime.

NUTRITIONAL INFORMATION

Calories 138	Sugars 5g
Protein 2g	Fat 6g
Carbohydrate ...20g	Saturates 1g

10 MINS • 20 MINS

SERVES 4

INGREDIENTS

4 waxy potatoes

2 tbsp vegetable oil

1 yellow (bell) pepper, diced

1 red (bell) pepper, diced

1 carrot, cut into matchstick strips

1 courgette (zucchini), cut into
   matchstick strips

2 garlic cloves, crushed

1 red chilli, sliced

1 bunch spring onions (scallions),
   halved lengthways

8 tbsp coconut milk

1 tsp chopped lemon grass

2 tsp lime juice

finely grated rind of 1 lime

1 tbsp chopped fresh coriander
   (cilantro)

1 Using a sharp knife, cut the potatoes into small dice.

2 Bring a large saucepan of water to the boil and cook the diced potatoes for 5 minutes. Drain thoroughly.

3 Heat the vegetable oil in a wok or large frying pan (skillet), swirling the oil around the base of the wok until it is really hot.

4 Add the potatoes, diced (bell) peppers, carrot, courgette (zucchini), garlic and chilli to the wok and stir-fry the vegetables for 2-3 minutes.

5 Stir in the spring onions, (scallions), coconut milk, chopped lemon grass and lime juice and stir-fry the mixture for a further 5 minutes.

6 Add the lime rind and coriander (cilantro) and stir-fry for 1 minute. Serve hot.

COOK'S TIP

Check that the potatoes are not overcooked in step 2, otherwise the potato pieces will disintegrate when they are stir-fried in the wok.

Leeks with Yellow Bean Sauce

This is a simple side dish which is ideal with other main meal vegetarian dishes.

NUTRITIONAL INFORMATION

Calories 131	Sugars 3g
Protein 6g	Fat 9g
Carbohydrate 7g	Saturates 2g

5 MINS   10 MINS

SERVES 4

INGREDIENTS

450 g/1 lb leeks

175 g/6 oz baby corn cobs

6 spring onions (scallions)

3 tbsp groundnut oil

225 g/8 oz Chinese leaves (cabbage), shredded

4 tbsp yellow bean sauce

1 Using a sharp knife, slice the leeks, halve the baby corn cobs and thinly slice the spring onions (scallions).

2 Heat the groundnut oil in a large preheated wok or frying pan (skillet) until smoking.

3 Add the leeks, shredded Chinese leaves (cabbage) and baby corn cobs to the wok or frying pan (skillet).

4 Stir-fry the vegetables over a high heat for about 5 minutes or until the edges of the vegetables are slightly brown.

5 Add the spring onions (scallions) to the wok or frying pan (skillet), stirring to combine.

6 Add the yellow bean sauce to the wok or frying pan (skillet).

7 Stir-fry the mixture in the wok for a further 2 minutes, or until heated through and the vegetables are thoroughly coated in the sauce.

8 Transfer the vegetables and sauce to warm serving dishes and serve immediately.

COOK'S TIP

Yellow bean sauce adds an authentic Chinese flavour to stir-fries. It is made from crushed salted soya beans mixed with flour and spices to make a thick paste. It is mild in flavour and is excellent with a range of vegetables.

Vegetables in Coconut Milk

This is a deliciously crunchy way to prepare a mixture of raw vegetables.

NUTRITIONAL INFORMATION

Calories 201	Sugars 10g
Protein 9g	Fat 13g
Carbohydrate . . .13g	Saturates 3g

 5 MINS   5 MINS

SERVES 4

I N G R E D I E N T S

1 red chilli, deseeded and chopped

1 tsp coriander seeds

1 tsp cumin seeds

2 garlic cloves, crushed

juice of 1 lime

250 ml/9 fl oz/1 cup coconut milk

125 g/4½ oz/2 cups bean sprouts

125 g/4½ oz/2 cups white cabbage,
shredded

125 g/4½ oz mangetout (snow peas),
trimmed

125 g/4½ oz/1¼ cups carrots,
sliced thinly

125 g/4½ oz/1¼ cups cauliflower florets

grated or shaved coconut, to serve

3 tbsp peanut butter

1 Grind together the chopped red chilli, coriander and cumin seeds, crushed garlic and lime juice in a pestle and mortar or food processor until a smooth paste is formed.

2 Put the spice paste into a medium-sized saucepan and heat gently for about 1 minute, or until fragrant.

3 Add the coconut milk to the saucepan and stir constantly until just about to boil.

4 Meanwhile, mix together the bean sprouts, shredded white cabbage, trimmed mangetout (snow peas), sliced carrots and cauliflower florets in a large mixing bowl.

5 Stir the peanut butter into the coconut mixture until well blended and then pour into the pan, stirring to coat the vegetables. Serve garnished with grated or shaved coconut.

COOK'S TIP

If you prefer, the cauliflower, carrots and mangetout (snow peas) may be blanched first for less bite.

This dish is ideal as a buffet dish as the quantity of dressing is quite sparse, and is only intended to coat.

Sweet & Sour Cauliflower

Although sweet and sour flavourings are mainly associated with pork, they are ideal for flavouring vegetables as in this tasty recipe.

NUTRITIONAL INFORMATION

Calories	154	Sugars	........16g
Protein	.........6g	Fat	...........7g
Carbohydrate	...17g	Saturates	.......1g

5 MINS   20 MINS

SERVES 4

INGREDIENTS

450 g/1 lb cauliflower florets

2 tbsp sunflower oil

1 onion, sliced

225 g/8 oz carrots, sliced

100 g/3½ oz mangetout (snow peas)

1 ripe mango, sliced

100 g/3½ oz/1 cup bean sprouts

3 tbsp chopped fresh coriander (cilantro)

3 tbsp fresh lime juice

1 tbsp clear honey

6 tbsp coconut milk

1 Bring a large saucepan of water to the boil. Add the cauliflower to the pan and cook for 2 minutes. Drain the cauliflower thoroughly.

2 Heat the sunflower oil in a large preheated wok.

3 Add the onion and carrots to the wok and stir-fry for about 5 minutes.

4 Add the drained cauliflower and mangetout (snow peas) to the wok and stir-fry for 2–3 minutes.

5 Add the mango and bean sprouts to the wok and stir-fry for about 2 minutes.

6 Mix together the coriander (cilantro), lime juice, honey and coconut milk in a bowl.

7 Add the coriander (cilantro) and coconut mixture to the wok and stir-fry for about 2 minutes or until the juices are bubbling.

8 Transfer the sweet and sour cauliflower stir-fry to serving dishes and serve immediately.

VARIATION

Use broccoli instead of the cauliflower as an alternative, if you prefer.

Ginger & Orange Broccoli

Thinly sliced broccoli florets are lightly stir-fried and served in a ginger and orange sauce.

NUTRITIONAL INFORMATION

Calories . . . . . . .133 Sugars 6g
Protein . . . . .9g Fat 7g
Carbohydrate . . .10g Saturates 1g

5 MINS   10 MINS

SERVES 4

INGREDIENTS

750 g/1 lb 10 oz broccoli

2 thin slices ginger root

2 garlic cloves

1 orange

2 tsp cornflour (cornstarch)

1 tbsp light soy sauce

½ tsp sugar

2 tbsp vegetable oil

1 Divide the broccoli into small florets. Peel the stems, using a vegetable peeler, and then cut the stems into thin slices, using a sharp knife.

2 Cut the ginger root into matchsticks and slice the garlic.

3 Peel 2 long strips of zest from the orange and cut into thin strips. Place the strips in a bowl, cover with cold water and set aside.

4 Squeeze the juice from the orange and mix with the cornflour (cornstarch), light soy sauce, sugar and 4 tablespoons water.

5 Heat the vegetable oil in a wok or large frying pan (skillet). Add the broccoli stem slices and stir-fry for 2 minutes.

6 Add the ginger root slices, garlic and broccoli florets, and stir-fry for a further 3 minutes.

7 Stir the orange sauce mixture into the wok and cook, stirring constantly, until the sauce has thickened and coated the broccoli.

8 Drain the reserved orange rind and stir into the wok before serving.

VARIATION

This dish could be made with cauliflower, if you prefer, or a mixture of cauliflower and broccoli.

Carrot & Orange Stir-Fry

Carrots and oranges have long been combined in Oriental cooking, the orange juice bringing out the sweetness of the carrots.

NUTRITIONAL INFORMATION

Calories 341	Sugars 26g
Protein 10g	Fat 21g
Carbohydrate . . .28g	Saturates 4g

 10 MINS 10 MINS

SERVES 4

I N G R E D I E N T S

2 tbsp sunflower oil

450 g/1 lb carrots, grated

225 g/8 oz leeks, shredded

2 oranges, peeled and segmented

2 tbsp tomato ketchup

1 tbsp demerara (brown crystal) sugar

2 tbsp light soy sauce

100 g/3½ oz/½ cup chopped peanuts

1 Heat the sunflower oil in a large preheated wok.

2 Add the grated carrot and leeks to the wok and stir-fry for 2–3 minutes, or until the vegetables have just softened.

3 Add the orange segments to the wok and heat through gently, ensuring that you do not break up the orange segments as you stir the mixture.

4 Mix the tomato ketchup, demerara (brown crystal) sugar and soy sauce together in a small bowl.

5 Add the tomato and sugar mixture to the wok and stir-fry for a further 2 minutes.

6 Transfer the stir-fry to warm serving bowls and scatter with the chopped peanuts. Serve immediately.

VARIATION

You could use pineapple instead of orange, if you prefer. If using canned pineapple, make sure that it is in natural juice not syrup as it will spoil the fresh taste of this dish.

Green & Black Bean Stir-fry

A terrific side dish, the variety of greens in this recipe make it as attractive as it is tasty.

NUTRITIONAL INFORMATION

Calories	88	Sugars	.........2g
Protein	.........2g	Fat	...........7g
Carbohydrate	....4g	Saturates	.......4g

  5 MINS   10 MINS

SERVES 4

INGREDIENTS

225 g/8 oz fine green beans, sliced

4 shallots, sliced

100 g/3½ oz shiitake mushrooms, thinly
sliced

1 clove garlic, crushed

1 Iceberg lettuce, shredded

1 tsp chilli oil

25 g/1 oz/2 tbsp butter

4 tbsp black bean sauce

1 Using a sharp knife, slice the fine green beans, shallots and shiitake mushrooms. Crush the garlic in a pestle and mortar and shred the Iceberg lettuce.

2 Heat the chilli oil and butter in a large preheated wok or frying pan (skillet).

3 Add the green beans, shallots, garlic and mushrooms to the wok and stir-fry for 2–3 minutes.

4 Add the shredded lettuce to the wok or frying pan (skillet) and stir-fry until the leaves have wilted.

5 Stir the black bean sauce into the mixture in the wok and heat through, tossing gently to mix, until the sauce is bubbling.

6 Transfer the green and black bean stir-fry to a warm serving dish and serve immediately.

COOK'S TIP

If possible, use Chinese green beans which are tender and can be eaten whole. They are available from specialist Chinese stores.

Vegetable Stir-fry with Eggs

Known as Gado Gado in China, this is a true classic which never fades from popularity. A delicious warm salad with a peanut sauce.

NUTRITIONAL INFORMATION

Calories 269	Sugars 12g
Protein 12g	Fat 19g
Carbohydrate ...14g	Saturates 3g

10 MINS   15 MINS

SERVES 4

INGREDIENTS

2 eggs

225 g/8 oz carrots

350 g/12 oz white cabbage

2 tbsp vegetable oil

1 red (bell) pepper, deseeded and thinly sliced

150 g/5½ oz/1½ cups bean sprouts

1 tbsp tomato ketchup

2 tbsp soy sauce

75 g/2¾ oz/⅓ cup salted peanuts, chopped

1 Bring a small saucepan of water to the boil. Add the eggs to the pan and cook for about 7 minutes. Remove the eggs from the pan and leave to cool under cold running water for 1 minute. Peel the shell from the eggs and then cut the eggs into quarters.

2 Peel and coarsley grate the carrots.

3 Remove any outer leaves from the white cabbage and cut out the stem, then shred the leaves very finely, either with a sharp knife or by using the fine slicing blade on a food processor.

4 Heat the vegetable oil in a large preheated wok or large frying pan (skillet).

5 Add the carrots, white cabbage and (bell) pepper to the wok and stir-fry for 3 minutes.

6 Add the bean sprouts to the wok and stir-fry for 2 minutes.

7 Combine the tomato ketchup and soy sauce in a small bowl and add to the wok or frying pan (skillet).

8 Add the chopped peanuts to the wok and stir-fry for 1 minute.

9 Transfer the stir-fry to warm serving plates and garnish with the hard-boiled (hard-cooked) egg quarters. Serve immediately.

COOK'S TIP

The eggs are cooled in cold water immediately after cooking in order to prevent the egg yolk blackening around the edges.

Spinach with Mushrooms

For best results, use straw mushrooms, available in cans from oriental shops. If these are unavailable, use button mushrooms instead.

NUTRITIONAL INFORMATION

Calories 201	Sugars 8g
Protein 7g	Fat 15g
Carbohydrate . . .10g	Saturates 2g

 5 MINS   10 MINS

SERVES 4

I N G R E D I E N T S

25 g/1 oz/¼ cup pine kernels (nuts)

500 g/1 lb 2 oz fresh spinach leaves

1 red onion

2 garlic cloves

3 tbsp vegetable oil

425 g/15 oz can straw mushrooms, drained

25 g/1 oz/3 tbsp raisins

2 tbsp soy sauce

salt

1 Heat a wok or large, heavy-based frying pan (skillet).

2 Dry-fry the pine kernels (nuts) in the wok until lightly browned. Remove with a perforated spoon and set aside until required.

3 Wash the spinach thoroughly, picking the leaves over and removing long stalks. Drain thoroughly and pat dry with absorbent kitchen paper (paper towels).

4 Using a sharp knife, slice the red onion and the garlic.

5 Heat the vegetable oil in the wok or frying pan (skillet). Add the onion and garlic slices and stir-fry for 1 minute until slightly softened.

6 Add the spinach and mushrooms, and continue to stir-fry until the leaves have wilted. Drain off any excess liquid.

7 Stir in the raisins, reserved pine kernels (nuts) and soy sauce. Stir-fry until thoroughly heated and all the ingredients are well combined.

8 Season to taste with salt, transfer to a warm serving dish and serve.

COOK'S TIP

Soak the raisins in 2 tablespoons dry sherry before using. This helps to plump them up as well as adding extra flavour to the stir-fry.

Broccoli & Black Bean Sauce

Broccoli works well with the black bean sauce in this recipe, while the almonds add extra crunch and flavour.

NUTRITIONAL INFORMATION

Calories	139	Sugars	.........3g
Protein	.........7g	Fat	..........10g
Carbohydrate	....5g	Saturates	.......1g

5 MINS   15 MINS

SERVES 4

I N G R E D I E N T S

450 g/1 lb broccoli florets

2 tbsp sunflower oil

1 onion, sliced

2 cloves garlic, thinly sliced

25 g/1 oz/¼ cup flaked (slivered) almonds

1 head Chinese leaves (cabbage), shredded

4 tbsp black bean sauce

1 Bring a large saucepan of water to the boil.

2 Add the broccoli florets to the pan and cook for 1 minute. Drain the broccoli thoroughly.

3 Meanwhile, heat the sunflower oil in a large preheated wok.

4 Add the onion and garlic slices to the wok and stir-fry until just beginning to brown.

5 Add the drained broccoli florets and the flaked (slivered) almonds to the mixture in the wok and stir-fry for a further 2–3 minutes.

6 Add the shredded Chinese leaves (cabbage) to the wok and stir-fry for a further 2 minutes, stirring the leaves briskly around the wok.

7 Stir the black bean sauce into the vegetables in the wok, tossing to coat the vegetables thoroughly in the sauce and cook until the juices are just beginning to bubble.

8 Transfer the vegetables to warm serving bowls and serve immediately.

VARIATION

Use unsalted cashew nuts instead of the almonds, if preferred.

Vegetable & Nut Stir-fry

A colourful selection of vegetables are stir-fried in a creamy peanut sauce and sprinkled with nuts to serve.

NUTRITIONAL INFORMATION

Calories ....325 Sugars 6g
Protein ....11g Fat 21g
Carbohydrate ...26g Saturates 4g

10 MINS   15 MINS

SERVES 4

INGREDIENTS

3 tbsp crunchy peanut butter

150 ml/¼ pint/⅔ cup water

1 tbsp soy sauce

1 tsp sugar

1 carrot

½ red onion

4 baby courgettes (zucchini)

1 red (bell) pepper

250 g/9 oz egg thread noodles

25 g/1 oz/¼ cup peanuts, chopped roughly

2 tbsp vegetable oil

1 tsp sesame oil

1 small green chilli, deseeded and sliced thinly

1 garlic clove, sliced thinly

225 g/8 oz can water chestnuts, drained and sliced

175 g/6 oz/3 cups bean sprouts

salt

1 Gradually blend the peanut butter with the water in a small bowl. Stir in the soy sauce and sugar. Set aside.

2 Cut the carrot into thin matchsticks and slice the red onion. Slice the courgettes (zucchini) on the diagonal and cut the (bell) pepper into chunks.

3 Bring a large pan of water to the boil and add the egg noodles. Remove from the heat immediately and leave to stand for 4 minutes, stirring occasionally to separate the noodles.

4 Heat a wok or large frying pan (skillet), add the peanuts and dry-fry until they are beginning to brown. Remove with a perforated spoon and set aside until required.

5 Add the oils to the pan and heat. Add the carrot, onion, courgette (zucchini), (bell) pepper, chilli and garlic, and stir-fry for 2–3 minutes. Add the water chestnuts, bean sprouts and peanut sauce. Bring to the boil and heat thoroughly. Season with salt to taste.

6 Drain the noodles and serve with the vegetable and nut stir-fry. Sprinkle with the reserved peanuts.

Quorn & Vegetable Stir-fry

Quorn, like tofu (bean curd), absorbs all of the flavours in a dish, making it ideal for this recipe which is packed with classic Chinese flavourings.

NUTRITIONAL INFORMATION

Calories 167   Sugars 8g
Protein ....12g   Fat 9g
Carbohydrate ...10g   Saturates 1g

30 MINS   10 MINS

SERVES 4

I N G R E D I E N T S

1 tbsp grated fresh root ginger

1 tsp ground ginger

1 tbsp tomato purée (paste)

2 tbsp sunflower oil

1 clove garlic, crushed

2 tbsp soy sauce

350 g/12 oz Quorn or soya cubes

225 g/8 oz carrots, sliced

100 g/3½ oz green beans, sliced

4 stalks celery, sliced

1 red (bell) pepper, deseeded and
   sliced

boiled rice, to serve

COOK'S TIP

Ginger root will keep for several weeks in a cool, dry place. Ginger root can also be kept frozen – break off lumps as needed.

1 Place the grated fresh root ginger, ground ginger, tomato purée (paste), 1 tablespoon of the sunflower oil, garlic, soy sauce and Quorn or soya cubes in a large bowl. Mix well to combine, stirring carefully so that you don't break up the Quorn or soya cubes. Cover and leave to marinate for 20 minutes.

2 Heat the remaining sunflower oil in a large preheated wok.

3 Add the marinated Quorn mixture to the wok and stir-fry for about 2 minutes.

4 Add the carrots, green beans, celery and red (bell) pepper to the wok and stir-fry for a further 5 minutes.

5 Transfer the stir-fry to warm serving dishes and serve immediately with freshly cooked boiled rice.

Creamy Green Vegetables

This dish is very quick to make. A dash of cream is added to the sauce, but this may be omitted, if preferred.

NUTRITIONAL INFORMATION

Calories 111   Sugars 2g
Protein ....5g   Fat 8g
Carbohydrate ....7g   Saturates 2g

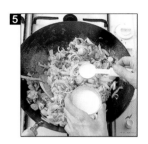

5 MINS   20 MINS

SERVES 4

I N G R E D I E N T S

450 g/1 lb Chinese leaves (cabbage), shredded

2 tbsp peanut oil

2 leeks, shredded

4 garlic cloves, crushed

300 ml/½ pint/1¼ cups vegetable stock

1 tbsp light soy sauce

2 tsp cornflour (cornstarch)

4 tsp water

2 tbsp single (light) cream or natural (unsweetened) yogurt

1 tbsp chopped coriander (cilantro)

1 Blanch the Chinese leaves (cabbage) in boiling water for 30 seconds. Drain, rinse under cold running water, then drain thoroughly again.

2 Heat the oil in a preheated wok and add the Chinese leaves (cabbage), leeks and garlic. Stir-fry for 2–3 minutes.

3 Add the stock and soy sauce to the wok, reduce the heat to low, cover and simmer for 10 minutes.

4 Remove the vegetables from the wok with a slotted spoon and set aside. Bring the stock to the boil and boil vigorously until reduced by about half.

5 Blend the cornflour (cornstarch) with the water and stir into the wok. Bring to the boil, and cook, stirring constantly, until thickened and clear.

6 Reduce the heat and stir in the vegetables and cream or yogurt. Cook over a low heat for 1 minute.

7 Transfer to a serving dish, sprinkle over the chopped coriander (cilantro) and serve.

COOK'S TIP

Do not boil the sauce once the cream or yogurt has been added, as it will separate.

Crispy Cabbage & Almonds

This dish is better known as crispy seaweed. It does not actually contain seaweed, but consists of spring greens (collard greens) or pak choi.

NUTRITIONAL INFORMATION

Calories 431   Sugars 17g
Protein . . . . .9g   Fat 37g
Carbohydrate . . .17g   Saturates 4g

  10 MINS   10 MINS

SERVES 4

INGREDIENTS

1.25 kg/2 lb 12 oz pak choi or spring greens (collard greens)

700 ml/1¼ pints/3 cups vegetable oil

75 g/2¾ oz/¾ cup blanched almonds

1 tsp salt

1 tbsp light brown sugar

pinch of ground cinnamon

1 Separate the leaves from the pak choi or spring greens (collard greens) and rinse them well. Drain thoroughly and pat dry with absorbent kitchen paper (paper towels).

2 Shred the greens (collard greens) into thin strips, using a sharp knife.

3 Heat the vegetable oil in a preheated wok or large, heavy-based frying pan (skillet) until the oil is almost smoking.

4 Reduce the heat and add the pak choi or spring greens (collard greens). Cook for 2–3 minutes, or until the greens begin to float in the oil and are crisp.

5 Remove the greens from the oil with a slotted spoon and leave to drain thoroughly on absorbent kitchen paper (paper towels).

6 Add the blanched almonds to the oil in the wok and cook for 30 seconds. Remove the almonds from the oil with a slotted spoon and drain thoroughly on absorbent kitchen paper (paper towels).

7 Mix together the salt, light brown sugar and ground cinnamon and sprinkle on to the greens.

8 Toss the almonds into the greens.

9 Transfer the greens and almonds to a warm serving dish and serve immediately.

COOK'S TIP

Ensure that the greens are completely dry before adding them to the oil, otherwise it will spit. The greens will not become crisp if they are wet when placed in the oil.

Chilli Aubergines (Eggplants)

Strips of aubergine (eggplant) are deep-fried, then served in a fragrant chilli sauce with carrot matchsticks and spring onions (scallions).

NUTRITIONAL INFORMATION

Calories 119	Sugars 2g	
Protein 1g	Fat 11g	
Carbohydrate 3g	Saturates 1g	

🕒 5 MINS   🕐 15 MINS

SERVES 4

I N G R E D I E N T S

1 large aubergine (eggplant)

vegetable oil, for deep-frying

2 carrots

4 spring onions (scallions)

2 large garlic cloves

1 tbsp vegetable oil

2 tsp chilli sauce

1 tbsp soy sauce

1 tbsp dry sherry

red chilli flower, to garnish (see page 269)

1 Slice the aubergine (eggplant) and then cut into strips about the size of potato chips (French fries).

2 Heat enough oil in a large heavy-based saucepan to deep-fry the aubergine (eggplant) in batches until just browned. Remove the strips with a perforated spoon and drain on kitchen paper (paper towels).

3 Using a sharp knife, cut the carrots into thin matchsticks. Trim and slice the spring onions (scallions) diagonally. Slice the garlic cloves.

4 Heat 1 tablespoon of oil in a wok or large frying pan (skillet). Add the carrots and stir-fry for 1 minute.

5 Add the chopped spring onions (scallions) and garlic to the wok and stir-fry for a further minute.

6 Stir in the chilli sauce, soy sauce and sherry, then stir in the drained aubergine (eggplant). Mix well to ensure that the vegetables are heated through.

7 Transfer to a serving dish, garnish with a red chilli flower and serve.

COOK'S TIP

For a milder dish, substitute hoisin sauce for the chilli sauce. This can be bought ready-made from all supermarkets.

Honey-fried Spinach

This stir-fry is the perfect accompaniment to tofu (bean curd) dishes, and it is so quick and simple to make.

NUTRITIONAL INFORMATION

Calories 146	Sugars 9g
Protein 4g	Fat 9g
Carbohydrate ...10g	Saturates 2g

 5 MINS   15 MINS

SERVES 4

INGREDIENTS

4 spring onions (scallions)

3 tbsp groundnut oil

350 g/12 oz shiitake mushrooms, sliced

2 cloves garlic, crushed

350 g/12 oz baby leaf spinach

2 tbsp dry sherry

2 tbsp clear honey

1 Using a sharp knife, slice the spring onions (scallions).

2 Heat the groundnut oil in a large preheated wok or heavy-based frying pan (skillet).

3 Add the shiitake mushrooms to the wok and stir-fry for about 5 minutes, or until the mushrooms have softened.

COOK'S TIP

Single-flower honey has a better, more individual flavour than blended honey. Acacia honey is typically Chinese, but you could also try clover, lemon blossom, lime flower or orange blossom.

4 Stir the crushed garlic into the wok or frying pan (skillet).

5 Add the baby leaf spinach to the wok or pan and stir-fry for a further 2–3 minutes, or until the spinach leaves have just wilted.

6 Mix together the dry sherry and clear honey in a small bowl until well combined. Drizzle the sherry and honey mixture over the spinach and heat through, stirring to coat the spinach leaves thoroughly in the mixture.

7 Transfer the stir-fry to warm serving dishes, scatter with the chopped spring onions (scallions) and serve immediately.

Chinese Fried Vegetables

The Chinese are known for their colourful, crisp vegetables, quickly stir-fried. In this recipe, they are tossed in a tasty soy and hoisin sauce.

NUTRITIONAL INFORMATION

Calories 137	Sugars 7g	
Protein 8g	Fat 7g	
Carbohydrate ...10g	Saturates 11g	

5 MINS   10 MINS

SERVES 4

INGREDIENTS

2 tbsp peanut oil

350 g/12 oz broccoli florets

1 tbsp chopped fresh root ginger

2 onions, cut into 8

3 celery sticks, sliced

175 g/6 oz baby spinach

125 g/4½ oz mangetout (snow peas)

6 spring onions (scallions), quartered

2 garlic cloves, crushed

2 tbsp light soy sauce

2 tsp caster (superfine) sugar

2 tbsp dry sherry

1 tbsp hoisin sauce

150 ml/¼ pint/⅔ cup vegetable stock

1 Heat the peanut oil in a preheated wok until it is almost smoking.

2 Add the broccoli florets, chopped root ginger, onions and celery to the wok and stir-fry for 1 minute.

3 Add the spinach, mangetout (snow peas), spring onions (scallions) and garlic and stir-fry for 3–4 minutes.

4 Mix together the soy sauce, caster (superfine) sugar, sherry, hoisin sauce and vegetable stock.

5 Pour the stock mixture into the wok, mixing well to coat the vegetables.

6 Cover the wok and cook over a medium heat for 2–3 minutes, or until the vegetables are cooked through, but still crisp.

7 Transfer the Chinese fried vegetables to a warm serving dish and serve immediately.

COOK'S TIP

You could use this mixture to fill Chinese pancakes. They are available from Chinese food stores and can be reheated in a steamer in 2–3 minutes.

Chestnut & Vegetable Stir-Fry

In this colourful stir-fry, vegetables are cooked in a wonderfully aromatic sauce which combines peanuts, chilli, coconut, coriander and turmeric.

NUTRITIONAL INFORMATION

Calories	446	Sugars	........17g
Protein	........14g	Fat	..........25g
Carbohydrate	...42g	Saturates	.......5g

 10 MINS   15 MINS

SERVES 4

INGREDIENTS

125 g/4½ oz/1 cup unsalted roasted peanuts

2 tsp hot chilli sauce

175 ml/6 fl oz/¾ cup coconut milk

2 tbsp soy sauce

1 tbsp ground coriander

pinch of ground turmeric

1 tbsp dark muscovado sugar

3 tbsp sesame oil

3-4 shallots, finely sliced

1 garlic clove, finely sliced

1-2 red chillies, deseeded and finely chopped

1 large carrot, cut into fine strips

1 yellow and 1 red (bell) pepper, sliced

1 courgette (zucchini), cut into fine strips

125 g/4½ oz sugar-snap peas, trimmed

7.5-cm/3-inch piece cucumber, cut into strips

250 g/9 oz oyster mushrooms,

250 g/9 oz canned chestnuts, drained

2 tsp grated ginger root

finely grated rind and juice of 1 lime

1 tbsp chopped fresh coriander (cilantro)

salt and pepper

slices of lime, to garnish

1 To make the peanut sauce, grind the peanuts in a blender, or chop very finely. Put into a small pan with the hot chilli sauce, coconut milk, soy sauce, ground coriander, ground turmeric and dark muscovado sugar. Heat gently and simmer for 3–4 minutes. Keep warm and set aside until required.

2 Heat the sesame oil in a wok or large frying pan (skillet). Add the shallots, garlic and chillies and stir-fry for 2 minutes.

3 Add the carrot, (bell) peppers, courgette (zucchini) and sugar-snap peas to the wok or pan (skillet) and stir-fry for 2 more minutes.

4 Add the cucumber, mushrooms, chestnuts, ginger, lime rind and juice and fresh coriander (cilantro) to the wok or pan (skillet) and stir-fry briskly for about 5 minutes, or until the vegetables are crisp, yet crunchy.

5 Season to taste with salt and pepper.

6 Divide the stir-fry between four warmed serving plates, and garnish with slices of lime. Transfer the peanut sauce to a serving dish and serve with the vegetables.

Garlic Spinach

This has to be one of the simplest recipes, yet it is so tasty. Spinach is fried with garlic and lemon grass and tossed in soy sauce and sugar.

NUTRITIONAL INFORMATION

Calories 118   Sugars 6g
Protein . . . . .7g   Fat 7g
Carbohydrate . . . .7g   Saturates 1g

 5 MINS   10 MINS

SERVES 4

INGREDIENTS

2 garlic cloves

1 tsp lemon grass

900 g/2 lb fresh spinach

2 tbsp peanut oil

salt

1 tbsp dark soy sauce

2 tsp brown sugar

1 Peel the garlic cloves and crush them in a pestle and mortar. Set aside until required.

2 Using a sharp knife, finely chop the lemon grass. Set aside until required.

3 Carefully remove the stems from the spinach. Rinse the spinach leaves and drain them thoroughly, patting them dry with absorbent kitchen paper (paper towels).

4 Heat the peanut oil in a preheated wok or large frying pan (skillet) until it is almost smoking.

5 Reduce the heat slightly, add the garlic and lemon grass and stir-fry for 30 seconds.

6 Add the spinach leaves and a pinch of salt to the wok or frying pan (skillet)

and stir-fry for 2–3 minutes, or until the spinach leaves have just wilted.

7 Stir the dark soy sauce and brown sugar into the mixture in the wok or frying pan (skillet) and cook for a further 3–4 minutes.

8 Transfer the garlic spinach to a warm serving dish and serve as an accompaniment to a main dish.

COOK'S TIP

Lemon grass is available fresh, dried and canned or bottled. Dried lemon grass must be soaked for 2 hours before using. The stems are hard and are usually used whole and removed from the dish before serving. The roots can be crushed or finely chopped.

Stir-fried Aubergines

This dish would go well with rice and another vegetable dish such as stir-fried baby corn and green beans.

NUTRITIONAL INFORMATION

Calories 115   Sugars 2g
Protein . . . . .3g   Fat 9g
Carbohydrate . . . .6g   Saturates 1g

12³/₄ HOURS   1¹/₄ HOURS

SERVES 4

I N G R E D I E N T S

60 g/2 oz/generous ⅓ cup dried black beans

425 ml/¾ pint/scant 2 cups vegetable stock

1 tbsp malt vinegar

1 tbsp dry sherry

1 tbsp soy sauce

1 tbsp sugar

1½ tsp cornflour (cornstarch)

1 red chilli, deseeded and chopped

1 cm/½ inch piece ginger root, chopped

2 aubergines (eggplants)

2 tsp salt

3 tbsp vegetable oil

2 garlic cloves, sliced

4 spring onions (scallions), cut diagonally

shredded radishes, to garnish

1 Soak the beans overnight in plenty of cold water. Drain and place in a saucepan. Cover with cold water, bring to the boil and boil rapidly, uncovered, for 10 minutes. Drain. Return the beans to the saucepan with the vegetable stock and bring to the boil.

2 Blend together the vinegar, sherry, soy sauce, sugar, cornflour (cornstarch), chilli and ginger in a small bowl. Add to

the saucepan, cover and simmer for 40 minutes, or until the beans are tender and the sauce has thickened. Stir occasionally.

3 Cut the aubergines (eggplants) into chunks and place in a colander. Sprinkle over the salt and leave to drain for 30 minutes. Rinse well to remove the salt and dry on kitchen paper (paper towels). This process removes the bitter juices which would otherwise spoil the flavour of the dish.

4 Heat the vegetable oil in a wok or large frying pan (skillet). Add the aubergine (eggplant) chunks and garlic. Stir-fry for 3–4 minutes until the aubergine (eggplant) has started to brown.

5 Add the sauce to the aubergine (eggplant) with the spring onions (scallions). Heat thoroughly, stirring to coat the aubergine (eggplant), garnish with radish shreds and serve.

Vegetable with Hoisin

This vegetable stir-fry has rice added to it and it can be served as a meal in itself.

NUTRITIONAL INFORMATION

Calories 120	Sugars 6g
Protein 4g	Fat 6g
Carbohydrate ...12g	Saturates 1g

20 MINS   10 MINS

SERVES 4

I N G R E D I E N T S

1 red onion

100 g/3½ oz carrots

1 yellow (bell) pepper

2 tbsp sunflower oil

50 g/1¾ oz/1 cup cooked brown rice

175 g/6 oz mangetout (snow peas)

175 g/6 oz/1½ cups bean sprouts

4 tbsp hoisin sauce

1 tbsp snipped fresh chives

1 Using a sharp knife, thinly slice the red onion.

2 Thinly slice the carrots.

3 Deseed and dice the yellow (bell) pepper.

4 Heat the sunflower oil in a large preheated wok or heavy-based frying pan (skillet).

5 Add the red onion slices, carrots and yellow (bell) pepper to the wok and stir-fry for about 3 minutes.

6 Add the cooked brown rice, mangetout (snow peas) and bean sprouts to the mixture in the wok and stir-

fry for a further 2 minutes. Stir briskly to ensure that the ingredients are well mixed and the rice grains are separated.

7 Stir the hoisin sauce into the vegetables and mix until well combined and completely heated through.

8 Transfer the vegetable stir-fry to warm serving dishes and scatter with the snipped fresh chives. Serve immediately.

COOK'S TIP

Hoisin sauce is a dark brown, reddish sauce made from soy beans, garlic, chilli and various other spices, and is commonly used in Chinese cookery. It may also be used as a dipping sauce.

Sweet & Sour Vegetables

Select vegetables from the suggested list, including spring onions (scallions) and garlic. For a hotter, spicier sauce add chilli sauce.

NUTRITIONAL INFORMATION

Calories 160	Sugars 16g	
Protein 6g	Fat 7g	
Carbohydrate ...18g	Saturates 1g	

5 MINS   10 MINS

SERVES 4

INGREDIENTS

5-6 vegetables from the following:

1 (bell) pepper, red, green or yellow, cored, seeded and sliced

125 g/4½ oz French (green) beans, cut into 2-3 pieces

125 g/4½ oz mangetout (snow peas), cut into 2-3 pieces

250 g/9 oz broccoli or cauliflower, divided into tiny florets

250 g/9 oz courgettes (zucchini), cut into thin 5 cm/2 inch lengths

175 g/6 oz carrots, cut into julienne strips

125 g/4½ oz baby sweetcorn, sliced thinly

2 leeks, sliced thinly and cut into matchsticks

125 g/4½ oz button or closed cup mushrooms, thinly sliced

1 x 200 g/7 oz can water chestnuts or bamboo shoots, drained and sliced

1 x 425 g/15 oz can bean sprouts

4 spring onions (scallions) trimmed and thinly sliced

1 garlic clove, crushed

2 tbsp sunflower oil

SWEET & SOUR SAUCE

2 tbsp wine vinegar

2 tbsp clear honey

1 tbsp tomato purée (paste)

2 tbsp soy sauce

2 tbsp sherry

1-2 tsp sweet chilli sauce (optional)

2 tsp cornflour (cornstarch)

1 Cut the selected vegetables into uniform lengths. Mix the sauce ingredients in a bowl. Heat the oil in the wok, add the spring onions (scallions) and garlic and stir-fry for 1 minute.

2 Add the prepared vegetables – the harder and firmer ones first – and stir-fry for 2 minutes. Then add the softer ones such as mushrooms and mangetout (snow peas) and stir-fry for 2 minutes.

3 Add the sweet and sour mixture to the wok and bring to the boil quickly, tossing all the vegetables until they are thoroughly coated and the sauce has thickened. Serve hot.

Butternut Squash Stir-fry

Butternut squash is as its name suggests, deliciously buttery and nutty in flavour. If the squash is not in season, use sweet potatoes instead.

NUTRITIONAL INFORMATION

Calories	.301	Sugars	.4g
Protein	.9g	Fat	.22g
Carbohydrate	.19g	Saturates	.4g

 5 MINS   25 MINS

SERVES 4

INGREDIENTS

1 kg/2 lb 4 oz butternut squash, peeled

3 tbsp groundnut oil

1 onion, sliced

2 cloves garlic, crushed

1 tsp coriander seeds

1 tsp cumin seeds

2 tbsp chopped coriander (cilantro)

150 ml/¼ pint/⅔ cup coconut milk

100 ml/3½ fl oz/½ cup water

100 g/3½ oz/⅓ cup salted cashew nuts

TO GARNISH

freshly grated lime zest

fresh coriander (cilantro)

lime wedges

1 Using a sharp knife, slice the butternut squash into small, bite-sized cubes.

2 Heat the groundnut oil in a large preheated wok.

3 Add the butternut squash, onion and garlic to the wok and stir-fry for 5 minutes.

4 Stir in the coriander seeds, cumin seeds and fresh coriander (cilantro) and stir-fry for 1 minute.

5 Add the coconut milk and water to the wok and bring to the boil. Cover the wok and leave to simmer for 10–15 minutes, or until the squash is tender.

6 Add the cashew nuts and stir to combine.

7 Transfer to warm serving dishes and garnish with freshly grated lime zest, fresh coriander (cilantro) and lime wedges. Serve hot.

COOK'S TIP

If you do not have coconut milk, grate some creamed coconut into the dish with the water in step 5.

Green Stir-fry

The basis of this recipe is pak choi, also known as bok choy or Chinese greens. If unavailable, use Swiss chard or Savoy cabbage instead.

NUTRITIONAL INFORMATION

Calories . . . . .107 Sugars 6g
Protein . . . . .4g Fat 8g
Carbohydrate . . . .6g Saturates 1g

 5 MINS   🕐 10 MINS

SERVES 4

I N G R E D I E N T S

2 tbsp peanut oil

2 garlic cloves, crushed

½ tsp ground star anise

1 tsp salt

350 g/12 oz pak choi, shredded

225 g/8 oz baby spinach

25 g/1 oz mangetout (snow peas)

1 celery stick, sliced

1 green (bell) pepper, seeded and
   sliced

50 ml/2 fl oz/¼ cup vegetable stock

1 tsp sesame oil

1 Heat the peanut oil in a preheated wok or large frying pan (skillet), swirling the oil around the base of the wok until it is really hot.

2 Add the crushed garlic to the wok or frying pan (skillet) and stir-fry for about 30 seconds.

3 Stir in the ground star anise, salt, shredded pak choi, spinach, mangetout (snow peas), celery and green (bell) pepper and stir-fry for 3–4 minutes.

4 Add the vegetable stock, cover the wok and cook for 3–4 minutes.

5 Remove the lid from the wok and stir in the sesame oil. Mix thoroughly to combine all the ingredients.

6 Transfer the green vegetable stir-fry to a warm serving dish and serve.

COOK'S TIP

Star anise is an important ingredient in Chinese cuisine. The attractive star-shaped pods are often used whole to add a decorative garnish to dishes. The flavour is similar to liquorice, but with spicy undertones and is quite strong.

Vegetable Stir-Fry

A range of delicious flavours are captured in this simple recipe which is ideal if you are in a hurry.

NUTRITIONAL INFORMATION

Calories ....138　Sugars 5g
Protein ....3g　Fat 12g
Carbohydrate ....5g　Saturates 2g

5 MINS　　25 MINS

SERVES 4

INGREDIENTS

3 tbsp vegetable oil

8 baby onions, halved

1 aubergine (eggplant), cubed

225 g/8 oz courgettes (zucchini), sliced

225 g/8 oz open-cap mushrooms, halved

2 cloves garlic, crushed

400 g/14 oz can chopped tomatoes

2 tbsp sundried tomato purée (paste)

2 tbsp soy sauce

1 tsp sesame oil

1 tbsp Chinese rice wine or dry sherry

freshly ground black pepper

fresh basil leaves, to garnish

1 Heat the vegetable oil in a large preheated wok or frying pan (skillet).

2 Add the baby onions and aubergine (eggplant) to the wok or frying pan (skillet) and stir-fry for 5 minutes, or until the vegetables are golden and just beginning to soften.

3 Add the sliced courgettes (zucchini), mushrooms, garlic, chopped tomatoes and tomato purée (paste) to the wok and stir-fry for about 5 minutes. Reduce the heat and leave to simmer for 10 minutes, or until the vegetables are tender.

4 Add the soy sauce, sesame oil and rice wine or sherry to the wok, bring back to the boil and cook for 1 minute.

5 Season the vegetable stir-fry with freshly ground black pepper and scatter with fresh basil leaves. Serve immediately.

COOK'S TIP

Basil has a very strong flavour which is perfect with vegetables and Chinese flavourings. Instead of using basil simply as a garnish in this dish, try adding a handful of fresh basil leaves to the stir-fry in step 4.

Stir-fried Spinach

This is an easy recipe to make as a quick accompaniment to a main course. The water chestnuts give a delicious crunch to the greens.

NUTRITIONAL INFORMATION

Calories	85	Sugars	.........2g
Protein	.........4g	Fat	...........4g
Carbohydrate	....9g	Saturates	.......1g

 5 MINS   10 MINS

SERVES 4

INGREDIENTS

1 tbsp sunflower oil

1 garlic clove, halved

2 spring onions (scallions), sliced finely

225 g/8 oz can water chestnuts, drained and sliced finely (optional)

500 g/1 lb 2 oz spinach, any tough stalks removed

1 tsp sherry vinegar

1 tsp light soy sauce

pepper

1 Heat the sunflower oil in a wok or large, heavy frying pan (skillet) over a high heat, swirling the oil around the base of the wok until it is really hot.

2 Add the halved garlic clove and cook, stirring, for 1 minute. If the garlic should brown, remove it immediately.

3 Add the finely sliced spring onions (scallions) and water chestnuts, if using, and stir for 2–3 minutes.

4 Add the spinach leaves and stir into the wok.

5 Add the sherry vinegar, soy sauce and a sprinkling of pepper. Cook, stirring, until the spinach is tender. Remove the garlic.

6 Using a slotted spoon, drain off the excess liquid from the wok and serve the stir-fried greens immediately.

COOK'S TIP

Several types of oriental greens (for example, choi sam and pak choi) are widely available and any of these can be successfully substituted for the spinach.

Stir-fried Mixed Vegetables

The Chinese carefully select vegetables to achieve a harmonious balance of contrasting colours and textures.

NUTRITIONAL INFORMATION

Calories 534	Sugars 8g	
Protein 14g	Fat 45g	
Carbohydrate ...19g	Saturates 5g	

 5 MINS   5 MINS

SERVES 4

I N G R E D I E N T S

60g/2 oz mangetout (snow peas)

1 small carrot

125 g/4½ oz Chinese leaves (cabbage)

60 g/2 oz black or white mushrooms

60 g/2 oz canned bamboo shoots, rinsed and drained

3-4 tbsp vegetable oil

125 g/4½ oz fresh bean sprouts

1 tsp salt

1 tsp sugar

1 tbsp oyster sauce or light soy sauce

a few drops sesame oil (optional)

dip sauce, to serve (optional)

1 Prepare the vegetables: top and tail the mangetout (snow peas), and cut the carrot, Chinese leaves (cabbage), mushrooms and bamboo shoots into roughly the same shape and size as the mangetout (snow peas).

2 Heat the vegetable oil in a preheated wok or large frying pan (skillet) and add the carrot. Stir-fry for a few seconds, then add the mangetout (snow peas) and Chinese leaves (cabbage) and stir-fry for about 1 minute.

3 Add the bean sprouts, mushrooms and bamboo shoots to the wok or

frying pan (skillet) and continue to stir-fry for another minute.

4 Add the salt and sugar, continue stirring for another minute, then add the oyster sauce or light soy sauce, blending well.

5 Sprinkle the vegetables with sesame oil (if using) and serve hot or cold, with a dip sauce, if liked.

COOK'S TIP

Oyster sauce is used in many Cantonese dishes. It is worth buying an expensive brand as it will be noticeably better. Good oyster sauce has a rich, almost beefy flavour. Once opened, a bottle of oyster sauce can be kept for months in the refrigerator.

Deep-fried Vegetables

Choose a selection of your favourite seasonal vegetables, coat them in a light batter and deep-fry them until crispy to make this delightful dish.

NUTRITIONAL INFORMATION

Calories 333	Sugars 9g
Protein 7g	Fat 16g
Carbohydrate . . .38g	Saturates 2g

40 MINS   15 MINS

SERVES 4

INGREDIENTS

500 g/1 lb 2 oz selection of fresh
    vegetables, such as red and green (bell)
    peppers, courgettes (zucchini), carrots,
    spring onions (scallions), cauliflower,
    broccoli and mushrooms

oil, for deep-frying

BATTER

125 g/4½ oz/1 cup plain (all-purpose) flour

½ tsp salt

1 tsp caster (superfine) sugar

1 tsp baking powder

3 tbsp vegetable oil

200 ml/7 fl oz/scant 1 cup tepid water

SAUCE

1 tbsp light muscovado sugar

2 tbsp soy sauce

4 tbsp cider vinegar

4 tbsp medium sherry

1 tbsp cornflour (cornstarch)

1 tsp finely grated fresh ginger root

TO GARNISH

spring onion (scallion) brushes
    (see page 305)

chopped spring onions (scallions)

1 To make the batter, sift the flour, salt, sugar and baking powder into a large bowl. Add the oil and most of the water. Whisk together to make a smooth batter, adding extra water to give it the consistency of single (light) cream. Chill for 20–30 minutes.

2 To make the sauce, put all the ingredients into a small saucepan. Heat, stirring, until thickened and smooth.

3 Cut all the vegetables into even, bite-sized pieces. Heat the oil in a wok or deep fat fryer. Dip the vegetables into the batter and fry them in the hot oil, a few at a time, until golden brown and crispy, about 2 minutes. Drain on kitchen paper (paper towels).

4 Garnish and serve the vegetables on a warmed platter accompanied by the dipping sauce.

Spiced Aubergine (Eggplant)

This is a spicy and sweet dish, flavoured with mango chutney and heated up with chillies for a really wonderful combination of flavours.

NUTRITIONAL INFORMATION

Calories 208	Sugars 17g
Protein 1g	Fat 15g
Carbohydrate . . .17g	Saturates 2g

5 MINS   25 MINS

SERVES 4

I N G R E D I E N T S

3 tbsp groundnut oil

2 onions, sliced

2 cloves garlic, chopped

2 aubergines (eggplants), diced

2 red chillies, deseeded and very finely chopped

2 tbsp demerara (brown crystal) sugar

6 spring onions (scallions), sliced

3 tbsp mango chutney

oil, for deep-frying

2 cloves garlic, sliced, to garnish

1 Heat the groundnut oil in a large preheated wok or heavy-based frying pan (skillet), swirling the oil around the base of the wok until it is really hot.

2 Add the onions and chopped garlic to the wok, stirring well.

3 Add the diced aubergine (eggplant) and chillies to the wok and stir-fry for 5 minutes.

4 Add the demerara (brown crystal) sugar, spring onions (scallions) and mango chutney to the wok, stirring well.

5 Reduce the heat, cover and leave to simmer, stirring from time to time, for 15 minutes or until the aubergine (eggplant) is tender.

6 Transfer the stir-fry to serving bowls and keep warm.

7 Heat the oil for deep-frying in the wok and quickly stir-fry the slices of garlic, until they brown slightly. Garnish the stir-fry with the deep-fried garlic and serve immediately.

COOK'S TIP

The 'hotness' of chillies varies enormously so always use with caution, but as a general guide the smaller they are the hotter they will be. The seeds are the hottest part and so are usually discarded.

Tofu

A popular ingredient in Chinese cooking, tofu (bean curd) is made from puréed and pressed yellow soya beans. Although it has a bland flavour it blends well with other ingredients and absorbs the flavours of spices and sauces. Tofu (bean curd) is extremely versatile – it can be stir-fried, deep-fried or added to soups. It is also a healthy

substitute for meat and fish, being high in protein and low in fat. Tofu (bean curd) is sold in cakes and dried form, and it is also available marinated or smoked. The recipes in this chapter combine tofu (bean curd) with a variety of flavours and ingredients to create a selection of tasty snacks together with more filling main dishes, for example Fried Tofu (Bean Curd) with Peanut Sauce, Braised Tofu (Bean Curd) Homestyle and Chinese Vegetable Casserole.

Fried Tofu with Peanut Sauce

This is a very sociable dish if put in the centre of the table where people can help themselves with cocktail sticks.

NUTRITIONAL INFORMATION

Calories	338	Sugars	.........9g
Protein	........16g	Fat	..........22g
Carbohydrate	...21g	Saturates	.......4g

5 MINS   20 MINS

SERVES 4

INGREDIENTS

500 g/1 lb 2 oz marinated or plain tofu (bean curd)

2 tbsp rice vinegar

2 tbsp sugar

1 tsp salt

3 tbsp smooth peanut butter

½ tsp chilli flakes

3 tbsp barbecue sauce

1 litre/1¾ pints/4 cups sunflower oil

2 tbsp sesame oil

BATTER

4 tbsp plain (all-purpose) flour

2 eggs, beaten

4 tbsp milk

½ tsp baking powder

½ tsp chilli powder

COOK'S TIP

Tofu (bean curd) is made from puréed soya beans. It is white, with a soft cheese-like texture, and is sold in blocks, either fresh or vacuum-packed. Although it has a bland flavour, it blends well with other ingredients, and absorbs the flavours of spices and sauces.

1 Cut the tofu (bean curd) into 2.5 cm/1 inch triangles. Set aside until required.

2 Combine the rice vinegar, sugar and salt in a saucepan. Bring to the boil and then simmer for 2 minutes.

3 Remove the sauce from the heat and add the smooth peanut butter, chilli flakes and barbecue sauce, stirring well until thoroughly blended.

4 To make the batter, sift the plain (all-purpose) flour into a bowl, make a well in the centre and add the eggs. Draw in the flour, adding the milk slowly. Stir in the baking powder and chilli powder.

5 Heat both the sunflower oil and sesame oil in a deep-fryer or large saucepan until a light haze appears on top.

6 Dip the tofu (bean curd) triangles into the batter and deep-fry until golden brown. You may need to do this in batches. Drain on absorbent kitchen paper (paper towels).

7 Transfer the tofu (bean curd) triangles to a serving dish and serve with the peanut sauce.

Tofu Sandwiches

Slices of tofu (beancurd) are sandwiched together with a cucumber and cream cheese filling and coated in batter.

NUTRITIONAL INFORMATION

Calories 398   Sugars 8g
Protein . . . . .13g   Fat 24g
Carbohydrate . . .35g   Saturates 7g

40 MINS   15 MINS

MAKES 28

I N G R E D I E N T S

4 Chinese dried mushrooms (if unavailable, use thinly sliced open-cup mushrooms)

275 g/9½ oz tofu (bean curd)

½ cucumber, grated

1 cm/½ inch piece ginger root, grated

60 g/2 oz/¼ cup cream cheese

salt and pepper

B A T T E R

125 g/4½ oz/1 cup plain (all-purpose) flour

1 egg, beaten

125 ml/4 fl oz/½ cup water

½ tsp salt

2 tbsp sesame seeds

vegetable oil for deep-frying

S A U C E

150 ml/¼ pint/⅔ cup natural (unsweetened) yogurt

2 tsp honey

2 tbsp chopped fresh mint

1 Place the dried mushrooms in a small bowl and cover with warm water. Leave to soak for 20–25 minutes.

2 Drain the mushrooms, squeezing out the excess water. Remove the tough centres and chop the mushrooms.

3 Drain the tofu (bean curd) and slice thinly. Then cut each slice to make 2.5 cm/1 inch squares.

4 Squeeze the excess liquid from the cucumber and mix the cucumber with the mushrooms, grated ginger and cream cheese. Season well with salt and pepper. Use as a filling to sandwich slices of tofu (bean curd) together to make about 28 sandwiches.

5 To make the batter, sift the flour into a bowl. Beat in the egg, water and salt to make a thick batter. Stir in the sesame seeds. Heat the oil in a wok. Coat the sandwiches in the batter and deep-fry in batches until golden. Remove and drain on kitchen paper (paper towels).

6 To make the dipping sauce, combine the yogurt, honey and mint. Serve with the tofu (bean curd) sandwiches.

Tofu with Hot & Sweet Sauce

Golden pieces of tofu (bean curd) are served in a hot and creamy peanut and chilli sauce for a classic vegetarian starter.

NUTRITIONAL INFORMATION

Calories 367	Sugars 5g	
Protein 18g	Fat 30g	
Carbohydrate 8g	Saturates 5g	

5 MINS   15 MINS

SERVES 4

INGREDIENTS

450 g/1 lb tofu (bean curd), cubed

oil, for frying

SAUCE

6 tbsp crunchy peanut butter

1 tbsp sweet chilli sauce

150 ml/¼ pint/⅔ cup coconut milk

1 tbsp tomato purée (paste)

25 g/1 oz/¼ cup chopped salted peanuts

1 Pat away any moisture from the tofu (bean curd), using absorbent kitchen paper (paper towels).

2 Heat the oil in a large wok or frying pan (skillet) until very hot.

3 Add the tofu (bean curd) to the wok and cook, in batches, for about 5 minutes, or until golden and crispy.

4 Remove the tofu (bean curd) with a slotted spoon, transfer to absorbent kitchen paper (paper towels) and leave to drain.

5 To make the peanut and chilli sauce, mix together the crunchy peanut butter, sweet chilli sauce, coconut milk, tomato purée (paste) and chopped salted peanuts in a bowl. Add a little boiling water if necessary to achieve a smooth consistency. Stir well until the ingredients are thoroughly blended.

6 Transfer the tofu (bean curd) to serving plates and pour the sauce over the top. Alternatively, pour the sauce into a serving dish and serve separately.

COOK'S TIP

Make sure that all of the moisture has been absorbed from the tofu (bean curd) before frying, otherwise it will not crispen.

Cook the peanut and chilli sauce in a saucepan over a gentle heat before serving, if you prefer.

Ma-po Tofu

Ma-Po was the wife of a Szechuan chef who created this popular dish in the middle of the 19th century.

NUTRITIONAL INFORMATION

Calories ....235 Sugars 1g
Protein ....16g Fat 18g
Carbohydrate ....3g Saturates 4g

3½ HOURS   15 MINS

SERVES 4

I N G R E D I E N T S

3 cakes tofu (bean curd)

3 tbsp vegetable oil

125 g/4½ oz coarsely minced (ground) beef

½ tsp finely chopped garlic

1 leek, cut into short sections

½ tsp salt

1 tbsp black bean sauce

1 tbsp light soy sauce

1 tsp chilli bean sauce

3-4 tbsp Chinese Stock (see page 30) or water

2 tsp cornflour (cornstarch) paste (see page 31)

a few drops sesame oil

black pepper

finely chopped spring onions (scallions), to garnish

1 Cut the tofu (bean curd) into 1 cm/ ½ inch cubes, handling it carefully.

2 Bring some water to the boil in a small pan or a wok, add the tofu (bean curd) and blanch for 2-3 minutes to harden. Remove and drain well.

3 Heat the oil in a preheated wok. Add the minced (ground) beef and garlic and stir-fry for about 1 minute, or until the colour of the beef changes. Add the leek, salt and sauces and blend well.

4 Add the stock or water followed by the tofu (bean curd). Bring to the boil and braise gently for 2-3 minutes.

5 Add the cornflour (cornstarch) paste, and stir until the sauce has thickened. Sprinkle with sesame oil and black pepper, garnish and serve hot.

COOK'S TIP

Tofu has been an important element in Chinese cooking for more than 1000 years. It is made of yellow soya beans, which are soaked, ground and mixed with water. Tofu is highly nutritious, being rich in protein and low in fat.

Braised Vegetables with Tofu

Also known Buddha's Delight, the original recipe calls for 18 different vegetables to represent the 18 Buddhas – but 6-8 are quite acceptable!

NUTRITIONAL INFORMATION

Calories 300	Sugars 2g
Protein 8g	Fat 28g
Carbohydrate 6g	Saturates 3g

3¾ HOURS   10 MINS

SERVES 4

INGREDIENTS

5 g/¼ oz dried wood ears (exotic mushrooms)

1 cake tofu (bean curd)

60 g/2 oz mangetout (snow peas)

125 g/4½ oz Chinese leaves (cabbage)

1 small carrot

90 g/3 oz canned baby sweetcorn, drained

90 g/3 oz canned straw mushrooms, drained

60 g/2 oz canned water chestnuts, drained

300 ml/½ pint/1¼ cups vegetable oil

1 tsp salt

½ tsp sugar

1 tbsp light soy sauce or oyster sauce

2-3 tbsp Chinese Stock (see page 30) or water

a few drops sesame oil

1 Soak the wood ears (mushrooms) in warm water for 15-20 minutes, then rinse and drain, discarding any hard bits, and dry on kitchen paper (paper towels).

2 Cut the cake of tofu into about 18 small pieces.

3 Top and tail the mangetout (snow peas). Cut the Chinese leaves (cabbage) and the carrot into slices roughly the same size and shape as the mangetout (snow peas). Cut the baby sweetcorn, the straw mushrooms and the water chestnuts in half.

4 Heat the oil in a preheated wok. Add the tofu (bean curd) and deep-fry for about 2 minutes until it turns slightly golden. Remove and drain.

5 Pour off the oil, leaving about 2 tablespoons in the wok. Add the carrot, Chinese leaves (cabbage) and mangetout (snow peas) and stir-fry for about 1 minute.

6 Add the sweetcorn, mushrooms and water chestnuts. Stir gently for 2 more minutes, then add the salt, sugar, soy sauce or oyster sauce and Chinese stock or water. Bring to the boil and stir-fry for 1 more minute. Sprinkle with sesame oil and serve hot or cold.

Braised Tofu Home Style

The pork used in the recipe can be replaced by chicken or prawns (shrimps), or it can be omitted altogether.

NUTRITIONAL INFORMATION

Calories 218	Sugars 1g
Protein 17g	Fat 16g
Carbohydrate 2g	Saturates 2g

10 MINS   10 MINS

SERVES 4

I N G R E D I E N T S

3 cakes tofu (bean curd)

125 g/4½ oz boneless pork (or any other type of meat)

1 leek

a few small dried whole chillies, soaked

vegetable oil, for deep-frying

1-2 spring onions (scallions), cut into short sections

2 tbsp crushed yellow bean sauce

1 tbsp light soy sauce

2 tsp rice wine or dry sherry

a few drops sesame oil

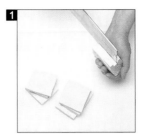

1 Split each cake of tofu (bean curd) into 3 slices crosswise, then cut each slice diagonally into 2 triangles.

2 Cut the pork into small thin slices or shreds; cut the leek into thin strips.

3 Drain the chillies, remove the seeds using the tip of a knife, then cut into small shreds.

4 Heat the oil in a preheated wok until smoking, then deep-fry the tofu (bean curd) triangles for 2-3 minutes, or until golden brown all over. Remove with a slotted spoon and drain on kitchen paper (paper towels).

5 Pour off the hot oil, leaving about 1 tablespoon in the wok. Add the pork strips, spring onions (scallions) and chillies and stir-fry for about 1 minute or until the pork changes colour.

6 Add the leek, tofu (bean curd), yellow bean sauce, soy sauce and wine or sherry and braise for 2-3 minutes, stirring gently to blend well. Finally sprinkle on the sesame oil and serve.

COOK'S TIP

Tofu (bean curd) is sold in 2 forms: as firm cakes, or as a thickish junket, known as silken tofu (bean curd). It is the solid kind that is used for braising and stir-frying. Silken tofu (bean curd) is usually added to soups or sauces.

Tofu with Mushrooms

Chunks of cucumber and smoked tofu (beancurd) stir-fried with straw mushrooms, mangetout (snow peas) and corn in a yellow bean sauce.

NUTRITIONAL INFORMATION

Calories 130	Sugars 2g
Protein 9g	Fat 9g
Carbohydrate 3g	Saturates 1g

 15 MINS   10 MINS

SERVES 4

I N G R E D I E N T S

1 large cucumber

1 tsp salt

225 g/8 oz smoked tofu (bean curd)

2 tbsp vegetable oil

60 g/2 oz mangetout (snow peas)

125 g/4½ oz/8 baby corn

1 celery stick, sliced diagonally

425 g/15 oz can straw mushrooms, drained

2 spring onions (scallions), cut into strips

1 cm/½ inch piece ginger root, chopped

1 tbsp yellow bean sauce

1 tbsp light soy sauce

1 tbsp dry sherry

1 Halve the cucumber lengthways and remove the seeds, using a teaspoon or melon baller.

2 Cut the cucumber into cubes, place in a colander and sprinkle over the salt. Leave to drain for 10 minutes. Rinse thoroughly in cold water to remove the salt and drain thoroughly on absorbent kitchen paper (paper towels).

3 Cut the tofu (bean curd) into cubes.

4 Heat the vegetable oil in a wok or large frying pan (skillet) until smoking.

5 Add the tofu (bean curd), mangetout (snow peas), baby corn and celery to the wok. Stir until the tofu (bean curd) is lightly browned.

6 Add the straw mushrooms, spring onions (scallions) and ginger, and stir-fry for a further minute.

7 Stir in the cucumber, yellow bean sauce, light soy sauce, dry sherry and 2 tablespoons of water. Stir-fry for 1 minute and ensure that all the vegetables are coated in the sauces before serving.

COOK'S TIP

Straw mushrooms are available in cans from oriental suppliers and some supermarkets. If unavailable, substitute 250 g/ 9 oz baby button mushrooms.

Chinese Vegetable Casserole

This mixed vegetable casserole is very versatile and is delicious with any combination of vegetables of your choice.

NUTRITIONAL INFORMATION

Calories . . . . .218 Sugars 4g
Protein . . . . .7g Fat 14g
Carbohydrate . . .12g Saturates 2g

5 MINS   30 MINS

SERVES 4

I N G R E D I E N T S

4 tbsp vegetable oil

2 medium carrots, sliced

1 courgette (zucchini), sliced

4 baby corn cobs, halved lengthways

125 g/4½ oz cauliflower florets

1 leek, sliced

125 g/4½ oz water chestnuts, halved

225 g/8 oz tofu (bean curd), diced

300 ml/½ pint/1¼ cups vegetable stock

1 tsp salt

2 tsp dark brown sugar

2 tsp dark soy sauce

2 tbsp dry sherry

1 tbsp cornflour (cornstarch)

2 tbsp water

1 tbsp chopped coriander (cilantro), to garnish

1 Heat the oil in a preheated wok until it is almost smoking. Lower the heat slightly, add the carrots, courgette (zucchini), corn cobs, cauliflower and leek to the wok and stir-fry for 2–3 minutes.

2 Stir in the water chestnuts, tofu (bean curd), stock, salt, sugar, soy sauce and sherry and bring to the boil. Reduce the heat, cover and simmer for 20 minutes.

3 Blend the cornflour (cornstarch) with the water to form a smooth paste.

4 Stir the cornflour (cornstarch) mixture into the wok. Bring the sauce to the boil and cook, stirring constantly until it thickens and clears.

5 Transfer the casserole to a warm serving dish, sprinkle with chopped coriander (cilantro) and serve immediately.

COOK'S TIP

If there is too much liquid remaining, boil vigorously for 1 minute before adding the cornflour (cornstarch) to reduce it slightly.

Oysters with Tofu

Oysters are often eaten raw, but are delicious when quickly cooked as in this recipe, and mixed with salt and citrus flavours.

NUTRITIONAL INFORMATION

Calories 175   Sugars 2g
Protein . . . . .18g   Fat 10g
Carbohydrate . . . .3g   Saturates 1g

 5 MINS   10 MINS

SERVES 4

INGREDIENTS

225 g/8 oz leeks

350 g/12 oz tofu (bean curd)

2 tbsp sunflower oil

350 g/12 oz shelled oysters

2 tbsp fresh lemon juice

1 tsp cornflour (cornstarch)

2 tbsp light soy sauce

100 ml/3½ fl oz/⅓ cup fish stock

2 tbsp chopped fresh coriander (cilantro)

1 tsp finely grated lemon zest

1 Using a sharp knife, trim and slice the leeks.

2 Cut the tofu (bean curd) into bite-sized pieces.

3 Heat the sunflower oil in a large preheated wok or frying pan (skillet). Add the leeks to the wok and stir-fry for about 2 minutes.

4 Add the tofu (bean curd) and oysters to the wok or frying pan (skillet) and stir-fry for 1–2 minutes.

5 Mix together the lemon juice, cornflour (cornstarch), light soy sauce and fish stock in a small bowl, stirring until well blended.

6 Pour the cornflour (cornstarch) mixture into the wok and cook, stirring occasionally, until the juices start to thicken.

7 Transfer to serving bowls and scatter the coriander (cilantro) and lemon zest on top. Serve immediately.

VARIATION

Shelled clams or mussels could be used instead of the oysters, if you prefer.

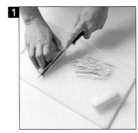

Tofu & Vegetable Stir-Fry

This is a quick dish to prepare, making it ideal as a mid-week supper dish, after a busy day at work!

NUTRITIONAL INFORMATION

Calories	124	Sugars	........2g
Protein	.........6g	Fat	..........6g
Carbohydrate	....11g	Saturates	.......1g

  5 MINS   25 MINS

SERVES 4

I N G R E D I E N T S

175 g/6 oz/1¼ cups potatoes, cubed

1 tbsp vegetable oil

1 red onion, sliced

225 g/8 oz firm tofu (bean curd), diced

2 courgettes (zucchini), diced

8 canned artichoke hearts, halved

150 ml/¼ pint/⅔ cup passata (sieved tomatoes)

1 tbsp sweet chilli sauce

1 tbsp soy sauce

1 tsp caster (superfine) sugar

2 tbsp chopped basil

salt and pepper

1 Cook the potatoes in a saucepan of boiling water for 10 minutes. Drain thoroughly and set aside until required.

2 Heat the vegetable oil in a wok or large frying pan (skillet) and sauté the red onion for 2 minutes until the onion has softened, stirring.

3 Stir in the diced tofu (bean curd) and courgettes (zucchini) and cook for 3–4 minutes until they begin to brown slightly.

4 Add the cooked potatoes to the wok or frying pan (skillet), stirring to mix.

5 Stir in the artichoke hearts, passata (sieved tomatoes), sweet chilli sauce, soy sauce, sugar and basil.

6 Season to taste with salt and pepper and cook for a further 5 minutes, stirring well.

7 Transfer the tofu (bean curd) and vegetable stir-fry to serving dishes and serve immediately.

COOK'S TIP

Canned artichoke hearts should be drained thoroughly and rinsed before use because they often have salt added.

Black Bean Casserole

This colourful Chinese-style casserole is made with tofu (beancurd), vegetables and black bean sauce.

NUTRITIONAL INFORMATION

Calories 513	Sugars 5g
Protein 19g	Fat 25g
Carbohydrate . . .56g	Saturates 4g

🥟 30 MINS   🕐 30 MINS

SERVES 4

INGREDIENTS

6 Chinese dried mushrooms

275 g/9½ oz tofu (bean curd)

3 tbsp vegetable oil

1 carrot, cut into thin strips

125 g/4½ oz mangetout (snow peas)

125 g/4½ oz/8 baby corn, halved lengthways

225 g/8 oz can sliced bamboo shoots, drained

1 red (bell) pepper, cut into chunks

125 g/4½ oz Chinese leaves (cabbage), shredded

1 tbsp soy sauce

1 tbsp black bean sauce

1 tsp sugar

1 tsp cornflour (cornstarch)

vegetable oil for deep-frying

250 g/9 oz Chinese rice noodles

salt

1 Soak the dried mushrooms in a bowl of warm water for 20–25 minutes. Drain and squeeze out the excess water, reserving the liquid. Remove the tough centres and slice the mushrooms thinly.

2 Cut the tofu (bean curd) into cubes. Boil in a pan of lightly salted water for 2–3 minutes to firm up and then drain.

3 Heat half the oil in a saucepan. Add the tofu (bean curd) and fry until lightly browned. Remove and drain on kitchen paper (paper towels).

4 Add the remaining oil and stir-fry the mushrooms, carrot, mangetout (snow peas), baby corn, bamboo shoots and (bell) pepper for 2–3 minutes. Add the Chinese leaves (cabbage) and tofu (bean curd), and stir-fry for a further 2 minutes.

5 Stir in the sauces and sugar, and season with salt. Add 6 tbsp of the reserved mushroom liquid mixed with the cornflour (cornstarch). Bring to the boil, reduce the heat, cover and braise for 2–3 minutes until the sauce thickens slightly.

6 Heat the oil for deep-frying in a large pan. Deep-fry the noodles, in batches, until puffed up and lightly golden. Drain and serve with the casserole.

Spicy Fried Tofu Triangles

Marinated tofu (bean curd) is ideal in this recipe for added flavour, although the spicy coating is very tasty with plain tofu (bean curd).

NUTRITIONAL INFORMATION

Calories . . . . . . .224 Sugars 17g
Protein . . . . .10g Fat 13g
Carbohydrate . . .18g Saturates 2g

1¼ HOURS   10 MINS

SERVES 4

INGREDIENTS

1 tbsp sea salt

4½ tsp Chinese five-spice powder

3 tbsp light brown sugar

2 garlic cloves, crushed

1 tsp grated fresh root ginger

2 x 225 g/8 oz cakes tofu (bean curd)

vegetable oil, for deep-frying

2 leeks, shredded and halved

shredded leek, to garnish

1 Mix together the salt, Chinese five-spice powder, sugar, garlic and ginger in a bowl and transfer to a plate.

2 Cut the tofu (bean curd) cakes in half diagonally to form two triangles. Cut each triangle in half and then in half again to form 16 triangles.

3 Roll the tofu (bean curd) triangles in the spice mixture, turning to coat thoroughly. Set aside for 1 hour.

4 Heat the vegetable oil for deep-frying in a wok until it is almost smoking.

5 Reduce the heat slightly, add the tofu (bean curd) triangles and fry for 5 minutes, until golden brown. Remove

the tofu (bean curd) from the wok with a slotted spoon, set aside and keep warm until required.

6 Add the leeks to the wok and stir-fry for 1 minute. Remove from the wok and drain on kitchen paper (paper towels).

7 Arrange the leeks on a warm serving plate and place the fried tofu (bean curd) on top. Garnish with the fresh shredded leek and serve immediately.

COOK'S TIP

Fry the tofu (bean curd) in batches and keep each batch warm until all of the tofu (bean curd) has been fried and is ready to serve.

Microwave Tofu Casserole

In this quick recipe, all the cooking is done in a microwave – there is not a wok in sight!

NUTRITIONAL INFORMATION

Calories	222	Sugars 3g
Protein	........11g	Fat 13g
Carbohydrate	...16g	Saturates 2g

1¼ HOURS   15 MINS

SERVES 4

I N G R E D I E N T S

275 g/9½ oz smoked tofu (bean curd), cubed

2 tbsp soy sauce

1 tbsp dry sherry

1 tsp sesame oil

4 dried Chinese mushrooms

250 g/9 oz egg noodles

1 carrot, cut into thin sticks

1 celery stick, cut into thin sticks

125 g/4½ oz (16–18) baby sweetcorn, halved lengthwise

2 tbsp oil

1 courgette (zucchini), sliced

4 spring onions (scallions), chopped

125 g/4½ oz/1⅓ cups mangetout (snow peas), each cut into 3 pieces

2 tbsp black bean sauce

1 tsp cornflour (cornstarch)

salt and pepper

1 tbsp toasted sesame seeds, to garnish

1 Marinate the tofu (bean curd) in the soy sauce, sherry and sesame oil for 30 minutes.

2 Place the mushrooms in a small bowl and pour over boiling water to cover. Leave to soak for 20 minutes.

3 Place the egg noodles in a large bowl. Pour over enough boiling water to cover by 2.5 cm/1 inch. Add ½ teaspoon salt, cover and cook on HIGH power for 4 minutes.

4 Place the carrot, celery, sweetcorn and oil in a large bowl. Cover and cook on HIGH power for 1 minute.

5 Drain the mushrooms, reserving 1 tablespoon of the liquid. Squeeze out excess water from the mushrooms and discard the hard cores. Thinly slice the mushrooms.

6 Add the mushrooms to the bowl of vegetables with the courgette (zucchini), spring onions (scallions) and mangetout (snow peas). Mix well. Cover and cook on HIGH power for 4 minutes, stirring every minute. Add the black bean sauce to the vegetables, stirring to coat the vegetables in the sauce.

7 Mix the cornflour (cornstarch) with reserved mushroom water and stir into the vegetables with the tofu (bean curd) and marinade. Cover and cook on HIGH power for 2–3 minutes until heated through and the sauce has thickened slightly. Season with salt and pepper to taste. Drain the noodles. Garnish the vegetables with sesame seeds and serve with the noodles.

Tofu with (Bell) Peppers

Tofu (bean curd) is perfect for marinating as it readily absorbs flavours for a great tasting main dish.

NUTRITIONAL INFORMATION

Calories ....267 Sugars 2g
Protein ....9g Fat 23g
Carbohydrate ....5g Saturates 3g

 25 MINS   15 MINS

SERVES 4

I N G R E D I E N T S

350 g/12 oz tofu (bean curd)

2 cloves garlic, crushed

4 tbsp soy sauce

1 tbsp sweet chilli sauce

6 tbsp sunflower oil

1 onion, sliced

1 green (bell) pepper, deseeded
  and diced

1 tbsp sesame oil

1 Using a sharp knife, cut the tofu (bean curd) into bite-sized pieces. Place the tofu (bean curd) in a shallow non-metallic dish.

2 Mix together the garlic, soy sauce and sweet chilli sauce and drizzle over the tofu (bean curd). Toss well to coat and leave to marinate for about 20 minutes.

3 Meanwhile, heat the sunflower oil in a large preheated wok.

4 Add the onion to the wok and stir-fry over a high heat until brown and crispy. Remove the onion with a slotted spoon and leave to drain on absorbent kitchen paper (paper towels).

5 Add the tofu (bean curd) to the hot oil and stir-fry for about 5 minutes.

6 Remove all but 1 tablespoon of the sunflower oil from the wok. Add the (bell) pepper to the wok and stir-fry for 2–3 minutes, or until softened.

7 Return the tofu (bean curd) and onions to the wok and heat through, stirring occasionally.

8 Drizzle with sesame oil. Transfer to serving plates and serve immediately.

COOK'S TIP

If you are in a real hurry, buy ready-marinated tofu (bean curd) from your supermarket.

Sweet & Sour Tofu

Sweet-and-sour sauce was one of the first Chinese sauces introduced to Western diets, and remains one of the most popular.

NUTRITIONAL INFORMATION

Calories ....205 Sugars 12g
Protein ....11g Fat 11g
Carbohydrate ...17g Saturates 1g

5 MINS   10 MINS

SERVES 4

I N G R E D I E N T S

2 celery sticks

1 carrot

1 green (bell) pepper, seeded

75 g/2¾ oz mangetout (snow peas)

2 tbsp vegetable oil

2 garlic cloves, crushed

8 baby corn cobs

125 g/4½ oz bean sprouts

450 g/1 lb tofu (bean curd), cubed

rice or noodles, to serve

S A U C E

2 tbsp light brown sugar

2 tbsp wine vinegar

225 ml/8 fl oz/1 cup vegetable stock

1 tsp tomato purée (paste)

1 tbsp cornflour (cornstarch)

1 Using a sharp knife, thinly slice the celery, cut the carrot into thin strips, dice the (bell) pepper and cut the mangetout (snow peas) in half diagonally.

2 Heat the vegetable oil in a preheated wok until it is almost smoking. Reduce the heat slightly, add the crushed garlic, celery, carrot, (bell) pepper, mangetout (snow peas) and corn cobs and stir-fry for 3–4 minutes.

3 Add the bean sprouts and tofu (bean curd) to the wok and cook for 2 minutes, stirring well.

4 To make the sauce, combine the sugar, wine vinegar, stock, tomato purée (paste) and cornflour (cornstarch), stirring well to mix. Stir into the wok, bring to the boil and cook, stirring, until the sauce thickens and clears. Continue to cook for 1 minute. Serve with rice or noodles.

COOK'S TIP

Be careful not to break up the tofu (bean curd) when stirring.

Fried Tofu & Vegetables

Tofu (bean curd) is available in different forms from both Chinese and Western supermarkets. The cake form of tofu is used in this recipe.

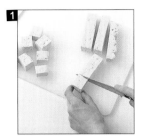  

5 MINS   15 MINS

SERVES 4

INGREDIENTS

450 g/1 lb tofu (bean curd)

150 ml/¼ pint/⅔ cup vegetable oil

1 leek, sliced

4 baby corn cobs, halved lengthways

60 g/2 oz mangetout (snow peas)

1 red (bell) pepper, seeded and diced

60 g/2 oz canned bamboo shoots, drained and rinsed

rice or noodles, to serve

SAUCE

1 tbsp Chinese rice wine or dry sherry

4 tbsp oyster sauce

3 tsp light soy sauce

2 tsp caster (superfine) sugar

pinch of salt

50 ml/2 fl oz/¼ cup vegetable stock

1 tsp cornflour (cornstarch)

2 tsp water

1 Rinse the tofu (bean curd) in cold water and pat dry with kitchen paper (paper towels). Cut the tofu (bean curd) into 2.5-cm/1-inch cubes.

2 Heat the oil in a preheated wok until almost smoking. Reduce the heat, add the tofu (bean curd) and stir-fry until golden brown. Remove from the wok with a slotted spoon and drain on absorbent kitchen paper (paper towels).

3 Pour all but 2 tablespoons of the oil from the wok and return to the heat. Add the leek, corn cobs, mangetout (snow peas), (bell) pepper and bamboo shoots and stir-fry for 2–3 minutes.

4 Add the Chinese rice wine or sherry, oyster sauce, soy sauce, sugar, salt and stock to the wok and bring to the boil. Blend the cornflour (cornstarch) with the water to form a smooth paste and stir it into the sauce. Bring the sauce to the boil and cook, stirring constantly, until thickened and clear.

5 Stir the tofu (bean curd) into the mixture in the wok and cook for about 1 minute until hot. Serve with rice or noodles.

Tofu Casserole

Tofu (bean curd) is ideal for absorbing all the other flavours in this dish. If marinated tofu (bean curd) is used, it will add a flavour of its own.

NUTRITIONAL INFORMATION

Calories 228	Sugars 3g	
Protein 16g	Fat 15g	
Carbohydrate 7g	Saturates 2g	

 5 MINS   15 MINS

SERVES 4

I N G R E D I E N T S

450 g/1 lb tofu (bean curd)

2 tbsp peanut oil

8 spring onions (scallions), cut
   into batons

2 celery sticks, sliced

125 g/4½ oz broccoli florets

125 g/4½ oz courgettes
   (zucchini), sliced

2 garlic cloves, thinly sliced

450 g/1 lb baby spinach

rice, to serve

S A U C E

425 ml/¾ pint/2 cups vegetable stock

2 tbsp light soy sauce

3 tbsp hoisin sauce

½ tsp chilli powder

1 tbsp sesame oil

VARIATION

This recipe has a green vegetable theme, but alter the colour and flavour by adding your favourite vegetables. Add 75 g/2¾ oz fresh or canned and drained straw mushrooms with the vegetables in step 2.

1 Cut the tofu (bean curd) into 2.5-cm/1-inch cubes and set aside until required.

2 Heat the peanut oil in a preheated wok or large frying pan (skillet).

3 Add the spring onions (scallions), celery, broccoli, courgettes (zucchini), garlic, spinach and tofu (bean curd) to the wok or frying pan (skillet) and stir-fry for 3–4 minutes.

4 To make the sauce, mix together the vegetable stock, soy sauce, hoisin sauce, chilli powder and sesame oil in a flameproof casserole and bring to the boil.

5 Add the stir-fried vegetables and tofu (bean curd) to the saucepan, reduce the heat, cover and simmer for 10 minutes.

6 Transfer the tofu (bean curd) and vegetables to a warm serving dish and serve with rice.

Tofu with Mushrooms & Peas

Chinese mushrooms are available from Chinese supermarkets and health food shops and add a unique flavour to Oriental dishes.

NUTRITIONAL INFORMATION

Calories 218	Sugars 1g
Protein 12g	Fat 14g
Carbohydrate . . .13g	Saturates 2g

15 MINS   15 MINS

SERVES 4

INGREDIENTS

25 g/1 oz dried Chinese mushrooms

450 g/1 lb tofu (bean curd)

25 g/1 oz/4 tbsp cornflour (cornstarch)

oil, for deep-frying

2 cloves garlic, finely chopped

2.5 cm/1 inch piece root ginger, grated

100 g/3½ oz/¾ cup frozen or fresh peas

1 Place the Chinese mushrooms in a large bowl. Pour in enough boiling water to cover and leave to stand for about 10 minutes.

2 Meanwhile, cut the tofu (bean curd) into bite-sized cubes, using a sharp knife.

3 Place the cornflour (cornstarch) in a large bowl.

4 Add the tofu (bean curd) to the bowl and toss in the cornflour (cornstarch) until evenly coated.

5 Heat the oil for deep-frying in a large preheated wok.

6 Add the cubes of tofu (bean curd) to the wok and deep-fry, in batches, for 2–3 minutes or until golden and crispy. Remove the tofu (bean curd) with a

slotted spoon and leave to drain on absorbent kitchen paper (paper towels).

7 Drain off all but 2 tablespoons of oil from the wok. Add the garlic, ginger and Chinese mushrooms to the wok and stir-fry for 2–3 minutes.

8 Return the cooked tofu (bean curd) to the wok and add the peas. Heat through for 1 minute then serve hot.

COOK'S TIP

Chinese dried mushrooms add flavour and a distinctive aroma. Sold dried in packets, they can be expensive but only a few are needed per dish and they store indefinitely. If they are unavailable, use open-cap mushrooms instead.

Rice

Together with noodles, rice forms the central part of a Chinese meal, particularly in southern China. In the north, the staple foods tend to be more wheat-based. For an everyday meal, plain rice is served with one or two dishes and a soup. Rice can be boiled and then steamed or it can be fried with other ingredients such as eggs, prawns

(shrimp), meat and vegetables and then flavoured with soy sauce. The most common type of rice used in Chinese cooking is short-grain or glutinous rice, which become slightly sticky when cooked and is therefore ideal for eating with chopsticks. This chapter includes some delicious rice dishes which can be eaten on their own or as an accompaniment. Fried rice is a particular favourite in Western restaurants so several variations are included here.

Egg Fried Rice

In this classic Chinese dish, boiled rice is fried with peas, spring onions (scallions) and egg and flavoured with soy sauce.

NUTRITIONAL INFORMATION

Calories 203   Sugars 1g
Protein . . . . .9g   Fat 11g
Carbohydrate . . .19g   Saturates 2g

  20 MINS   10 MINS

SERVES 4

I N G R E D I E N T S

150 g/5½ oz/⅔ cup long-grain rice

3 eggs, beaten

2 tbsp vegetable oil

2 garlic cloves, crushed

4 spring onions (scallions), chopped

125 g/4½ oz/1 cup cooked peas

1 tbsp light soy sauce

pinch of salt

shredded spring onion (scallion),
  to garnish

1 Cook the rice in a pan of boiling water for 10-12 minutes, until almost cooked, but not soft. Drain well, rinse under cold water and drain again.

2 Place the beaten eggs in a saucepan and cook over a gentle heat, stirring until softly scrambled.

3 Heat the vegetable oil in a preheated wok or large frying pan (skillet), swirling the oil around the base of the wok until it is really hot.

4 Add the crushed garlic, spring onions (scallions) and peas and sauté, stirring occasionally, for 1-2 minutes. Stir the rice into the wok, mixing to combine.

5 Add the eggs, light soy sauce and a pinch of salt to the wok or frying pan (skillet) and stir to mix the egg in thoroughly.

6 Transfer the egg fried rice to serving dishes and serve garnished with the shredded spring onion (scallion).

COOK'S TIP

The rice is rinsed under cold water to wash out the starch and prevent it from sticking together.

Fried Rice with Pork

This dish is a meal in itself, containing pieces of pork, fried with rice, peas, tomatoes and mushrooms.

NUTRITIONAL INFORMATION

Calories . . . . . . .285 Sugars 2g
Protein . . . . .18g Fat 16g
Carbohydrate . . .19g Saturates 4g

10 MINS   30 MINS

SERVES 4

I N G R E D I E N T S

150 g/5½ oz/⅔ cup long-grain rice

3 tbsp peanut oil

1 large onion, cut into 8

225 g/8 oz pork tenderloin, thinly sliced

2 open-cap mushrooms, sliced

2 garlic cloves, crushed

1 tbsp light soy sauce

1 tsp light brown sugar

2 tomatoes, skinned, seeded and
  chopped

60 g/2 oz/½ cup cooked peas

2 eggs, beaten

1 Cook the rice in a saucepan of boiling water for about 15 minutes, until tender, but not soft. Drain well, rinse under cold running water and drain again thoroughly.

2 Heat the peanut oil in a preheated wok. Add the sliced onion and pork and stir-fry for 3-4 minutes, until just beginning to colour.

3 Add the mushrooms and garlic to the wok and stir-fry for 1 minute.

4 Add the soy sauce and sugar to the mixture in the wok and stir-fry for a further 2 minutes.

5 Stir in the rice, tomatoes and peas, mixing well. Transfer the mixture to a warmed dish.

6 Stir the eggs into the wok and cook, stirring with a wooden spoon, for 2-3 minutes, until beginning to set.

7 Return the rice mixture to the wok and mix well. Transfer to serving dishes and serve immediately.

COOK'S TIP

You can cook the rice in advance and chill or freeze it until required.

Chilli Fried Rice

Not so much a side dish as a meal in itself, this delicious fried rice can be served on its own or as an accompaniment to many Chinese dishes.

NUTRITIONAL INFORMATION

Calories	290	Sugars	.........2g
Protein	........11g	Fat	..........14g
Carbohydrate	...26g	Saturates	.......2g

  20 MINS   15 MINS

SERVES 4

I N G R E D I E N T S

250 g/9 oz/generous 1 cup long-grain rice

4 tbsp vegetable oil

2 garlic cloves, chopped finely

1 small red chilli, deseeded and chopped finely

8 spring onions (scallions), trimmed and sliced finely

1 tbsp red curry paste or 2 tsp chilli sauce

1 red (bell) pepper, cored, deseeded and chopped

90 g/3 oz/¾ cup dwarf green beans, chopped

250 g/9 oz/1½ cups cooked peeled prawns (shrimp) or chopped cooked chicken

2 tbsp fish sauce

T O   G A R N I S H

cucumber slices

shredded spring onion (scallion)

COOK'S TIP

Cook the rice the day before if you can remember – it will give an even better result. Alternatively, use rice left over from another dish to make this recipe.

1 Cook the rice in plenty of boiling, lightly salted water until tender, about 12 minutes. Drain, rinse with cold water and drain thoroughly.

2 Heat the vegetable oil in a wok or large frying pan (skillet) until the oil is really hot.

3 Add the garlic to the wok and fry gently for 2 minutes until golden.

4 Add the chilli and spring onions (scallions) and cook, stirring, for 3–4 minutes.

5 Add the red curry paste or chilli sauce to the wok or frying pan (skillet) and fry for 1 minute, then add the red (bell) pepper and dwarf green beans. Stir-fry briskly for 2 minutes.

6 Tip the cooked rice into the wok or frying pan (skillet) and add the prawns (shrimp) or chicken and the fish sauce. Stir-fry over a medium-high heat for about 4–5 minutes, until the rice is hot.

7 Transfer the chilli fried rice to warm serving dishes, garnish with cucumber slices and shredded spring onion (scallion) and serve.

Rice with Seven Spice Beef

Beef fillet is used in this recipe as it is very suitable for quick cooking and has a wonderful flavour.

NUTRITIONAL INFORMATION

Calories	171	Sugars	.........8g
Protein	........28g	Fat	..........15g
Carbohydrate	...60g	Saturates	.......6g

 5 MINS   30 MINS

SERVES 4

I N G R E D I E N T S

225 g/8 oz/1 cup long-grain white rice

600 ml/1 pint/2½ cups water

350 g/12 oz beef fillet

2 tbsp soy sauce

2 tbsp tomato ketchup

1 tbsp seven spice seasoning

2 tbsp groundnut oil

1 onion, diced

225 g/8 oz carrots, diced

100 g/3½ oz/¾ cup frozen peas

2 eggs, beaten

2 tbsp cold water

1 Rinse the rice under cold running water, then drain thoroughly. Place the rice in a saucepan with 600 ml/ 1 pint/2½ cups of water, bring to the boil, cover and leave to simmer for 12 minutes. Turn the cooked rice out on to a tray and leave to cool.

2 Using a sharp knife, thinly slice the beef fillet.

3 Mix together the soy sauce, tomato ketchup and seven spice seasoning. Spoon over the beef and toss well to coat.

4 Heat the oil in a preheated wok. Add the beef and stir-fry for 3–4 minutes.

5 Add the onion, carrots and peas to the wok and stir-fry for a further 2–3 minutes. Add the cooked rice to the wok and stir to combine.

6 Beat the eggs with 2 tablespoons of cold water. Drizzle the egg mixture over the rice and stir-fry for 3–4 minutes, or until the rice is heated through and the egg has set. Transfer to a warm serving bowl and serve immediately.

VARIATION

You can use pork fillet or chicken instead of the beef, if you prefer.

Chinese Fried Rice

It is essential to use cold, dry rice with separate grains to make this recipe properly.

NUTRITIONAL INFORMATION

Calories ....475 Sugars 3g
Protein ....16g Fat 16g
Carbohydrate ...72g Saturates 3g

5 MINS   30 MINS

SERVES 4

INGREDIENTS

700 ml/1¼ pints/3 cups water

½ tsp salt

300 g/10½ oz/1½ cups long-grain rice

2 eggs

4 tsp cold water

3 tbsp sunflower oil

4 spring onions (scallions), sliced diagonally

1 red, green or yellow (bell) pepper, cored, seeded and thinly sliced

3-4 lean rashers bacon, rinded and cut into strips

200 g/7 oz fresh bean sprouts

125 g/4½ oz frozen peas, defrosted

2 tbsp soy sauce (optional)

salt and pepper

1 Pour the water into the wok with the salt and bring to the boil. Rinse the rice in a sieve under cold water until the water runs clear, drain well and add to the boiling water. Stir well, then cover the wok tightly with the lid, and simmer gently for 12-13 minutes. (Don't remove the lid during cooking or the steam will escape and the rice will not be cooked.)

2 Remove the lid, give the rice a good stir and spread out on a large plate or baking tray (cookie sheet) to cool and dry.

3 Beat each egg separately with salt and pepper and 2 teaspoons of cold water. Heat 1 tablespoon of oil in the wok, pour in the first egg, swirl it around and leave to cook undisturbed until set. Remove to a board and cook the second egg. Cut the omelettes into thin slices.

4 Add the remaining oil to the wok and when really hot add the spring onions (scallions) and (bell) pepper and stir-fry for 1-2 minutes. Add the bacon and continue to stir-fry for a further 1-2 minutes. Add the bean sprouts and peas and toss together thoroughly; stir in the soy sauce, if using.

5 Add the rice and seasoning and stir-fry for 1 minute or so, then add the strips of omelette and continue to stir for about 2 minutes or until the rice is piping hot. Serve at once.

Chinese Risotto

Risotto is a creamy Italian dish made with arborio or risotto rice. This Chinese version is simply delicious!

NUTRITIONAL INFORMATION

Calories	436	Sugars	.........7g
Protein	........13g	Fat	..........14g
Carbohydrate	...70g	Saturates	.......4g

5 MINS   25 MINS

SERVES 4

INGREDIENTS

2 tbsp groundnut oil

1 onion, sliced

2 cloves garlic, crushed

1 tsp Chinese five-spice powder

225 g/8 oz Chinese sausage, sliced

225 g/8 oz carrots, diced

1 green (bell) pepper, deseeded and diced

275 g/9½ oz/1⅓ cups risotto rice

850 ml/1½ pints/1¾ cups vegetable or chicken stock

1 tbsp fresh chives

1 Heat the groundnut oil in a large preheated wok or heavy-based frying pan (skillet).

2 Add the onion slices, crushed garlic and Chinese five-spice powder to the wok or frying pan (skillet) and stir-fry for 1 minute.

3 Add the Chinese sausage, carrots and green (bell) pepper to the wok and stir to combine.

4 Stir in the risotto rice and cook for 1 minute.

5 Gradually add the vegetable or chicken stock, a little at a time, stirring constantly until the liquid has been completely absorbed and the rice grains are tender.

6 Snip the chives with a pair of clean kitchen scissors and stir into the wok with the last of the stock.

7 Transfer the Chinese risotto to warm serving bowls and serve immediately.

COOK'S TIP

Chinese sausage is highly flavoured and is made from chopped pork fat, pork meat and spices. Use a spicy Portuguese sausage if Chinese sausage is unavailable.

Fragrant Coconut Rice

This fragrant, sweet rice is delicious served with meat, vegetable or fish dishes as part of a Chinese menu.

NUTRITIONAL INFORMATION

Calories	306	Sugars	.........2g
Protein	.........5g	Fat	...........6g
Carbohydrate	...61g	Saturates	.......4g

5 MINS   15 MINS

SERVES 4

INGREDIENTS

275 g/9½ oz long-grain white rice

600 ml/1 pint/2½ cups water

½ tsp salt

100 ml/3½ fl oz/⅓ cup coconut milk

25 g/1 oz/¼ cup desiccated (shredded) coconut

1 Rinse the rice thoroughly under cold running water until the water runs completely clear.

2 Drain the rice thoroughly in a sieve set over a large bowl. This is to remove some of the starch and to prevent the grains from sticking together.

3 Place the rice in a wok with 600 ml/ 1 pint/2½ cups water.

4 Add the salt and coconut milk to the wok and bring to the boil.

5 Cover the wok with a lid or a lid made of foil, curved into a domed shape and resting on the sides of the wok. Reduce the heat and leave to simmer for 10 minutes.

6 Remove the lid from the wok and fluff up the rice with a fork – all of the liquid should be absorbed and the rice grains should be tender. If not, add more water and continue to simmer for a few more minutes until all the liquid has been absorbed.

7 Spoon the rice into a warm serving bowl and scatter with the desiccated (shredded) coconut. Serve immediately.

COOK'S TIP

Coconut milk is not the liquid found inside coconuts – that is called coconut water. Coconut milk is made from the white coconut flesh soaked in water and milk and then squeezed to extract all of the flavour. You can make your own or buy it in cans.

Stir-Fried Rice with Sausage

This is a very quick rice dish as it uses pre-cooked rice. It is therefore ideal when time is short or for a quick lunch-time dish.

NUTRITIONAL INFORMATION

Calories .... .383	Sugars 9g
Protein 19g	Fat .... .17g
Carbohydrate ...42g	Saturates 4g

5 MINS   20 MINS

SERVES 4

I N G R E D I E N T S

350 g/12 oz Chinese sausage

2 tbsp sunflower oil

2 tbsp soy sauce

1 onion, sliced

175 g/6 oz carrots, cut into thin sticks

175 g/6 oz/1¼ cups peas

100 g/3½ oz/¾ cup canned pineapple cubes, drained

275 g/9½ oz/4¾ cups cooked long-grain rice

1 egg, beaten

1 tbsp chopped fresh parsley

1 Using a sharp knife, thinly slice the Chinese sausage.

2 Heat the sunflower oil in a large preheated wok. Add the sausage to the wok and stir-fry for 5 minutes.

3 Stir in the soy sauce and allow to bubble for about 2–3 minutes, or until syrupy.

4 Add the onion, carrots, peas and pineapple to the wok and stir-fry for a further 3 minutes.

5 Add the cooked rice to the wok and stir-fry the mixture for about 2–3 minutes, or until the rice is completely heated through.

6 Drizzle the beaten egg over the top of the rice and cook, tossing the ingredients in the wok, until the egg sets.

7 Transfer the stir-fried rice to a large, warm serving bowl and scatter with plenty of chopped fresh parsley. Serve immediately.

COOK'S TIP

Cook extra rice and freeze it in prepration for some of the other rice dishes included in this book as it saves time and enables a meal to be prepared in minutes. Be sure to cool any leftover cooked rice quickly before freezing to avoid food poisoning.

Egg Fu-Yung with Rice

In this dish, cooked rice is mixed with scrambled eggs and Chinese vegetables. It is a great way of using up leftover cooked rice.

NUTRITIONAL INFORMATION

Calories 258   Sugars 1g
Protein ....8g   Fat 16g
Carbohydrate ...21g   Saturates 3g

30 MINS   25 MINS

SERVES 4

INGREDIENTS

175 g/6 oz/generous ¾ cup long-grain rice

2 Chinese dried mushrooms
(if unavailable, use thinly sliced open-cap mushrooms)

3 eggs, beaten

3 tbsp vegetable oil

4 spring onions (scallions), sliced

½ green (bell) pepper, chopped

60 g/2 oz/⅓ cup canned bamboo shoots

60 g/2 oz/⅓ cup canned water chestnuts, sliced

125 g/4½ oz/2 cups bean sprouts

2 tbsp light soy sauce

2 tbsp dry sherry

2 tsp sesame oil

salt and pepper

1 Cook the rice in lightly salted boiling water according to the packet instructions.

2 Place the Chinese dried mushrooms in a small bowl, cover with warm water and leave to soak for about 20–25 minutes.

3 Mix the beaten eggs with a little salt. Heat 1 tablespoon of the oil in a preheated wok or large frying pan (skillet). Add the eggs and stir until just set. Remove and set aside.

4 Drain the mushrooms and squeeze out the excess water. Remove the tough centres and chop the mushrooms.

5 Heat the remaining oil in a clean wok or frying pan (skillet). Add the mushrooms, spring onions (scallions) and green (bell) pepper, and stir-fry for 2 minutes. Add the bamboo shoots, water chestnuts and bean sprouts. Stir-fry for 1 minute.

6 Drain the rice thoroughly and add to the pan with the remaining ingredients. Mix well, heating the rice thoroughly. Season to taste with salt and pepper. Stir in the reserved eggs and serve.

COOK'S TIP

To wash bean sprouts, place them in a bowl of cold water and swirl with your hand. Remove any long tail ends then rinse and drain thoroughly.

Rice with Crab & Mussels

Shellfish makes an ideal partner for rice. Mussels and crab add flavour and texture to this spicy dish.

NUTRITIONAL INFORMATION

Calories 336	Sugars 4g
Protein 32g	Fat 10g
Carbohydrate . . .33g	Saturates 1g

20 MINS   10 MINS

SERVES 4

INGREDIENTS

300 g/10½ oz/1½ cups long-grain rice

175 g/6 oz white crab meat, fresh, canned or frozen (defrosted if frozen), or 8 crab sticks, defrosted if frozen

2 tbsp sesame or sunflower oil

2.5 cm/1 inch piece ginger root, grated

4 spring onions (scallions), thinly sliced diagonally

125 g/4½ oz mangetout (snow peas), cut into 2-3 pieces

½ tsp turmeric

1 tsp ground cumin

2 x 200 g/7 oz jars mussels, well drained, or 350 g/12 oz frozen mussels, defrosted

1 x 425 g/15 oz can bean sprouts, well drained

salt and pepper

1 Cook the rice in boiling salted water, following the instructions given in Chinese Fried Rice (see page 416).

2 Extract the crab meat, if using fresh crab (see right). Flake the crab meat or cut the crab sticks into 3 or 4 pieces.

3 Heat the oil in a preheated wok and stir-fry the ginger and spring onions (scallions) for a minute or so. Add the mangetout (snow peas) and continue to cook for a further minute. Sprinkle the turmeric, cumin and seasoning over the vegetables and mix well.

4 Add the crab meat and mussels and stir-fry for 1 minute. Stir in the cooked rice and bean sprouts and stir-fry for 2 minutes or until hot and well mixed.

5 Adjust the seasoning to taste and serve immediately.

COOK'S TIP

To prepare fresh crab, twist off the claws and legs, crack with a heavy knife and pick out the meat with a skewer. Discard the gills and pull out the under shell; discard the stomach sac. Pull the soft meat from the shell. Cut open the body section and prise out the meat with a skewer.

Rice with Five-Spice Chicken

This dish has a wonderful colour obtained from the turmeric, and a great spicy flavour, making it very appealing all round.

NUTRITIONAL INFORMATION

Calories 412   Sugars 1g
Protein . . . . .23g   Fat 13g
Carbohydrate . . .53g   Saturates 2g

 5 MINS   20 MINS

SERVES 4

INGREDIENTS

1 tbsp Chinese five-spice powder

2 tbsp cornflour (cornstarch)

350 g/12 oz boneless, skinless chicken breasts, cubed

3 tbsp groundnut oil

1 onion, diced

225 g/8 oz/1 cup long-grain white rice

½ tsp turmeric

600 ml/1 pint/2½ cups chicken stock

2 tbsp snipped fresh chives

1 Place the Chinese five-spice powder and cornflour (cornstarch) in a large bowl. Add the chicken pieces and toss to coat all over.

COOK'S TIP

Be careful when using turmeric as it can stain the hands and clothes a distinctive shade of yellow.

2 Heat 2 tablespoons of the groundnut oil in a large preheated wok. Add the chicken pieces to the wok and stir-fry for 5 minutes. Using a slotted spoon, remove the chicken and set aside.

3 Add the remaining groundnut oil to the wok.

4 Add the onion to the wok and stir-fry for 1 minute.

5 Add the rice, turmeric and chicken stock to the wok and gently bring to the boil.

6 Return the chicken pieces to the wok, reduce the heat and leave to simmer for 10 minutes, or until the liquid has been absorbed and the rice is tender.

7 Add the snipped fresh chives, stir to mix and serve hot.

Green Rice

Spinach is used in this recipe to give the rice a wonderful green colouring. Tossed with the carrot strips, it is a really appealing dish.

NUTRITIONAL INFORMATION

Calories	582	Sugars	........11g
Protein	........15g	Fat	..........12g
Carbohydrate	...110g	Saturates	.......4g

 1¼ HOURS   20 MINS

SERVES 4

I N G R E D I E N T S

2 tbsp olive oil

500 g/1 lb 2 oz/2¼ cups Basmati rice, soaked for 1 hour, washed and drained

700 ml/1¼ pints/3 cups coconut milk

1 tsp salt

1 bay leaf

2 tbsp chopped fresh coriander (cilantro)

2 tbsp chopped fresh mint

2 green chillies, deseeded and chopped finely

1 Heat the olive oil in a saucepan.

2 Add the Basmati rice to the saucepan and stir with a wooden spatula until the rice becomes translucent.

3 Add the coconut milk, salt and bay leaf. Bring to the boil and cook until all the liquid is absorbed.

4 Lower the heat as much as possible, cover the saucepan tightly and cook for 10 minutes.

5 Remove the bay leaf and stir in the coriander (cilantro), mint and chopped green chillies. Fork through the rice gently and serve.

COOK'S TIP

Two segments of fresh lime would make an attractive garnish for this dish and would complement the coriander (cilantro) perfectly.

Hot & Spicy Chicken Rice

Chicken is cooked with rice and vegetables and flavoured with red curry paste, ginger, coriander and lime for a deliciously spicy dish.

NUTRITIONAL INFORMATION

Calories	350	Sugars	.........2g
Protein	........26g	Fat	..........16g
Carbohydrate	...27g	Saturates	.......3g

10 MINS   30 MINS

SERVES 4

INGREDIENTS

250 g/9 oz/generous 1 cup white
   long-grain rice

4 tbsp vegetable oil

2 garlic cloves, chopped finely

6 shallots, sliced finely

1 red (bell) pepper, deseeded and diced

125 g/4½ oz French (green) beans,
   cut into 2.5 cm/1 inch lengths

1 tbsp red curry paste

350 g/12 oz cooked skinless, boneless
   chicken, chopped

½ tsp ground coriander seeds

1 tsp finely grated fresh ginger root

2 tbsp fish sauce

finely grated rind of 1 lime

3 tbsp lime juice

1 tbsp chopped fresh coriander
   (cilantro)

salt and pepper

TO GARNISH

lime wedges

sprigs of fresh coriander (cilantro)

1 Cook the rice in plenty of boiling, lightly salted water for 12–15 minutes until tender. Drain, rinse in cold water and drain thoroughly.

2 Heat the vegetable oil in a large preheated wok or frying pan (skillet).

3 Add the garlic and shallots to the wok or frying pan (skillet) and fry gently for 2–3 minutes until golden.

4 Add the (bell) pepper and French (green) beans and stir-fry for 2 minutes. Add the red curry paste and stir-fry for 1 minute.

5 Add the cooked rice to the wok or frying pan (skillet), then add the cooked chicken, ground coriander seeds, ginger, fish sauce, lime rind and juice, and fresh coriander (cilantro).

6 Stir-fry the mixture in the wok over a medium-high heat for about 4–5 minutes, until the rice and chicken are thoroughly reheated. Season to taste.

7 Transfer the chicken and rice mixture to a warm serving dish, garnish with lime wedges and fresh coriander (cilantro) and serve immediately.

Chinese Vegetable Rice

This rice can either be served as a meal in itself or as an accompaniment to other vegetable recipes.

NUTRITIONAL INFORMATION

Calories 228	Sugars 5g	
Protein 5g	Fat 7g	
Carbohydrate ...37g	Saturates 1g	

 5 MINS   25 MINS

SERVES 4

INGREDIENTS

350 g/12 oz/1¾ cups long-grain white rice

1 tsp turmeric

2 tbsp sunflower oil

225 g/8 oz courgettes (zucchini), sliced

1 red (bell) pepper, deseeded and sliced

1 green (bell) pepper, deseeded and sliced

1 green chilli, deseeded and finely chopped

1 medium carrot, coarsley grated

150 g/5½ oz/1½ cups bean sprouts

6 spring onions (scallions), sliced, plus extra
to garnish (optional)

2 tbsp soy sauce

salt

1 Place the rice and turmeric in a pan of lightly salted water and bring to the boil. Reduce the heat and leave to simmer until the rice is just tender. Drain the rice thoroughly and press out any excess water with a sheet of kitchen paper (paper towels). Set aside until required.

2 Heat the sunflower oil in a large preheated wok.

3 Add the courgettes (zucchini) to the wok and stir-fry for about 2 minutes.

4 Add the (bell) peppers and chilli to the wok and stir-fry for 2–3 minutes.

5 Add the cooked rice to the mixture in the wok, a little at a time, tossing well after each addition.

6 Add the carrots, bean sprouts and spring onions (scallions) to the wok and stir-fry for a further 2 minutes.

7 Drizzle with soy sauce and serve at once, garnished with extra spring onions (scallions), if desired.

COOK'S TIP

For real luxury, add a few saffron strands infused in boiling water instead of the turmeric.

Green-fried Rice

Spinach is used in this recipe to give the rice a wonderful green colouring. Tossed with the carrot strips, it is a really appealing dish.

NUTRITIONAL INFORMATION

Calories 139	Sugars 2g	
Protein 3g	Fat 7g	
Carbohydrate ...18g	Saturates 1g	

5 MINS   20 MINS

SERVES 4

INGREDIENTS

150 g/5½ oz/⅔ cup long-grain rice

2 tbsp vegetable oil

2 garlic cloves, crushed

1 tsp grated fresh root ginger

1 carrot, cut into matchsticks

1 courgette (zucchini), diced

225 g/8 oz baby spinach

2 tsp light soy sauce

2 tsp light brown sugar

1 Cook the rice in a saucepan of boiling water for about 15 minutes. Drain the rice well, rinse under cold running water and then rinse the rice thoroughly again. Set aside until required.

2 Heat the vegetable oil in a preheated wok or large, heavy-based frying pan (skillet).

3 Add the crushed garlic and grated fresh root ginger to the wok or frying pan (skillet) and stir-fry for about 30 seconds.

4 Add the carrot matchsticks and diced courgette (zucchini) to the mixture in the wok and stir-fry for about 2 minutes, so the vegetables still retain their crunch.

5 Add the baby spinach and stir-fry for 1 minute, until wilted.

6 Add the rice, soy sauce and sugar to the wok and mix together well.

7 Transfer the green-fried rice to serving dishes and serve immediately.

COOK'S TIP

Light soy sauce has more flavour than the sweeter, dark soy sauce, which gives the food a rich, reddish colour.

 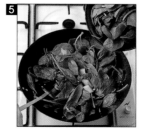 

Fruity Coconut Rice

A pale yellow rice flavoured with coconut and spices to serve as an accompaniment – or as a main dish with added diced chicken or pork.

NUTRITIONAL INFORMATION

Calories 578	Sugars 17g	
Protein 8g	Fat 31g	
Carbohydrate 71g	Saturates 15g	

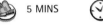

🍲 5 MINS   🕐 35 MINS

SERVES 4

INGREDIENTS

90 g/3 oz creamed coconut

700 ml/1¼ pints/3 cups boiling water

1 tbsp sunflower oil (or olive oil for a
   stronger flavour)

1 onion, thinly sliced or chopped

250 g/9 oz/generous 1 cup long-grain rice

¼ tsp turmeric

6 whole cloves

1 cinnamon stick

½ tsp salt

60-90 g/2-3 oz/½ cup raisins or sultanas

60 g/2 oz/½ cup walnut or pecan halves,
   roughly chopped

2 tbsp pumpkin seeds (optional)

1 Blend the creamed coconut with half the boiling water until smooth, then stir in the remainder until well blended.

2 Heat the oil in a preheated wok, add the onion and stir-fry gently for 3-4 minutes until the onion begins to soften.

3 Rinse the rice thoroughly under cold running water, drain well and add to the wok with the turmeric. Cook for 1-2 minutes, stirring all the time.

4 Add the coconut milk, cloves, cinnamon stick and salt and bring to the boil. Cover and simmer very gently for 10 minutes.

5 Add the raisins, nuts and pumpkin seeds, if using, and mix well. Cover the wok again and continue to cook for a further 5-8 minutes or until all the liquid has been absorbed and the rice is tender. Remove from the heat and leave to stand, still tightly covered, for 5 minutes. Remove the cinnamon stick and serve.

COOK'S TIP

Add 250 g/9 oz/1 cup cooked chicken or pork cut into dice or thin slivers with the raisins to turn this into a main dish. The addition of coconut milk makes the cooked rice slightly sticky.

Chinese Chicken Rice

This is a really colourful main meal or side dish which tastes just as good as it looks.

NUTRITIONAL INFORMATION

Calories ....324 Sugars 4g
Protein ....24g Fat 10g
Carbohydrate ...37g Saturates 2g

5 MINS   25 MINS

SERVES 4

INGREDIENTS

350 g/12 oz/1¾ cups long-grain white rice

1 tsp turmeric

2 tbsp sunflower oil

350 g/12 oz skinless, boneless chicken breasts or thighs, sliced

1 red (bell) pepper, deseeded and sliced

1 green (bell) pepper, deseeded and sliced

1 green chilli, deseeded and finely chopped

1 medium carrot, coarsely grated

150 g/5½ oz/1½ cups bean sprouts

6 spring onions (scallions), sliced, plus extra to garnish

2 tbsp soy sauce

salt

1 Place the rice and turmeric in a large saucepan of lightly salted water and cook until the grains of rice are just tender, about 10 minutes. Drain the rice thoroughly and press out any excess water with kitchen paper (paper towels)

2 Heat the sunflower oil in a large preheated wok or frying pan (skillet).

3 Add the strips of chicken to the wok or frying pan (skillet) and stir-fry over a high heat until the chicken is just beginning to turn a golden colour.

4 Add the sliced (bell) peppers and green chilli to the wok and stir-fry for 2–3 minutes.

5 Add the cooked rice to the wok, a little at a time, tossing well after each addition until well combined and the grains of rice are separated.

6 Add the carrot, bean sprouts and spring onions (scallions) to the wok and stir-fry for a further 2 minutes.

7 Drizzle with the soy sauce and toss to combine.

8 Transfer the Chinese chicken rice to a warm serving dish, garnish with extra spring onions (scallions), if wished and serve at once.

Fried Rice in Pineapple

This looks very impressive on a party buffet. Mix the remaining pineapple flesh with paw-paw (papaya) and mango for an exotic fruit salad.

NUTRITIONAL INFORMATION

Calories 197   Sugars 8g
Protein . . . . .5g   Fat 8g
Carbohydrate . . .29g   Saturates 1g

20 MINS   10 MINS

SERVES 4

INGREDIENTS

1 large pineapple

1 tbsp sunflower oil

1 garlic clove, crushed

1 small onion, diced

½ celery stick, sliced

1 tsp coriander seeds, ground

1 tsp cumin seeds, ground

150 g/5½ oz/1½ cups button
   mushrooms, sliced

250 g/9 oz/1⅓ cups cooked rice

2 tbsp light soy sauce

½ tsp sugar

½ tsp salt

25 g/1 oz/¼ cup cashew nuts

TO GARNISH

1 spring onion (scallion),
   sliced finely

fresh coriander (cilantro) leaves

mint sprig

1 Using a sharp knife, halve the pineapple lengthways and cut out the flesh to make 2 boat-shaped shells.

2 Cut the flesh into cubes and reserve 125 g/4½ oz/1 cup to use in this recipe. (Any remaining pineapple cubes can be served separately.)

3 Heat the sunflower oil in a wok or large, heavy frying pan (skillet).

4 Cook the garlic, onion and celery over a high heat, stirring constantly, for 2 minutes. Stir in the coriander and cumin seeds, and the mushrooms.

5 Add the reserved pineapple cubes and cooked rice to the wok or frying pan (skillet) and stir well.

6 Stir in the soy sauce, sugar, salt and cashew nuts.

7 Using 2 spoons, lift and stir the rice for about 4 minutes until it is thoroughly heated.

8 Spoon the rice mixture into the pineapple boats. Garnish with sliced spring onion (scallion), coriander (cilantro) leaves and a mint sprig.

Chatuchak Fried Rice

An excellent way to use up leftover rice. Pop it in the freezer as soon as it is cool, and it will be ready to reheat at any time.

NUTRITIONAL INFORMATION

Calories 241   Sugars 5g
Protein . . . . .7g   Fat 5g
Carbohydrate . . .46g   Saturates 1g

25 MINS   15 MINS

SERVES 4

INGREDIENTS

1 tbsp sunflower oil

3 shallots, chopped finely

2 garlic cloves, crushed

1 red chilli, deseeded and chopped finely

2.5-cm/1-inch piece ginger root, shredded finely

½ green (bell) pepper, deseeded and sliced finely

150 g/5½ oz/2-3 baby aubergines (eggplants), quartered

90 g/3 oz sugar snap peas or mangetout (snow peas), trimmed and blanched

90 g/3 oz/6 baby sweetcorn, halved lengthways and blanched

1 tomato, cut into 8 pieces

90 g/3 oz/1½ cups bean sprouts

500 g/1 lb 2 oz/3 cups cooked jasmine rice

2 tbsp tomato ketchup

2 tbsp light soy sauce

TO GARNISH

fresh coriander (cilantro) leaves

lime wedges

1 Heat the sunflower oil in a wok or large, heavy frying pan (skillet) over a high heat.

2 Add the shallots, garlic, chilli and ginger to the wok or frying pan (skillet). Stir until the shallots have softened.

3 Add the green (bell) pepper and baby aubergines (eggplants) and stir well.

4 Add the sugar snap peas or mangetout (snow peas), baby sweetcorn, tomato and bean sprouts. Stir-fry for 3 minutes.

5 Add the cooked jasmine rice to the wok, and lift and stir with two spoons for 4–5 minutes, until no more steam is released.

6 Stir the tomato ketchup and soy sauce into the mixture in the wok.

7 Serve the Chatuchak fried rice immediately, garnished with coriander (cilantro) leaves and lime wedges to squeeze over.

Curried Rice with Tofu

Cooked rice is combined with marinated tofu (bean curd), vegetables and peanuts to make this deliciously rich curry.

NUTRITIONAL INFORMATION

Calories 598   Sugars 2g
Protein ....16g   Fat 25
Carbohydrate ...81g   Saturates 4g

15 MINS   15 MINS

SERVES 4

INGREDIENTS

1 tsp coriander seeds

1 tsp cumin seeds

1 tsp ground cinnamon

1 tsp cloves

1 whole star anise

1 tsp cardamom pods

1 tsp white peppercorns

1 tbsp oil

6 shallots, chopped very roughly

6 garlic cloves, chopped very roughly

5-cm/2-inch piece lemon grass, sliced

4 fresh red chillies, deseeded and chopped

grated rind of 1 lime

1 tsp salt

3 tbsp sunflower oil

250 g/9 oz/1 cup marinated tofu (bean curd), cut into 2.5 cm/1 inch cubes

125 g/4½ oz green beans, cut into 2.5cm/ 1 inch lengths

1 kg/2 lb 4 oz/6 cups cooked rice (300 g/10½ oz/1½ cups raw weight)

3 shallots, diced finely and deep-fried

1 spring onion (scallion), chopped finely

2 tbsp chopped roast peanuts

1 tbsp lime juice

1 To make the curry paste, grind together the seeds and spices in a pestle and mortar or spice grinder.

2 Heat the sunflower oil in a preheated wok until it is really hot. Add the shallots, garlic and lemon grass and cook over a low heat until soft, about 5 minutes. Add the chillies and grind together with the dry spices. Stir in the lime rind and salt.

3 To make the curry, heat the oil in a wok or large, heavy frying pan (skillet). Cook the tofu (bean curd) over a high heat for 2 minutes to seal. Stir in the curry paste and beans. Add the rice and stir over a high heat for about 3 minutes.

4 Transfer to a warmed serving dish. Sprinkle with the deep-fried shallots, spring onion (scallion) and peanuts. Squeeze over the lime juice.

Crab Congee

This is a typical Chinese breakfast dish although it is probably best served as a lunch or supper dish at a Western table!

5 MINS   1¼ HOURS

SERVES 4

I N G R E D I E N T S

225 g/8 oz/1 cup short-grain rice

1.5 litres/2¾ pints/6¼ cups
    fish stock

½ tsp salt

100 g/3½ oz Chinese sausage,
    thinly sliced

225 g/8 oz white crab meat

6 spring onions (scallions), sliced

2 tbsp chopped fresh coriander
    (cilantro)

freshly ground black pepper,
    to serve

1 Place the short-grain rice in a large preheated wok or frying pan (skillet).

2 Add the fish stock to the wok or frying pan (skillet) and bring to the boil.

3 Reduce the heat, then simmer gently for 1 hour, stirring the mixture from time to time.

4 Add the salt, sliced Chinese sausage, white crab meat, sliced spring onions (scallions) and chopped fresh coriander (cilantro) to the wok and heat through for about 5 minutes.

5 Add a little more water to the wok if the congee "porridge" is too thick, stirring well.

6 Transfer the crab congee to warm serving bowls, sprinkle with freshly ground black pepper and serve immediately.

COOK'S TIP

Always buy the freshest possible crab meat; fresh is best, although frozen or canned will work for this recipe. In the West, crabs are almost always sold ready-cooked. The crab should feel heavy for its size, and when it is shaken, there should be no sound of water inside.

Curried Rice with Pork

This rice dish is flavoured with vegetables and pork, soy sauce and curry spices with strips of omelette added as a topping.

NUTRITIONAL INFORMATION

Calories 436   Sugars 2g
Protein ....30g   Fat 20g
Carbohydrate ...37g   Saturates 5g

10 MINS   35 MINS

SERVES 4

INGREDIENTS

300 g/10½ oz/1½ cups long-grain rice

350-500 g/12 oz-1 lb 2 oz pork fillet or lean pork slices

3 tomatoes, peeled, quartered and seeded

2 eggs

4 tsp water

3 tbsp sunflower oil

1 onion, thinly sliced

1-2 garlic cloves, crushed

1 tsp medium or mild curry powder

½ tsp ground coriander

¼ tsp medium chilli powder or 1 tsp bottled sweet chilli sauce

2 tbsp soy sauce

125 g/4½ oz frozen peas, defrosted

salt and pepper

1 Cook the rice in boiling salted water, following the instructions given in Chinese Fried Rice (see page 416) and keep warm until required.

2 Meanwhile, cut the pork into narrow strips across the grain, discarding any fat. Slice the tomatoes.

3 Beat each egg separately with 2 teaspoons cold water and salt and pepper. Heat 2 teaspoons of oil in the wok until really hot. Pour in the first egg, swirl it around and cook undisturbed until set. Remove to a plate or board and repeat with the second egg. Cut the omelettes into strips about 1 cm/½ inch wide.

4 Heat the remaining oil in the wok and when really hot add the onion and garlic and stir-fry for 1-2 minutes. Add the pork and continue to stir-fry for about 3 minutes or until almost cooked.

5 Add the curry powder, coriander, chilli powder or chilli sauce and soy sauce to the wok and cook for a further minute, stirring constantly.

6 Stir in the rice, tomatoes and peas and stir-fry for about 2 minutes until piping hot. Adjust the seasoning to taste and turn into a heated serving dish. Arrange the strips of omelette on top and serve at once.

Steamed Rice in Lotus Leaves

The fragrance of the leaves penetrates the rice, giving it a unique taste. Lotus leaves can be bought from specialist Chinese shops.

NUTRITIONAL INFORMATION

Calories	163	Sugars	.......0.1g
Protein	.........5g	Fat	...........6g
Carbohydrate	...2.1g	Saturates	.......1g

🍲 1 HOUR   🕐 40 MINS

SERVES 4

INGREDIENTS

2 lotus leaves

4 Chinese dried mushrooms (if unavailable, use thinly sliced open-cup mushrooms)

175 g/6 oz/generous ¾ cup long-grain rice

1 cinnamon stick

6 cardamom pods

4 cloves

1 tsp salt

2 eggs

1 tbsp vegetable oil

2 spring onions (scallions), chopped

1 tbsp soy sauce

2 tbsp sherry

1 tsp sugar

1 tsp sesame oil

1 Unfold the lotus leaves carefully and cut along the fold to divide each leaf in half. Lay on a large baking sheet and pour over enough hot water to cover. Soak for about 30 minutes until softened.

2 Place the dried mushrooms in a small bowl and cover with warm water. Leave to soak for 20–25 minutes.

3 Cook the rice in a saucepan of boiling water with the cinnamon stick, cardamom pods, cloves and salt for about

10 minutes – the rice should be partially cooked. Drain thoroughly and remove the cinnamon stick. Place the rice in a bowl

4 Beat the eggs lightly. Heat the oil in a wok and cook the eggs quickly, stirring until set. Remove and set aside.

5 Drain the mushrooms, squeezing out the excess water. Remove the tough centres and chop the mushrooms. Stir into

the rice with the cooked egg, spring onions (scallions), soy sauce, sherry, sugar and sesame oil.

6 Drain the lotus leaves and divide the rice into four portions. Place a portion in the centre of each leaf and fold up to form a parcel (packet). Place in a steamer, cover and steam over simmering water for 20 minutes. To serve, cut the tops of the lotus leaves open to expose the rice inside.

Vegetable Fried Rice

This dish can be served as part of a substantial meal for a number of people or as a vegetarian meal in itself for four.

NUTRITIONAL INFORMATION

Calories	175	Sugars	.........3g
Protein	.........3g	Fat	..........10g
Carbohydrate	...20g	Saturates	.......2g

 10 MINS   20 MINS

SERVES 4

I N G R E D I E N T S

125 g/4½ oz/⅔ cup long-grain white rice

3 tbsp peanut oil

2 garlic cloves, crushed

½ tsp Chinese five-spice powder

60 g/2 oz/⅓ cup green beans

1 green (bell) pepper, seeded and chopped

4 baby corn cobs, sliced

25 g/1 oz bamboo shoots, chopped

3 tomatoes, skinned, seeded and chopped

60 g/2 oz/½ cup cooked peas

1 tsp sesame oil

1 Bring a large saucepan of water to the boil.

2 Add the long-grain white rice to the saucepan and cook for about 15 minutes. Drain the rice well, rinse under cold running water and drain thoroughly again.

3 Heat the peanut oil in a preheated wok or large frying pan (skillet). Add the garlic and Chinese five-spice and stir-fry for 30 seconds.

4 Add the green beans, chopped green (bell) pepper and sliced corn cobs and stir-fry the ingredients in the wok for 2 minutes.

5 Stir the bamboo shoots, tomatoes, peas and rice into the mixture in the wok and stir-fry for 1 further minute.

6 Sprinkle with sesame oil and transfer to serving dishes. Serve immediately.

VARIATION

Use a selection of vegetables of your choice in this recipe, cutting them to a similar size in order to ensure that they cook in the same amount of time.

Coconut Rice with Lentils

Rice and green lentils are cooked with coconut, lemon grass and curry leaves. It will serve 2 people as a main course or 4 as a side dish.

NUTRITIONAL INFORMATION

Calories	.511	Sugars	.3g
Protein	.12g	Fat	.24g
Carbohydrate	...67g	Saturates	...15g

 5 MINS   50 MINS

SERVES 4

I N G R E D I E N T S

90 g/3 oz/⅓ cup green lentils

250 g/9 oz/generous 1 cup long-grain rice

2 tbsp vegetable oil

1 onion, sliced

2 garlic cloves, crushed

3 curry leaves

1 stalk lemon grass, chopped (if unavailable, use grated rind of ½ lemon)

1 green chilli, deseeded and chopped

½ tsp cumin seeds

1½ tsp salt

90 g/3 oz/⅓ cup creamed coconut

600 ml/1 pint/2½ cups hot water

2 tbsp chopped fresh coriander (cilantro)

T O   G A R N I S H

shredded radishes

shredded cucumber

1 Wash the lentils and place in a saucepan. Cover with cold water, bring to the boil and boil rapidly for 10 minutes.

2 Wash the rice thoroughly and drain well. Set aside until required.

3 Heat the vegetable oil in a large saucepan which has a tight-fitting lid

and fry the onion for 3–4 minutes. Add the garlic, curry leaves, lemon grass, chilli, cumin seeds and salt, and stir well.

4 Drain the lentils and rinse. Add to the onion and spices with the rice and mix well.

5 Add the creamed coconut to the hot water and stir until dissolved. Stir the coconut liquid into the rice mixture and bring to the boil. Turn down the heat to

low, put the lid on tightly and leave to cook undisturbed for 15 minutes.

6 Without removing the lid, remove the pan from the heat and leave to rest for 10 minutes to allow the rice and lentils to finish cooking in their own steam.

7 Stir in the coriander (cilantro) and remove the curry leaves. Serve garnished with the radishes and cucumber.

Fried Rice with Prawns

Use either large peeled prawns (shrimp) or tiger prawns (jumbo shrimp) for this rice dish.

NUTRITIONAL INFORMATION

Calories 599	Sugars 0g
Protein 26g	Fat 16g
Carbohydrate ...94g	Saturates 3g

5 MINS   35 MINS

SERVES 4

I N G R E D I E N T S

300 g/10½ oz/1½ cups long-grain rice

2 eggs

4 tsp cold water

salt and pepper

3 tbsp sunflower oil

4 spring onions (scallions), thinly sliced diagonally

1 garlic clove, crushed

125 g/4½ oz closed-cup or button mushrooms, thinly sliced

2 tbsp oyster or anchovy sauce

1 x 200 g/7 oz can water chestnuts, drained and sliced

250 g/9 oz peeled prawns (shrimp), defrosted if frozen

½ bunch watercress, roughly chopped

watercress sprigs, to garnish (optional)

1 Cook the rice in boiling salted water, following the instructions given in Chinese Fried Rice (see page 416) and keep warm.

2 Beat each egg separately with 2 teaspoons of cold water and salt and pepper.

3 Heat 2 teaspoons of sunflower oil in a wok or large frying pan (skillet), swirling it around until really hot. Pour in the first egg, swirl it around and leave to cook undisturbed until set. Remove to a plate or board and repeat with the second egg. Cut the omelettes into 2.5 cm/1 inch squares.

4 Heat the remaining oil in the wok and when really hot add the spring onions (scallions) and garlic and stir-fry for 1 minute. Add the mushrooms and continue to cook for a further 2 minutes.

5 Stir in the oyster or anchovy sauce and seasoning and add the water chestnuts and prawns (shrimp); stir-fry for 2 minutes.

6 Stir in the cooked rice and stir-fry for 1 minute, then add the watercress and omelette squares and stir-fry for a further 1-2 minutes until piping hot. Serve at once garnished with sprigs of watercress, if liked.

Chicken & Rice Casserole

This is a quick-cooking, spicy casserole of rice, chicken, vegetables and chilli in a soy and ginger flavoured liquor.

NUTRITIONAL INFORMATION

Calories	502	Sugars	.........2g
Protein	........55g	Fat	..........9g
Carbohydrate	...52g	Saturates	.......3g

35 MINS   50 MINS

SERVES 4

INGREDIENTS

150 g/5½ oz/⅔ cup long-grain rice

1 tbsp dry sherry

2 tbsp light soy sauce

2 tbsp dark soy sauce

2 tsp dark brown sugar

1 tsp salt

1 tsp sesame oil

900 g/2 lb skinless, boneless chicken meat, diced

850 ml/1½ pints/3¾ cups chicken stock

2 open-cap mushrooms, sliced

60 g/2 oz water chestnuts, halved

75 g/2¾ oz broccoli florets

1 yellow (bell) pepper, sliced

4 tsp grated fresh root ginger

whole chives, to garnish

VARIATION

This dish would work equally well with beef or pork. Chinese dried mushrooms may be used instead of the open-cap mushrooms, if rehydrated before adding to the dish.

1 Cook the rice in a saucepan of boiling water for about 15 minutes. Drain well, rinse under cold water and drain again thoroughly.

2 Mix together the sherry, soy sauces, sugar, salt and sesame oil.

3 Stir the chicken into the soy mixture, turning to coat the chicken well. Leave to marinate for about 30 minutes.

4 Bring the stock to the boil in a saucepan or preheated wok. Add the chicken with the marinade, mushrooms, water chestnuts, broccoli, (bell) pepper and ginger.

5 Stir in the rice, reduce the heat, cover and cook for 25-30 minutes, until the chicken and vegetables are cooked through. Transfer to serving plates, garnish with chives and serve.

Special Fried Rice

This dish is a popular choice in Chinese restaurants. Ham and prawns (shrimp) are mixed with vegetables in a soy-flavoured rice.

NUTRITIONAL INFORMATION

Calories 301   Sugars 1g
Protein . . . . .26g   Fat 13g
Carbohydrate . . .21g   Saturates 3g

5 MINS   30 MINS

SERVES 4

INGREDIENTS

150 g/5½ oz/⅔ cup long-grain rice

2 tbsp vegetable oil

2 eggs, beaten

2 garlic cloves, crushed

1 tsp grated fresh root ginger

3 spring onions (scallions), sliced

75 g/2¾ oz/¾ cup cooked peas

150 g/5½ oz/⅔ cup bean sprouts

225 g/8 oz/1⅓ cups shredded ham

150 g/5½ oz peeled, cooked prawns (shrimp)

2 tbsp light soy sauce

1 Cook the rice in a saucepan of boiling water for about 15 minutes. Drain well, rinse under cold water and drain thoroughly again.

2 Heat 1 tablespoon of the vegetable oil in a preheated wok.

3 Add the beaten eggs and a further 1 teaspoon of oil. Tilt the wok so that the egg covers the base to make a thin pancake.

4 Cook until lightly browned on the underside, then flip the pancake over and cook on the other side for 1 minute. Remove from the wok and leave to cool.

5 Heat the remaining oil in the wok and stir-fry the garlic and ginger for 30 seconds. Add the spring onions (scallions), peas, bean sprouts, ham and prawns (shrimp). Stir-fry for 2 minutes.

6 Stir in the soy sauce and rice and cook for a further 2 minutes. Transfer the rice to serving dishes. Roll up the pancake, slice it very thinly and use to garnish the rice. Serve immediately.

COOK'S TIP

As this recipe contains meat and fish, it is ideal served with simpler vegetable dishes.

Sweet Chilli Pork Fried Rice

This is a variation of egg fried rice which may be served as an accompaniment to a main meal dish.

NUTRITIONAL INFORMATION

Calories	366	Sugars	.........5g
Protein	........29g	Fat	..........16g
Carbohydrate	...28g	Saturates	.......4g

 25 MINS   20 MINS

SERVES 4

INGREDIENTS

450 g/1 lb pork tenderloin

2 tbsp sunflower oil

2 tbsp sweet chilli sauce, plus extra to serve

1 onion, sliced

175 g/6 oz carrots, cut into thin sticks

175 g/6 oz courgettes (zucchini), cut into sticks

100 g/3½ oz/1 cup canned bamboo shoots, drained

275 g/9½ oz/4¾ cups cooked long-grain rice

1 egg, beaten

1 tbsp chopped fresh parsley

1 Using a sharp knife, cut the pork tenderloin into thin slices.

2 Heat the sunflower oil in a large preheated wok or frying pan (skillet).

3 Add the pork to the wok and stir-fry for 5 minutes.

4 Add the chilli sauce to the wok and allow to bubble, stirring, for 2–3 minutes or until syrupy.

5 Add the onion, carrots, courgettes (zucchini) and bamboo shoots to the wok and stir-fry for a further 3 minutes.

6 Add the cooked rice and stir-fry for 2–3 minutes, or until the rice is heated through.

7 Drizzle the beaten egg over the top of the fried rice and cook, tossing the ingredients in the wok with two spoons, until the egg sets.

8 Scatter with chopped fresh parsley and serve immediately, with extra sweet chilli sauce, if desired.

COOK'S TIP

For a really quick dish, add frozen mixed vegetables to the rice instead of the freshly prepared vegetables.

Crab Fried Rice

Canned crabmeat is used in this recipe for convenience, but fresh white crabmeat could be used - quite deliciously - in its place.

NUTRITIONAL INFORMATION

Calories	225	Sugars	.........1g
Protein	........12g	Fat	...........11g
Carbohydrate	...20g	Saturates	.......2g

 5 MINS   25 MINS

SERVES 4

INGREDIENTS

150 g/5½ oz/⅔ cup long-grain rice

2 tbsp peanut oil

125 g/4½ oz canned white crabmeat, drained

1 leek, sliced

150 g/5½ oz/⅔ cup bean sprouts

2 eggs, beaten

1 tbsp light soy sauce

2 tsp lime juice

1 tsp sesame oil

salt

sliced lime, to garnish

1 Cook the rice in a saucepan of boiling salted water for 15 minutes. Drain well, rinse under cold running water and drain again thoroughly.

2 Heat the peanut oil in a preheated wok until it is really hot.

3 Add the crabmeat, leek and bean sprouts to the wok and stir-fry for 2-3 minutes. Remove the mixture from the wok with a slotted spoon and set aside until required.

4 Add the eggs to the wok and cook, stirring occasionally, for 2-3 minutes, until they begin to set.

5 Stir the rice and the crabmeat, leek and bean sprout mixture into the eggs in the wok.

6 Add the soy sauce and lime juice to the mixture in the wok. Cook for 1 minute, stirring to combine, and sprinkle with the sesame oil.

7 Transfer the crab fried rice to a serving dish, garnish with the sliced lime and serve immediately.

VARIATION

Cooked lobster may be used instead of the crab for a really special dish.

Noodles

Noodles are a symbol of longevity in China and are always served at birthday and New Year celebrations. It is considered bad luck to cut noodles into shorter lengths because the Chinese believe the longer they are the longer and happier your life will be. Noodles are available in several varieties, both fresh and dried, made from wheat,

buckwheat or rice flours, or you can even make your own if you have time! They come in fine threads, strings or flat ribbons and can be bought from large supermarkets or oriental food shops. Like rice, noodles are very versatile and can be boiled, fried, added to soups, or served plain. Noodles are precooked as part of the manufacturing process so most only need soaking in hot water to rehydrate them.

Beef Chow Mein

Chow Mein must be the best-known and most popular noodle dish on any Chinese menu. You can use any meat or vegetables instead of beef.

NUTRITIONAL INFORMATION

Calories	.341	Sugars	.3g
Protein	.27g	Fat	.17g
Carbohydrate	.20g	Saturates	.4g

 10 MINS   20 MINS

SERVES 4

INGREDIENTS

450 g/1 lb egg noodles

4 tbsp peanut oil

450 g/1 lb lean beef steak, cut into thin strips

2 garlic cloves, crushed

1 tsp grated fresh root ginger

1 green (bell) pepper, thinly sliced

1 carrot, thinly sliced

2 celery sticks, sliced

8 spring onions (scallions)

1 tsp dark brown sugar

1 tbsp dry sherry

2 tbsp dark soy sauce

few drops of chilli sauce

VARIATION

A variety of different vegetables may be used in this recipe for colour and flavour – try broccoli, red (bell) peppers, green beans or baby sweetcorn cobs.

1 Cook the noodles in a saucepan of boiling salted water for 4-5 minutes. Drain well, rinse under cold running water and drain again thoroughly.

2 Toss the noodles in 1 tablespoon of the peanut oil.

3 Heat the remaining oil in a preheated wok. Add the beef and stir-fry for 3-4 minutes, stirring constantly.

4 Add the crushed garlic and grated fresh root ginger to the wok and stir-fry for 30 seconds.

5 Add the (bell) pepper, carrot, celery and spring onions (scallions) and stir-fry for about 2 minutes.

6 Add the dark brown sugar, dry sherry, dark soy sauce and chilli sauce to the mixture in the wok and cook, stirring, for 1 minute.

7 Stir in the noodles, mixing well, and cook until completely warmed through.

8 Transfer the noodles to warm serving bowls and serve immediately.

Cellophane Noodles & Prawns

Tiger prawns (jumbo shrimp) are cooked with orange juice, (bell) peppers, soy sauce and vinegar and served on a bed of cellophane noodles.

NUTRITIONAL INFORMATION

Calories 118	Sugar 4g	
Protein 7g	Fat 4g	
Carbohydrate ...15g	Saturates 1g	

10 MINS   25 MINS

SERVES 4

INGREDIENTS

175 g/6 oz cellophane noodles

1 tbsp vegetable oil

1 garlic clove, crushed

2 tsp grated fresh root ginger

24 raw tiger prawns (jumbo shrimp), peeled and deveined

1 red (bell) pepper, seeded and thinly sliced

1 green (bell) pepper, seeded and thinly sliced

1 onion, chopped

2 tbsp light soy sauce

juice of 1 orange

2 tsp wine vinegar

pinch of brown sugar

150 ml/¼ pint/⅔ cup fish stock

1 tbsp cornflour (cornstarch)

2 tsp water

orange slices, to garnish

1 Cook the noodles in a pan of boiling water for 1 minute. Drain well, rinse under cold water and then drain again.

2 Heat the oil in a wok and stir-fry the garlic and ginger for 30 seconds.

3 Add the prawns (shrimp) and stir-fry for 2 minutes. Remove with a slotted spoon and keep warm.

4 Add the (bell) peppers and onion to the wok and stir-fry for 2 minutes. Stir in the soy sauce, orange juice, vinegar, sugar and stock. Return the prawns (shrimp) to the wok and cook for 8-10 minutes, until cooked through.

5 Blend the cornflour (cornstarch) with the water and stir into the wok. Bring to the boil, add the noodles and cook for 1-2 minutes. Garnish and serve.

VARIATION

Lime or lemon juice and slices may be used instead of the orange. Use 3-5½ tsp of these juices.

Cantonese Fried Noodles

This dish is usually served as a snack or light meal. It may also be served as an accompaniment to plain meat and fish dishes.

NUTRITIONAL INFORMATION

Calories	385	Sugars	.........6g
Protein	........38g	Fat	..........17g
Carbohydrate	...21g	Saturates	.......4g

 5 MINS   15 MINS

SERVES 4

INGREDIENTS

350 g/12 oz egg noodles

3 tbsp vegetable oil

675 g/1½lb lean beef steak, cut into thin
  strips

125 g/4½ oz green cabbage, shredded

75 g/2¾ oz bamboo shoots

6 spring onions (scallions), sliced

25 g/1 oz green beans, halved

1 tbsp dark soy sauce

2 tbsp beef stock

1 tbsp dry sherry

1 tbsp light brown sugar

2 tbsp chopped parsley, to garnish

1 Cook the noodles in a saucepan of boiling water for 2-3 minutes. Drain well, rinse under cold running water and drain thoroughly again.

2 Heat 1 tablespoon of the oil in a preheated wok or frying pan (skillet), swirling it around until it is really hot

3 Add the noodles and stir-fry for 1-2 minutes. Drain the noodles and set aside until required.

4 Heat the remaining oil in the wok. Add the beef and stir-fry for 2-3 minutes. Add the cabbage, bamboo shoots, spring onions (scallions) and beans to the wok and stir-fry for 1-2 minutes.

5 Add the soy sauce, beef stock, dry sherry and light brown sugar to the wok, stirring to mix well.

6 Stir the noodles into the mixture in the wok, tossing to mix well. Transfer to serving bowls, garnish with chopped parsley and serve immediately.

VARIATION

You can vary the vegetables in this dish depending on seasonal availability or whatever you have at hand – try broccoli, green (bell) pepper or spinach.

Sweet & Sour Noodles

This delicious dish combines sweet and sour flavours with the addition of egg, rice noodles, king prawns (shrimp) and vegetables for a real treat.

NUTRITIONAL INFORMATION

Calories ....352 Sugars 14g
Protein ....23g Fat 17g
Carbohydrate ...29g Saturates 3g

10 MINS   10 MINS

SERVES 4

INGREDIENTS

3 tbsp fish sauce

2 tbsp distilled white vinegar

2 tbsp caster (superfine) or palm sugar

2 tbsp tomato purée (paste)

2 tbsp sunflower oil

3 cloves garlic, crushed

350 g/12 oz rice noodles, soaked in boiling
   water for 5 minutes

8 spring onions (scallions), sliced

175 g/6 oz carrot, grated

150 g/5½ oz/1¼ cups bean sprouts

2 eggs, beaten

225 g/8 oz peeled king prawns (shrimp)

50 g/1¾ oz/½ cup chopped peanuts

1 tsp chilli flakes, to garnish

1 Mix together the fish sauce, vinegar, sugar and tomato purée (paste).

2 Heat the sunflower oil in a large preheated wok.

3 Add the garlic to the wok and stir-fry for 30 seconds.

4 Drain the noodles thoroughly and add them to the wok together with the fish sauce and tomato purée (paste) mixture. Mix well to combine.

5 Add the spring onions (scallions), carrot and bean sprouts to the wok and stir-fry for 2–3 minutes.

6 Move the contents of the wok to one side, add the beaten eggs to the empty part of the wok and cook until the egg sets. Add the noodles, prawns (shrimp) and peanuts to the wok and mix well. Transfer to warm serving dishes and garnish with chilli flakes. Serve hot.

COOK'S TIP

Chilli flakes may be found in the spice section of large supermarkets.

Noodles with Chilli & Prawn

This is a simple dish to prepare and is packed with flavour, making it an ideal choice for special occasions.

NUTRITIONAL INFORMATION

Calories	.259	Sugars	.9g
Protein	.28g	Fat	.8g
Carbohydrate	.20g	Saturates	.1g

 10 MINS 5 MINS

SERVES 4

INGREDIENTS

250 g/9 oz thin glass noodles

2 tbsp sunflower oil

1 onion, sliced

2 red chillies, deseeded and very finely chopped

4 lime leaves, thinly shredded

1 tbsp fresh coriander (cilantro)

2 tbsp palm or caster (superfine) sugar

2 tbsp fish sauce

450 g/1 lb raw tiger prawns (jumbo shrimp), peeled

1 Place the noodles in a large bowl. Pour over enough boiling water to cover the noodles and leave to stand for 5 minutes. Drain thoroughly and set aside until required.

COOK'S TIP

If you cannot buy raw tiger prawns (jumbo shrimp), use cooked prawns (shrimp) instead and cook them with the noodles for 1 minute only, just to heat through.

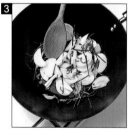  

2 Heat the sunflower oil in a large preheated wok or frying pan (skillet) until it is really hot.

3 Add the onion, red chillies and lime leaves to the wok and stir-fry for 1 minute.

4 Add the coriander (cilantro), palm or caster (superfine) sugar, fish sauce and prawns (shrimp) to the wok or frying pan (skillet) and stir-fry for a further 2 minutes or until the prawns (shrimp) turn pink.

5 Add the drained noodles to the wok, toss to mix well, and stir-fry for 1–2 minutes or until heated through.

6 Transfer the noodles and prawns (shrimp) to warm serving bowls and serve immediately.

Chicken & Noodle One-Pot

Flavoursome chicken and vegetables cooked with Chinese egg noodles in a coconut sauce. Serve in deep soup bowls.

NUTRITIONAL INFORMATION

Calories 256   Sugars 7g
Protein ....30g   Fat 8g
Carbohydrate ...18g   Saturates 2g

5 MINS   20 MINS

SERVES 4

INGREDIENTS

1 tbsp sunflower oil

1 onion, sliced

1 garlic clove, crushed

2.5 cm/1 inch root ginger, peeled and grated

1 bunch spring onions (scallions), sliced diagonally

500 g/1 lb 2 oz chicken breast fillet, skinned and cut into bite-sized pieces

2 tbsp mild curry paste

450 ml/16 fl oz/2 cups coconut milk

300 ml/½ pint/1¼ cups chicken stock

250 g/9 oz Chinese egg noodles

2 tsp lime juice

salt and pepper

basil sprigs, to garnish

1 Heat the sunflower oil in a wok or large, heavy-based frying pan (skillet).

2 Add the onion, garlic, ginger and spring onions (scallions) to the wok and stir-fry for 2 minutes until softened.

3 Add the chicken and curry paste and stir-fry for 4 minutes, or until the vegetables and chicken are golden brown. Stir in the coconut milk, stock and salt and pepper to taste, and mix well.

4 Bring to the boil, break the noodles into large pieces, if necessary, add to the pan, cover and simmer for about 6-8 minutes until the noodles are just tender, stirring occasionally.

5 Add the lime juice and adjust the seasoning, if necessary.

6 Serve the chicken and noodle one-pot at once in deep soup bowls, garnished with basil sprigs.

COOK'S TIP

If you enjoy hot flavours, substitute the mild curry paste in the above recipe with hot curry paste (found in most supermarkets) but reduce the quantity to 1 tablespoon.

Quick Chicken Chow Mein

A quick stir-fry of chicken and vegetables which are mixed with Chinese egg noodles and a dash of sesame oil.

NUTRITIONAL INFORMATION

Calories	300	Sugars	.........5g
Protein	........23g	Fat	..........15g
Carbohydrate	...18g	Saturates	.......2g

 20 MINS ⏱ 15 MINS

SERVES 4

INGREDIENTS

2 tbsp sesame seeds

250 g/9 oz thread egg noodles

175 g/6 oz broccoli florets

3 tbsp sunflower oil

1 garlic clove, sliced

2.5 cm/1 inch piece ginger root, peeled and chopped

250 g/9 oz chicken fillet, sliced thinly

1 onion, sliced

125 g/4½ oz shiitake mushrooms, sliced

1 red (bell) pepper, deseeded and cut into thin strips

1 tsp cornflour (cornstarch)

2 tbsp water

425 g/15 oz can baby sweetcorn, drained and halved

2 tbsp dry sherry

2 tbsp soy sauce

1 tsp sesame oil

COOK'S TIP

As well as adding protein, vitamins and useful fats to the diet, nuts and seeds add important flavour and texture.

1 Put the sesame seeds in a heavy-based frying pan (skillet) and cook for 2–3 minutes until they turn brown and begin to pop. Cover the pan so the seeds do not jump out and shake them constantly to prevent them burning. Remove from the pan and set aside until required.

2 Put the noodles in a bowl, cover with boiling water and leave to stand for 4 minutes. Drain thoroughly.

3 Meanwhile, blanch the broccoli in boiling salted water for 2 minutes, then drain.

4 Heat the sunflower oil in a wok or large frying pan (skillet), add the garlic, ginger, chicken and onion and stir-fry for 2 minutes until the chicken is golden and the onion softened.

5 Add the broccoli, mushrooms and red (bell) pepper and stir-fry for a further 2 minutes.

6 Mix the cornflour (cornstarch) with the water then stir into the pan with the baby sweetcorn, sherry, soy sauce, drained noodles and sesame oil and cook, stirring, until the sauce is thickened and the noodles warmed through. Sprinkle with the sesame seeds and serve.

Lamb with Noodles

Lamb is quick fried, coated in a soy sauce and served on a bed of transparent noodles for a richly flavoured dish.

NUTRITIONAL INFORMATION

Calories 285   Sugars 1g
Protein ....27g   Fat 16g
Carbohydrate ...10g   Saturates 6g

5 MINS   15 MINS

SERVES 4

I N G R E D I E N T S

150 g/5½ oz cellophane noodles

2 tbsp peanut oil

450 g/1 lb lean lamb, thinly sliced

2 garlic cloves, crushed

2 leeks, sliced

3 tbsp dark soy sauce

250 ml/9 fl oz/1 cup lamb stock

dash of chilli sauce

red chilli strips, to garnish

1 Bring a large saucepan of water to the boil. Add the cellophane noodles and cook for 1 minute. Drain the noodles well, place in a sieve, rinse under cold running water and drain thoroughly again. Set aside until required.

2 Heat the peanut oil in a preheated wok or frying pan (skillet), swirling the oil around until it is really hot.

3 Add the lamb to the wok or frying pan (skillet) and stir-fry for about 2 minutes.

4 Add the crushed garlic and sliced leeks to the wok and stir-fry for a further 2 minutes.

5 Stir in the dark soy sauce, lamb stock and chilli sauce and cook for 3-4

minutes, stirring frequently, until the meat is cooked through.

6 Add the drained cellophane noodles to the wok or frying pan (skillet) and cook for about 1 minute, stirring, until heated through.

7 Transfer the lamb and cellophane noodles to serving plates, garnish with red chilli strips and serve.

COOK'S TIP

Transparent noodles are available in Chinese supermarkets. Use egg noodles instead if transparent noodles are unavailable, and cook them according to the instructions on the packet.

Fried Vegetable Noodles

In this recipe, noodles are first boiled and then deep-fried for a crisply textured dish, and tossed with fried vegetables.

NUTRITIONAL INFORMATION

Calories 229   Sugars 4g
Protein . . . . .5g   Fat 15g
Carbohydrate . . .20g   Saturates 2g

     5 MINS   25 MINS

SERVES 4

INGREDIENTS

350 g/12 oz/3 cups dried egg noodles

2 tbsp peanut oil

2 garlic cloves, crushed

½ tsp ground star anise

1 carrot, cut into matchsticks

1 green (bell) pepper, cut into matchsticks

1 onion, quartered and sliced

125 g/4½ oz broccoli florets

75 g/2¾ oz bamboo shoots

1 celery stick, sliced

1 tbsp light soy sauce

150 ml/¼ pint/⅔ cup vegetable stock

oil, for deep-frying

1 tsp cornflour (cornstarch)

2 tsp water

1 Cook the noodles in a saucepan of boiling water for 1–2 minutes. Drain well and rinse under cold running water. Leave the noodles to drain thoroughly in a colander until required.

2 Heat the peanut oil in a preheated wok until smoking. Reduce the heat, add the crushed garlic and ground star anise and stir-fry for 30 seconds. Add the remaining vegetables and stir-fry for 1–2 minutes.

3 Add the soy sauce and vegetable stock to the wok and cook over a low heat for 5 minutes.

4 Heat the oil for deep-frying in a separate wok to 180°C/350°F, or until a cube of bread browns in 30 seconds.

5 Using a fork, twist the drained noodles and form them into rounds. Deep-fry them in batches until crisp, turning once. Leave to drain on kitchen paper (paper towels).

6 Blend the cornflour (cornstarch) with the water to form a paste and stir into the vegetables. Bring to the boil, stirring until the sauce is thickened and clear.

7 Arrange the noodles on a warm serving plate, spoon the vegetables on top and serve immediately.

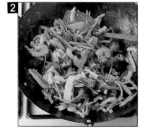

Pork Chow Mein

This is a basic recipe – the meat and/or vegetables can be varied as much as you like.

NUTRITIONAL INFORMATION

Calories 239	Sugars 1g
Protein 17g	Fat 14g
Carbohydrate . . .12g	Saturates 2g

15 MINS   15 MINS

SERVES 4

I N G R E D I E N T S

250 g/9 oz egg noodles

4–5 tbsp vegetable oil

250 g/9 oz pork fillet, cooked

125g/4½ oz French (green) beans

2 tbsp light soy sauce

1 tsp salt

½ tsp sugar

1 tbsp Chinese rice wine or dry sherry

2 spring onions (scallions), finely shredded

a few drops sesame oil

chilli sauce, to serve (optional)

1 Cook the noodles in boiling water according to the instructions on the packet, then drain and rinse under cold water. Drain again then toss with 1 tablespoon of the oil.

2 Slice the pork into thin shreds and top and tail the beans.

3 Heat 3 tablespoons of oil in a preheated wok until hot. Add the noodles and stir-fry for 2–3 minutes with 1 tablespoon soy sauce, then remove to a serving dish. Keep warm.

4 Heat the remaining oil and stir-fry the beans and meat for 2 minutes. Add the salt, sugar, wine or sherry, the remaining soy sauce and about half the spring onions (scallions) to the wok.

5 Stir the mixture in the wok, adding a little stock if necessary, then pour on top of the noodles, and sprinkle with sesame oil and the remaining spring onions (scallions).

6 Serve the chow mein hot or cold with chilli sauce, if desired.

COOK'S TIP

Chow Mein literally means 'stir-fried noodles' and is highly popular in the West as well as in China. Almost any ingredient can be added, such as fish, meat, poultry or vegetables. It is very popular for lunch and makes a tasty salad served cold.

Fried Noodles (Chow Mein)

This is a basic recipe for Chow Mein. Additional ingredients such as chicken or pork etc can be added if liked.

NUTRITIONAL INFORMATION

Calories 716	Sugars 2g	
Protein 4g	Fat 12g	
Carbohydrate . . .14g	Saturates 1g	

5 MINS 15 MINS

SERVES 4

I N G R E D I E N T S

275 g/9½ oz egg noodles

3-4 tbsp vegetable oil

1 small onion, finely shredded

125 g/4½ oz fresh bean sprouts

1 spring onion (scallion),
  finely shredded

2 tbsp light soy sauce

a few drops of sesame oil

salt

1 Bring a wok or saucepan of salted water to the boil.

2 Add the egg noodles to the saucepan or wok and cook according to the instructions on the packet (usually no more than 4-5 minutes).

3 Drain the noodles well and rinse in cold water; drain thoroughly again, then transfer to a large mixing bowl and toss with a little vegetable oil.

4 Heat the remaining vegetable oil in a preheated wok or large frying pan (skillet) until really hot.

5 Add the shredded onion to the wok and stir-fry for about 30-40 seconds.

6 Add the bean sprouts and drained noodles to the wok, stir and toss for 1 more minute.

7 Add the shredded spring onion (scallion) and light soy sauce and blend well.

8 Transfer the noodles to a warm serving dish, sprinkle with the sesame oil and serve immediately.

COOK'S TIP

Noodles, a symbol of longevity, are made from wheat or rice flour, water and egg. Handmade noodles are made by an elaborate process of kneading, pulling and twisting the dough, and it takes years to learn the art.

Noodles with Prawns (Shrimp)

This is a simple dish using egg noodles and large prawns (shrimp), which give the dish a wonderful flavour, texture and colour.

NUTRITIONAL INFORMATION

Calories 142   Sugars 0.4g
Protein ....11g   Fat 7g
Carbohydrate ....11g   Saturates 1g

 5 MINS   10 MINS

SERVES 4

INGREDIENTS

225 g/8 oz thin egg noodles

2 tbsp peanut oil

1 garlic clove, crushed

½ tsp ground star anise

1 bunch spring onions (scallions), cut into 5-cm/2-inch pieces

24 raw tiger prawns (jumbo shrimp), peeled with tails intact

2 tbsp light soy sauce

2 tsp lime juice

lime wedges, to garnish

1 Blanch the noodles in a saucepan of boiling water for about 2 minutes.

2 Drain the noodles well, rinse under cold water and drain thoroughly again. Keep warm and set aside until required.

3 Heat the peanut oil in a preheated wok or large frying pan (skillet) until almost smoking.

4 Add the crushed garlic and ground star anise to the wok and stir-fry for 30 seconds.

5 Add the spring onions (scallions) and tiger prawns (jumbo shrimp) to the wok and stir-fry for 2-3 minutes.

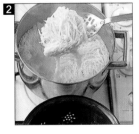  

6 Stir in the light soy sauce, lime juice and noodles and mix well.

7 Cook the mixture in the wok for about 1 minute until thoroughly heated through and all the ingredients are thoroughly incorporated.

8 Spoon the noodle and prawn mixture into a warm serving dish. Transfer to serving bowls, garnish with lime wedges and serve immediately.

COOK'S TIP

If fresh egg noodles are available, these require very little cooking: simply place in boiling water for about 3 minutes, then drain and toss in oil. Noodles can be boiled and eaten plain, or stir-fried with meat and vegetables for a light meal or snack.

Homemade Noodles

These noodles are simple to make; you do not need a pasta-making machine as they are rolled out by hand.

20 MINS   15 MINS

SERVES 2–4

INGREDIENTS

NOODLES

125 g/4½ oz/1 cup plain (all-purpose) flour

2 tbsp cornflour (cornstarch)

½ tsp salt

125 ml/4 fl oz/½ cup boiling water

5 tbsp vegetable oil

STIR-FRY

1 courgette (zucchini), cut into thin sticks

1 celery stick, cut into thin sticks

1 carrot, cut into thin sticks

125 g/4½ oz open-cup mushrooms, sliced

125 g/4½ oz broccoli florets and stalks, peeled and thinly sliced

1 leek, sliced

125 g/4½ oz/2 cups bean sprouts

1 tbsp soy sauce

2 tsp rice wine vinegar

½ tsp sugar

1 To prepare the noodles, sift the flour, cornflour (cornstarch) and salt into a bowl. Make a well in the centre and pour in the boiling water and 1 teaspoon of oil. Mix quickly to make a soft dough. Cover and leave for 5–6 minutes.

2 Make the noodles by breaking off small pieces of dough and rolling into balls. Roll each ball across a very lightly oiled work surface (counter) with the palm of your hand to form thin noodles. Do not worry if some of the noodles break into shorter lengths. Set the noodles aside.

3 Heat 3 tablespoons of oil in a wok. Add the noodles in batches and fry over a high heat for 1 minute. Reduce the heat and cook for a further 2 minutes. Remove and drain on kitchen paper (paper towels). Set aside.

4 Heat the remaining oil in the pan. Add the courgette (zucchini), celery and carrot, and stir-fry for 1 minute. Add the mushrooms, broccoli and leek, and stir-fry for a further minute. Stir in the remaining ingredients and mix well until thoroughly heated.

5 Add the noodles and cook over a high heat, tossing to mix the ingredients. Serve immediately.

Special Noodles

This dish combines meat, vegetables, prawns (shrimp) and noodles in a curried coconut sauce. Serve as a main meal or as an accompaniment.

NUTRITIONAL INFORMATION

Calories	....	409
Protein	....	24g
Carbohydrate	...	28g

Sugars	....	12g
Fat	....	23g
Saturates	....	8g

 5 MINS   25 MINS

SERVES 4

INGREDIENTS

250 g/9 oz thin rice noodles

4 tbsp groundnut oil

2 cloves garlic, crushed

2 red chillies, deseeded and very finely chopped

1 tsp grated fresh ginger

2 tbsp Madras curry paste

2 tbsp rice wine vinegar

1 tbsp caster (superfine) sugar

225 g/8 oz cooked ham, finely shredded

100 g/3½ oz/1¼ cups canned water chestnuts, sliced

100 g/3½ oz mushrooms, sliced

100 g/3½ oz/¾ cup peas

1 red (bell) pepper, deseeded and thinly sliced

100 g/3½ oz peeled prawns (shrimp)

2 large eggs

4 tbsp coconut milk

25 g/1 oz/¼ cup desiccated (shredded) coconut

2 tbsp chopped fresh coriander (cilantro)

1 Place the rice noodles in a large bowl, cover with boiling water and leave to soak for about 10 minutes. Drain the noodles thoroughly, then toss with 2 tablespoons of groundnut oil.

2 Heat the remaining groundnut oil in a large preheated wok until the oil is really hot.

3 Add the garlic, chillies, ginger, curry paste, rice wine vinegar and caster (superfine) sugar to the wok and stir-fry for 1 minute.

4 Add the ham, water chestnuts, mushrooms, peas and red (bell) pepper to the wok and stir-fry for 5 minutes.

5 Add the noodles and prawns (shrimps) to the wok and stir-fry for 2 minutes.

6 In a small bowl, beat together the eggs and coconut milk. Drizzle over the mixture in the wok and stir-fry until the egg sets.

7 Add the desiccated (shredded) coconut and chopped fresh coriander (cilantro) to the wok and toss to combine. Transfer the noodles to warm serving dishes and serve immediately.

Seafood Chow Mein

Use whatever seafood is available for this delicious noodle dish – mussels or crab would also be suitable.

NUTRITIONAL INFORMATION

Calories 281   Sugars 1g
Protein . . . . .15g   Fat 18g
Carbohydrate . . .16g   Saturates 2g

15 MINS   15 MINS

SERVES 4

INGREDIENTS

90 g/3 oz squid, cleaned

3-4 fresh scallops

90 g/3 oz raw prawns (shrimp), shelled

½ egg white, lightly beaten

1 tbsp cornflour (cornstarch) paste (see page 31)

275 g/9½ oz egg noodles

5-6 tbsp vegetable oil

2 tbsp light soy sauce

60 g/2 oz mangetout (snow peas)

½ tsp salt

½ tsp sugar

1 tsp Chinese rice wine

2 spring onions (scallions), finely shredded

a few drops of sesame oil

COOK'S TIP

Chinese rice wine, made from glutinous rice, is also known as 'Yellow wine' because of its golden amber colour. If it is unavailable, a good dry or medium sherry is an acceptable substitute.

1 Open up the squid and score the inside in a criss-cross pattern, then cut into pieces about the size of a postage stamp. Soak the squid in a bowl of boiling water until all the pieces curl up. Rinse in cold water and drain.

2 Cut each scallop into 3-4 slices. Cut the prawns (shrimp) in half lengthways if large. Mix the scallops and prawns (shrimp) with the egg white and cornflour (cornstarch) paste.

3 Cook the noodles in boiling water according to the packet instructions, then drain and rinse under cold water. Drain well, then toss with about 1 tablespoon of oil.

4 Heat 3 tablespoons of oil in a preheated wok. Add the noodles and 1 tablespoon of the soy sauce and stir-fry for 2-3 minutes. Remove to a large serving dish.

5 Heat the remaining oil in the wok and add the mangetout (snow peas) and seafood. Stir-fry for about 2 minutes, then add the salt, sugar, wine, remaining soy sauce and about half the spring onions (scallions). Blend well and add a little stock or water if necessary. Pour the seafood mixture on top of the noodles and sprinkle with sesame oil. Garnish with the remaining spring onions (scallions) and serve.

Sesame Hot Noodles

Plain egg noodles are tossed in a dressing made with sesame oil, soy sauce, peanut butter, coriander (cilantro), lime, chilli and sesame seeds.

NUTRITIONAL INFORMATION

Calories	300	Sugars	.........1g
Protein	.........7g	Fat	..........21g
Carbohydrate	...21g	Saturates	.......3g

5 MINS   10 MINS

SERVES 4

INGREDIENTS

2 x 250 g/9 oz packets medium egg noodles

3 tbsp sunflower oil

2 tbsp sesame oil

1 garlic clove, crushed

1 tbsp smooth peanut butter

1 small green chilli, seeded and very finely chopped

3 tbsp toasted sesame seeds

4 tbsp light soy sauce

½ tbsp lime juice

salt and pepper

4 tbsp chopped fresh coriander (cilantro)

1 Place the noodles in a large pan of boiling water, then immediately remove from the heat. Cover and leave to stand for 6 minutes, stirring once halfway through the time. At the end of 6 minutes the noodles will be perfectly cooked. Alternatively, cook the noodles following the packet instructions.

2 Meanwhile, make the dressing. Mix together the sunflower oil, sesame oil, crushed garlic and peanut butter in a mixing bowl until smooth.

3 Add the chopped green chilli, sesame seeds and light soy sauce to the other

dressing ingredients. Add the lime juice, according to taste, and mix well. Season with salt and pepper.

4 Drain the noodles thoroughly then place in a heated serving bowl.

5 Add the dressing and chopped fresh coriander (cilantro) to the noodles and toss well to mix. Serve hot as a main meal accompaniment.

COOK'S TIP

If you are cooking the noodles ahead of time, toss the cooked, drained noodles in 2 teaspoons of sesame oil, then turn into a bowl. Cover and keep warm until required.

Mushroom & Pork Noodles

This dish benefits from the use of coloured oyster mushrooms. If these are unavailable, plain grey mushrooms will suffice.

NUTRITIONAL INFORMATION

Calories	286	Sugars	.........3g
Protein	........23g	Fat	..........13g
Carbohydrate	...21g	Saturates	.......3g

 10 MINS   20 MINS

SERVES 4

INGREDIENTS

450 g/1 lb thin egg noodles

2 tbsp peanut oil

350 g/12 oz pork fillet (tenderloin), sliced

2 garlic cloves, crushed

1 onion, cut into 8 pieces

225 g/8 oz oyster mushrooms

4 tomatoes, skinned, seeded and thinly sliced

2 tbsp light soy sauce

50 ml/2 fl oz/¼ cup pork stock

1 tbsp chopped fresh coriander (cilantro)

1 Cook the noodles in a saucepan of boiling water for 2-3 minutes. Drain well, rinse under cold running water and drain thoroughly again.

2 Heat 1 tablespoon of the oil in a preheated wok or frying pan (skillet).

3 Add the noodles to the wok or frying pan (skillet) and stir-fry for about 2 minutes.

4 Using a slotted spoon, remove the noodles from the wok, drain well and set aside until required.

5 Heat the remaining peanut oil in the wok. Add the pork slices and stir-fry for 4-5 minutes.

6 Stir in the crushed garlic and chopped onion and stir-fry for a further 2-3 minutes.

7 Add the oyster mushrooms, tomatoes, light soy sauce, pork stock and drained noodles. Stir well and cook for 1-2 minutes.

8 Sprinkle with chopped coriander (cilantro) and serve immediately.

COOK'S TIP

For crisper noodles, add 2 tablespoons of oil to the wok and fry the noodles for 5-6 minutes, spreading them thinly in the wok and turning half-way through cooking.

Beef with Crispy Noodles

Crispy noodles are terrific and may also be served on their own as a side dish, sprinkled with sugar and salt.

NUTRITIONAL INFORMATION

Calories 244   Sugars 9g
Protein ....20g   Fat 10g
Carbohydrate ...19g   Saturates 2g

5 MINS   30 MINS

SERVES 4

INGREDIENTS

225 g/8 oz medium egg noodles

350 g/12 oz beef fillet

2 tbsp sunflower oil

1 tsp ground ginger

1 clove garlic, crushed

1 red chilli, deseeded and very finely chopped

100 g/3½ oz carrots, cut into thin sticks

6 spring onions (scallions), sliced

2 tbsp lime marmalade

2 tbsp soy sauce

oil, for frying

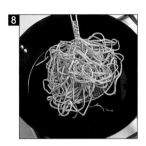

1 Place the noodles in a large dish or bowl. Pour over enough boiling water to cover the noodles and leave to stand for about 10 minutes while you stir-fry the rest of the ingredients.

2 Using a sharp knife, thinly slice the beef fillet.

3 Heat the sunflower oil in a large preheated wok or frying pan (skillet).

4 Add the beef and ground ginger to the wok or frying pan (skillet) and stir-fry for about 5 minutes.

5 Add the crushed garlic, chopped red chilli, carrots and spring onions (scallions) to the wok and stir-fry for a further 2–3 minutes.

6 Add the lime marmalade and soy sauce to the wok and allow to bubble for 2 minutes. Remove the chilli beef and ginger mixture, set aside and keep warm until required.

7 Heat the oil for frying in the wok or frying pan (skillet).

8 Drain the noodles thoroughly and pat dry with absorbent kitchen paper (paper towels). Carefully lower the noodles into the hot oil and cook for 2–3 minutes or until crispy. Drain the noodles on absorbent kitchen paper (paper towels).

9 Divide the noodles between 4 warm serving plates and top with the chilli beef and ginger mixture. Serve immediately.

Egg Noodles with Beef

Quick and easy, this mouth-watering Chinese-style noodle dish can be cooked in minutes.

10 MINS   15 MINS

SERVES 4

INGREDIENTS

285 g/10 oz egg noodles

3 tbsp walnut oil

2.5 cm/1 inch piece fresh root ginger,
   cut into thin strips

5 spring onions (scallions), finely
   shredded

2 garlic cloves, finely chopped

1 red (bell) pepper, cored, seeded and
   thinly sliced

100 g/3½ oz button mushrooms, thinly
   sliced

350 g/12 oz fillet steak, cut into
   thin strips

1 tbsp cornflour (cornstarch)

5 tbsp dry sherry

3 tbsp soy sauce

1 tsp soft brown sugar

225 g/8 oz/1 cup bean sprouts

1 tbsp sesame oil

salt and pepper

spring onion (scallion) strips,
   to garnish

1 Bring a large saucepan of water to the boil. Add the egg noodles and cook according to the instructions on the packet. Drain the noodles, rinse under cold running water, drain thoroughly again and set aside.

2 Heat the walnut oil in a preheated wok until it is really hot.

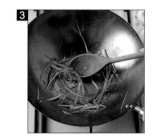

3 Add the grated fresh root ginger, shredded spring onions (scallions) and chopped garlic and stir-fry for 45 seconds.

4 Add the red (bell) pepper, button mushrooms and steak and stir-fry for 4 minutes. Season to taste with salt and pepper.

5 Mix together the cornflour (cornstarch), dry sherry and soy sauce in a small jug to form a paste, and pour into the wok. Sprinkle over the brown sugar and stir-fry all of the ingredients for a further 2 minutes.

6 Add the bean sprouts, drained noodles and sesame oil to the wok, stir and toss together for 1 minute.

7 Transfer the stir-fry to warm serving dishes, garnish with strips of spring onion (scallion) and serve.

Chilli (Small) Shrimp Noodles

Cellophane or 'glass' noodles are made from mung beans. They are sold dried, so they need soaking before use.

NUTRITIONAL INFORMATION

Calories ....152 Sugars 2g
Protein ....11g Fat 8g
Carbohydrate ...10g Saturates 1g

 25 MINS   10 MINS

SERVES 4

INGREDIENTS

2 tbsp light soy sauce

1 tbsp lime or lemon juice

1 tbsp fish sauce

125 g/4½ oz firm tofu (bean curd), cut into chunks

125 g/4½ oz cellophane noodles

2 tbsp sesame oil

4 shallots, sliced finely

2 garlic cloves, crushed

1 small red chilli, deseeded and chopped finely

2 celery sticks, sliced finely

2 carrots, sliced finely

125 g/4½ oz/⅔ cup cooked, peeled (small) shrimps

60 g/2 oz/1 cup bean sprouts

TO GARNISH

celery leaves

fresh chillies

1 Mix together the light soy sauce, lime or lemon juice and fish sauce in a small bowl. Add the tofu (bean curd) cubes and toss them until coated in the mixture. Cover and set aside for 15 minutes.

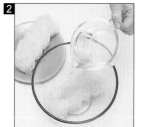

2 Put the noodles into a large bowl and cover with warm water. Leave them to soak for about 5 minutes, and then drain them well.

3 Heat the sesame oil in a wok or large frying pan (skillet). Add the shallots, garlic and red chilli, and stir-fry for 1 minute.

4 Add the sliced celery and carrots to the wok or pan and stir-fry for a further 2–3 minutes.

5 Tip the drained noodles into the wok or frying pan (skillet) and cook, stirring, for 2 minutes, then add the (small) shrimps, bean sprouts and tofu (bean curd), with the soy sauce mixture. Cook over a medium high heat for 2–3 minutes until heated through.

6 Transfer the mixture in the wok to a serving dish and garnish with celery leaves and chillies.

Noodles with Cod & Mango

Fish and fruit are tossed with a trio of (bell) peppers in this spicy dish served with noodles for a quick, healthy meal.

NUTRITIONAL INFORMATION

Calories	274	Sugars	........11g
Protein	........25g	Fat	..........8g
Carbohydrate	...26g	Saturates	.......1g

  10 MINS   25 MINS

SERVES 4

INGREDIENTS

250 g/9 oz packet egg noodles

450 g/1 lb skinless cod fillet

1 tbsp paprika

2 tbsp sunflower oil

1 red onion, sliced

1 orange (bell) pepper, deseeded and sliced

1 green (bell) pepper, deseeded and sliced

100 g/3½ oz baby corn cobs, halved

1 mango, sliced

100 g/3½ oz/1 cup bean sprouts

2 tbsp tomato ketchup

2 tbsp soy sauce

2 tbsp medium sherry

1 tsp cornflour (cornstarch)

1 Place the egg noodles in a large bowl and cover with boiling water. Leave to stand for about 10 minutes.

2 Rinse the cod fillet and pat dry with absorbent kitchen paper (paper towels). Cut the cod flesh into thin strips.

3 Place the cod strips in a large bowl. Add the paprika and toss well to coat the fish.

4 Heat the sunflower oil in a large preheated wok.

 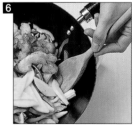 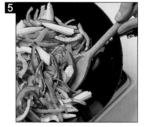

5 Add the onion, (bell) peppers and baby corn cobs to the wok and stir-fry for about 5 minutes.

6 Add the cod to the wok together with the sliced mango and stir-fry for a further 2–3 minutes or until the fish is tender.

7 Add the bean sprouts to the wok and toss well to combine.

8 Mix together the tomato ketchup, soy sauce , sherry and cornflour (cornstarch). Add the mixture to the wok and cook, stirring occasionally, until the juices thicken.

9 Drain the noodles thoroughly and transfer to warm serving bowls. Transfer the cod and mango stir-fry to separate serving bowls and serve immediately.

Chicken Noodles

Rice noodles are used in this recipe. They are available in large supermarkets or specialist Chinese supermarkets.

NUTRITIONAL INFORMATION

Calories ....169 Sugars 2g
Protein ....14g Fat 7g
Carbohydrate ...12g Saturates 2g

5 MINS   **15 MINS**

SERVES 4

INGREDIENTS

225 g/8 oz rice noodles

2 tbsp peanut oil

225 g/8 oz skinless, boneless chicken breast, sliced

2 garlic cloves, crushed

1 tsp grated fresh root ginger

1 tsp Chinese curry powder

1 red (bell) pepper, seeded and thinly sliced

75 g/2¾ oz mangetout (snow peas), shredded

1 tbsp light soy sauce

2 tsp Chinese rice wine

2 tbsp chicken stock

1 tsp sesame oil

1 tbsp chopped fresh coriander (cilantro)

1 Soak the rice noodles for 4 minutes in warm water. Drain thoroughly and set aside until required.

2 Heat the peanut oil in a preheated wok or large heavy-based frying pan (skillet) and stir-fry the chicken slices for 2-3 minutes.

3 Add the garlic, ginger and Chinese curry powder and stir-fry for a further 30 seconds. Add the red (bell) pepper and mangetout (snow peas) to the mixture in the wok and stir-fry for 2-3 minutes.

4 Add the noodles, soy sauce, Chinese rice wine and chicken stock to the wok and mix well, stirring occasionally, for 1 minute.

5 Sprinkle the sesame oil and chopped coriander (cilantro) over the noodles. Transfer to serving plates and serve.

VARIATION

You can use pork or duck in this recipe instead of the chicken, if you prefer.

Noodles in Soup

Noodles in soup are far more popular than fried noodles in China. You can use different ingredients for the dressing according to taste.

NUTRITIONAL INFORMATION

Calories 231	Sugars 1g
Protein 18g	Fat 11g
Carbohydrate . . .16g	Saturates 2g

4 HOURS   15 MINS

SERVES 4

I N G R E D I E N T S

250 g/9 oz chicken fillet, pork fillet, or any other ready-cooked meat

3-4 Chinese dried mushrooms, soaked

125 g/4½ oz canned sliced bamboo shoots, rinsed and drained

125 g/4½ oz spinach leaves, lettuce hearts, or Chinese leaves (cabbage), shredded

2 spring onions (scallions), finely shredded

250 g/9 oz egg noodles

about 600 ml/1 pint/2½ cups Chinese Stock (see page 30)

2 tbsp light soy sauce

2 tbsp vegetable oil

1 tsp salt

½ tsp sugar

2 tsp Chinese rice wine or dry sherry

a few drops sesame oil

1 tsp red chilli oil (optional)

1 Using a sharp knife or meat cleaver, cut the meat into thin shreds.

2 Squeeze dry the soaked Chinese mushrooms and discard the hard stalk.

3 Thinly shred the mushrooms, bamboo shoots, spinach leaves and spring onions (scallions).

4 Cook the noodles in boiling water according to the instructions on the packet, then drain and rinse under cold water. Place the noodles in a bowl.

5 Bring the Chinese stock to the boil, add about 1 tablespoon soy sauce and pour over the noodles. Keep warm.

6 Heat the vegetable oil in a preheated wok, add about half of the spring onions (scallions), the meat and the vegetables (mushrooms, bamboo shoots and greens). Stir-fry for about 2-3 minutes. Add all the seasonings and stir until well combined.

7 Pour the mixture in the wok over the noodles, garnish with the remaining spring onions (scallions) and serve immediately.

COOK'S TIP

Noodle soup is wonderfully satisfying and is ideal to serve on cold winter days.

Speedy Peanut Pan-fry

Thread egg noodles are the ideal accompaniment to this quick dish because they can be cooked quickly and easily while the stir-fry sizzles.

NUTRITIONAL INFORMATION

Calories	563	Sugars	.........7g
Protein	........45g	Fat	..........33g
Carbohydrate	...22g	Saturates	.......7g

🍚 5 MINS   🕐 15 MINS

SERVES 4

INGREDIENTS

300 g/10½ oz/2 cups courgettes (zucchini)

250 g/9 oz/1⅓ cups baby corn (corn-on-the-cob)

250 g/9 oz thread egg noodles

2 tbsp corn oil

1 tbsp sesame oil

8 boneless chicken thighs or 4 breasts, sliced thinly

300 g/10½ oz/3¾ cups button mushrooms

350 g/12 oz/1½ cups bean sprouts

4 tbsp smooth peanut butter

2 tbsp soy sauce

2 tbsp lime or lemon juice

60 g/2 oz/½ cup roasted peanuts

salt and pepper

coriander (cilantro), to garnish

1 Using a sharp knife, trim and thinly slice the courgettes (zucchini) and baby corn (corn-on-the-cob). Set the vegetables aside until required.

2 Cook the noodles in lightly salted boiling water for 3–4 minutes.

3 Meanwhile, heat the corn oil and sesame oil in a large wok or frying pan (skillet) and fry the chicken over a fairly high heat for 1 minute.

4 Add the courgettes (zucchini), corn and mushrooms and stir-fry for 5 minutes.

5 Add the bean sprouts, peanut butter, soy sauce, lime or lemon juice and pepper, then cook for a further 2 minutes.

6 Drain the noodles thoroughly. Scatter with the roasted peanuts and serve with the courgette (zucchini) and mushroom mixture. Garnish and serve.

COOK'S TIP

Try serving this stir-fry with rice sticks. These are broad, pale, translucent ribbon noodles made from ground rice.

Chicken Chow Mein

This classic dish requires no introduction as it is already a favourite amongst most Chinese food-eaters.

NUTRITIONAL INFORMATION

Calories 230	Sugars 2g
Protein 19g	Fat 11g
Carbohydrate . . .14g	Saturates 2g

5 MINS   20 MINS

SERVES 4

INGREDIENTS

250 g/9 oz packet medium egg noodles

2 tbsp sunflower oil

275 g/9½ oz cooked chicken breasts, shredded

1 clove garlic, finely chopped

1 red (bell) pepper, deseeded and thinly sliced

100 g/3½ oz shiitake mushrooms, sliced

6 spring onions (scallions), sliced

100 g/3½ oz/1 cup bean sprouts

3 tbsp soy sauce

1 tbsp sesame oil

VARIATION

You can make the chow mein with a selection of vegetables for a vegetarian dish, if you prefer.

1 Place the egg noodles in a large bowl or dish and break them up slightly. Pour over enough boiling water to cover the noodles and leave to stand.

2 Heat the sunflower oil in a large preheated wok. Add the shredded chicken, finely chopped garlic, (bell) pepper slices, mushrooms, spring onions (scallions) and bean sprouts to the wok and stir-fry for about 5 minutes.

3 Drain the noodles thoroughly. Add the noodles to the wok, toss well and stir-fry for a further 5 minutes.

4 Drizzle the soy sauce and sesame oil over the chow mein and toss until well combined.

5 Transfer the chicken chow mein to warm serving bowls and serve immediately.

  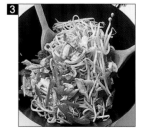

Garlic Pork & Noodles

This is a wonderful one-pot dish of stir-fried pork fillet with (small) shrimps and noodles that is made in minutes.

NUTRITIONAL INFORMATION

Calories ....424 Sugars 1g
Protein ....33g Fat 27g
Carbohydrate ...13g Saturates 5g

 5 MINS   15 MINS

SERVES 4

INGREDIENTS

250 g/9 oz packet medium egg noodles

3 tbsp vegetable oil

2 garlic cloves, crushed

350 g/12 oz pork fillet, cut into strips

4 tbsp/⅓ cup dried (small) shrimps, or 125 g/4½ oz peeled prawns (shrimp)

1 bunch spring onions (scallions), finely chopped

90 g/3 oz/¾ cup chopped roasted and shelled unsalted peanuts

3 tbsp fish sauce

1½ tsp palm or demerara (brown crystal) sugar

1-2 small red chillies, seeded and finely chopped (to taste)

3 tbsp lime juice

3 tbsp chopped fresh coriander (cilantro)

1 Place the noodles in a large pan of boiling water, then immediately remove from the heat. Cover and leave to stand for 6 minutes, stirring once halfway through the time. After 6 minutes the noodles will be perfectly cooked. Alternatively, follow the instructions on the packet. Drain and keep warm.

2 Heat the oil in a wok, add the garlic and pork and stir-fry until the pork strips are browned, about 2-3 minutes.

3 Add the dried (small) shrimps or shelled prawns (shrimp), spring onions (scallions), peanuts, fish sauce, palm or demerara (brown crystal) sugar, chillies to taste and lime juice. Stir-fry for a further 1 minute.

4 Add the cooked noodles and chopped fresh coriander (cilantro) and stir-fry until heated through, about 1 minute. Serve the stir-fry immediately.

COOK'S TIP

Fish sauce is made from pressed, salted fish and is widely available in super-markets and oriental stores. It is very salty, so no extra salt should be added.

Yellow Bean Noodles

Cellophane or thread noodles are excellent re-heated, unlike other noodles which must be served as soon as they are ready.

NUTRITIONAL INFORMATION

Calories	212	Sugars	.......0.5g
Protein	........28g	Fat	...........7g
Carbohydrate	...10g	Saturates	.......2g

5 MINS   30 MINS

SERVES 4

INGREDIENTS

175 g/6 oz cellophane noodles

1 tbsp peanut oil

1 leek, sliced

2 garlic cloves, crushed

450 g/1 lb minced (ground) chicken

425 ml/¾ pint/1 cup chicken stock

1 tsp chilli sauce

2 tbsp yellow bean sauce

4 tbsp light soy sauce

1 tsp sesame oil

chopped chives, to garnish

1 Place the cellophane noodles in a bowl, pour over boiling water and soak for 15 minutes.

COOK'S TIP

Cellophane noodles are available from many supermarkets and all Chinese supermarkets.

2 Drain the noodles thoroughly and cut into short lengths with a pair of kitchen scissors.

3 Heat the oil in a wok or frying pan (skillet) and stir-fry the leek and garlic for 30 seconds.

4 Add the chicken to the wok and stir-fry for 4-5 minutes, until the chicken is completely cooked through.

5 Add the chicken stock, chilli sauce, yellow bean sauce and soy sauce to the wok and cook for 3-4 minutes.

6 Add the drained noodles and sesame oil to the wok and cook, tossing to mix well, for 4-5 minutes.

7 Spoon the mixture into warm serving bowls, sprinkle with chopped chives and serve immediately.

Crispy Noodles & Tofu

This dish requires a certain amount of care and attention to get the crispy noodles properly cooked, but it is well worth the effort.

NUTRITIONAL INFORMATION

Calories 242	Sugars 2g
Protein 13g	Fat 17g
Carbohydrate . . .10g	Saturates 3g

 35 MINS   25 MINS

SERVES 4

INGREDIENTS

175 g/6 oz thread egg noodles

600 ml/1 pint/2½ cups sunflower oil, for deep-frying

2 tsp grated lemon peel

1 tbsp light soy sauce

1 tbsp rice vinegar

1 tbsp lemon juice

1½ tbsp sugar

250 g/9 oz/1 cup marinated tofu (bean curd), diced

2 garlic cloves, crushed

1 red chilli, sliced finely

1 red (bell) pepper, diced

4 eggs, beaten

red chilli flower, to garnish (see Cook's Tip page 269)

1 Blanch the egg noodles briefly in hot water, to which a little of the oil has been added. Drain the noodles and spread out to dry for at least 30 minutes. Cut into threads about 7 cm/3 inches long.

2 Combine the lemon peel, light soy sauce, rice vinegar, lemon juice and sugar in a small bowl. Set the mixture aside until required.

3 Heat the sunflower oil in a wok or large, heavy frying pan (skillet), and

test the temperature with a few strands of noodles. They should swell to many times their size, but if they do not, wait until the oil is hot enough; otherwise they will be tough and stringy, not puffy and light.

4 Cook the noodles in batches. As soon as they turn a pale gold colour, scoop them out and drain on plenty of absorbent kitchen paper (paper towels). Leave to cool.

5 Reserve 2 tablespoons of the oil and drain off the rest. Heat the reserved oil in the wok or pan (skillet).

6 Add the marinated tofu (bean curd) to the wok or frying pan (skillet) and cook quickly over a high heat to seal.

7 Add the crushed garlic cloves, sliced red chilli and diced red (bell) pepper to the wok. Stir-fry for 1–2 minutes.

8 Add the reserved vinegar mixture to the wok, stir to mix well and add the beaten eggs, stirring until they are set.

9 Serve the tofu (bean curd) mixture with the crispy fried noodles, garnished with a red chilli flower.

Twice-cooked Lamb

Here lamb is first boiled and then fried with soy sauce, oyster sauce and spinach and finally tossed with noodles for a richly flavoured dish.

NUTRITIONAL INFORMATION

Calories 315   Sugars 5g
Protein . . . . .27g   Fat 16g
Carbohydrate . . .16g   Saturates 6g

 5 MINS   30 MINS

SERVES 4

I N G R E D I E N T S

250 g/9 oz packet egg noodles

450 g/1 lb lamb loin fillet,
   thinly sliced

2 tbsp soy sauce

2 tbsp sunflower oil

2 cloves garlic, crushed

1 tbsp caster (superfine) sugar

2 tbsp oyster sauce

175 g/6 oz baby spinach

1 Place the egg noodles in a large bowl and cover with boiling water. Leave to soak for about 10 minutes.

2 Bring a large saucepan of water to the boil. Add the lamb and cook for 5 minutes. Drain thoroughly.

3 Place the slices of lamb in a bowl and mix with the soy sauce and 1 tablespoon of the sunflower oil.

4 Heat the remaining sunflower oil in a large preheated wok, swirling the oil around until it is really hot.

5 Add the marinated lamb and crushed garlic to the wok and stir-fry for about 5 minutes or until the meat is just beginning to brown.

6 Add the caster (superfine) sugar and oyster sauce to the wok and stir well to combine.

7 Drain the noodles thoroughly. Add the noodles to the wok and stir-fry for a further 5 minutes.

8 Add the spinach to the wok and cook for 1 minute or until the leaves just wilt. Transfer the lamb and noodles to serving bowls and serve hot.

COOK'S TIP

If using dried noodles, follow the instructions on the packet as they require less soaking.

Quick Chicken Noodles

Chicken and fresh vegetables are flavoured with ginger and Chinese five-spice powder in this speedy stir-fry.

10 MINS   15 MINS

SERVES 4

INGREDIENTS

175 g/6 oz Chinese thread egg noodles

2 tbsp sesame or vegetable oil

25 g/1 oz/¼ cup peanuts

1 bunch spring onions (scallions), sliced

1 green (bell) pepper, deseeded and cut into thin strips

1 large carrot, cut into matchsticks

125 g/4½ oz cauliflower, broken into small florets

350 g/12 oz skinless, boneless chicken, cut into strips

250 g/9 oz mushrooms, sliced

1 tsp finely grated ginger root

1 tsp Chinese five-spice powder

1 tbsp chopped fresh coriander (cilantro)

1 tbsp light soy sauce

salt and pepper

fresh chives, to garnish

1 Put the noodles in a large bowl and cover with boiling water. Leave to soak for 6 minutes.

2 Heat the oil in a wok and stir-fry the peanuts for 1 minute until browned. Remove from the wok and leave to drain.

3 Add the spring onions (scallions), (bell) pepper, carrot, cauliflower and chicken to the pan. Stir-fry over a high heat for 4–5 minutes.

4 Drain the noodles thoroughly and add to the wok. Add the mushrooms and stir-fry for 2 minutes. Add the ginger, five-spice and coriander (cilantro); stir-fry for 1 minute.

5 Season with soy sauce and salt and pepper. Sprinkle with the peanuts, garnish and serve.

VARIATION

Instead of ginger root, ½ teaspoon ground ginger can be used.

Vary the vegetables according to what is in season. Make the most of bargains bought from your greengrocer or market.

Oyster Sauce Noodles

Chicken and noodles are cooked and then tossed in an oyster sauce and egg mixture in this delicious recipe.

NUTRITIONAL INFORMATION

Calories . . . . . . .278 Sugars 2g
Protein . . . . .30g Fat 12g
Carbohydrate . . .13g Saturates 3g

5 MINS   25 MINS

SERVES 4

I N G R E D I E N T S

250 g/9 oz egg noodles

450 g/1 lb chicken thighs

2 tbsp groundnut oil

100 g/3½ oz carrots, sliced

3 tbsp oyster sauce

2 eggs

3 tbsp cold water

1 Place the egg noodles in a large bowl or dish. Pour enough boiling water over the noodles to cover and leave to stand for 10 minutes.

2 Meanwhile, remove the skin from the chicken thighs. Cut the chicken flesh into small pieces, using a sharp knife.

VARIATION

Flavour the eggs with soy sauce or hoisin sauce as an alternative to the oyster sauce, if you prefer.

3 Heat the groundnut oil in a large preheated wok or frying pan (skillet), swirling the oil around the base of the wok until it is really hot.

4 Add the pieces of chicken and the carrot slices to the wok and stir-fry for about 5 minutes.

5 Drain the noodles thoroughly. Add the noodles to the wok and stir-fry for a

further 2–3 minutes or until the noodles are heated through.

6 Beat together the oyster sauce, eggs and 3 tablespoons of cold water. Drizzle the mixture over the noodles and stir-fry for a further 2–3 minutes or until the eggs set.

7 Transfer the mixture in the wok to warm serving bowls and serve hot.

Satay Noodles

Rice noodles and vegetables are tossed in a crunchy peanut and chilli sauce for a quick satay-flavoured recipe.

NUTRITIONAL INFORMATION

Calories 281   Sugars 7g
Protein . . . . .9g   Fat 20g
Carbohydrate . . .18g   Saturates 4g

5 MINS   20 MINS

SERVES 4

I N G R E D I E N T S

275 g/9½ oz rice sticks (wide, flat rice noodles)

3 tbsp groundnut oil

2 cloves garlic, crushed

2 shallots, sliced

225 g/8 oz green beans, sliced

100 g/3¾ oz cherry tomatoes, halved

1 tsp chilli flakes

4 tbsp crunchy peanut butter

150 ml/¼ pint/⅔ cup coconut milk

1 tbsp tomato purée (paste)

sliced spring onions (scallions), to garnish

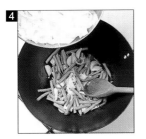

1 Place the rice sticks (wide, flat rice noodles) in a large bowl and pour over enough boiling water to cover. Leave to stand for 10 minutes.

2 Heat the groundnut oil in a large preheated wok or heavy-based frying pan (skillet).

3 Add the crushed garlic and sliced shallots to the wok or frying pan (skillet) and stir-fry for 1 minute.

4 Drain the rice sticks (wide, flat rice noodles) thoroughly. Add the green beans and drained noodles to the wok or frying pan (skillet) and stir-fry for about 5 minutes.

5 Add the cherry tomatoes to the wok and mix well.

6 Mix together the chilli flakes, peanut butter, coconut milk and tomato purée (paste).

7 Pour the chilli mixture over the noodles, toss well until all the ingredients are thoroughly combined and heat through.

8 Transfer the satay noodles to warm serving dishes and garnish with spring onion (scallion) slices and serve immediately.

Curried Rice Noodles

Rice noodles or vermicelli are also known as rice sticks. The ideal meat to use in this dish is Barbecue Pork (see page 115).

NUTRITIONAL INFORMATION

Calories	223	Sugars	.........2g
Protein	........15g	Fat	..........13g
Carbohydrate	....11g	Saturates	.......2g

15 MINS   15 MINS

SERVES 4

I N G R E D I E N T S

200 g/7 oz rice vermicelli

125 g/4½ oz cooked chicken or pork

60 g/2 oz peeled prawns (shrimp), defrosted if frozen

4 tbsp vegetable oil

1 medium onion, thinly shredded

125 g/4¼ oz fresh bean sprouts

1 tsp salt

1 tbsp mild curry powder

2 tbsp light soy sauce

2 spring onions (scallions), thinly shredded

1-2 small fresh green or red chilli peppers, seeded and thinly shredded

1 Soak the rice vermicelli in boiling water for about 8-10 minutes, then rinse in cold water and drain well. Set aside until required.

2 Using a sharp knife or meat cleaver, thinly slice the cooked meat.

3 Dry the prawns (shrimp) on absorbent kitchen paper (paper towels).

4 Heat the vegetable oil in a preheated wok or large frying pan (skillet).

5 Add the shredded onion to the wok or pan and stir-fry until opaque. Add the bean sprouts and stir-fry for 1 minute.

6 Add the drained noodles with the meat and prawns (shrimp), and continue stirring for another minute.

7 Mix together the salt, curry powder and soy sauce in a little bowl.

8 Blend the sauce mixture into the wok, followed by the spring onions (scallions) and chilli peppers. Stir-fry for one more minute, then serve immediately.

COOK'S TIP

Rice noodles are very delicate noodles made from rice flour. They become soft and pliable after being soaked for about 15 minutes. If you wish to store them after they have been soaked, toss them in a few drops of sesame oil then place them in a sealed container in the refrigerator.

Hot & Crispy Noodles

These crispy noodles will add a delicious crunch to your Chinese meal.
They can be served as a side dish or as an appetizer for people to share.

NUTRITIONAL INFORMATION

Calories 104   Sugars 0.3g
Protein . . . . .2g   Fat 6g
Carbohydrate . . . .11g   Saturates 1g

 5 MINS   🕐 15 MINS

SERVES 4

I N G R E D I E N T S

250 g/9 oz rice noodles

oil, for deep-frying

2 garlic cloves, chopped finely

8 spring onions (scallions), trimmed and
    chopped finely

1 small red or green chilli, deseeded and
    chopped finely

2 tbsp fish sauce

2 tbsp light soy sauce

2 tbsp lime or lemon juice

2 tbsp molasses sugar

TO GARNISH

spring onions (scallions), shredded

cucumber, sliced thinly

fresh chillies

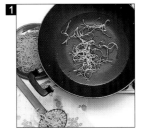

1 Break the noodles into smaller pieces with your hands. Heat the oil for deep-frying in a wok or large frying pan (skillet) and fry small batches of the noodles until pale golden brown and puffed up. Lift the noodles out with a perforated spoon and leave to drain on kitchen paper (paper towels).

2 When all of the noodles are cooked, pour off the oil, leaving 3 tbsp in the wok. Add the garlic, spring onions (scallions) and chilli, and stir-fry for 2 minutes.

3 Mix together the fish sauce, soy sauce, lime or lemon juice and sugar. Add to the wok or frying pan (skillet) and cook for 2 minutes, until the sugar has dissolved. Tip all the noodles back into the wok and toss lightly to coat with the sauce mixture.

4 Serve the noodles garnished with shredded spring onions (scallions), thinly sliced cucumber and chillies.

VARIATION

Stir-fry some uncooked peeled prawns (shrimp) or chopped raw chicken with the spring onions (scallions) and garlic in step 2. Cook for an extra 3–4 minutes to make sure they are thoroughly cooked.

Chicken on Crispy Noodles

Blanched noodles are fried in the wok until crisp and brown, and then topped with a shredded chicken sauce for a delightfully tasty dish.

NUTRITIONAL INFORMATION

Calories	376	Sugars	.........2g
Protein	........15g	Fat	..........27g
Carbohydrate	...17g	Saturates	.......4g

 35 MINS   25 MINS

SERVES 4

I N G R E D I E N T S

225 g/8 oz skinless, boneless chicken breasts, shredded

1 egg white

5 tsp cornflour (cornstarch)

225 g/8 oz thin egg noodles

300 ml/½ pint/1⅓ cups vegetable oil

600 ml/1 pint/2½ cups chicken stock

2 tbsp dry sherry

2 tbsp oyster sauce

1 tbsp light soy sauce

1 tbsp hoisin sauce

1 red (bell) pepper, seeded and very thinly sliced

2 tbsp water

3 spring onions (scallions), chopped

1 Mix together the chicken, egg white and 2 teaspoons of the cornflour (cornstarch) in a bowl. Leave to stand for at least 30 minutes.

2 Blanch the noodles in boiling water for 2 minutes, then drain thoroughly.

3 Heat the vegetable oil in a preheated wok. Add the noodles, spreading them to cover the base of the wok. Cook over a low heat for about 5 minutes, until the noodles are browned on the underside.

Flip the noodles over and brown on the other side. Remove from the wok when crisp and browned, place on a serving plate and keep warm. Drain the oil from the wok.

4 Add 300 ml/½ pint/1¼ cups of the chicken stock to the wok. Remove from the heat and add the chicken, stirring well so that it does not stick. Return to the heat and cook for 2 minutes. Drain, discarding the stock.

5 Wipe the wok with kitchen paper (paper towels) and return to the heat. Add the sherry, sauces, (bell) pepper and the remaining stock and bring to the boil. Blend the remaining cornflour (cornstarch) with the water and stir it into the mixture.

6 Return the chicken to the wok and cook over a low heat for 2 minutes. Place the chicken on top of the noodles and sprinkle with spring onions (scallions).

Chilli Pork Noodles

This is quite a spicy dish, with a delicious peanut flavour. Increase or reduce the amount of chilli to your liking.

NUTRITIONAL INFORMATION

Calories . . . . .421 Sugars 3g
Protein . . . . .27g Fat 26g
Carbohydrate . . .20g Saturates 6g

35 MINS   10 MINS

SERVES 4

INGREDIENTS

350 g/12 oz minced (ground) pork

1 tbsp light soy sauce

1 tbsp dry sherry

350 g/12 oz egg noodles

2 tsp sesame oil

2 tbsp vegetable oil

2 garlic cloves, crushed

2 tsp grated fresh root ginger

2 fresh red chillies, sliced

1 red (bell) pepper, seeded and finely sliced

25 g/1 oz/¼ cup unsalted peanuts

3 tbsp peanut butter

3 tbsp dark soy sauce

dash of chilli oil

300 ml/½ pint/1¼ cups pork stock

1 Mix together the pork, light soy sauce and dry sherry in a large bowl. Cover and leave to marinate for 30 minutes.

2 Meanwhile, cook the noodles in a saucepan of boiling water for 4 minutes. Drain well, rinse in cold water and drain again. Toss the noodles in the sesame oil.

3 Heat the vegetable oil in a preheated wok and stir-fry the garlic, ginger, chillies and (bell) pepper for 30 seconds.

4 Add the pork to the mixture in the wok, together with the marinade. Continue cooking for about 1 minute, until the pork is sealed.

5 Add the peanuts, peanut butter, soy sauce, chilli oil and stock and cook for 2-3 minutes.

6 Toss the noodles in the mixture and serve at once.

VARIATION

Minced (ground) chicken or lamb would also be excellent in this recipe instead of the pork.

Curried Prawn Noodles

Athough these noodles are almost a meal in themselves, if served as an accompaniment, they are ideal with plain vegetable or fish dishes.

NUTRITIONAL INFORMATION

Calories	246	Sugars	.........1g
Protein	........17g	Fat	..........14g
Carbohydrate	...14g	Saturates	.......2g

5 MINS   15 MINS

SERVES 4

I N G R E D I E N T S

225 g/8 oz rice noodles

4 tbsp vegetable oil

1 onion, sliced

2 ham slices, shredded

2 tbsp Chinese curry powder

150 ml/¼ pint/⅔ cups fish stock

225 g/8 oz peeled, raw prawns (shrimp)

2 garlic cloves, crushed

6 spring onions (scallions), chopped

1 tbsp light soy sauce

2 tbsp hoisin sauce

1 tbsp dry sherry

2 tsp lime juice

fresh snipped chives, to garnish

COOK'S TIP

Hoisin sauce is made from soy beans, sugar, flour, vinegar, salt, garlic, chilli and sesame seed oil. Sold in cans or jars, it will keep in the refrigerator for several months.

1 Cook the noodles in a pan of boiling water for 3-4 minutes. Drain well, rinse under cold water and drain again.

2 Heat 2 tablespoons of the oil in a wok. Add the onion and ham and stir-fry for 1 minute. Add the curry powder and stir-fry for a further 30 seconds.

3 Stir the noodles and fish stock into the wok and cook for 2-3 minutes.

Remove the noodles from the wok and keep warm.

4 Heat the remaining oil in the wok. Add the prawns (shrimp), garlic and spring onions (scallions) and stir-fry for about 1 minute.

5 Stir in the remaining ingredients. Pour the mixture over the noodles, toss to mix and garnish with fresh chives.

Chilled Noodles & Peppers

This is a convenient dish to serve when you are arriving home just before family or friends. Quick to prepare and assemble, it is ready in minutes.

NUTRITIONAL INFORMATION

Calories	260	Sugars	.........4g
Protein	.........4g	Fat	..........21g
Carbohydrate	...15g	Saturates	.......4g

5 MINS   15 MINS

SERVES 4–6

INGREDIENTS

250 g/9 oz ribbon noodles, or Chinese egg noodles

1 tbsp sesame oil

1 red (bell) pepper

1 yellow (bell) pepper

1 green (bell) pepper

6 spring onions (scallions), cut into matchstick strips

salt

DRESSING

5 tbsp sesame oil

2 tbsp light soy sauce

1 tbsp tahini (sesame seed paste)

4-5 drops hot pepper sauce

1 Preheat the grill (broiler) to medium. Cook the noodles in a large pan of boiling, salted water until they are almost tender. Drain them in a colander, run cold water through them and drain thoroughly. Tip the noodles into a bowl, stir in the sesame oil, cover and chill.

2 Cook the (bell) peppers under the grill (broiler), turning them frequently, until they are blackened on all sides. Plunge into cold water, then skin them. Cut in half, remove the core and seeds and cut the flesh into thick strips. Set aside in a covered container.

3 To make the dressing, mix together the sesame oil, light soy sauce, tahini (sesame seed paste) and hot pepper sauce until well combined.

4 Pour the dressing on the noodles, reserving 1 tablespoon, and toss well. Turn the noodles into a serving dish, arrange the grilled (bell) peppers over the noodles and spoon on the reserved dressing. Scatter on the spring onion (scallion) strips.

COOK'S TIP

If you have time, another way of skinning (bell) peppers is to first grill (broil) them, then place in a plastic bag, seal and leave for about 20 minutes. The skin will then peel off easily.

Desserts

Desserts are rarely eaten in ordinary Chinese households except on special occasions. Sweet dishes are usually served as snacks between main meals, but fresh fruit is considered to be very refreshing at the end of a meal. The recipes in this chapter are adaptations of Imperial recipes or use Chinese cooking methods and ingredients to

produce mouthwatering desserts that round off any meal perfectly. There are delicious dinner party desserts which look as good as they taste, pastries which can be eaten as a tea-time snack

and a selection of refreshing fruit salads. Among the recipes to choose from are Sweet Fruit Wontons in which a sweet date filling is sealed in wonton wrappers and laced with honey, or Battered Bananas in which pieces of banana are deep-fried and then sprinkled with brown sugar.

Sweet Fruit Wontons

These sweet wontons are very adaptable and may be filled with whole, small fruits or a spicy chopped mixture as here.

NUTRITIONAL INFORMATION

Calories . . . . . . .244 Sugars 25g
Protein . . . . .2g Fat 12g
Carbohydrate . . .35g Saturates 3g

10 MINS   15 MINS

SERVES 4

I N G R E D I E N T S

12 wonton wrappers

2 tsp cornflour (cornstarch)

6 tsp cold water

oil, for deep-frying

2 tbsp clear honey

selection of fresh fruit (such as kiwi fruit, limes, oranges, mango and apples), sliced, to serve

F I L L I N G

175 g/6 oz/1 cup chopped dried, stoned (pitted) dates

2 tsp dark brown sugar

½ tsp ground cinnamon

1 To make the filling, mix together the dates, sugar and cinnamon in a bowl.

2 Spread out the wonton wrappers on a chopping board and spoon a little of the filling into the centre of each wrapper.

COOK'S TIP

Wonton wrappers may be found in Chinese supermarkets. Alternatively, make 1 quantity of the dough used for Shrimp Dumpling Soup (see page 51).

3 Blend the cornflour (cornstarch) and water and brush this mixture around the edges of the wrappers.

4 Fold the wrappers over the filling, bringing the edges together, then bring the two corners together, sealing with the cornflour (cornstarch) mixture.

5 Heat the oil for deep-frying in a wok to 180°C/350°F, or until a cube of bread browns in 30 seconds. Fry the wontons, in batches, for 2–3 minutes, until golden. Remove the wontons from the oil with a slotted spoon and leave to drain on absorbent kitchen paper (paper towels).

6 Place the honey in a bowl and stand it in warm water, to soften it slightly. Drizzle the honey over the sweet fruit wontons and serve with a selection of fresh fruit.

Mango Mousse

This is a light, softly set and tangy mousse, which is perfect for clearing the palate after a Chinese meal of mixed flavours.

NUTRITIONAL INFORMATION

Calories 346   Sugars 27g
Protein . . . . .7g   Fat 24g
Carbohydrate . . .27g   Saturates 15g

🍲 40 MINS   🕐 0 MINS

SERVES 4

I N G R E D I E N T S

400 g/14 oz can mangoes in syrup

2 pieces stem (preserved) ginger, chopped

200 ml/7 fl oz/1 cup double (heavy) cream

20 g/¾ oz/4 tsp powdered gelatine

2 tbsp hot water

2 egg whites

1½ tbsp light brown sugar

stem (preserved) ginger and lime zest, to decorate

1 Drain the mangoes, reserving the syrup. Blend the mango pieces and ginger in a food processor or blender for 30 seconds, or until smooth.

2 Measure the purée and make up to 300 ml/½ pint/1¼ cups with the reserved mango syrup.

3 In a separate bowl, whip the cream until it forms soft peaks. Fold the mango mixture into the cream until well combined.

4 Dissolve the gelatine in the hot water and leave to cool slightly.

5 Pour the gelatine into the mango mixture in a steady stream, stirring.

Leave to cool in the refrigerator for 30 minutes, until almost set.

6 Beat the egg whites in a clean bowl until they form soft peaks, then beat in the sugar. Gently fold the egg whites into the mango mixture with a metal spoon.

7 Spoon the mousse into individual serving dishes, decorate with stem (preserved) ginger and lime zest and serve.

COOK'S TIP

The gelatine must be stirred into the mango mixture in a gentle, steady stream to prevent it from setting in lumps when it comes into contact with the cold mixture.

Lychees With Orange Sorbet

This dish is truly delicious! The fresh flavour of the sorbet perfectly complements the spicy lychees.

NUTRITIONAL INFORMATION

Calories . . . . .313 Sugars 82g
Protein . . . . .1g Fat 0g
Carbohydrate . . .82g Saturates 0g

  10½ HOURS   5 MINS

SERVES 4

INGREDIENTS

SORBET

225 g/8 oz/¼ cups caster (superfine)
   sugar

425 ml/¾ pint/2 cups cold water

350 g/12 oz can mandarins,
   in natural juice

2 tbsp lemon juice

STUFFED LYCHEES

425 g/15 oz can lychees, drained

60 g/2 oz stem (preserved) ginger,
   drained and finely chopped

lime zest, cut into diamond shapes,
   to decorate

1 To make the sorbet, place the sugar and water in a saucepan and stir over a low heat until the sugar has dissolved. Bring the mixture to the boil and boil vigorously for 2-3 minutes.

2 Blend the mandarins in a food processor or blender until smooth. Press the purée through a sieve then stir into the syrup, together with the lemon juice. Set aside to cool. Once cooled, pour the mixture into a rigid, plastic container and freeze until set, stirring occasionally.

3 Meanwhile, drain the lychees on absorbent kitchen paper (paper towels). Spoon the chopped ginger into the centre of the lychees.

4 Arrange the lychees on serving plates and serve with scoops of orange sorbet. Decorate with lime zest.

COOK'S TIP

It is best to leave the sorbet in the refrigerator for 10 minutes, so that it softens slightly, allowing you to scoop it to serve.

Exotic Fruit Pancakes

These pancakes are filled with an exotic array of tropical fruits. Decorate lavishly with tropical flowers or mint sprigs.

NUTRITIONAL INFORMATION

Calories 382   Sugars 24g
Protein ....7g   Fat 17g
Carbohydrate ...53g   Saturates 3g

 40 MINS   35 MINS

SERVES 4

INGREDIENTS

BATTER

125 g/4½ oz/1 cup plain flour

pinch of salt

1 egg

1 egg yolk

300 ml/½ pint/1¼ cups coconut milk

4 tsp vegetable oil, plus oil for frying

FILLING

1 banana

1 paw-paw (papaya)

juice of 1 lime

2 passion fruit

1 mango, peeled, stoned and sliced

4 lychees, stoned and halved

1-2 tbsp honey

flowers or mint sprigs, to decorate

1 Sift the flour and salt into a bowl. Make a well in the centre and add the egg, egg yolk and a little of the coconut milk. Gradually draw the flour into the egg mixture, beating well and slowly adding the remaining coconut milk to make a smooth batter. Stir in the oil. Cover and chill for 30 minutes.

2 Peel and slice the banana and place in a bowl. Peel and slice the paw-paw (papaya), discarding the seeds. Add to the banana with the lime juice and mix well. Cut the passion-fruit in half and scoop out the flesh and seeds into the fruit bowl. Stir in the mango, lychees and honey.

3 Heat a little oil in a 15 cm/6 inch frying pan (skillet). Pour in just enough of the pancake batter to cover the base of the pan and tilt so that it spreads thinly and evenly. Cook until the pancake is just set and the underside is lightly browned, turn and briefly cook the other side. Remove from the pan and keep warm. Repeat with the remaining batter to make a total of 8 pancakes.

4 To serve, place a little of the prepared fruit filling along the centre of each pancake and then roll it into a cone shape. Lay seam-side down on warmed serving plates, decorate with flowers or mint sprigs and serve.

Mango & Passion-fruit Salad

The rich Mascarpone Cream which accompanies the exotic fruit salad gives this Chinese dessert an Italian twist.

NUTRITIONAL INFORMATION

Calories 211   Sugars 18g
Protein . . . . .6g   Fat 10g
Carbohydrate . . .18g   Saturates 6g

    1¼ HOURS   0 MINS

SERVES 4

I N G R E D I E N T S

1 large mango

2 oranges

4 passion-fruit

2 tbsp orange-flavoured liqueur such as Grand Marnier

mint or geranium leaves, to decorate

M A S C A R P O N E   C R E A M

125 g/4½ oz/½ cup Mascarpone cheese

1 tbsp clear honey

4 tbsp thick, natural (unsweetened) yogurt

few drops vanilla flavouring (extract)

1 Using a sharp knife, cut the mango in half lengthwise as close to the stone (pit) as possible. Remove the stone (pit), using a sharp knife.

2 Peel off the mango skin, cut the flesh into slices and place into a large bowl.

3 Peel the oranges, removing all the pith, and cut into segments. Add to the bowl with any juices.

4 Halve the passion-fruit, scoop out the flesh and add to the bowl with the orange-flavoured liqueur. Mix together all the ingredients in the bowl.

5 Cover the bowl with cling film (plastic wrap) and chill in the refrigerator for 1 hour. Turn into glass serving dishes.

6 To make the Mascarpone cream, blend the Mascarpone cheese and honey together. Stir in the natural (unsweetened) yogurt and vanilla flavouring (extract) until thoroughly blended.

7 Serve the fruit salad with the Mascarpone cream, decorated with mint or geranium leaves.

COOK'S TIP

Passion-fruit are ready to eat when their skins are well dimpled. They are most readily available in the summer. Substitute guava or pineapple for the passion-fruit, if you prefer.

Baked Coconut Rice Pudding

A wonderful baked rice pudding cooked with flavoursome coconut milk and a little lime rind. Serve hot or chilled with fresh or stewed fruit.

NUTRITIONAL INFORMATION

Calories 211	Sugars 27g
Protein 5g	Fat 2g
Carbohydrate . . .46g	Saturates 1g

 5 MINS   2¹/₂ HOURS

SERVES 4–6

I N G R E D I E N T S

90 g/3 oz/scant ⅓ cup short or round-grain pudding rice

600 ml/1 pint/2½ cups coconut milk

300 ml/½ pint/1¼ cups milk

1 large strip lime rind

60 g/2 oz/¼ cup caster (superfine) sugar

knob of butter

pinch of ground star anise (optional)

fresh or stewed fruit, to serve

1 Lightly grease a 1.4 litre/2¹/₂ pint shallow ovenproof dish.

2 Mix the pudding rice with the coconut milk, milk, lime rind and caster (superfine) sugar until all the ingredients are well blended.

3 Pour the rice mixture into the greased ovenproof dish and dot the surface with a little butter. Bake in the oven for about 30 minutes.

4 Remove the dish from the oven. Remove and discard the strip of lime from the rice pudding.

5 Stir the pudding well, add the pinch of ground star anise, if using, return to the oven and cook for a further 1-2

hours or until almost all the milk has been absorbed and a golden brown skin has baked on the top of the pudding.

6 Cover the top of the pudding with foil if it starts to brown too much towards the end of the cooking time.

7 Serve the baked coconut rice pudding warm, or chilled if you prefer, with fresh or stewed fruit.

COOK'S TIP

As the mixture cools it thickens. If you plan to serve the rice chilled then fold in about 3 tablespoons cream or extra coconut milk before serving to give a thinner consistency.

Passion-Fruit Rice

This creamy rice pudding, adapted for the microwave, is spiced with cardamom, cinnamon and bay leaf and served with passion-fruit.

NUTRITIONAL INFORMATION

Calories ....534 Sugars 42g
Protein ....9g Fat 22g
Carbohydrate ...80g Saturates 13g

1¼ HOURS   30 MINS

SERVES 4

INGREDIENTS

175 g/6 oz/scant 1 cup jasmine fragrant rice

600 ml/1 pint/2½ cups milk

125 g/4½ oz/½ cup caster (superfine) sugar

6 cardamom pods, split open

1 dried bay leaf

1 cinnamon stick

150 ml/¼ pint/⅔ cup double (heavy) cream, whipped

4 passion-fruit

soft berry fruits, to decorate

1 Place the jasmine fragrant rice in a large bowl with the milk, caster (superfine) sugar, cardamom pods, bay leaf and cinnamon stick. Cover and cook on medium power for 25–30 minutes, stirring occasionally. The rice should be just tender

and have absorbed most of the milk. Add a little extra milk, if necessary.

2 Leave the rice to cool, still covered. Remove the bay leaf, cardamom husks and cinnamon stick.

3 Gently fold the cream into the cooled rice mixture.

4 Halve the passion-fruits and scoop out the centres into a bowl.

5 Layer the rice with the passion-fruit in 4 tall glasses, finishing with a layer of passion-fruit. Leave to chill in the refrigerator for 30 minutes.

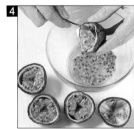

6 Decorate the passion-fruit rice with soft berry fruits and serve immediately.

COOK'S TIP

If you are unable to obtain passion-fruit, you can use a purée of another fruit of your choice, such as kiwi fruit, raspberry or strawberry.

Chinese Fruit Salad

The syrup for this colourful dish is filled with Chinese flavours for a refreshing dessert.

NUTRITIONAL INFORMATION

Calories	405	Sugars	.......81g
Protein	.........3g	Fat	...........6g
Carbohydrate	...83g	Saturates	.......1g

1¾ HOURS   10 MINS

SERVES 4

I N G R E D I E N T S

75 ml/3 fl oz Chinese rice wine or dry sherry

rind and juice of 1 lemon

850 ml/1½ pints water

225 g/8 oz caster (superfine) sugar

2 cloves

2.5-cm/1-inch piece cinnamon stick, bruised

1 vanilla pod (bean)

pinch of mixed (apple pie) spice

1 star anise pod

2.5-cm/1-inch piece fresh ginger root, sliced

50 g/1¾ oz unsalted cashew nuts

2 kiwi fruits

1 star fruit

115 g/4 oz strawberries

400 g/14 oz can lychees in syrup, drained

1 piece stem (preserved) ginger, drained and sliced

chopped mint, to decorate

1 Put the Chinese rice wine or sherry, lemon rind and juice and water in a saucepan.

2 Add the caster (superfine) sugar, cloves, cinnamon stick, vanilla pod (bean), mixed (apple pie) spice, star anise and fresh ginger root to the saucepan.

3 Heat the mixture in the pan gently, stirring constantly, until the sugar has dissolved and then bring to the boil. Reduce the heat and simmer for 5 minutes. Set aside to cool completely.

4 Strain the syrup, discarding the flavourings. Stir in the cashew nuts, cover with cling film (plastic wrap) and chill in the refrigerator.

5 Meanwhile, prepare the fruits: halve and slice the kiwi fruit, slice the star fruit, and hull and slice the strawberries.

6 Spoon the prepared fruit into a dish with the lychees and ginger. Stir through gently to mix.

7 Pour the syrup over the fruit, decorate with chopped mint and serve.

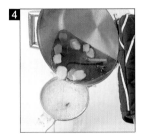

Banana Pastries

These pastries require a little time to prepare, but are well worth the effort. A sweet banana filling is wrapped in dough and baked.

NUTRITIONAL INFORMATION

Calories . . . . . . .745 Sugars 24g
Protein . . . . .13g Fat 30g
Carbohydrate . . .112g Saturates 15g

  45 MINS   25 MINS

SERVES 4

I N G R E D I E N T S

D O U G H

450 g/1 lb/4 cups plain (all-purpose) flour

60 g/2 oz/4 tbsp lard (shortening)

60 g/2 oz/4 tbsp unsalted butter

125 ml/4 fl oz/½ cup water

F I L L I N G

2 large bananas

75 g/2¾ oz/⅓ cup finely chopped
    no-need-to-soak dried apricots

pinch of nutmeg

dash of orange juice

1 egg yolk, beaten

icing (confectioners') sugar, for dusting

cream or ice cream, to serve

VARIATION

Use a fruit filling of your choice, such as apple or plum, as an alternative.

1 To make the dough, sift the flour into a large mixing bowl. Add the lard (shortening) and butter and rub into the flour with the fingertips until the mixture resembles breadcrumbs. Gradually blend in the water to make a soft dough. Wrap in cling film (plastic wrap) and chill in the refrigerator for 30 minutes.

2 Mash the bananas in a bowl with a fork and stir in the apricots, nutmeg and orange juice, mixing well.

3 Roll the dough out on a lightly floured surface and cut out 16 x 10-cm/4-inch rounds.

4 Spoon a little of the banana filling on to one half of each round and fold the dough over the filling to make semi-circles. Pinch the edges together and seal by pressing with the prongs of a fork.

5 Arrange the pastries on a non-stick baking tray (cookie sheet) and brush them with the beaten egg yolk. Cut a small slit in each pastry and cook in a preheated oven, 180°C/350°F/Gas 4, for about 25 minutes, or until golden brown.

6 Dust the banana pastries with icing (confectioners') sugar and serve with cream or ice cream.

Fruit Salad with Ginger Syrup

This is a very special fruit salad made from the most exotic and colourful fruits that are soaked in a syrup made with fresh ginger and ginger wine.

NUTRITIONAL INFORMATION

Calories 225   Sugars 45g
Protein . . . . .2g   Fat 4g
Carbohydrate . . .45g   Saturates 3g

 4¹/₂ HOURS 5 MINS

SERVES 4

INGREDIENTS

2.5 cm/1 inch ginger root, peeled and chopped

60 g/2 oz/¼ cup caster sugar

150 ml/¼ pint/⅔ cup water

grated rind and juice of 1 lime

4 tbsp/⅓ cup ginger wine

1 fresh pineapple, peeled, cored and cut into bite-sized pieces

2 ripe mangoes, peeled, stoned and diced

4 kiwi fruit, peeled and sliced

1 paw-paw (papaya), peeled, seeded and diced

2 passion-fruit, halved and flesh removed

350 g/12 oz lychees, peeled and stoned

¼ fresh coconut, grated

60 g/2 oz Cape gooseberries, to decorate (optional)

coconut ice-cream, to serve (optional)

 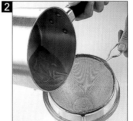 

1 Place the ginger, sugar, water and lime juice in a pan and bring slowly to the boil. Simmer for 1 minute, remove from the heat and allow to cool slightly.

2 Sieve (strain) the syrup, add the ginger wine and mix well. Cool completely.

3 Place the prepared fruit in a serving bowl. Add the cold syrup and mix well. Cover and chill in the refrigerator for 2–4 hours.

4 Just before serving, add half of the grated coconut to the salad and mix well. Sprinkle the remainder on top.

5 If using Cape gooseberries to decorate the salad, peel back each calyx to form a flower. Wipe the berries clean, then arrange them around the side of the fruit salad before serving.

COOK'S TIP

Despite their name, Cape gooseberries are golden in colour and more similar in appearance to ground cherries. They make a delightful decoration to many fruit-based desserts.

Honeyed Rice Puddings

These small rice puddings are quite sweet, but have a wonderful flavour because of the combination of ginger, honey and cinnamon.

NUTRITIONAL INFORMATION

Calories	199	Sugars	........15g
Protein	.........3g	Fat	...........1g
Carbohydrate	...46g	Saturates	.......0g

  10 MINS 50 MINS

SERVES 4

INGREDIENTS

300 g/10½ oz/1½ cups pudding rice

2 tbsp clear honey, plus extra
    for drizzling

large pinch of ground cinnamon

15 no-need-to-soak dried apricots,
    chopped

3 pieces stem (preserved) ginger, drained
    and chopped

8 whole no-need-to-soak dried apricots,
    to decorate

1 Put the rice in a saucepan and just cover with cold water. Bring to the boil, reduce the heat, cover and cook for about 15 minutes, or until the water has been absorbed. Stir the honey and cinnamon into the rice.

2 Grease 4 x 150 ml/¼ pint/⅔ cup ramekin dishes.

3 Blend the chopped dried apricots and ginger in a food processor to make a smooth paste.

4 Divide the paste into 4 equal portions and shape each into a flat round to fit into the base of the ramekin dishes.

5 Divide half of the rice between the ramekin dishes and place the apricot paste on top.

6 Cover the apricot paste with the remaining rice. Cover the ramekins with greaseproof (wax) paper and foil and steam for 30 minutes, or until set.

7 Remove the ramekins from the steamer and let stand for 5 minutes.

8 Turn the puddings out on to warm serving plates and drizzle with honey. Decorate with dried apricots and serve.

COOK'S TIP

The puddings may be left to chill in their ramekin dishes in the refrigerator, then turned out and served with ice cream or cream.

Green Fruit Salad

This delightfully refreshing fruit salad is the perfect finale for a Chinese meal. It has a lovely light syrup made with fresh mint and honey.

NUTRITIONAL INFORMATION

Calories 157	Sugars 34g
Protein 1g	Fat 0.2g
Carbohydrate ...34g	Saturates 0g

30 MINS   15 MINS

SERVES 4

I N G R E D I E N T S

1 small Charentais or honeydew melon

2 green apples

2 kiwi fruit

125 g/4½ oz/1 cup seedless white grapes

fresh mint sprigs, to decorate

S Y R U P

1 lemon

150 ml/¼ pint/⅔ cup white wine

150 ml/¼ pint/⅔ cup water

4 tbsp clear honey

few sprigs of fresh mint

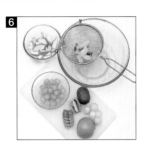

1 To make the syrup, pare the rind from the lemon using a potato peeler.

2 Put the lemon rind in a saucepan with the white wine, water and clear honey. Bring to the boil, then simmer gently for 10 minutes.

3 Remove the syrup from the heat. Add the sprigs of mint and leave to cool.

4 To prepare the fruit, first slice the melon in half and scoop out the seeds. Use a melon baller or a teaspoon to make melon balls.

5 Core and chop the apples. Peel and slice the kiwi fruit.

6 Strain the cooled syrup into a serving bowl, removing and reserving the lemon rind and discarding the mint sprigs.

7 Add the apple, grapes, kiwi fruit and melon to the serving bowl. Stir through gently to mix.

8 Serve the fruit salad, decorated with sprigs of fresh mint and some of the reserved lemon rind.

COOK'S TIP

Single-flower honey has a better, more individual flavour than blended honey. Acacia honey is typically Chinese, but you could also try clove, lemon blossom, lime flower or orange blossom.

Chinese Custard Tarts

These small tarts are irresistible – a custard is baked in a rich, sweet pastry. The tarts may be served warm or cold.

NUTRITIONAL INFORMATION

Calories 474   Sugars 30g
Protein . . . . .9g   Fat 22g
Carbohydrate . . .64g   Saturates 12g

 20 MINS   30 MINS

SERVES 4

INGREDIENTS

DOUGH

175 g/6 oz/1½ cups plain (all-purpose) flour

3 tbsp caster (superfine) sugar

60 g/2 oz/4 tbsp unsalted butter

25 g/1 oz/2 tbsp lard (shortening)

2 tbsp water

CUSTARD

2 small eggs

60 g/2 oz/¼ cup caster (superfine) sugar

175 ml/6 fl oz/¾ cup pint milk

½ tsp ground nutmeg, plus extra for sprinkling

cream, to serve

1 To make the dough, sift the plain (all-purpose) flour into a bowl. Add the caster (superfine) sugar and rub in the butter and lard (shortening) until the mixture resembles breadcrumbs. Add the water and mix to form a firm dough.

2 Transfer the dough to a lightly floured surface and knead for 5 minutes, until smooth. Cover with cling film (plastic wrap) and leave to chill in the refrigerator while you prepare the filling.

3 To make the custard, beat the eggs and sugar together. Gradually add the milk and ground nutmeg and beat until well combined.

4 Separate the dough into 15 even-sized pieces. Flatten the dough pieces into rounds and press into shallow patty tins (pans).

5 Spoon the custard into the pastry cases (tart shells) and cook in a preheated oven, at 150°C/300°F/Gas 2, for 25-30 minutes.

6 Transfer the Chinese custard tarts to a wire rack, leave to cool slightly, then sprinkle with nutmeg. Serve hot or cold with cream.

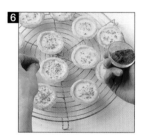

COOK'S TIP

For extra convenience, make the dough in advance, cover and leave to chill in the refrigerator until required.

Coconut Bananas

This elaborate dessert is the perfect finale for a Chinese banquet. Bananas are fried in a citrus-flavoured butter and served with coconut.

NUTRITIONAL INFORMATION

Calories 514   Sugars 70g
Protein . . . . .4g   Fat 21g
Carbohydrate . . .75g   Saturates 14g

10 MINS   10 MINS

SERVES 4

I N G R E D I E N T S

3 tbsp shredded fresh coconut

60 g/2 oz/¼ cup unsalted butter

1 tbsp grated ginger root

grated zest of 1 orange

60 g/2 oz/¼ cup caster (superfine) sugar

4 tbsp fresh lime juice

6 bananas

6 tbsp orange liqueur (Cointreau or Grand Marnier, for example)

3 tsp toasted sesame seeds

lime slices, to decorate

ice-cream, to serve (optional)

1 Heat a small non-stick frying pan (skillet) until hot. Add the coconut and cook, stirring constantly, for 1 minute until lightly coloured. Remove from the pan and allow to cool.

2 Melt the butter in a large frying pan (skillet) and add the ginger, orange zest, sugar and lime juice. Mix well.

3 Peel and slice the bananas length-ways (and halve if they are very large). Place the bananas cut-side down in the butter mixture and cook for 1-2 minutes or until the sauce mixture starts to become sticky. Turn the bananas to coat in the sauce.

4 Remove the bananas and place on heated serving plates. Keep warm.

5 Return the pan to the heat and add the orange liqueur, blending well. Ignite with a taper, allow the flames to die down, then pour over the bananas.

6 Sprinkle with the reserved coconut and sesame seeds and serve at once, decorated with slices of lime.

COOK'S TIP

For a very special treat try serving this with a flavoured ice-cream such as coconut, ginger or praline.

Exotic Fruit Salad

This is a sophisticated fruit salad that makes use of some of the exotic fruits that can now be seen in the supermarket.

NUTRITIONAL INFORMATION

Calories 149   Sugars 39g
Protein . . . . .1g   Fat 0.1g
Carbohydrate . . .39g   Saturates 0g

10 MINS   15 MINS

SERVES 6

INGREDIENTS

3 passion-fruit

125 g/4 oz/½ cup caster (superfine) sugar

150 ml/¼ pint/⅔ cup water

1 mango

10 lychees, canned or fresh

1 star-fruit

1 Halve the passion-fruit and press the flesh through a sieve (strainer) into a saucepan.

2 Add the sugar and water to the pan and bring to a gentle boil, stirring.

3 Put the mango on a chopping board and cut a thick slice from either side, cutting as near to the stone (pit) as possible. Cut away as much flesh as possible in large chunks from the stone (pit) section.

COOK'S TIP

A delicious accompaniment to any exotic fruit dish is cardamom cream. Crush the seeds from 8 cardamom pods, add 300 ml/½ pint/1¼ cups whipping cream and whip until soft peaks form.

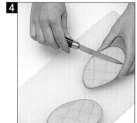 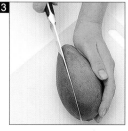 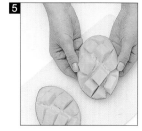

4 Take the 2 side slices and make 3 cuts through the flesh but not the skin, and 3 more at right angles to make a lattice pattern.

5 Push inside out so that the cubed flesh is exposed and you can easily cut it off.

6 Peel and stone (pit) the lychees and cut the star-fruit into 12 slices.

7 Add all the mango flesh, the lychees and star-fruit to the passion-fruit syrup and poach gently for 5 minutes. Remove the fruit with a perforated spoon.

8 Bring the syrup to the boil and cook for 5 minutes until it thickens slightly.

9 To serve, transfer all the fruit to individual serving glasses, pour over the sugar syrup and serve warm.

Sweet Rice

This dessert is served at banquets and celebratory meals in China, as it looks wonderful when sliced.

NUTRITIONAL INFORMATION

Calories	213	Sugars	. . . . .15g
Protein	. . . . .2g	Fat	. . . . .7g
Carbohydrate	. . .37g	Saturates	. . . . . . .4g

20 MINS

1¼ HOURS

SERVES 4

I N G R E D I E N T S

175 g/6 oz/¾ cup pudding rice

25 g/1 oz/2 tbsp unsalted butter

1 tbsp caster (superfine) sugar

8 dried dates, pitted and chopped

1 tbsp raisins

5 glacé (candied) cherries, halved

5 pieces angelica, chopped

5 walnut halves

125 g/4½ oz/½ cup canned chestnut
   purée (paste)

S Y R U P

150 ml/¼ pint/⅔ cup water

2 tbsp orange juice

4½ tsp light brown sugar

1½ tsp cornflour (cornstarch)

1 tbsp cold water

1 Put the rice in a saucepan, cover with cold water and bring to the boil. Reduce the heat, cover and simmer for about 15 minutes, or until the water has been absorbed. Stir in the butter and caster (superfine) sugar.

2 Grease a 600 ml/1 pint heatproof pudding basin (bowl). Cover the base and sides of the basin (bowl) with a thin layer of the rice, pressing with the back of a spoon.

3 Mix the fruit and walnuts together and press them into the rice.

4 Spread a thicker layer of rice on top and then fill the centre with the chestnut purée (paste). Cover with the remaining rice, pressing the top down to seal in the purée (paste) completely.

5 Cover the basin (bowl) with pleated greaseproof (wax) paper and foil and secure with string. Place in a steamer, or stand the basin (bowl) in a pan and fill with hot water until it reaches halfway up the sides of the basin (bowl). Cover and steam for 45 minutes. Leave to stand for 10 minutes.

6 Before serving, gently heat the water and orange juice in a small saucepan. Add the light brown sugar and stir to dissolve. Bring the syrup to the boil.

7 Mix the cornflour (cornstarch) with the cold water to form a smooth paste, then stir into the boiling syrup. Cook for 1 minute until thickened and clear.

8 Turn the pudding out on to a serving plate. Pour the syrup over the top, cut into slices and serve.

Mango Dumplings

Fresh mango and canned lychees fill these small steamed dumplings, making a really colourful and tasty treat.

NUTRITIONAL INFORMATION

Calories 434	Sugars 16g
Protein 12g	Fat 4g
Carbohydrate ...93g	Saturates 1g

🍲 🍲 🍲 🍲

🍲 1¾ HOURS   🕐 25 MINS

SERVES 4

I N G R E D I E N T S

D O U G H

2 tsp baking powder

1 tbsp caster (superfine) sugar

150 ml/¼ pint/⅔ cup water

150 ml/¼ pint/⅔ cup milk

400 g/14 oz/3½ cups plain
(all-purpose) flour

FILLING AND SAUCE

1 small mango

100 g/3½ oz can lychees, drained

1 tbsp ground almonds

4 tbsp orange juice

ground cinnamon, for dusting

1 To make the dough, place the baking powder and caster (superfine) sugar in a large mixing bowl.

2 Mix the water and milk together and then stir this mixture into the baking powder and sugar mixture until well combined. Gradually stir in the plain (all-purpose) flour to make a soft dough. Set the dough aside in a warm place for about 1 hour.

3 To make the filling, peel the mango and cut the flesh from the stone (pit). Roughly chop the mango flesh; reserve half and set aside for the sauce.

4 Chop the lychees and add to half of the chopped mango, together with the ground almonds. Leave to stand for 20 minutes.

5 Meanwhile, make the sauce. Blend the reserved mango and the orange juice in a food processor until smooth. Using the back of a spoon, press the mixture through a sieve to make a smooth sauce.

6 Divide the dough into 16 equal pieces. Roll each piece out on a lightly floured surface into 7.5-cm/3-inch rounds.

7 Spoon a little of the mango and lychee filling on to the centre of each round and fold the dough over the filling to make semi-circles. Pinch the edges together to seal firmly.

8 Place the dumplings on a heatproof plate in a steamer, cover and steam for about 20-25 minutes, or until cooked through.

9 Remove the mango dumplings from the steamer, dust with a little ground cinnamon and serve with the mango sauce.

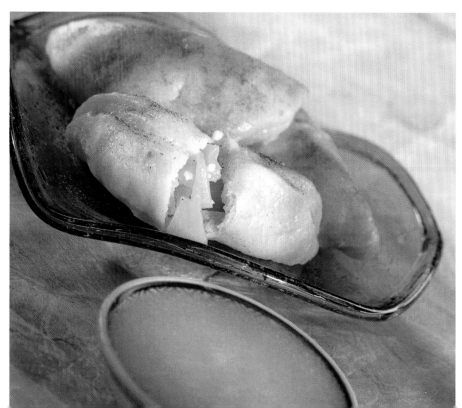

Battered Bananas

These bananas are quite irresistible, therefore it may be wise to make double quantities for weak-willed guests!

NUTRITIONAL INFORMATION

Calories	.... .562	Sugars	.... .79g
Protein	.... .6g	Fat	.... .10g
Carbohydrate	...118g	Saturates	.... .1g

10 MINS   20 MINS

SERVES 4

I N G R E D I E N T S

8 medium bananas

2 tsp lemon juice

75 g/2¾ oz/⅔ cup self-raising flour

75 g/2¾ oz/⅔ cup rice flour

1 tbsp cornflour (cornstarch)

½ tsp ground cinnamon

250 ml/9 fl oz/1 cup water

oil, for deep-frying

4 tbsp light brown sugar

cream or ice cream, to serve

1 Cut the bananas into even-sized chunks and place them in a large mixing bowl.

2 Sprinkle the lemon juice over the bananas to prevent discoloration.

3 Sift the self-raising flour, rice flour, cornflour (cornstarch) and cinnamon into a mixing bowl. Gradually stir in the water to make a thin batter.

4 Heat the oil in a preheated wok until smoking, then reduce the heat slightly.

5 Place a piece of banana on the end of a fork and carefully dip it into the batter, draining off any excess. Repeat with the remaining banana pieces.

6 Sprinkle the light brown sugar on to a large plate.

7 Carefully place the banana pieces in the oil and cook for 2-3 minutes, until golden. Remove the banana pieces from the oil with a slotted spoon and roll them in the sugar.

8 Transfer the battered bananas to serving bowls and serve immediately with cream or ice cream.

COOK'S TIP

Rice flour can be bought from wholefood shops or from Chinese supermarkets.

Melon & Kiwi Salad

A refreshing fruit salad, ideal to serve after a rich meal. Charentais or cantaloup melons are also good.

NUTRITIONAL INFORMATION

Calories 88   Sugars 17g
Protein ....1g   Fat 0.2g
Carbohydrate ...17g   Saturates 0g

 1¼ HOURS   0 MINS

SERVES 4

I N G R E D I E N T S

½ Galia melon

2 kiwi fruit

125 g/4½ oz/1 cup white (green)
    seedless grapes

1 paw-paw (papaya), halved

3 tbsp orange-flavoured liqueur such
    as Cointreau

1 tbsp chopped lemon verbena,
    lemon balm or mint

sprigs of lemon verbena or Cape
    gooseberries, to decorate

1 Remove the seeds from the melon, cut into 4 slices and cut away the skin. Cut the flesh into cubes and put into a bowl.

2 Peel the kiwi fruit and cut across into slices. Add to the melon with the white grapes.

3 Remove the seeds from the paw-paw (papaya) and cut off the skin. Slice the flesh thickly and cut into diagonal pieces. Add to the fruit bowl and mix well.

4 Mix together the liqueur and lemon verbena, pour over the fruit and leave for 1 hour, stirring occasionally.

5 Spoon the fruit salad into glasses, pour over the juices and decorate with lemon verbena sprigs or Cape gooseberries.

COOK'S TIP

Lemon balm or sweet balm is a fragrant lemon-scented plant with slightly hairy serrated leaves and a pronounced lemon flavour. Lemon verbena can also be used – this has an even stronger lemon flavour and smooth elongated leaves.

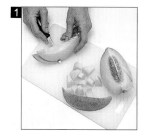

Poached Allspice Pears

These pears are moist and delicious after poaching in a sugar and allspice mixture. They are wonderful served hot or cold.

NUTRITIONAL INFORMATION

Calories 157	Sugars 17g	
Protein 5g	Fat 19g	
Carbohydrate ...17g	Saturates 12g	

 5 MINS   15 MINS

SERVES 4

I N G R E D I E N T S

4 large, ripe pears

300 ml/½ pint/1¼ cups orange juice

2 tsp ground allspice

60 g/2 oz/⅓ cup raisins

2 tbsp light brown sugar

grated orange rind, to decorate

1 Cut the bananas into even-sized chunks and place them in a large mixing bowl.

2 Sprinkle the lemon juice over the bananas to prevent discoloration.

3 Sift the self-raising flour, rice flour, cornflour (cornstarch) and cinnamon into a mixing bowl. Gradually stir in the water to make a thin batter.

4 Heat the oil in a preheated wok until smoking, then reduce the heat slightly.

5 Place a piece of banana on the end of a fork and carefully dip it into the batter, draining off any excess. Repeat with the remaining banana pieces.

6 Sprinkle the light brown sugar on to a large plate.

7 Carefully place the banana pieces in the oil and cook for 2-3 minutes, until golden. Remove the banana pieces from the oil with a slotted spoon and roll them in the sugar.

8 Transfer the battered bananas to serving bowls and serve immediately with cream or ice cream.

COOK'S TIP

The Chinese do not usually have desserts to finish off a meal, except at banquets and special occasions. Sweet dishes are usually served in between main meals as snacks, but fruit is refreshing at the end of a big meal.

Mangoes with Sticky Rice

These delightful rice puddings make a lovely dessert or afternoon snack. You can have fun experimenting with different-shaped rice moulds.

NUTRITIONAL INFORMATION

Calories ....202 Sugars 31g
Protein ....2g Fat 2g
Carbohydrate ...47g Saturates 0.3g

12³/₄ HOURS   50 MINS

SERVES 4

I N G R E D I E N T S

125 g/4½ oz/generous ½ cup glutinous (sticky) rice

250 ml/9 fl oz/1 cup coconut milk

60 g/2 oz/⅓ cup light muscovado sugar

½ tsp salt

1 tsp sesame seeds, toasted

4 ripe mangoes, peeled, halved, stoned (pitted) and sliced

1 Put the glutinous (sticky) rice into a colander and rinse well with plenty of cold water until the water runs clear. Transfer the rice to a large bowl, cover with cold water and leave to soak overnight, or for at least 12 hours. Drain the rice thoroughly.

2 Line a bamboo basket or steamer with muslin (cheesecloth) or finely woven cotton cloth. Add the rice and steam over a pan of gently simmering water until the rice is tender, about 40 minutes.

3 Remove the rice from the heat and transfer to a large mixing bowl.

4 Reserve 4 tablespoons of the coconut milk and put the remainder into a small saucepan with the light muscovado sugar and salt. Heat and simmer gently for about 8 minutes until reduced by about one third.

5 Pour the coconut milk mixture over the rice, fluffing up the rice with a fork so that the mixture is absorbed. Set aside for 10–15 minutes.

6 Pack the rice into individual moulds and then invert them on to serving plates.

7 Pour a little reserved coconut milk over each rice mound and sprinkle with the sesame seeds.

8 Arrange the sliced mango on the plates and serve, decorated with pieces of mango cut into different shapes with tiny cutters.

COOK'S TIP

Glutinous or sticky rice is available from stockists of Thai ingredients, although you can try making this recipe with short-grain pudding rice instead.

Lime Mousse with Mango

Lime-flavoured cream moulds, served with a fresh mango and lime sauce, make a stunning dessert.

NUTRITIONAL INFORMATION

Calories	254	Sugars 17g
Protein	.........5g	Fat 19g
Carbohydrate	...17g	Saturates 12g

10 MINS   0 MINS

SERVES 4

I N G R E D I E N T S

250 g/9 oz/1 cup fromage frais

grated rind of 1 lime

1 tbsp caster (superfine) sugar

125 ml/4 fl oz/½ cup double (heavy) cream

M A N G O   S A U C E

1 mango

juice of 1 lime

4 tsp caster (superfine) sugar

T O   D E C O R A T E

4 Cape gooseberries

strips of lime rind

1 Put the fromage frais, lime rind and sugar in a bowl and mix together.

2 Whisk the double (heavy) cream in a separate bowl and fold into the fromage frais.

3 Line 4 decorative moulds or ramekin dishes with muslin (cheesecloth) or cling film (plastic wrap) and divide the mixture evenly between them. Fold the muslin (cheesecloth) over the top and press down firmly.

4 To make the sauce, slice through the mango on each side of the large flat stone, then cut the flesh from the stone. Remove the skin.

5 Cut off 12 thin slices and set aside. Chop the remaining mango, put into a food processor with the lime juice and sugar. Blend until smooth. Alternatively, push the mango through a sieve (strainer) then mix with the lime juice and sugar.

6 Turn out the moulds on to serving plates. Arrange 3 slices of mango on each plate, pour some sauce around, decorate and serve.

COOK'S TIP

Cape gooseberries have a tart and mildly scented flavour and make an excellent decoration for many desserts. Peel back the papery husks to expose the bright orange fruits.

Index

Index compiled by Hilary Bird.